LANGUAGE AND LINGUISTICS

AN INTRODUCTION

LANGUAGE AND LINGUISTICS

AN INTRODUCTION

JOHN LYONS

Professor of Linguistics, University of Sussex

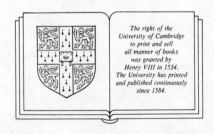

The right of the
University of Cambridge
to print and sell
all manner of books
was granted by
Henry VIII in 1534.
The University has printed
and published continuously
since 1584.

CAMBRIDGE UNIVERSITY PRESS

CAMBRIDGE

LONDON   NEW YORK   NEW ROCHELLE

MELBOURNE   SYDNEY

Published by the Press Syndicate of the University of Cambridge
The Pitt Building, Trumpington Street, Cambridge CB2 1RP
32 East 57th Street, New York, NY 10022, USA
296 Beaconsfield Parade, Middle Park, Melbourne 3206, Australia

© Cambridge University Press 1981

First published 1981
Reprinted 1982 (twice), 1983, 1984

Printed in the United States of America

British Library Cataloguing in Publication Data
Lyons, John
Language and linguistics
1. Linguistics
I. Title
410   P121   80-42002

ISBN 0 521 23034 9 hard covers
ISBN 0 521 29775 3 paperback

Contents

Preface

This book is designed for the course, entitled 'Language and Linguistics', which my colleagues and I teach to first-year students at the University of Sussex. Very few of these students come to the University with the intention of taking a degree in Linguistics. Some of them, having had their interest aroused by the course, do in fact transfer into Linguistics from other subjects. The vast majority, however, go on to complete their degree-work, as we expect that they will, in the discipline which they originally chose as their major subject in applying for admission. Our aim, therefore, in teaching 'Language and Linguistics' is to introduce our students to some of the more important theoretical concepts and empirical findings of modern linguistics, but to do so at a relatively non-technical level and in a way that emphasizes the connections between linguistics and the many other academic disciplines that are concerned, for their own purposes and from their own point of view, with the study of language. I trust that this book will prove to be equally suitable for similar courses on language, which now exist at many universities, polytechnics and colleges of education, both in this country and abroad. I hope that it will be of some interest also to the general reader who wishes to learn something of modern linguistics.

This book is broader in coverage, and less demanding in its central chapters, than my *Introduction to Theoretical Linguistics* (1968). It is correspondingly less detailed in its treatment of many topics. But I have appended to each chapter a list of suggestions for further reading. This should be comprehensive enough for lecturers and instructors using the book to make a selection according to their knowledge of the field and their theoretical preferences; and they can add to my list of books a number of important journal articles which, unless they have been reprinted in accessible publications, I have as a matter of policy excluded. The Bibliography is geared to the annotated Suggestions for Further Reading and is representative of most, if not all, points of view. For the benefit of students using the book without specialized guidance, and to help the interested general reader who wishes to go further into the subject, I have picked out about twenty general textbooks and collections of articles and asterisked these in the Bibliography. Here too I have been careful to make a representative selection – representative both of different theoretical viewpoints and of different levels of exposition.

Each chapter has associated with it a set of Questions and Exercises. Some of these are straightforward revision questions that can be answered without further reading. Some – especially those containing quotations from other works on linguistics – will oblige the student to consider and evaluate opinions different from those which I put forward myself in this book. A few of the questions are quite difficult; I would not expect students to be able to answer them, without assistance, on the basis of a ten-week course in Linguistics. On the other hand, I think it is important that students taking such courses should be given some sense of what Linguistics is like at a more advanced, though not necessarily more technical, level; and it is surprising what can be achieved by means of a little Socratic midwifery!

I would make the same comment in respect of the one problem that I have included (after the chapter on Grammar). I invented this many years ago, when I was teaching a course at Indiana University, and it has been used since then, by me and by others, as a fairly demanding exercise in linguistic analysis. Anyone who can come up with a solution that satisfies the demands of observational and explanatory adequacy in less than two hours will not need to read the central chapters of this book!

Although *Language and Linguistics* is very different from my *Introduction to Theoretical Linguistics*, it is informed with the same sense of the continuity of linguistic theory from the earliest times to the present day. I have not included a chapter on the history of linguistics as such, but within the limits of the space available for this I have tried to set some of the more important theoretical issues in their historical context. And I have written a brief chapter on structuralism, functionalism and generativism in linguistics, since the relations among these movements are, in my view, either neglected or misrepresented in most textbooks. In particular, generative grammar is commonly confused, on the one hand, with a certain kind of transformational-generative grammar, formalized by Chomsky, and, on the other, with what I have here called 'generativism', also propagated largely by Chomsky. In my own very brief treatment of generative grammar in this book, as also in my *Chomsky* (1977a) and elsewhere, I have tried to maintain the necessary distinctions. Personally, I am fully committed to the aims of those who use generative grammars as models for the description – for theoretical, rather than practical, purposes – of the grammatical structure of natural languages. As will be evident from this book, I reject many, though not all, of the tenets of generativism. Nevertheless, I have presented them as fairly and as objectively as I can. My aim, throughout, has been to give equal weight to both the cultural and the biological basis of language. There has been a tendency in recent years to emphasize the latter to the detriment of the former.

I must here record my appreciation of the assistance given to me in the writing of this book by my colleagues, Dr Richard Coates and Dr Gerald Gazdar. They have both read the whole work in draft and made many helpful critical comments, as well as supplying me with advice in areas where their expertise is greater than mine. Needless to say, they are not to be held responsible for any of the opinions expressed in the final version, the more so, as – I am happy to affirm publicly – we still disagree on a number of theoretical issues.

I should also like to express my indebtedness to my wife, who has not only given me the necessary moral support and love while I was writing the book, but has also served as my model general reader for several chapters and has corrected most of the proofs for me. Once again, I have had the benefit of the specialized and sympathetic editorial advice of Dr Jeremy Mynott and Mrs Penny Carter of Cambridge University Press; and I am very grateful to them.

Falmer, Sussex
January 1981

I
Language

1.1 *What is language?*

Linguistics is the scientific study of language. At first sight this definition – which is one that will be found in most textbooks and general treatments of the subject – is straightforward enough. But what exactly is meant by 'language' and 'scientific'? And can linguistics, as it is currently practised, be rightly described as a science?

The question "What is language?" is comparable with – and, some would say, hardly less profound than – "What is life?", the presuppositions of which circumscribe and unify the biological sciences. Of course, "What is life?" is not the kind of question that the biologist has constantly before his mind in his everyday work. It has more of a philosophical ring to it. And the biologist, like other scientists, is usually too deeply immersed in the details of some specific problem to be pondering the implications of such general questions. Nevertheless, the presumed meaningfulness of the question "What is life?" – the presupposition that all living things share some property or set of properties which distinguishes them from non-living things – establishes the limits of the biologist's concerns and justifies the autonomy, or partial autonomy, of his discipline. Although the question "What is life?" can be said, in this sense, to provide biology with its very reason for existence, it is not so much the question itself as the particular interpretation that the biologist puts upon it and the unravelling of its more detailed implications within some currently accepted theoretical framework that nourish the biologist's day-to-day speculations and research. So it is for the linguist in relation to the question "What is language?"

The first thing to notice about the question "What is language?" is that it uses the word 'language' in the singular without the indefinite article. Formulated as it is in English, it thus differs grammatically, if not in meaning, from the superficially similar question "What is a language?" Several European languages have two words, not one, to translate the English word 'language': cf. French 'langage' : 'langue', Italian 'linguaggio' : 'lingua'; Spanish 'lenguaje' : 'lengua'. In each case, the difference between the two words correlates, up to a point, with the difference in the two senses of the English word 'language'. For example, in French the word 'langage' is used to refer to language in general and the word 'langue' is applied to particular languages. It so happens that English allows its speakers to say, of some person, not only that he possesses a language (English, Chinese, Malay, Swahili, etc.), but that he possesses language. Philosophers, psychologists and linguists commonly make the point that it is the possession of language which most clearly distinguishes man from other animals. We shall be looking into the substance of this claim in the present chapter. Here I wish to emphasize the obvious, but important, fact that one cannot possess (or use) natural language without possessing (or using) some particular natural language.

I have just used the term 'natural language'; and this brings us to another point. The word 'language' is applied, not only to English, Chinese, Malay, Swahili, etc. – i.e. to what everyone will agree are languages properly so called – but to a variety of other systems of communication, notation or calculation, about which there is room for dispute. For example, mathematicians, logicians and computer scientists frequently construct, for particular purposes, notational systems which, whether they are rightly called languages or not, are artificial, rather than natural. So too, though it is based on pre-existing natural languages and is incontrovertibly a language, is Esperanto, which was invented in the late nineteenth century for the purpose of international communication. There are other systems of communication, both human and non-human, which are quite definitely natural rather than artificial, but which do not seem to be languages in the strict sense of the term, even though the word 'language' is commonly used with reference to them. Consider such phrases as 'sign language', 'body language' or 'the language of the bees' in this connection. Most people would probably say that the word 'language' is here being used metaphorically or figuratively. Interestingly enough, it is 'langage', rather than 'langue', that would normally be used in translating such phrases into French. The French word 'langage' (like the Italian 'linguaggio' and the Spanish 'lenguaje') is more general than the other member of the pair, not only in that it is used to refer to language in general, but also in that it is applied to systems of communication, whether they are natural or artificial, human or non-human, for which the English word 'language' is employed in what appears to be an extended sense.

The linguist is concerned primarily with natural languages. The question "What is language?" carries with it the presupposition that each of the several thousand recognizably distinct natural languages spoken throughout the world is a specific instance of something more general. What the linguist wants to know is whether all natural languages have something in common not shared by other systems of communication, human or non-human, such that it is right to apply to each of them the word 'language' and to deny the application of the term to other systems of communication – except in so far as they are based, like Esperanto, on pre-existing natural languages. This is the question with which we shall be dealing in the present chapter.

1.2 *Some definitions of 'language'*

Definitions of language are not difficult to find. Let us look at some. Each of the following statements about language, whether it was intended as a definition or not, makes one or more points that we will take up later. The statements all come from classic works by well-known linguists. Taken together, they will serve to give some preliminary indication of the properties that linguists at least tend to think of as being essential to language.

(i) According to Sapir (1921: 8): "Language is a purely human and non-instinctive method of communicating ideas, emotions and desires by means of voluntarily produced symbols." This definition suffers from several defects. However broadly we construe the terms 'idea', 'emotion' and 'desire', it seems clear that there is much that is communicated by language which is not covered by any of them; and 'idea' in particular is inherently imprecise. On the other hand, there are many systems of voluntarily produced symbols that we only count as languages in what we feel to be an extended or metaphorical sense of the word 'language'. For example, what is now popularly referred to by means of the expression 'body language' – which makes use of gestures, postures, eye-gaze, etc. – would seem to satisfy this point of Sapir's definition. Whether it is purely human and non-instinctive is, admittedly, open to doubt. But so too, as we shall see, is the question whether languages properly so called are both purely human and non-instinctive. This is the main point to be noted in Sapir's definition.

(ii) In their *Outline of Linguistic Analysis* Bloch & Trager wrote (1942: 5): "A language is a system of arbitrary vocal symbols by means of which a social group co-operates." What is striking about this definition, in contrast with Sapir's, is that it makes no appeal, except indirectly and by implication, to the communicative function of language. Instead, it puts all the emphasis upon its social function; and, in doing so, as we shall see later, it takes a rather narrow view of the role that language plays in society. The Bloch & Trager definition differs from Sapir's in that it brings in the property of arbitrariness and explicitly restricts language to spoken language (thus making the phrase 'written language' contradictory). The term 'arbitrariness' is here being used in a rather special sense: we will come back to this presently. We will also come back to the question of the relation that holds between language and speech. All that needs to be said at this point is that, as far as natural languages are concerned, there is a close connection between language and speech. Logically, the latter presupposes the former: one cannot speak without using language (i.e. without speaking in a particular language), but one can use language without speaking. However, granted that language is logically independent of speech, there are good grounds for saying that, in all natural languages as we know them, speech is historically, and perhaps biologically, prior to writing. And this is the view that most linguists take.

(iii) In his *Essay on Language*, Hall (1968: 158), tells us that language is "the institution whereby humans communicate and interact with each other by means of habitually used oral–auditory arbitrary symbols". Among the points to notice here are, first of all, the fact that both communication and interaction are introduced into the definition ('interaction' being broader than and, in this respect, better than 'co-operation') and, second, that the term 'oral–auditory' can be taken to be roughly equivalent to 'vocal', differing from it only in that 'oral–auditory' makes reference to the hearer as well as to the speaker (i.e. to the receiver as well as the sender of the vocal signals that we identify as language-utterances). Hall, like Sapir, treats language as a purely human institution; and the term 'institution' makes explicit the view that the language that is used by a particular society is part of that society's culture. The property of arbitrariness is, once again, singled out for mention.

What is most noteworthy in Hall's definition, however, is his employment of the term 'habitually used'; and there are historical reasons for this. Linguistics and the psychology of language were strongly influenced, for about thirty years or so, especially in America, by the stimulus–response theories of the behaviourists; and within the theoretical framework of behaviourism the term 'habit' acquired a rather special sense. It was used with reference to bits of behaviour that were identifiable as statistically predictable responses to particular stimuli. Much that we would not normally think of as being done as a matter of habit was brought within the scope of the behaviourists' term; and many textbooks of linguistics reflect this more or less technical use of the term and, with its adoption, commit themselves, by implication at least, to some version or other of the behaviourists' stimulus–response theory of language-use and language-acquisition. It is now generally accepted that this theory is, if not wholly inapplicable, of very restricted applicability both in linguistics and in the psychology of language.

Hall presumably means by language 'symbols' the vocal signals that are actually transmitted from sender to receiver in the process of communication and interaction. But it is now clear that there is no sense of the term 'habit', technical or non-technical, in which the utterances of a language are either themselves habits or constructed by means of habits. If 'symbol' is being used to refer, not to language-utterances, but to the words or phrases of which they are composed, it would still be wrong to imply that a speaker uses such and such a word, as a matter of habit, on such and such an occasion. One of the most important facts about language is that there is, in general, no connection between words and the situations in which they are used such that occurrence of particular words is predictable, as habitual behaviour is predictable, from the situations themselves. For example, we do nuï habitually produce an utterance containing the word 'bird' whenever we happen to find ourselves in a situation in which we see a bird; indeed, we are no more likely to use the word 'bird' in such situations than we are in all sorts of other situations. Language, as we shall see later, is **stimulus-free**.

(iv) Robins (1979a: 9–14) does not give a formal definition of language: he rightly points out that such definitions "tend to be trivial and uninformative, unless they presuppose . . . some general theory of language and of linguistic analysis". But he does list and discuss a number of salient facts that "must be taken into account in any seriously intended theory of language". Throughout successive editions of this standard textbook, he notes that languages are "symbol systems . . . almost wholly based on pure or arbitrary convention", but lays special emphasis on their flexibility and adaptability.[1] There is perhaps no logical incompatibility between the view that languages are systems of habit ('habit' being construed in a particular sense) and the view expressed by Robins. It is after all conceivable that a habit-system should itself change over time, in response to the changing needs of its users. But the term 'habit' is not one that we usually associate with adaptable behaviour. We shall need to look a little more closely at the notion of infinite extensibility later. And we shall then see that a distinction must be drawn between the extensibility and modifiability of a system and the extensibility or modifiability of the products of that system. It is also important to recognize that, as far as the system is concerned, some kinds of extension and modification are theoretically more interesting than others. For example, the fact that new words can enter the vocabulary of a language at any time is of far less theoretical interest than is the fact that new grammatical constructions can, and do, arise in the course of time. One of the central issues in linguistics is whether there are any limits to this latter kind of modifiability and, if so, what the limits are.

(v) The last definition to be quoted here strikes a very different

---

[1] In earlier editions (1964: 14; 1971: 13), he says: "Languages are infinitely extendable and modifiable according to the changing needs and conditions of the speakers." In the most recent edition 'adaptable' replaces 'infinitely extendable'.

note: "From now on I will consider a language to be a set (finite or infinite) of sentences, each finite in length and constructed out of a finite set of elements." This definition is taken from Chomsky's *Syntactic Structures* (1957: 13), whose publication inaugurated the movement known as transformational grammar. Unlike the other definitions, it is intended to cover much else besides natural languages. But, according to Chomsky, all natural languages, in either their spoken or their written form, are languages in the sense of his definition: since (a) each natural language has a finite number of sounds in it (and a finite number of letters in its alphabet – on the assumption that it has an alphabetic writing system); and (b), although there may be infinitely many distinct sentences in the language, each sentence can be represented as a finite sequence of these sounds (or letters). It is the task of the linguist describing some particular natural language to determine which of the finite sequences of elements in that language are sentences and which are non-sentences. And it is the task of the theoretical linguist who interprets the question "What is language?" as meaning "What is natural language?" to discover, if he can, the structural properties, if there are any, whereby natural languages differ from what, in contrast with them, may be called non-natural languages.

It is Chomsky's belief – and he has stressed this increasingly in his more recent work – not only that there are indeed such structural properties, but that they are so abstract, so complex and so highly specific to their purpose that they could not possibly be learned from scratch by an infant grappling with the problem of acquiring his native language. They must be known to the child, in some sense, prior to and independently of his experience of any natural language, and used by him in the process of language acquisition. It is because Chomsky holds this view that he describes himself as a rationalist, rather than an empiricist. We will come back to this point (cf. 7.4).

Chomsky's definition of 'language' has been quoted here largely for the contrast that it provides with the others, both in style and in content. It says nothing about the communicative function of either natural or non-natural languages; it says nothing about the symbolic nature of the elements or sequences of them. Its purpose is to focus attention upon the purely structural properties of languages and to suggest that these properties can be investigated from a mathematically precise point of view. It is Chomsky's major contribution to linguistics to have given particular emphasis to what he calls the **structure-dependence** of the processes whereby sentences are constructed in natural languages and to have formulated a general theory of grammar which is based upon a particular definition of this property (cf. 4.6).

The five definitions of 'language' quoted and briefly discussed above have served to introduce some of the properties which some linguists have taken to be essential features of languages as we know them. Most of them have taken the view that languages are systems of symbols designed, as it were, for the purpose of communication. And this is how we will look at languages below, in the section entitled 'The semiotic point of view': semiotics, as we shall see, is the discipline or branch of study that is devoted to the investigation of symbolic and communicative behaviour. The question that will concern us at that point will be whether there is any simple property or set of properties that distinguishes natural languages from other **semiotic** systems. Some of the properties that have been mentioned here are arbitrariness, flexibility and modifiability, freedom from stimulus control, and structure-dependence. Others will be added to this list in due course. The relation between language and speech will be dealt with in 1.4.

1.3 *Language-behaviour and language-systems*

It is now time, however, to draw some necessary distinctions of sense within the term 'language'. I have already referred to the distinction between language in general ('langage', to use the French term) and a particular language ('langue'). The adjective 'linguistic' is similarly ambiguous (even when it is relatable to 'language' rather than 'linguistics'). For example, the phrase 'linguistic competence', which has been employed by Chomsky and, following him, others to refer to a person's mastery of a particular language is no less naturally construed in everyday English as having reference to the ability or facility that someone might have for the acquisition or use, not of a language, but of language. (And whenever the word 'language' is used adjectivally in compound nouns it is subject to the same kind of ambiguity: cf. 'language-competence', 'language-acquisition'.) Very often the ambiguity is of no consequence or is resolved by the context. When it is important to keep the two senses of 'language' apart, I shall do so.

To use one particular language rather than another is to behave in one way rather than another. Both language in general and particular languages may be looked at as behaviour, or activity, some of which at least is observable, and recognizable as **language-behaviour**, not only by participant-observers (i.e. speakers and hearers in so far as we are restricting our attention to spoken language), but also by observers who are not themselves involved at the time in this characteristically interactive and communicative behaviour. Furthermore, although it is of the essence of language-behaviour that it should be, in general, if not on each and every occasion, communicative, it is usually possible for external observers to recognize language-behaviour for what it is, even when they do not know the particular language that is being used and cannot interpret the utterances that are the product of the behaviour that is being observed.

Language, then, can be considered, legitimately enough, from a behavioural (though not necessarily a behaviouristic) point of view. But language in general and particular languages can be considered from at least two other points of view. One of these is associated with the terminological distinction that Chomsky has drawn between 'competence' and 'performance'; the other, with the somewhat different distinction that Ferdinand de Saussure drew in French, at the beginning of the century, between 'langue' and 'parole'.

When we say of someone that he speaks English, we can mean one of two things: either (a) that he, habitually or occasionally, engages in a particular kind of behaviour or (b) that he has the ability (whether he exercises it or not) to engage in this particular kind of behaviour. Referring to the former as **performance** and the latter as **competence**, we can say that performance presupposes competence, whereas competence does not presuppose performance. Put like this, the distinction between competence and performance is relatively uncontroversial. So too is Chomsky's further point that, however broadly we construe the term 'linguistic competence', we must recognize that the language-behaviour of particular persons on particular occasions is determined by many other factors over and above their linguistic competence. There is much in Chomsky's more detailed formulation of the notion of linguistic competence that is highly controversial. But this need not concern us at present (cf. 7.4). Here it is sufficient to note that, for Chomsky, what linguists are describing when they are describing a particular language is, not the performance as such (i.e. behaviour), but the competence of its speakers, in so far as it is purely linguistic, which underlies and makes possible their performance. One's linguistic competence is one's knowledge of a particular language. Since linguistics is concerned with identifying and giving a satisfactory theoretical account of the determinants of linguistic competence it is to be classified, according to Chomsky, as a branch of cognitive psychology.

The distinction between 'langue' and 'parole', as it was originally drawn by Saussure, subsumed a number of logically independent distinctions. Most important of these were the distinction between what is potential and what is actual, on the one hand, and the distinction between what is social and what is individual, on the other (cf. 7.2). What Saussure called a 'langue' is any particular language that is the common possession of all the members of a given **language-community** (i.e. of all those who are acknowledged to speak the same language). The French term 'langue', which, as we have seen, is simply one of the ordinary words meaning "language", is usually left untranslated in English when it is being employed technically in its Saussurean sense. We will introduce the term 'language-system' in place of it; and we will contrast this with 'language-behaviour', initially at least, in the way that Saussure contrasted 'langue' and 'parole'. A **language-system** is a social phenomenon, or institution, which of itself is purely abstract, in that it has no physical existence, but which is actualized on particular occasions in the **language-behaviour** of individual members of the language-community. Up to a point, what Chomsky calls linguistic competence can be identified, readily enough, not with the language-system, but with the typical speaker's knowledge of the language-system. But Saussure gave special emphasis to the social or institutional character of language-systems. Therefore, he thought of linguistics as being closer to sociology and social psychology than it is to cognitive psychology. Many other linguists have taken the same view. Others, however, have held that language-systems can, and should be, studied independently of their psychological or sociological correlates. We return to this point in Chapter 2. Let us for the present simply note that, when we say that the linguist is interested in language, we imply that he is interested, primarily, in the structure of language-systems.

1.4 *Language and speech*

It is one of the cardinal principles of modern linguistics that spoken language is more basic than written language. This does not mean, however, that language is to be identified with speech. A distinction must be drawn between language-signals and the **medium** in which the signals are realized. Thus it is possible to read aloud what is written and, conversely, to write down what is spoken. Literate native speakers of a language can tell, in general, whether this process of transferring a language-signal from one medium to the other has been correctly carried out or not. In so far as language is independent, in this sense, of the medium in which language-signals are realized, we will say that language has the property of **medium-transferability**. This is a most important property – one to which far too little attention has been paid in general discussions of the nature of language. It is a property which, as we shall see, depends upon others and which, with them, contributes to the flexibility and adaptability of language-systems.

In what sense, then, is spoken language more basic than written language? And why is it that many linguists are inclined to make it a defining feature of natural languages that they should be systems of vocal signals?

First of all, linguists see it as their duty to correct the bias of traditional grammar and traditional language-teaching. Until recently, grammarians have been concerned almost exclusively with the language of literature and have taken little account of everyday colloquial speech. All too often they have treated the norms of literary usage as the norms of correctness for the language itself and have condemned colloquial usage, in so far as it differs from literary usage, as ungrammatical, slovenly or even illogical. In the course of the nineteenth century, great progress was made in the investigation of the historical development of languages. Scholars came to realize more clearly than before that changes in the language of written texts of different periods – changes of the kind that over the centuries transformed Latin into French, Italian or Spanish, for example – could be explained in terms of changes that had taken place in the corresponding spoken language. The continuity and ubiquity of language-change is considerably obscured in the written texts of the past that have come down to us by the conservatism of scribal traditions in many cultures, and by the continued use over long periods, in legal and religious documents and in literature, of an increasingly archaic style of writing. All the great literary languages of the world are derived, ultimately, from the spoken language of particular communities. Furthermore, it is a matter of historical accident that the usage of one region or of one social class should have served as the basis for the development of a standard literary language in particular communities and that, consequently, the dialects of other regions or of other social classes should now be regarded, as they often are, as inferior, or substandard, varieties of the language. Such is the force of the traditional prejudice in favour of the standard language in its written form, that it is very difficult for linguists to persuade laymen of the fact that non-standard dialects are, in general, no less regular or systematic than standard literary languages and have their own norms of correctness, imman-ent in the usage of their native speakers. One of the first and most difficult tasks for students of linguistics is to acquire the ability to consider spoken language on its own terms, as it were, without thinking that the pronunciation of a word or phrase is, or should be, determined by its spelling.

The desire to redress the balance in favour of the unprejudiced investigation of speech and spoken language does not of course justify the adoption of the principle that spoken language is more basic – and not simply no less basic – than written language. So what does 'basic' mean? The **historical priority** of speech over writing admits of little doubt. There is no human society known to exist or to have existed at any time in the past without the capacity of speech. Although languages, as we know them today in most parts of the world, may be either written or spoken, the vast majority of societies have, until recently, been either totally or very largely illiterate. Historical priority, however, is far less important than other kinds of priority implied by the term 'basic' in this context: structural, functional and, arguably, biological.

The **structural priority** of spoken language may be explained as follows. If we neglect, for the moment, any differences of style that there might be between corresponding written and spoken languages and make the assumption that every acceptable spoken sentence can be converted into an acceptable written sentence, and conversely, then we have no reason to think of either as being derived, except as a matter of historical fact, from the other. The structure of written sentences depends upon identifiable distinctions of shape; the structure of spoken sentences upon identifiable distinctions of sound. In the theoretically ideal case of a one-to-one correspondence holding between the spoken and the written sentences of a language, each written sentence will be **isomorphic** with (i.e. have the same internal structure as) the corresponding spoken sentence. For example, if the written sentences make use of an alphabetic writing-system, particular letters will stand in correspondence with particular sounds and particular combinations of letters will be in one-to-one correspondence, as words or phrases, with particular combinations of sounds. Not all combinations of letters are acceptable; nor are all combinations of sounds. But there is an important difference between letters and sounds in this respect. The potentiality that the sounds used in a particular language have for combining with one another depends in part upon the properties of the medium itself (certain combinations of sounds are either unpronounceable or difficult to pronounce) and in part upon the more specific restrictions that hold for that language alone. The potentiality that letters have for combining with one another is totally unpredictable in terms of their shape. It is predictable, however, to a greater or less extent, in all languages that make use of an alphabetic writing-system in terms of the association of particular shapes with particular sounds and of the potentiality that the sounds have for combining with one another in speech. In this respect, therefore, spoken language is structurally more basic than written language, even though the two might be isomorphic, in the theoretical ideal at least, at the level of such larger units as words and phrases. It should be noted that this point does not hold with respect to languages that make use of writing-systems in which there is no association of particular shapes with particular sounds as such, but with words. It does not hold, for example, with respect to Classical Chinese, written in the traditional characters, or Ancient Egyptian, written in hieroglyphs. It is because there is, in general, no structural priority of spoken language over written language, as far as Chinese is concerned, that much the same written language can be put into correspondence with quite distinct and mutually incomprehensible spoken dialects.

Functional priority is easier to explain and understand. Even today in the most literate of modern industrialized and bureaucratic societies, the spoken language is used for a wider range of purposes than the written, and writing serves as a functional substitute for speech only in situations which make vocal–auditory communication impossible, unreliable or inefficient. And the invention of the telephone and tape-recorder has made possible the use of the spoken language in circumstances in which the written language would have been employed in the past. It was for the purposes of reliable communication at a distance and the preservation of important legal, religious and commercial documents that writing was originally invented. The fact that written texts have been used for such important purposes throughout history and are more reliable and more enduring than spoken utterances (or were so until modern methods of recording sound were developed) has contributed to the greater formality and prestige of written language in many cultures.

We now come to the more controversial question of **biological priority**. There is much to suggest that human beings are genetically pre-programmed, not only to acquire language, but also, and as part of the same process, to produce and recognize speech-sounds. It has often been pointed out that what the linguist commonly refers to as the speech organs (or vocal organs) – the lungs, the vocal cords, the teeth, the tongue, etc. – all serve some biologically more basic function than that of producing vocal signals. This is indisputably the case: the lungs are used in breathing, the teeth in chewing food, and so on. None the less, all babies start babbling when they are a few months old (unless they suffer from some inhibiting mental or physical disability); and babbling, which involves the production of a much wider range of sounds than may be found in the speech of those with whom the child comes into contact, cannot be satisfactorily explained in terms of the child's parrot-like imitation of the sounds that he hears around him. Furthermore, it has now been demonstrated experimentally that babies are capable, in the very first weeks of life, of distinguishing speech sounds from other sounds and are predisposed, as it were, to pay attention to them. Man's nearest relatives among the higher primates, though they have much the same physiological apparatus, do not show the same predisposition to produce or distinguish the sounds characteristic of human speech. This may be the principal reason why attempts to teach spoken language to chimpanzees have failed, though a considerable measure of success has been achieved in teaching them languages, or language-like systems, whose signals are produced manually and interpreted visually. (It is now known that, in their natural habitat, chimpanzees communicate among themselves by means of gestures as well as with vocal signals; and their gestural signals appear to be much more richly differentiated than their vocal calls: cf. 1.7.) Finally, there is the fact that the two hemispheres of the human brain are functionally asymmetrical after childhood, one of them being dominant with respect to the performance of particular operations. In most people it is the left hemisphere that is dominant; and the left hemisphere carries out much of the processing of language-signals and is better at processing speech-sounds, though not other kinds of sound, than the right hemisphere (cf. 8.3).

Evidence of this kind, though not conclusive, is highly suggestive. According to one plausible hypothesis, human language developed, at some point in the evolution of the species, out of a gestural, rather than a vocal, system of communication; and there are many reasons why this might have happened. Whether this hypothesis is correct or not, the evidence summarized in the preceding paragraph points to the conclusion that, for man in his present state of evolutionary development, sound, and more particularly the range of audible sound that can be produced by the human speech organs, is the natural, or biologically basic, medium in which language is realized. If this is so, linguists are justified, not only in their use of the term 'speech organs', but also in their postulation of a non-contingent relation between languages and speech.

The fact remains, however, that there is a difference between biological and logical priority. As has been emphasized already, language has to a very high degree the property of medium-transferability. In the normal course of events, children acquire a command of the spoken language naturally (i.e. by virtue of their biological endowment and without special training), whereas reading and writing are special skills in which children are given special instruction based upon their prior knowledge of a spoken language. Nevertheless, not only children, but also adults, can learn to read and write without excessive difficulty; and it is quite possible, though unusual, to learn a written language without having a prior command of the associated spoken language. It is also possible to learn gestural systems of communication that are based upon neither a spoken nor a written language, as are some of the systems used by the deaf and dumb. If we were to discover a society using a written or gestural system of communication that had all the other distinguishing properties of language, but was never realized in the spoken medium, we would surely refer to this system of communication as a language. One should not, therefore, place too much emphasis on the biological priority of speech.

Furthermore, when it comes to the problem of describing particular languages, there is good reason for the linguist to treat the corresponding written and spoken languages as more or less, rather than absolutely, isomorphic. It is only in the theoretical ideal, as I said earlier, that there is complete isomorphism. No writing-system yet devised (other than the systems of transcription designed by phoneticians for this very purpose) provides for the representation of all the significant distinctions of speech. It follows that there are generally several non-equivalent ways of pronouncing the same written sentence, differing in stress, intonation, etc. Punctuation-marks and the use of italics or capitals serve much the same purpose in written language as do stress and intonation in spoken language, but the former can never adequately represent the latter. Due recognition must also be given to the fact that there are always both functional and structural differences between corresponding spoken and written languages. The extent of the difference varies, for historical and cultural reasons, from one language to another. In Arabic and Tamil, for example, the difference in both grammar and vocabulary is very considerable. It is less striking in English. Even in English, however, there are words, phrases and grammatical constructions that are felt to be too colloquial for the written language (e.g. 'load of old cobblers') or, conversely, too literary for the spoken language (e.g. 'any arrangements made heretofore notwithstanding').

The terms 'colloquial' and 'literary' are revealing. There is a clear distinction to be drawn, in principle, between 'colloquial' and 'spoken', on the one hand, and between 'literary' and 'written' on the other. The distinction is hard to maintain in practice; and for some languages the distinction between differences of medium ('spoken' vs. 'written') and differences of style ('colloquial' vs. 'literary') does not make much sense. Nor does the distinction between differences of medium and differences of dialect ('standard' vs. 'non-standard', etc.). The theoretical postulate of isomorphism between written and spoken language is part and parcel of what is referred to below as the fiction of homogeneity (cf. 1.6).

1.5 *The semiotic point of view*

Semiotics has been variously described: as the science of signs, of symbolic behaviour or of communication-systems. There has been much discussion, within semiotics, of the difference between signs, symbols and signals; and of the scope of the term 'communication'. For present purposes, we will think of semiotics as having to do with communication-systems; and we will construe 'communication', fairly broadly, as not necessarily implying the **intention** to inform. It is only if the term is construed in this way that one can talk about animal communication without begging some controversial philosophical questions.

There are certain concepts relevant to the investigation of all communication-systems, human and non-human, natural and artificial. A **signal** is transmitted from a **sender** to a **receiver** (or group of receivers) along a **channel** of communication. The signal will have a particular **form** and will convey a particular **meaning** (or **message**). The connection between the form of the signal and its meaning is established by what (in a rather general sense of the term) is commonly referred to in semiotics as the **code**: the message is encoded by the sender and decoded by the receiver.

Looked at from this point of view, natural languages are codes, and they may be compared with other codes in all sorts of ways: in terms of the channel along which the signals are transmitted; in terms of the form, or structure, of the signals; in terms of the kind or range of the messages that may be encoded; and so on. The problem lies in deciding what properties of the codes, or of the communication-systems in which they operate, are significant for the purpose of comparison and what properties are either insignificant or of less importance. This problem is aggravated by the fact that many of the properties that one might select as criterial are gradable, so that it may be more important to compare codes in terms of the degree to which a certain property is present than in terms simply of whether the property is present or not. Rather absurd comparisons between languages and the communication-systems used by particular species of birds and animals have sometimes been made on the basis of the selection of certain properties to the exclusion of others and the failure to pay attention to the gradability of properties.

As far as the channel of communication is concerned, little need be said, except that, unlike the codes used by many, if not all, animals, language has the property, to a very high degree, of medium-transferability. This point was made in the previous section. The notions of medium and channel are, of course, intrinsically connected, in that the properties of the medium derive from the properties of the normal channel of transmission. It is nevertheless important to distinguish the two notions in respect of language. Both written and spoken language can be transmitted along a variety of channels. When we use the term 'medium', rather than 'channel', we are not concerned with the actual transmission of signals on particular occasions, but with the systematic functional and structural differences between what is characteristically written or characteristically spoken. Paradoxical though it may appear at first sight, written English can be transmitted along the vocal–auditory channel (i.e. by means of speech) and spoken English can be transmitted in writing (though not very satisfactorily in the normal orthographic script).

Perhaps the most striking characteristic of language by comparison with other codes or communication-systems is its flexibility and versatility. We can use language to give vent to our emotions and feelings; to solicit the co-operation of our fellows; to make threats or promises; to issue commands, ask questions or make statements. We can make reference to the past, present and future; to things far removed from the situation of utterance – even to things that need not exist and could not exist. No other system of communication, human or non-human, would seem to have anything like the same degree of flexibility and versatility. Among the more specific properties that contribute to the flexibility and versatility of language (i.e. of each and every language-system), there are four that have frequently been singled out for mention: arbitrariness, duality, discreteness and productivity.

(i) The term 'arbitrary' is here being used in a rather special sense, to mean something like "inexplicable in terms of some more general principle". The most obvious instance of **arbitrariness** in language – and the one that is most frequently mentioned – has to do with the link between form and meaning, between the signal and the message. There are sporadic instances in all languages of what is traditionally referred to as onomatopoeia: cf. the non-arbitrary connection between the form and the meaning of such onomatopoeic words as 'cuckoo', 'peewit', 'crash', in English. But the vast majority of the words in all languages are non-onomatopoeic: the connection between their form and their meaning is arbitrary in that, given the form, it is impossible to predict the meaning and, given the meaning, it is impossible to predict the form.

It is obvious that arbitrariness, in this sense, increases the flexibility and versatility of a communication-system in that the extension of the vocabulary is not constrained by the necessity of matching form and meaning in terms of some more general principle. On the other hand, the fact that the link between form and meaning at the level of the vocabulary-units of language-systems is, in general, arbitrary has the effect that a considerable burden is placed upon memory in the language-acquisition process. The association of a particular form with a particular meaning must be learned for each vocabulary-unit independently. Looked at from a semiotic point of view, then, arbitrariness of this kind has both advantages and disadvantages: it makes the system more flexible and adaptable, but it also makes it more difficult and laborious to learn. There is the further point that arbitrariness in a semiotic system makes the signals more difficult to interpret for anyone intercepting them who does not know the system. This too has both advantages and disadvantages for the normal users of the system. Presumably the advantages must have outweighed the disadvantages in the development of language. In most animal communication-systems there is a non-arbitrary link between the form of a signal and its meaning.

Arbitrariness is not restricted, as far as language is concerned, to the link between form and meaning. It also holds, to some considerable degree, with respect to much of the grammatical structure of particular languages, in so far as languages differ grammatically one from another. If this were not the case, it would be much easier to learn foreign languages than it is.

More controversial is Chomsky's thesis that a good deal of what is common to the grammatical structure of all human languages, including the operation of a very specific kind of structure-dependency, is also arbitrary, in the sense that it cannot be explained or predicted in terms of the functions of language, the environmental conditions in which language is acquired and used, the nature of human cognitive processes in general, or any factor of this kind. It is Chomsky's view that human beings are genetically endowed with a knowledge of the allegedly arbitrary general principles which determine the grammatical structure of all languages. All that needs to be said about this hypothesis here is that not all linguists agree that such general principles as can be established are arbitrary in the intended sense, and that much current research in theoretical linguistics is devoted to the attempt to show that they are not. We will return to this point in Chapter 8.

(ii) By **duality** is meant the property of having two **levels** of structure, such that **units** of the primary level are composed of **elements** of the secondary level and each of the two levels has its own principles of organization. It will be noticed that I have introduced a terminological distinction here between 'element' and 'unit'. This is not a standard terminological distinction of linguistics. However, it has a certain expository convenience; and it will be maintained throughout this book.

For the present, we can think of the elements of spoken language as sounds (more precisely, as what will be identified in Chapter 3 as phonemes). The sounds do not of themselves convey meaning. Their sole function is to combine with one another to make units which do, in general, have a particular meaning. It is because the smaller, lower-level elements are meaningless whereas the larger, higher-level, units generally, if not invariably, have a distinct and identifiable meaning that the elements are described as secondary and the units as primary. All communication-systems have such primary units; but these units are not necessarily made up of elements. It is only if a system has both units and elements that it has the property of duality. Most animal communication-systems, apparently, do not; and those that do are such that the units are not combined with one another in the way that words are combined with one another to form phrases and sentences in all human languages.

The advantage of duality is obvious: a large number of different units can be formed out of a small number of elements – many thousands of words, for example, out of thirty or forty sounds. If these primary units can be combined systematically in various ways the number of distinct signals that can be transmitted – and consequently the number of different messages – is increased enormously. As we shall see presently, there is no limit to the number of distinct language-signals that can be constructed in particular languages.

(iii) **Discreteness** is opposed to continuity, or continuous variation. In the case of language, discreteness is a property of the secondary elements. To illustrate: the two words 'bit' and 'bet' differ in form, in both the written and the spoken language. It is quite possible to produce a vowel-sound that is half-way between the vowels that normally occur in the pronunciation of these two words. But if we substitute this intermediate sound for the vowel of 'bit' or 'bet' in the same context, we shall not thereby have pronounced some third word distinct from either or sharing the characteristics of both. We shall have pronounced something that is not recognized as a word at all or, alternatively, something that is identified as a mispronounced version of one or the other. Identity of form in language is, in general, a matter of all or nothing, not of more or less.

Though discreteness is not logically dependent upon arbitrariness, it interacts with it to increase the flexibility and efficiency of language-systems. For example it would be possible in principle for two words differing minimally, but discretely, in form to be very similar in meaning. Generally speaking, this does not happen: 'bet' and 'bit' are no more similar in meaning than are any randomly selected pairs of English words. The fact that words differing minimally in form will usually differ considerably, rather than minimally, in meaning has the effect of enhancing the discreteness of the formal difference between them: in most contexts the occurrence of one will be far more probable than the occurrence of the other, and this reduces the possibility of misunderstanding in poor conditions of signal-transmission. In animal communication-systems non-discreteness (i.e. continuous variation) is often associated with non-arbitrariness.

(iv) The **productivity** of a communication-system is the property which makes possible the construction and interpretation of new signals: i.e. of signals that have not been previously encountered and are not to be found on some list – however large that list might be – of prefabricated signals, to which the user has access. Most animal communication-systems appear to be highly restricted with respect to the number of different signals that their users can send and receive. All language-systems, on the other hand, enable their users to construct and understand indefinitely many utterances that they have never heard or read before.

The importance of productivity has been stressed in the recent linguistic literature, especially by Chomsky, with particular reference to the problem of accounting for the acquisition of language by children. The fact that children, at a quite early age, are able to produce utterances that they have never heard before is proof that language is not learned solely by means of imitation and memorization.

It must be emphasized, in the discussion of productivity, that it is not so much the ability to construct new utterances that is of crucial importance in the evaluation of language-systems. For example, to say that the communication-system used by the honey-bee in indicating the source of nectar has the property of productivity is quite misleading if it means that the system is, in this respect, like human languages. The bee produces indefinitely many different signals (varying with respect to the vibrations of its body and the angle that it adopts in relation to the sun). But there is continuous variation in the signals, a non-arbitrary link between the signal and the message, and the system cannot be used by the bee to convey information about anything other than the distance and direction of the source of nectar.

What is striking about the productivity of natural languages, in so far as it is manifest in their grammatical structure, is the extreme complexity and heterogeneity of the principles which guarantee and constitute it. But, as Chomsky more than anyone else has insisted, this complexity and heterogeneity is not unconstrained: it is **rule-governed**. Within the limits set by the rules of the grammar, which are perhaps partly universal and partly specific to particular languages, native speakers of a language are free to act creatively – in what Chomsky would say is a distinctively human way – to construct indefinitely many utterances. This notion of rule-governed creativity is closely associated with that of productivity (cf. 7.4); it has been of great importance in the development of generativism.

The four general properties that have been listed and briefly discussed above – arbitrariness, duality, discreteness and productivity – are all interconnected in various ways. Not only are they present, as far as we know, in all languages, but they are present to a very high degree. Whether they are all found in any communication-system other than language is questionable. But, if they are, they do not appear to be present to the same degree or to be interconnected in the same way.

It is also worth pointing out, however, that these four properties, which are completely independent of both channel and medium, are less characteristic of the non-verbal part of language-signals. Utterances are not just sequences of words. Superimposed upon the string of words (i.e. the **verbal** part) in any spoken utterance there will be two more or less distinguishable kinds of vocal phenomena: **prosodic** and **paralinguistic**. The prosodic features include such things as stress and intonation; the paralinguistic, such phenomena as tempo, loudness, etc. There will also be associated with the spoken utterance a variety of non-vocal phenomena (eye-movements, head-nods, facial expressions, gestures, body-posture, etc.) which further determine the structure or meaning of the utterance and may also be described as paralinguistic. It is only the prosodic phenomena that the linguist normally treats, with the verbal features, as being determined by the language-system as such. Both prosodic and paralinguistic phenomena, however, are an integral part of all normal language-behaviour in the spoken medium. In so far as they lack the four general properties of arbitrariness, duality, discreteness and productivity – or at least do not manifest them to the same degree as does the verbal part of language – the prosodic and paralinguistic features of language-behaviour more closely resemble the features of various kinds of animal communication.

Is language unique, then, to man? The answer to this question, like the answer to the question "Is man unique among animals?", depends very much upon what properties one decides to concentrate upon and make criterial in the definition of language. It is equally legitimate to stress either the striking differences, both of degree and of kind, between language and non-language or the no less striking similarities. The linguist, the psychologist and the philosopher may tend to emphasize the former; the ethologist, the zoologist and the semiotician would probably stress the latter.

1.6 *The fiction of homogeneity*

So far we have been operating with what I will refer to as the fiction of homogeneity: the belief or assumption that all members of the same language-community speak exactly the same language. It is, of course, possible to define the term 'language-community' in such a way that it is made a matter of definition that there should be no systematic differences of pronunciation, grammar or vocabulary in the speech of its members. But if the term is interpreted as referring to any group of people who would normally be said to speak the same language, e.g. English, French or Russian, it then becomes a matter of empirical discovery whether all the members of a particular language-community speak alike in all respects or not.

In all but the smallest language-communities throughout the world there are more or less obvious differences of **accent** and **dialect**. Of the terms 'accent' and 'dialect', the former is more restricted than the latter: it refers solely to the way in which the language is pronounced and carries no implications whatsoever with respect to grammar and vocabulary. For example, it is possible, and by no means uncommon, for a foreigner to be immediately identifiable as such by his accent and yet speak the language, as far as grammar and vocabulary are concerned, indistinguishably from its native speakers. And it is possible for two native speakers to use what is otherwise the same dialect, but to speak it with a recognizably different accent. This is especially common if the dialect in question has, for historical reasons, acquired the status of a national or regional **standard**. For example, most educated native-born inhabitants of England speak a dialect of English which approximates more or less closely to a particular kind of Standard English, but they will speak it with an accent which reveals their geographical or social provenance. There is a distinction to be drawn, in everyday usage at least, between 'accent' and 'dialect'. Many linguists, however, subsume differences of accent under differences of dialect. This purely terminological point is, in itself, of no consequence. But it is important to realize that what is otherwise the same dialect can be pronounced in strikingly different ways. It is no less important to realize that, where there is no acknowledged and long-established national and regional standard, differences of dialect, not only in pronunciation, but also in grammar and vocabulary, tend to be much more striking than they are in most of the English-speaking language-community today.

Though the linguist uses the term 'dialect' and, like the layman, relates it to the term 'language' by saying that a language may be composed of several different dialects, he does not accept the implications commonly associated with the term 'dialect' in everyday usage. Most important of all, he does not accept that the dialect of a particular region or a particular social class is a debased or degenerate version of the standard dialect: he knows that from a historical point of view the standard dialect – to which the layman may prefer to apply the term 'language', rather than 'dialect' – is, in origin, though not in its subsequent development, no different in kind from the non-standard dialects. He knows too that, as long as they serve a fairly broad range of functions in the daily life of the locality or social class in which they operate, non-standard dialects are no less systematic than the regional or national standard. These points were made earlier. We will come back to them, in order to develop and exemplify them – and, on occasion, to introduce certain qualifications – in later chapters of this book: looked at from a contemporary social and cultural point of view, a regional or national standard is rightly regarded as being very different in character from the associated non-standard dialects to which it is historically related.

Very often in everyday usage of the terms 'dialect' and 'language', the distinction between them is based very largely upon political or cultural considerations. For example, Mandarin and Cantonese are called dialects of Chinese, but they are more distinct from one another than, say, Danish and Norwegian or, even more strikingly, Dutch, Flemish and Afrikaans, which are frequently described as different languages. It might be thought that the criterion of intercomprehensibility would suffice to draw a politically and culturally neutral line of demarcation between languages. This is indeed the major criterion that a practising linguist would apply in establishing the limits of a language-community. But there are problems. It very often happens that dialect variation is gradual, and more or less continuous, over a wide area. Thus, speakers from two widely separated regions might be unable to understand one another, but there might be no point between any two adjacent dialects at which intercomprehensibility breaks down. Then there is the further, more troublesome problem that comprehensibility is not always symmetrical; nor is it a matter of all or nothing. It is quite possible, and indeed quite common, for X to understand most of what Y says and for Y to understand little or nothing of what X says, when each speaks to the other in his own dialect. For various reasons, then, it is often very difficult to draw a sharp distinction between distinct languages and different dialects of the same language.

Indeed, it is very often the case that no sharp distinction can be drawn between the dialect of one region and that of another, usually neighbouring region. However narrowly we circumscribe the dialect area by means of social, as well as geographical, criteria, we shall always find, if we investigate the matter, a certain amount of systematic variation in the speech of those who are thereby established as speakers of the same dialect. In the last resort, we should have to admit that everyone has his own individual dialect: that he has his own **idiolect**, as linguists put it. Every idiolect will differ from every other, certainly in vocabulary and pronunciation and perhaps also, to a smaller degree, in grammar. Furthermore, one's idiolect is not fixed once and for all at the end of what we normally think of as the period of language-acquisition: it is subject to modification and extension right through life.

In addition to what can be accounted for in terms of the scale language–dialect–idiolect, there is another dimension of systematic variation in the utterances of the members of a language-community: the dimension of **style**. Stylistic differences have already been referred to in connection with the distinction between the literary and the colloquial – a distinction which derives from, but is by no means coincident with, the distinction between written and spoken language. But there is much more to stylistic variation than this. Whenever we speak or write in our native language we do so in one style rather than another, according to the situation, the relations that hold between us and the person to whom we are speaking or writing, the purpose and nature of what we have to communicate, and several other factors. Whether the stylistic choices that we make are conscious or unconscious, they are none the less both systematic and identifiable; and making the appropriate stylistic choices is an important part of using a language correctly and effectively. There is a sense, therefore, in which every native speaker of a language is stylistically multilingual. Just as it is, in principle, possible to think of each idiolect as a separate language-system, so it is possible – and no less reasonable – to think of each distinguishable style as a distinct language-system.

1.7   There are no primitive languages

It is still fairly common to hear laymen talking about primitive languages and even repeating the discredited myth that there are some peoples whose language consists of a couple of hundred words supplemented by gestures. The truth is that every language so far studied, no matter how primitive or uncivilized the society using it might appear to us in other respects, has proved upon investigation to be a complex and highly developed system of communication. Of course, the whole notion of cultural evolution from barbarism to

civilization is itself highly questionable. But it is not for the linguist
to pronounce upon its validity. What he can say is that no correlation has yet been discovered between the different stages of cultural
development through which societies have passed and the type of
language spoken at these stages of cultural development. For
example, there is no such thing as a Stone Age type of language; or,
as far as its general grammatical structure is concerned, a type of
language that is characteristic of food-gathering or pastoral
societies, on the one hand, or modern industrialized societies, on
the other.

There was a good deal of speculation in the nineteenth century
about the development of languages from structural complexity to
simplicity or, alternatively, from simplicity to complexity. Most
linguists these days refrain from speculating about the evolutionary
development of languages in such general terms. They know that, if
there has been any directionality in the evolution of language from
its origins in the prehistory of man to the present day, there is no
evidence of any such directionality recoverable from the study of
contemporary spoken languages or of those languages of the past
of which we have any knowledge. Many of the earlier speculations
of scholars about the evolution of languages were biased in favour of
so called inflecting languages like Latin and Greek.

Something should be said, at this point, about the origin of
language, which is a problem that has exercised the mind and
imagination of man from time immemorial. It was extensively
debated in secular, as distinct from religious or supernatural, terms
by the Greek philosophers and at various times since then, notably
in the eighteenth century, from a broadly similar point of view. The
earlier debates played an important part in the development of
traditional grammar. Late eighteenth-century discussion by the
French philosopher Condillac and the German philosopher Herder
helped to prepare the way for a better understanding of the interdependence of language, thought and culture. Since the nineteenth
century, most linguists have, with very few exceptions, tended to
dismiss the whole question of the origin of language as one that is
forever beyond the scope of scientific investigation. The reason is
that, as we have just seen, in the course of the nineteenth century
linguists came to realize that, however far back one traced the

history of particular languages in the texts that have come down to us, it was impossible to discern in them any signs of evolutionary development from a more primitive to a more advanced state.

But there is other evidence, some of it new. And the origin of language is, once again, the subject of scholarly debate. It is perhaps premature to talk of solutions. What can be said, however, is that it now seems much more plausible than it did a few years ago that language originated as a gestural, rather than a vocal, system of communication. One piece of evidence is the success that psychologists have had in teaching chimpanzees to understand and use quite complex and, up to a point, language-like gestural systems. It now appears that the failure of chimpanzees to acquire speech in similar experiments in the past is, in part at least, explained by relatively small, but important, differences in the vocal organs of man and chimpanzee. It also appears, from the study of fossils, that the vocal organs of Neanderthal man were more similar than ours are to those of chimpanzees and other primates, which have a restricted range of vocal calls, but communicate with one another in the wild quite extensively by means of gestures. What this and other evidence suggests is that language may have first developed as a gestural system at a time when man's ancestors were adopting an upright posture, thus freeing the hands, and the brain was both increasing in size and acquiring the potential for the specialization of complex processing functions in the dominant hemisphere. At some point, and for biologically plausible reasons, the gestural system would have been converted into a vocal system and would have subsequently acquired the property of duality which, as we have seen, permits a very considerable increase in vocabulary. It follows that not all characteristic properties of languages, as we know them, may have been present from the start and that language did indeed evolve from non-language.

The fact remains, however, not only that in all known languages it is the vocal–auditory channel that is used primarily and naturally for their transmission, but also that all known languages are of roughly equal complexity, as far as their grammatical structure is concerned.

The only exception that must be made to the latter generalization is in respect of **pidgin** languages. These are specialized languages, used for trade or similar purposes by those who have no other common language. It is characteristic of pidgins that they have a simplified grammar and a highly restricted vocabulary by comparison with the language, or languages, upon which they are based. But they are used for very restricted purposes; and when, as has often happened, what originated as a pidgin comes to be used as the mother tongue of a language-community, it not only furnishes itself with a more extensive vocabulary, but also develops its own grammatical complexity. It is in this respect, rather than in terms of their origin, that pidgins are distinguished by linguists from what are called **creole** languages. Creoles may look, or sound, very much like pidgins, but they are no closer to being primitive languages – i.e. of rudimentary structure – than are any of the thousands of natural languages that did not originate, as far as we know, as pidgins (cf. 9.3).

There are, of course, considerable differences in the vocabularies of different languages. It may therefore be necessary to learn another language, or at least a specialized vocabulary, in order to study a particular subject or talk satisfactorily about it. In this sense, one language may be better adapted than another for particular purposes. This does not mean, however, that one language is intrinsically richer or poorer than another. All living languages, it may be assumed, are of their very nature efficient systems of communication. As the communicative needs of a society change, so their language will change to meet these new needs. The vocabulary will be extended, either by borrowing words from other languages or by creating them from existing words. The fact that many languages spoken in what are sometimes referred to as underdeveloped countries lack words for the concepts and material products of modern science and technology does not imply that the languages in question are more primitive than the languages that do have such words. It just means that certain languages have not been used, so far at least, by those involved in the development of science and technology.

It must be emphasized, in conclusion, that the principle that there are no primitive languages is not so much an empirical finding of linguistic research as a working hypothesis. We must allow for the possibility that languages do differ in grammatical complexity and that these differences have not so far been discovered by linguists. It would be as unscientific to deny that this possibility exists as it is to say that Latin is intrinsically nobler or more expressive than Hottentot or one of the Australian Aboriginal languages.

FURTHER READING

Most general introductions to language and linguistics cover in more or less detail, and from different points of view, the topics dealt with in Chapter 1: a selection of such works is included in the Bibliography.

Students new to the subject might begin with Aitchison (1978), chapters 1–2; Akmajian, Demers & Harnish (1979), chapters 1–5; Chao (1968); Crystal (1971), chapter 1; Fowler (1964), chapter 1; Fromkin & Rodman (1974), chapters 1–2; Lyons (1970), chapter 1; Robins (1974); Smith & Wilson (1979), chapter 1. They could then move on to some of the other textbooks and readers asterisked in the Bibliography, many of which contain relevant chapters or sections.

On speech and writing, see also Basso (1974); Gelb (1963); Haas (1976); Householder (1971), chapter 13; Lyons (1977b), sections 3.1–3.3; Uldall (1944); Vachek (1949, 1973); and some of the general works on phonetics listed in the Further reading for Chapter 3 below.

On the semiotic point of view (including animal communication), see also Aitchison (1976); Cherry (1957); Eco (1976); Hinde (1972), chapters 1–3; Hockett (1960); Hockett & Altmann (1968); Householder (1971), chapter 3; Lyons (1977b), sections 3.4, 4.1–4.2; McNeill (1970), chapter 4; Sebeok (1968, 1974a); Thorpe (1974).

On recent work with chimpanzees, see Akmajian, Demers & Harnish (1979), chapter 14; Brown (1970); Clark & Clark (1977; 520–3); Linden (1976); Premack (1977); Rumbaugh (1977).

On the sign-systems used by the deaf, see Klima & Bellugi (1978); Siple (1978); Stokoe (1961).

On the origin of language, see also Hewes (1977); Lieberman (1975); Stam (1977); Wescott (1974).

Other topics dealt with in this chapter are dealt with in more detail in Chapters 8–10, where further references are given.

QUESTIONS AND EXERCISES

1. Explain what is meant by **freedom from stimulus control**.

2. "performance presupposes competence, whereas competence does not presuppose performance" (p. 9). Discuss.

3. What distinction, if any, would you draw between **linguistic competence** and **fluency**?

4. "Often enough, the layman thinks that writing is somehow more basic than speech. Almost, the reverse is true" (Hockett, 1958: 4). Discuss (with particular reference to 'basic' and 'almost').

5. Language is sometimes called 'verbal behaviour'. Discuss the appropriateness of this term in respect of (a) 'verbal' and (b) 'behaviour'.

6. In what sense, and to what degree, is written English the same language as spoken English? What kinds of information is it impossible, or very difficult, to encode in writing, though it is naturally and normally encoded in speech?

7. Can you think of any English sentences which are ambiguous when written but kept distinct in the spoken language? Conversely, are there any sentences that are ambiguous in the spoken language, but not in the written language? (How is this question of medium-transferability affected (a) by differences of accent and dialect and (b) by giving due recognition to the distinction between the verbal and the non-verbal components of language?)

8. How does English compare with other languages known to you in respect of the relation that holds between spelling and pronunciation? What are the arguments for and against spelling reform?

9. Give some everyday examples of the transmission of written English along the vocal–auditory channel and conversely of the transmission of spoken English by means of writing.

10. "If I change the pronunciation of my name the law does not care, . . . ; but if I change the spelling, . . . , then I must go to court to make it legitimate. And public sentiment is behind the lawyers one hundred per cent . . ." (Householder, 1971: 353; cf. also Hockett, 1958: 549). Is it generally the case that only the written language is given legal recognition?

11. What other kinds of non-arbitrariness exist in natural languages in addition to **onomatopoeia**?

12. Is there any necessary connection between **duality** and meaningfulness?

13. Explain what is meant by **discreteness** with reference (a) to writing and (b) to speech.

14. What distinction, if any, would you draw between **productivity** and **creativity**?

15. "The most extensive and striking parallelism is that between language and bee dancing, which share productivity, some displacement, and some specialization" (Hockett, 1958: 581). Discuss.

16. "all normal humans acquire language, whereas acquisition of even its barest rudiments is quite beyond the capacities of an otherwise intelli-

gent ape" (Chomsky, 1972a: 66). Has this assertion been falsified by recent work with chimpanzees?

17. "Both deaf infants and chimps learn their first sign long before normal infants say their first word, which supports the notion that ontogenetically and phylogenetically we are equipped for gestural language before we are equipped for speech" (Linden, 1976: 72). Discuss.

18. Are the various sign-systems used by the deaf rightly called natural languages or not?

19. In general, how do accents differ from dialects? What sense can we attach, as linguists, to the statement that (a) a foreigner and (b) a native speaker "has no accent"? (These questions may be discussed non-technically at this point, but cf. 9.2.)

20. "There is room for regional dialects and room for the Queen's English. The place for the regional accent is the place in which it was born; it is right for the public bar, the football field, the village dance. Queen's English is for the BBC talk on Existentialism, the cocktail party, the interview for a better job" (Burgess, 1975: 16). Discuss.

2
Linguistics

2.1 *Branches of linguistics*

As we have seen, both language in general and particular languages can be studied from different points of view. Therefore, the field of linguistics as a whole can be divided into several subfields according to the point of view that is adopted or the special emphasis that is given to one set of phenomena, or assumptions, rather than another.

The first distinction to be drawn is between **general** and **descriptive** linguistics. This is in itself straightforward enough. It corresponds to the distinction between studying language in general and describing particular languages. The question "What is language?" which, in the previous chapter, was said to be the central defining question of the whole discipline is more properly seen as the central question in general linguistics. General linguistics and descriptive linguistics are by no means unrelated. Each depends, explicitly or implicitly upon the other: general linguistics supplies the concepts and categories in terms of which particular languages are to be analysed; descriptive linguistics, in its turn, provides the data which confirm or refute the propositions and theories put forward in general linguistics. For example, the general linguist might formulate the hypothesis that all languages have nouns and verbs. The descriptive linguist might refute this with empirical evidence that there is at least one language in the description of which the distinction between nouns and verbs cannot be established. But in order to refute, or confirm, the hypothesis the descriptive linguist must operate with some concepts of 'noun' and 'verb' which have been supplied to him by the general linguist.

There are of course all sorts of reasons why one might wish to describe a particular language. Many of those working in descriptive linguistics will be doing so, not because they are interested in

providing data for general linguistics or in testing conflicting
theories and hypotheses, but because they wish to produce a
reference grammar or dictionary for practical purposes. But this
fact does not affect the interdependence of the two complementary
subfields of general and descriptive linguistics.

Throughout the nineteenth century, linguists were very much
concerned with investigating the details of the historical development of particular languages and with formulating general hypotheses about language-change. The branch of the discipline that
deals with these matters is now known, naturally enough, as **historical** linguistics. It is obvious that in historical linguistics, as in
non-historical linguistics, one can be interested in language in
general or in particular languages. It is convenient to mention at this
point the more technical terms 'diachronic' and 'synchronic'. These
were first used by Saussure (whose distinction of 'langue' and
'parole' was referred to in the preceding chapter). A **diachronic**
description of a language traces the historical development of the
language and records the changes that have taken place in it between successive points in time: 'diachronic' is equivalent, therefore, to 'historical'. A **synchronic** description of a language is non-
historical: it presents an account of the language as it is at some
particular point in time.

A third dichotomy is that which holds between **theoretical** and
applied linguistics. Briefly, theoretical linguistics studies language
and languages with a view to constructing a theory of their structure
and functions and without regard to any practical applications that
the investigation of language and languages might have, whereas
applied linguistics has as its concerns the application of the concepts
and findings of linguistics to a variety of practical tasks, including
language-teaching. In principle, the distinction between the theoretical and the applied is independent of the other two distinctions
drawn so far. In practice, there is little difference made between the
terms 'theoretical linguistics' and 'general linguistics': it is taken for
granted by most of those who use the term 'theoretical linguistics'
that the goal of theoretical linguistics is the formulation of a satisfactory theory of the structure of language in general. As far as applied
linguistics is concerned, it is clear that it draws on both the general
and the descriptive branches of the subject.

The fourth, and final, dichotomy has to do with a narrower and a broader view of the scope of the subject. There is no generally accepted terminological distinction for this: we will use the terms 'microlinguistics' and 'macrolinguistics', saying that in **microlinguistics** one adopts the narrower view and in **macrolinguistics** the broader view. At its narrowest microlinguistics is concerned solely with the structure of language-systems, without regard to the way in which languages are acquired, stored in the brain or used in their various functions; without regard to the interdependence of language and culture; without regard to the physiological and psychological mechanisms that are involved in language-behaviour; in short, without regard to anything other than the language-system, considered (as Saussure, or rather his editors, put it) in itself and for itself. At its broadest, macrolinguistics is concerned with everything that pertains in any way at all to language and languages.

Since many disciplines other than linguistics are concerned with language, it is not surprising that several interdisciplinary areas should have been identified within macrolinguistics and given a distinctive name: sociolinguistics, psycholinguistics, ethnolinguistics, stylistics, etc.

One point that must be emphasized is that the distinction between microlinguistics and macrolinguistics is independent of the distinction between theoretical and applied linguistics. There is, in principle, a theoretical aspect to every branch of macrolinguistics. It so happens that in such areas of applied linguistics as language-teaching it is essential to take the broader, rather than the narrower, view of the structure and functions of languages. This is why some authors have incorporated what is here called macrolinguistics within applied linguistics.

We shall look at some areas of macrolinguistics in later chapters. It might be thought that, in view of the acknowledged importance of language to so many disciplines, linguistics ought to take the broadest possible view of its subject-matter. There is a sense in which this is true. The problem is that there is not yet, and may never be, a satisfactory theoretical framework within which we can view language simultaneously from a psychological, a sociological, a cultural, an aesthetic and a neurophysiological point of view (not to mention several other equally relevant viewpoints). Most linguists nowadays would say that it is theoretical synchronic microlinguistics that constitutes the core of their discipline and gives it whatever unity and coherence it has. Almost half of this book will be devoted to this central core; the rest will be concerned with historical linguistics and with selected areas of macrolinguistics.

2.2   Is linguistics a science?

Linguistics is usually defined as the science of language or, alternatively, as the scientific study of language (cf. 1.1). The very fact that there should be a section, in this book and in other introductions to linguistics, devoted explicitly to a discussion of the scientific status of the discipline should not pass without comment. After all, disciplines whose scientific status is unquestioned – physics, chemistry, biology, etc. – feel no need to justify their claim to be called sciences. Why should linguistics be so concerned to defend the validity of its title? And why is it that, in defending his scientific credentials, the linguist so often gives the impression of protesting too much? The reader has every right to be suspicious.

The first point that must be made is that the English word 'science' is much narrower in its coverage than many of its conventionally accepted translation-equivalents in other languages: such as 'Wissenschaft' in German, 'nauka' in Russian and even 'science' in French. Linguistics suffers more than most disciplines do from the very specific implications of the English words 'science' and 'scientific', which refer, first and foremost, to the natural sciences and the methods of investigation characteristic of them. This is still true, even though such phrases as 'the social sciences', 'the behavioural sciences' and even 'the human sciences' are increasingly common. Should we then interpret the word 'science' in the heading to this section to mean simply "properly constituted academic discipline"?

There is rather more to the question than this interpretation would suggest. Most linguists who subscribe to the definition of their discipline as the scientific study of language do so because they have in mind some distinction between a scientific and a non-scientific way of doing things. They may disagree about some of the implications of the term 'scientific', as do philosophers and historians of science. But they are in general agreement about the principal differences between the scientific and non-scientific study of language. Let us begin, then, with these points of agreement.

The first, and most important of these is that linguistics is **empirical**, rather than speculative or intuitive: it operates with publicly verifiable data obtained by means of observation or experiment. To be empirical, in this sense, is for most people the very hallmark of science. Closely related to the property of being empirically based is that of **objectivity**. Language is something that we tend to take for granted; something with which we are familiar from childhood in a practical, unreflecting manner. This practical familiarity with language tends to stand in the way of its objective examination. There are all sorts of social, cultural and nationalistic prejudices associated with the layman's view of language and of particular languages. For example, one accent or dialect of a particular language might be thought to be inherently purer than another; or again one language might be held to be more primitive than another. Objectivity demands, at the very least, that beliefs like these should be challenged and terms like 'pure' and 'primitive' either clearly defined or rejected.

Many of the ideas about language which the linguist calls into question, if he does not abandon them entirely, might appear to be a matter of downright common sense. But, as Bloomfield (1935: 3) remarked of the common-sense way of dealing with linguistic questions: "like much else that masquerades as common sense, it is in fact highly sophisticated and derives, at no great distance, from the speculations of ancient and medieval philosophers". Not all linguists have as low an opinion of these philosophical speculations about language as Bloomfield had. But his general point is valid. The terms that the layman uses to talk about language and the attitudes that he has with respect to language have a history to them. They would often seem less obviously applicable or self-evident if he knew something of their historical origin.

We shall not go into the history of linguistics in this book. Some general comments, however, are in order. It is customary for introductions to linguistics to draw a sharp distinction between **traditional grammar** and modern linguistics, contrasting the scientific status of the latter with the non-scientific status of the former. There is good reason to draw this distinction and to point out that

many of the popular misconceptions about language that are current in our society can be explained, historically, in terms of the
philosophical and cultural assumptions which determined the development of traditional grammar. Some of these misconceptions
will be listed and discussed in the following section. It must be
emphasized, however, that linguistics, like any other discipline,
builds on the past, not only by challenging and refuting traditional
doctrines but also by developing and reformulating them. Many
recent works on linguistics, in describing the great advances made
in the scientific investigation of language in the past hundred years
or so, have neglected to emphasize the continuity of Western linguistic theory from the earliest times to the present day. They have
often been somewhat anachronistic, too, in their failure to treat
traditional grammar in terms of the aims it set itself. It must not be
forgotten that the terms 'science' and 'scientific' (or their precur-
sors) have been construed differently at different periods.

   It should also be pointed out that what is generally referred to by
means of the term 'traditional grammar' – i.e. Western linguistic
theory going back through the Renaissance and the Middle Ages to
Roman and, before that, Greek scholarship – is much richer and
more variegated than is commonly realized. Furthermore, it was
very often a misunderstood and distorted version of traditional
grammar that was taught at school to generations of reluctant and
uninterested pupils. In the last few years linguists have begun to
take a more balanced view of the contribution that traditional
grammar – we shall continue to use the term – has made to the
development of their discipline. There is still much research to be
done on such of the original sources as have survived from the
earlier periods. But several histories of linguistics are now available
which give a more satisfactory account of the foundations and
development of traditional grammar than was readily available to
Bloomfield's generation and that of his immediate successors.

   Let us now return to the present state of linguistics. It is undoubtedly more empirical and objective, in its professed attitudes
and assumptions at any rate, than traditional grammar. We shall
look at some of these attitudes and assumptions in more detail in the
following section. But is it as empirical and objective in practice as it
claims to be? Here there is certainly room for doubt. There is also

room for dispute, at a more sophisticated level of discussion, as to the nature of scientific objectivity and the applicability to the study of language of what is commonly referred to as the scientific method.

Actually, it is no longer so widely accepted by scientists and philosophers of science that there is a single method of enquiry applicable in all branches of science. The very term itself, 'the scientific method', has a distinctly old-fashioned, even nineteenth-century, ring to it. It is sometimes suggested that scientific enquiry must necessarily proceed by means of inductive generalization on the basis of theoretically uncontrolled observation. Indeed, this is what many people hold to be implied by the term 'the scientific method'. But few scholars have ever worked in this way even in the natural sciences. Whatever scientific objectivity means it certainly does not imply that the scientist should refrain from theorizing and from the formulation of general hypotheses until he has amassed a sufficient amount of data. Scientific data, it has often been pointed out, are not given in experience, but taken from it. Observation implies selective attention. There is no such thing as theory-neutral and hypothesis-free observation and data collection. To use a currently fashionable phrase, originating with Popper, observation is, of necessity and from the outset, theory-laden.

The phrase is suggestive, but controversial. It was produced in reaction to the strongly empiricist view of science put forward by the logical positivists in the period preceding the Second World War. Students of linguistics should know a little about **empiricism** and **positivism**. Without such knowledge – though it need not be very detailed or profound – they cannot be expected to understand some of the theoretical and methodological issues that divide one school of linguistics from another at the present time. What follows is the necessary minimum of background information, presented, as far as this is possible, impartially and without commitment to either side in areas of known controversy. The controversies, it should be added, are relevant to the whole of science, not just to linguistics. But they have a special relevance for the linguist, in that recent developments in linguistics and the philosophy of language, associated with the work and ideas of Chomsky, have had a very considerable impact upon the more general discussion of empiricism and positivism both by philosophers and by psychologists and other social scientists (cf. 7.4).

Empiricism implies much more than the adoption of empirical methods of verification or confirmation: there is therefore a crucial distinction to be drawn between 'empiricist' and 'empirical'. The term 'empiricism' refers to the view that all knowledge comes from experience – the Greek word 'empeiria' means, roughly, "experience" – and, more particularly, from perception and sense-data. It is opposed, in a long-standing philosophical controversy to 'rationalism' – from the Latin 'ratio' meaning, in this context, "mind", "intellect" or "reason". The **rationalists** emphasize the role that the mind plays in the acquisition of knowledge. In particular, they hold that there are certain a priori concepts or propositions ('a priori' means, in its traditional interpretation, "known independently of experience") in terms of which the mind interprets the data of experience. We will come back to some more specific aspects of the controversy between empiricism and rationalism in our discussion of generativism (cf. 7.4).

No distinction need be drawn, for our purposes, between empiricism and positivism. The former has a longer history and is much broader in scope as a philosophical attitude. But the two are natural allies and are closely associated in all that concerns us here. Positivism rests upon the distinction between the so called positive data of experience and transcendental speculation of various kinds. It tends to be secular and anti-metaphysical in outlook and rejects any appeal to non-physical entities. It was the aim of the **logical positivists** of the Vienna Circle to produce a single system of unified science, in which the whole body of positive knowledge would be represented, ultimately, as a set of precisely formulated propositions.

Two more specific principles were central to this proposal. The first was the now famous **verification principle**: the principle that no statement was meaningful unless it could be verified by observation or standard scientific methods applied to the data provided by observation. The second was the principle of **reductionism**: the principle that, of the sciences, some were more basic than others – physics and chemistry being more basic than biology, biology being more basic than psychology and sociology, and so on – and that in the grand synthesis of unified science the concepts and propositions of the less basic sciences were to be reduced to (i.e. reinterpreted in terms of) the concepts and propositions of the more basic sciences. Reductionism, unlike the verification principle, was characteristic of a much wider group of scholars than the members of the Vienna Circle forty years ago.

The verification principle has now been abandoned (though it has played its part in the formation of the truth-conditional theory of meaning: cf. 5.6) and the principle of reductionism is far less generally accepted by scientists and philosophers of science than it was when Bloomfield wrote his classic textbook of linguistics in 1933. I mention Bloomfield at this point because, not surprisingly, he was strongly committed to empiricism and positivism. This is made very clear in the second chapter of his textbook. He was, in fact, closely associated with the Unity of Science movement and subscribed fully to the principle of reductionism. It was Bloomfield more than anyone else who set for linguistics, especially in America, the ideal of being truly scientific. There is therefore a historically explicable legacy of empiricism and positivism in linguistics.

Reductionism, and more generally positivism, is no longer as attractive to most scientists as it once was. It is now widely accepted that there is no such thing as a single scientific method applicable in all fields; that diverse approaches are not only to be tolerated, as a matter of short-term necessity, in different disciplines, but may be justifiable, in the long term too, by virtue of irreducible differences of subject-matter. Ever since the seventeenth century – from the time of Descartes and Hobbes – there have been doubts expressed by some philosophers of science about the positivists' programme of accounting for mental processes in terms of the methods and concepts characteristic of the physical sciences. Much of twentieth-century psychology and sociology, like much of twentieth-century linguistics, has been positivistic in spirit. But in all three disciplines, and most obviously in linguistics, positivism has recently come under attack as being either unworkable or sterile.

In short, the question whether a discipline is or is not scientific can no longer be satisfactorily answered, if it ever could be, by making reference to the so called scientific method. Every well established science employs its own characteristic theoretical constructs and its own methods of obtaining and interpreting the data. What was referred to in the previous chapter as a fiction – the language-system – can be described, in scientifically more respectable terms, as a **theoretical construct**. Questions can be asked about the reality of such constructs, just as they can be asked about the reality of the theoretical constructs of physics or biochemistry. It is more profitable, however, to enquire of each theoretical construct that is postulated what explanatory purpose it is fulfilling with respect to the data.

All that has just been said about empiricism, positivism and the current status of the so called scientific method is intended to be more or less factual and uncontroversial. We now turn to points of controversy.

The first has to do with the implication of Popper's notion of theory-laden observation. This is controversial in the use of the term 'theory'. What Popper had in mind, and was attacking, was the sharp distinction drawn by the logical positivists between observation, itself held to be theoretically neutral, and theory-construction, held to be a matter of inductive generalization. He was undoubtedly correct in challenging the sharpness of the distinction and, more especially, the view that observation and data-collection can, and must, proceed in advance of the formulation of hypotheses. It is commonly the case that the selection of data is determined by some hypothesis that the scientist wishes to test; and it does not matter how this hypothesis has been arrived at. The fact that the positivists' notion of unselective observation and data-collection is invalid does not mean that there is no distinction at all to be drawn between pretheoretical and theoretical concepts. It is an abuse of the term 'theory' to subsume under it all the preconceptions and expectations with which one approaches what is observable and makes one's selection. We will draw upon the distinction between pretheoretical and theoretical concepts at several places in later chapters; and we will assume that observation, though necessarily selective, can be made subject to satisfactory methodological controls, in linguistics as in other empirically based sciences.

A second point of controversy – and one that is of particular importance in linguistics at the present time – has to do with the role of intuition and the methodological problems that arise in this

connection. The term 'intuition' carries with it certain rather unfor-
tunate everyday associations. All that is meant when one refers to
the native speaker's intuitions about his language is his spontaneous
and untutored judgements about the acceptability or unacceptabil-
ity of utterances, the equivalence or non-equivalence of utterances,
and so on. There was a time when some linguists thought that it was
in principle possible to escape from the necessity of asking native
speakers to make such intuitive judgements about their language by
simply collecting a large enough **corpus** of naturally occurring data
and submitting it to an exhaustive and systematic analysis. Very few
linguists take this view nowadays. It has become clear that many
naturally occurring utterances are, for linguistically irrelevant
reasons, unacceptable and also that no corpus of material, however
large, will contain examples of every kind of acceptable utterance.
But the linguist's appeal to intuitive evidence remains controversial. There are two aspects to the controversy.

The first relates to the question whether the intuitions that the
linguist makes reference to are part of the native speaker's linguistic
competence as such. If so, on Chomsky's definition of 'competence'
and his formulation of the goals of linguistics, the intuitions themselves become part of what the description of any particular language must directly account for. Most linguists would probably not
want to say that the description of a language must treat the native
speaker's intuitions as data. We will come back to this question in
our discussion of generativism (cf. 7.4).

The second part of the controversy has to do with the reliability of
the native speaker's judgements, considered as reports or predictions of his own and others' language-behaviour. The general consensus of opinion among linguists would seem to be that such
judgements are, in particular respects at least, highly unreliable.
Not only do native speakers frequently disagree among themselves
about what is acceptable, when there is no other reason to believe
that they speak different dialects, but their judgements have been
shown to vary over time. Moreover, it often happens that a native
speaker will reject as unacceptable some utterance put to him by the
descriptive linguist and then be heard, or hear himself, producing
that very utterance in some natural context of use. As far as the
linguist's introspections about his language are concerned, they are

at least as unreliable, though often for other reasons, as the intuitions of the layman. The linguist may be less concerned than the layman about conventional standards of correct usage (e.g. admitting quite freely that he normally says *It's me*, rather than *It is I*). But his judgements are more likely to be distorted by his awareness of the implications that they have for this or that theoretical issue. The linguist's introspections about his own language-behaviour and that of others may very well be theory-laden, even if direct observation of spontaneous conversation is not.

There are in fact quite serious methodological problems attaching to the collection of reliable data for a whole range of issues in theoretical linguistics. But they are no more serious than the methodological problems that confront those working in psychology, sociology or the social sciences in general. And in certain respects the linguist is better off than most social scientists, since it is fairly clear how much of what is observable is language-behaviour and how much is not. Furthermore, there are very considerable areas, in the description of any language, for which the reliability of the native speaker's intuitions, and even of the linguist's introspections, is not a serious problem. One must not make too much, therefore, of the methodological problems that arise in the course of linguistic research.

Reference was made in the previous paragraph to psychology, sociology and the other social sciences. Many linguists, perhaps the majority, would classify their discipline among the social sciences. But linguistics is not readily classifiable within any division of academic research which takes as fundamental either the distinction between science and arts or the tripartite distinction of the natural sciences, the social sciences and the humanities. The increasing use of such phrases as 'the life sciences', 'the behavioural sciences', 'the human sciences' or 'the earth sciences' indicates that many disciplines feel the need for strategic or tactical regroupings which have little regard to the conventional distinctions. Whether linguistics, as a university subject, is housed in one faculty rather than another is largely a matter of administrative convenience. Linguistics, as has been emphasized before, has natural links with a wide range of academic disciplines. To say that linguistics is a science is not to deny that, by virtue of its subject-matter, it is closely related to such eminently humane disciplines as philosophy and literary criticism.

In the following sections, a number of principles will be mentioned and discussed which are generally taken for granted nowadays by linguists. For the most part, they can be seen as deriving from the scientific ideal of objectivity. Since modern linguistics, in asserting its objectivity, has so often proclaimed its distinctiveness in this respect from traditional grammar, they are frequently presented in contrast with the principles that determined the characteristic attitudes and assumptions of the traditional grammarian.

2.3 *Terminology and notation*

Every discipline has its own technical vocabulary. Linguistics is no exception. Most of the technical terms used by linguists arise in the course of their work and are easily understood by those who approach the subject sympathetically and without prejudice.

The objection is sometimes made that the terminology, or jargon, of linguistics is unnecessarily complex. Why is the linguist so prone to the creation of new terms? Why is he not content to talk about sounds, words and parts of speech, instead of inventing such new technical terms as 'phoneme', 'morpheme' and 'form class'? The answer is that most of the everyday terms that are used with reference to language – many of which, incidentally, originated as technical terms of traditional grammar – are imprecise or ambiguous. This is not to say that the linguist, like all specialists, may not be guilty at times of misplaced terminological pedantry. In principle, however, the specialized vocabulary of linguistics, if it is kept under control and properly used, serves to clarify, rather than to mystify. It eliminates a good deal of ambiguity and possible misunderstanding.

As with terminology, so with notation. We have to use language in order to talk both about language in general and about particular languages. In doing so, we need to be able to identify exactly what bits, parts or features of a language we are referring to. The use of special notational conventions makes this a lot easier. For example, we might need to distinguish between the meaning of a word and its form and between each of these and the word itself. There is unfortunately no generally accepted set of notational conventions by means of which these and other distinctions can be drawn. In the present work, we shall make distinctive use of single quotation-marks, double quotation-marks and italics. For example, we shall distinguish between "table" and *table*, the former being the meaning and the latter the form (or one of the forms) of the word 'table'. By making use of these conventions, we can keep distinct, as we shall see later, at least two of the senses of the word 'word': in the first sense it refers to something that we should expect to be listed in the dictionary of the language; in the second sense it refers to what would be printed between spaces as a sequence of letters in a written text.

Other notational conventions will be introduced later, enabling us to distinguish spoken forms from written forms; and spoken forms of one kind (phonetic) from spoken forms of another kind (phonological); and so on. The general point being made here is that various notational conventions are, if not absolutely essential, at least very useful for the purpose of referring to language-data and making it clear what is being talked about. They have the further advantage that they force the linguist to think carefully about certain distinctions that might otherwise pass unnoticed. Very often, it proves difficult to be absolutely consistent in the application of some particular notational convention; and this difficulty then leads to a re-assessment of the theoretical distinction for which the notational convention was first established. This is one of the ways in which progress in any discipline is made.

2.4   *Linguistics is descriptive, not prescriptive*

The term 'descriptive' is here being employed in a different sense from the sense in which it opposes either 'general', on the one hand, or 'historical', on the other. The contrast that is relevant here is the one that holds between **describing** how things are and **prescribing** how things ought to be. An alternative to 'prescriptive', in the sense in which it contrasts with 'descriptive', is 'normative'. To say that linguistics is a descriptive (i.e. non-normative) science is to say that the linguist tries to discover and record the rules to which the members of a language-community actually conform and does not seek to impose upon them other (i.e. extraneous) rules, or norms, of correctness.

It is perhaps confusing to use the term 'rule', as I have just done, in these two very different senses. Rightly or wrongly, linguists talk in these terms. It might be helpful, therefore, to illustrate the difference between the two kinds of rules – let us call them immanent and transcendent, respectively – from something other than the use of language. Let us take sexual behaviour in a given society. If we adopt the purely descriptive (i.e. non-normative) point of view in the investigation of sexual behaviour, we will try to find out how people actually behave: whether they practise premarital sex, and, if so, of what kind and from what age; whether husbands and wives are equally faithful or unfaithful to their partners; and so on. In so far as the behaviour of particular groups within the community is governed, in practice, by determinable principles – whether the members of these groups profess, or are even aware of, these principles or not – we can say that their behaviour is rule-governed: the rules are **immanent** in their actual behaviour. But such rules (if they are rightly called rules) are very different, in status if not in content, from the rules of conduct that the law, the established religion or simply explicit conventional morality might prescribe. People may or may not conform, in practice, to what I am calling the **transcendent** (i.e. extraneous or non-immanent) rules of sexual behaviour. Furthermore, there may be differences between how they behave and how they say, or even think, that they behave. All these differences have their correlates in respect of language-behaviour. The most important distinction, however, is the one that holds between transcendent (i.e. prescriptive) and immanent (i.e. descriptive) rules. Prescriptive *do*s and *don't*s are commands (*Do/Don't say X!*); descriptive *do*s and *don't*s are statements (*People do/don't say X*).

The reason why present-day linguists are so insistent about the distinction between descriptive and prescriptive rules is simply that traditional grammar was very strongly normative in character. The grammarian saw it as his task to formulate the standards of correctness and to impose these, if necessary, upon the speakers of the language. Many of the normative precepts of traditional grammar will be familiar to the reader: "You should never use a double-negative" (*I didn't do nothing*); "Don't end a sentence with a preposition" (*That's the man I was speaking to*); "The verb 'to be' takes the same case after it as before" (so that, by the application of this rule, *It's me* should be corrected to *It is I*); "*Ain't* is wrong"; "You should not split the infinitive" (as in *I want you to clearly understand* where *clearly* is inserted between *to* and *understand*).

Consideration of the above examples quickly shows that they are quite heterogeneous in character. There are some dialects of English in which the so called double-negative is never employed (i.e. in which *I didn't do nothing* is never used as the equivalent of Standard English *I didn't do anything*); there are others in which it is, from a purely descriptive point of view, the correct construction. When reasons are given for the condemnation of the double negative as incorrect, in terms of some prescriptive principle with reference to which actual usage may be judged and found wanting, logic is made the court of appeal. Logic tells us, it is said, that two negatives make a positive. This calls for several comments. First, it betrays a misunderstanding of what logic is and how it operates: but we need not go into the nature of logical axioms and the complex question of how the so-called natural logic of ordinary language-behaviour relates to the systems of logic that are constructed and investigated by logicians. The point is simply that there is nothing inherently illogical about the so-called double-negative construction. In the dialects in which it is regularly employed, it operates quite systematically according to the grammatical rules and principles of interpretation that are immanent in the behaviour of the dialect-communities in question. A second point to be borne in mind is that the so-called double-negative construction cannot be properly described, as it operates in certain dialects of English, without taking into account features of stress and intonation. The rules of Standard English (i.e. the rules immanent in the language-behaviour of the speakers of a particular dialect of English) permit *I didn't do nothing* (with the meaning, roughly, "It's not true that I did nothing") provided that *didn't* is stressed or, alternatively and with additional implications or presuppositions, *do* or *nothing* is pronounced with particularly heavy stress. In dialects in which *I didn't do nothing* (with normal unemphatic stress) can mean "I didn't do anything" it also has the meanings that it has in Standard

English, but stress and intonation prevent confusion. Finally, it may be noted that there are many languages in which the so-called double-negative construction occurs in the standard literary dialect: e.g. French, Italian, Spanish, Russian – to mention but a few of the more familiar modern European languages. Even the most prestigious dialect of Ancient Greek – Classical Greek as used in the writings of Plato, Sophocles, Thucydides or, the very founding father of logic, Aristotle himself – had a double-negative construction. And traditional grammar, after all, had its origins in the description of the literary dialects of Ancient Greece!

Other normative precepts of traditional grammar – such as the condemnation of the split infinitive (. . . *to clearly understand*) or of *It's me* – derive from the application to English of principles and categories established in the first place for the description of Greek and Latin. It so happens that the forms to which the term 'infinitive' is applied are one-word forms in Greek and Latin, as in French, German, Russian, etc. Traditionally, the two-word forms *to understand*, *to go*, etc., are also called infinitives, though their function is only partly comparable with the function of, say, the Latin infinitives. As we shall see later, whether a form can be split (in the sense in which we talk about the split infinitive) is one of the principal criteria which the linguist applies to decide whether the form in question is a one-word form or a two-word form. Given that, by other criteria and by the writing conventions of the written language, the so-called infinitives of English are two-word forms, there can be no objection, in principle, to splitting them. As to the castigation of *It's me*, etc., the fact of the matter is that what are referred to in traditional grammar as differences of case (*I* vs. *me*, *she* vs. *her*, *he* vs. *him*, etc.) are not found in all languages; nor is anything that can be identified in terms of its function and grammatical characteristics as a verb meaning "to be". Furthermore, in languages that have both case and a verb identifiable as the equivalent of the Latin 'esse' or English 'to be', the diversity of the constructions that are found is such that the traditional rule, "The verb 'to be' takes the same case after it as before", stands out immediately for what it is – a Latin-based normative rule which cannot be supported on more general grounds.

Interestingly enough, many speakers of what the traditionally minded grammarian would regard as good English will say and write *between you and I*, *He told you and I*, etc. Such constructions violate another traditional prescriptive rule for English: "Verbs and prepositions govern their object in the accusative." They result, presumably, from what is often called **hypercorrection**: the extension of some rule or principle, on the basis of a misunderstanding of its domain of application, to a range of phenomena to which, originally, it did not apply. The nature of the prescriptive rule is misunderstood – the more so as many speakers who might naturally say *You and me will go* would never say either *Me will go* or *He told I*. It is interpreted instead as an instruction (under pain of being considered a speaker of bad English) to substitute *you and I* for *you and me* (or *me and you*) in all positions of occurrence. This results in the production, not only of what the traditional grammarian would accept as correct, *You and I will go together*, etc., but also of what he would condemn, *between you and I*, *He told you and I*, etc. It is not being implied, of course, that every speaker of English who says *between you and I*, *He told you and I*, etc., has himself performed the operation of applying and misapplying the traditional rule. These constructions are now so common in the speech of middle-class and upper-class speakers of Standard English in England that they must have been learned naturally in the normal process of language-acquisition by perhaps the majority of those who use them. There is little doubt, however, that their origin lies in the process of hypercorrection.

Neither logic nor the grammar of Latin can properly serve as the court of appeal when it comes to deciding whether something is or is not correct in English. Nor can the unquestioned authority of tradition for tradition's sake ("That's what I was taught, and my parents, and my parents' parents") or the usage of what are thought to be the best writers in the language. It is a widely held view in our society, or has been until recently, that linguistic change necessarily involves a debasement or corruption of the language. This view is indefensible. All languages are subject to change. This is a matter of empirical fact; and it is the task of historical linguistics to investigate the details of language-change, when they are accessible to investigation, and, by constructing an explanatory theory of language-change, to contribute to our understanding of the nature of language. The factors that determine language-change are complex and, so far, only partly understood. But enough is known now – and has been known since the middle of the nineteenth century – for it to be clear to any unprejudiced observer of change in language that what is condemned at any one time as a corruption or debasement of traditional standards of usage can always be matched with an earlier change of the same kind which brought into being the usage that traditionalists themselves treat as unalterably correct.

As to the principle of conforming to the standards set by the acknowledged best writers, this principle too is indefensible – indefensible, that is to say, in relation to the use that is commonly made of it. There is no reason to believe that the writer, genius though he be, is vouchsafed, by special dispensation, a sure and certain knowledge of the transcendent rules of correctness that is denied to the rest of us. It so happens that traditional grammar had a very strong literary bias. The reason is that at several important periods in the development of European culture – from the period of Alexandrian scholarship in the second century B.C. to that of Renaissance humanism – grammatical description, first of Greek, then of Latin, was subordinated to the practical task of making the literature of an earlier age accessible to those who did not, and in the nature of things could not, speak naturally the dialect of Greek or Latin upon which the language of the classical texts was based. The literary bias of traditional grammar is not only historically explicable, but perfectly justifiable, as far as the description of Greek and Latin was concerned. It is quite unjustifiable when it comes to the grammatical description of modern spoken languages.

There are no absolute standards of correctness in language. We can say that a foreigner has made a mistake, if he says something that violates the rules immanent in the usage of native speakers. We can also say, if we wish, that a speaker of a non-standard social or regional dialect of English has spoken ungrammatically if his utterance violates the rules immanent in Standard English. But, in saying this, we are of course assuming that he was intending, or perhaps ought to have been intending, to use Standard English. And that is itself an assumption which requires justification.

It must now be emphasized – and this point is frequently misunderstood – that in drawing a distinction between description and prescription, the linguist is not saying that there is no place at all for the establishment and prescription of norms of usage. There are obvious administrative and educational advantages, in the modern world, in standardizing the principal dialect that is employed within a particular country or region. This process of standardization has taken place over a long period in many Western countries with or without government intervention. It is now happening on an accelerated scale, and as a matter of official policy, in several of the developing nations in Africa and Asia. The problem of selecting, standardizing and promoting one particular language or dialect at the expense of others is fraught with political and social difficulties. It is part of what has come to be called **language-planning** – an important area in the field of applied sociolinguistics.

Nor should it be thought that in denying that all change in language is for the worse, the linguist is implying that it must be for the better. He is merely calling into question the unthinking appeal to empirically discredited criteria. He concedes that it might be possible, in principle, to evaluate dialects and languages in terms of their relative flexibility, range of expression, precision and aesthetic potential; and he certainly accepts that the use that is made of their dialect or language by individual speakers and writers may be more or less effective. However, he cannot but report, on the basis of the more scientific work that has been done on language and languages in recent years, that most of the judgements that are made about such matters are extremely subjective. As an individual member of a language-community, the linguist will have his own prejudices, either personal to him or deriving from his social, cultural and geographical background; and he may be either conservative or progressive by temperament. His attitudes towards his own language will be no less subjective in this respect than those of the layman. He may find a particular accent or dialect pleasing or displeasing. He may even correct his children's speech, if he finds them using a pronunciation, a word or a grammatical construction that is frowned upon by purists. But, in doing so, if he is honest with himself, he will know that what he is correcting is not inherently incorrect, but only incorrect relative to some standard which, for reasons of social prestige or educational advantage, he wishes his children to adopt.

As far as his attitude to the literary language is concerned, the linguist is simply pointing out that language is used for many purposes and that its use in relation to these purposes should not be judged by criteria which are applicable, solely or primarily, to the literary language. This does not mean that he is in any way hostile to literature or to the study of literature in our schools and universities. On the contrary, many linguists have a particular interest in the investigation of the literary purposes to which language is put and its success in achieving those purposes. This is one part – and a very important part – of the branch of macrolinguistics known as **stylistics**.

2.5 *Priority of synchronic description*

The principle of the priority of synchronic description, which is characteristic of most twentieth-century linguistic theory, implies that historical considerations are irrelevant to the investigation of particular temporal states of a language. Saussure's terms 'synchronic' and 'diachronic' were introduced earlier in the chapter (cf. 2.1). We can use one of Saussure's own analogies to explain what is meant by the priority of the synchronic over the diachronic.

Let us compare the historical development of a particular language with a game of chess that is being played in front of us. The state of the board is constantly changing, as each player makes his move. At any one time, however, the state of the game can be fully described in terms of the positions occupied by the pieces. (Actually, this is not quite true. For example, the state of the game is affected, as far as the possibilities for castling are concerned, by moving the king from, and back to, its original position. We may neglect such minor points of detail in which Saussure's analogy breaks down.) It does not matter by what route the players have arrived at a given state of the game. Regardless of the number, nature or order of the previous moves, the present state of the game is synchronically describable without reference to them. So it is, according to Saussure, with the historical development of languages. All languages are constantly changing. But each of the successive states of a language can, and should, be described on its own terms without reference to what it has developed from or what it is likely to develop into.

All this may seem highly theoretical and abstract. But it has some very practical implications. The first has to do with what I will call the **etymological fallacy**. Etymology is the study of the origin and development of words. It had its source, as far as the Western grammatical tradition is concerned, in the speculations of certain Greek philosophers of the fifth century before Christ. The term 'etymology' is itself revealing. It contains a Latinized transcription of a form of the Greek word 'etumos' meaning "true" or "real". According to one school of fifth-century Greek philosophers all words were naturally, rather than conventionally, associated with what they signified. This might not be evident to the layman, they would say; but it could be demonstrated by the philosopher able to discern the reality that lay behind the appearance of things. To penetrate the often misleading appearances and, by careful analysis of changes that had taken place in the development of the form or meaning of a word, to discover the origin of a word and thereby its real meaning was to reveal one of the truths of nature. What I am referring to as the etymological fallacy is the assumption that the original form or meaning of a word is, necessarily and by virtue of that very fact, its correct form or meaning. This assumption is widely held. How often do we meet the argument that because such and such a word comes from Greek, Latin, Arabic, or whatever language it might be in the particular instance, the correct meaning of the word must be what it was in the language of origin! The argument is fallacious, because the tacit assumption of an originally true or appropriate correspondence between form and meaning, upon which the argument rests, cannot be substantiated.

Etymology was put on a sounder footing in the nineteenth century than it had been in previous periods. It is no longer fair to say, as Voltaire is reported to have done, that etymology is a science in which the vowels count for nothing and the consonants for very little! As it is nowadays practised, it is a respectable branch of historical, or diachronic, linguistics. As we shall see in Chapter 6, it has its own methodological principles, whose reliability depends upon the quality and quantity of the evidence upon which they are brought to bear. In favourable instances the reliability of etymological reconstruction is very high indeed.

One point that became clear to nineteenth-century etymologists and is now taken for granted by all linguists is that most words in the vocabulary of any language cannot be traced back to their origin. Words that are deliberately created, by borrowing forms from other languages or using any other principle, are untypical of the vocabulary as a whole, and certainly of what might be thought of as the more basic, non-technical vocabulary of a language. What the present-day etymologist does is to relate words of one synchronically describable state of a language to words, attested or reconstructed, of some earlier state of the same language or of some other language. But the words of the earlier state of the same language or of the earlier language have themselves developed from earlier words. Whether the form or meaning of these earlier words is recoverable by the techniques of etymology will depend upon the evidence that has survived. For example, we can relate the present-day English word 'ten' to the Old English word whose forms were either *ten* (with a long vowel) or *tien*. And we can relate the Old English word, through successive hypothetical states, to a reconstructed Proto-Indo-European word with the form *dek̂m*, also meaning "ten". But we cannot go back with any confidence beyond that. And yet the Proto-Indo-European word *dek̂m* – the prefixed asterisk indicates that it is reconstructed, not attested (cf. 6.3) – is obviously not the origin, in any absolute sense, of all the words that have developed from it in the languages that we can identify as belonging to the Indo-European family. It must itself have developed from a word (which may or may not have meant "ten" – there is no way of knowing) belonging to the vocabulary of some other language; and that word in turn from some earlier word in another language: and so on. Generally speaking, etymologists are not concerned nowadays with origins. Indeed, they would say that in many instances (e.g. the word 'ten') it does not make sense to enquire about the origin of a word. All that the etymologist can tell us, with greater or less confidence according to the evidence, is that such and such is the form or meaning of a particular word's earliest known or hypothetical ancestor.

This brings us to one of the more obvious ways in which Saussure's analogy breaks down. Every game of chess, played according to the rules and completed, has a determinate beginning and end. Languages are not like this. Not only is it not the case (as far as we know) that all languages started from the same state of the board, as it were, and then developed differently, but it is also impossible to date the beginning of a language except by arbitrary convention and very approximately. We cannot say, for example, at what point in time spoken Latin became Old French, or Italian, or Spanish. Nor can we say at what time a particular language ceased to exist – except in respect of languages which have become extinct, more or less suddenly, when their last native speakers died. Languages, considered from the diachronic point of view, do not have determinate beginnings or ends. In the last resort, it is a matter of convention and convenience whether we say that Old English and Modern English are two states of the same language or two different languages.

There is yet another way in which Saussure's analogy breaks down. The game of chess is governed by explicitly formulated rules and, within the limits imposed by these rules, the players determine the course of any particular game that is being played in opposition to one another and with reference to a recognized goal. As far as we know, there is no directionality in the diachronic development of languages. There may well be certain general principles which determine the transition from one state of a language to another. But, if there are such principles, they are not comparable with the rules of a man-made game like chess. We shall look at the so-called laws of language-change in Chapter 6.

The principle of the priority of synchronic description is usually understood to carry the implication that, whereas synchronic description is independent of diachronic description, diachronic description presupposes the prior synchronic analysis of the successive states through which languages have passed in the course of their historical development. This may not have been Saussure's view. But it follows from what are now widely accepted assumptions about the nature of language-systems.

Linguists sometimes talk, rather misleadingly, as if the passage of time was of itself sufficient to explain language-change. There are many different factors, both within a language and external to it, which may cause it to change from one synchronic state to another. Some of these factors and possibly the most important of them, are social. The passage of time merely allows for their complex interaction to bring about what is subsequently recognized as a transition from one state of the language to another.

Moreover the notion of diachronic development between successive states of a language makes sense only if it is applied with respect to language-states that are relatively far removed from one another in time. I have already referred to what I have called the fiction of homogeneity (cf. 1.6). Up to a point, this is both useful and necessary. However, if it is assumed that language-change involves the constant transformation through time of what is at any one time a perfectly homogeneous language-system, the whole process of change in language appears to be much more mysterious than it really is. What is characteristic of the speech of an apparently insignificant minority of the members of a language-community at one time may spread throughout most of the community in the course of a generation or two. It might be quite legitimate for the linguist describing the language synchronically at either of these two points in time to discount the speech of the divergent minority. But, if he does so, and then goes on to talk diachronically of one synchronically homogeneous language-system being transformed into another equally homogeneous language-system, he will be guilty of distorting the facts. Worse than that, he will run the risk of creating for himself insoluble theoretical pseudo-problems. Once we realize that no language is ever stable or uniform, we have made the first step towards accounting, theoretically, for the ubiquity and continuity of language-change. If we take two diachronically determined states of a language that are not widely separated in time we are likely to find that most of the differences between them are also present as synchronic variation at both the earlier and the later time. From the microscopic point of view – as distinct from the macroscopic point of view that one normally adopts in historical linguistics – it is impossible to draw a sharp distinction between diachronic change and synchronic variation.

In summary, the principle of the priority of synchronic description is valid. But, in so far as it rests upon the fiction of homogeneity, it must be applied sensibly and in full recognition of the theoretical status of the concept of the language-system. It is to this point that we now turn.

2.6 *Structure and system*

One of the definitions of 'language' that I quoted in Chapter 1 was Chomsky's "a set (finite or infinite) of sentences, each finite in length and constructed out of a finite set of elements" (cf. 1.2). Let us adopt this as a partial definition of the term 'language-system', which was introduced, it will be recalled, in order to eliminate some of the ambiguity that attaches to the English word 'language'.

In so far as they are by definition both stable and uniform, language-systems cannot be identified with real natural languages: they are theoretical constructs, postulated by the linguist in order to account for such regularities as he finds in the language-behaviour of the members of particular language-communities – more precisely in the language-signals that are the products of their language-behaviour. As we have seen, real natural languages are neither stable nor homogeneous. However, there is sufficient stability and homogeneity in the speech of those who would generally be considered to speak the same language for the linguist's postulation of a common underlying language-system to be useful and scientifically justifiable, except when he is dealing explicitly with synchronic and diachronic variation. Throughout the next three chapters, we shall take for granted the validity of the notion of the language-system as it is here defined and explained.

Among the language-signals produced by an English speaker, over a given period of time, some would be classified as **sentences** of the language and some would not. We need not enquire at this stage what are the criteria by virtue of which this division into sentences and non-sentences is made. Obviously, there are principles that determine the construction of larger texts and discourses. Furthermore, some of these principles are such that anyone violating them might reasonably be accused of breaking the rules of the language. Although it has not gone unchallenged in recent years, the traditional assumption that most, if not all, of what is involved in knowing a language can be accounted for in terms of the construction and interpretation of sentences is still accepted by the majority of linguists.

Sentences, let us say, are what would be conventionally punctuated as such in the written language. As we have seen, natural languages have the property of medium-transferability (cf. 1.4). This means that, in general, any sentence of the written language can be put into correspondence with a sentence of the spoken language and vice versa. Spoken sentences are not, of course, punctuated as such with anything that is strictly equivalent to the initial capital letter or the closing full-stop, or period, of written sentences. For present purposes, however, we can establish a rough and ready equivalence between the punctuation-marks of a written language and the **intonation-patterns** of the corresponding spoken language.

The term 'structure' figures prominently in modern linguistics, as it does in many disciplines. If we adopt the point of view that was first clearly expressed by Saussure and is now accepted by all those who subscribe to the principles of **structuralism**, we will say not only that a language-system has a structure, but that it is a structure. For example, in so far as written and spoken English are isomorphic (i.e. have the same structure), they are the same language: there is nothing but their structure that they have in common. The language-system itself is, in principle, independent of the medium in which it is manifest. It is, in this sense, a purely abstract structure.

Language-systems are two-level structures: they have the property of duality (cf. 1.5). Spoken sentences are not just combinations of phonological elements; they are also combinations of syntactic units. Chomsky's partial definition of a language-system as a set of sentences, each of which is finite in length and constructed out of a finite set of elements, must be extended to take account of this essential property of natural languages. It is logically possible for two language-systems to be isomorphic on one level without their being isomorphic on the other. Indeed, as has been pointed out already, it is because the so-called dialects of Chinese are sufficiently close to being syntactically isomorphic (though they are far from being phonologically isomorphic) that the same, non-alphabetic, written language can be put into correspondence more or less equally well with each of them. It is also possible for languages to be phonologically, but not syntactically, isomorphic. This possibility is actualized to a greater or less degree by, let us say, a native speaker of English speaking grammatically perfect French with a particularly bad English accent. More interestingly, the independence of syntax and phonology is demonstrated often quite dramatically in the process of creolization (cf. 9.3).

Natural languages, then, have two levels of structure and the levels are independent, in the sense that the phonological structure of a language is not determined by its syntactic structure and its syntactic structure is not determined by its phonological structure. It is unlikely, to say the least, that any two natural languages should exist such that every spoken or written sentence of the one can be heard or read as a sentence of the other (with or without the same meaning). But it frequently happens, as a consequence of the independence of phonological and syntactic structure, that the same combination of elements (sounds in speech and letters in alphabetic writing) realizes not one, but two or more, sentences. The sentences may be distinguished one from another by intonation or punctuation, as the case may be. Thus

(1) John says Peter has been here all the time

is distinguished from

(2) John, says Peter, has been here all the time

in written English by means of punctuation; and they would normally be distinguished from one another in spoken English by the intonation-pattern superimposed upon them. But even without differences of intonation or punctuation the same combination of elements can realize more than one sentence. For example,

(3) We watched her box

could be either of two different English sentences, in one of which *her* is an adjective-form (cf. *his*) and *box* a noun-form (cf. *suitcase*), in the other of which *her* is a pronoun-form (cf. *him*) and *box* is a verb-form (cf. *wrestle*). We need not bother about justifying the traditional syntactic analysis of (3) to which I have covertly appealed. This is something that will be taken up later. It suffices for the present that we should have established that sentences, as traditionally defined, cannot be identified, and distinguished one from another, in terms of the phonological elements of which they are composed. Indeed, as we can see from (3), they cannot even be identified in terms of the syntactic units of which they are composed without taking into account other aspects of syntactic structure, including the assignment of syntactic units to what are traditionally called **parts of speech** (noun, verb, adjective, etc.).

The syntactic units out of which sentences are constructed, unlike the phonological elements, are very numerous. Nevertheless, like the phonological elements, they are finite in number. Let us say that every language-system presupposes the existence of a finite **inventory** of elements and a finite **vocabulary** of (simple) units, together with a set of rules (of perhaps several kinds) which interrelate the two levels of structure and tell us which combinations of units are sentences of the language-system and, by implication, if not explicitly, which are not. It should be noted that, as we shall see later, the vocabulary of a natural language is much more than a set of syntactic units. None of the modifications or terminological refinements to be introduced in subsequent chapters affects the substance of what has been said here.

For the time being, what we have been calling syntactic units may be thought of as **forms**: i.e. as combinations of elements such that every distinguishable combination is a distinct form. But forms, in this sense of the term, have a meaning, and their meaning is far from being independent of their syntactic function. That this is so is clear in the case of the forms *her* and *box* in (3) above. The traditional view would be that there are (at least) two different words in the vocabulary of English, let us represent them (with single quotation-marks) as 'box$_1$' and 'box$_2$' respectively, which differ both in meaning and in syntactic function, but share the same form, *box*. We shall later make more precise this traditional distinction between a form and the unit of which it is a form; and, in doing so, we shall see that the term 'word', as used both by linguists and by laymen, is highly ambiguous (cf. 4.1).

Every sentence is by definition **well-formed**, both syntactically and phonologically, in the language-system of which it is a sentence. The term 'well-formed' is broader than, but subsumes, the more traditional term 'grammatical', as the latter is broader than, but subsumes, the term 'syntactically well-formed'. The nature and limits of **grammaticality** (i.e. grammatical well-formedness) will be discussed in Chapter 4. Here it is sufficient to make the point that well-formedness (including grammaticality) must not be confused with acceptability, potentiality for use or even meaningfulness. There are indefinitely many sentences of English and other natural languages that, for various reasons, would not normally occur: they might contain an unacceptable juxtaposition of obscene or blasphemous words; they might be stylistically awkward or excessively complex from a psychological point of view; they might be self-contradictory or describe situations which do not occur in the world inhabited by the society using the language in question. Any combination of elements or units of a given language, L, which is not well-formed in terms of the rules of L is **ill-formed** with respect to L. Ill-formed combinations of elements or units may be marked as such by means of a preceding asterisk.[1] Thus

(4) *He weren't doing nothing

is ill-formed, and indeed ungrammatical, with respect to Standard English. It is, however, grammatically well-formed in certain non-standard dialects of English. This example illustrates the more general point that different languages may be constructed out of the same elements and units, what is well-formed in one language being ill-formed with respect to another language. Although the point has been illustrated with reference to two dialects of the same language, it holds, in principle, for what would be thought of as quite different languages.

More could be said here about the structure of language-systems. It is best left for the chapters dealing with phonology, grammar and semantics, where the general points can be introduced gradually and exemplified in greater detail.[2]

We began this section by accepting Chomsky's definition of a language (i.e. a language-system) as a set of sentences. It is

---

[1] The use of the asterisk to indicate ill-formedness must not be confused with its equally common, and longer established, employment in historical linguistics to mark reconstructed forms (cf. 2.5). The context will make it clear which use is intended.

[2] The terms 'structure' and 'system' are frequently used, especially by British linguists, in a specialized sense: 'system' for any set of elements or units that can occur in the same position; 'structure' for any combination of elements and units that results from the appropriate selection in particular positions. Defined in this way 'structure' and 'system' are complementary: each presupposes the other. Systems are established for particular positions in structures; structures are identified in terms of the selections made from systems (cf. Berry, 1975). In this book, 'system' and 'structure' are employed in a more general sense.

preferable, however, to think of a language-system as being composed of an inventory of elements, a vocabulary of units and the rules which determine the well-formedness of sentences on both levels. And this is what we shall do from now on. Arguably, under the appropriate definition of 'sentence' the two ways of thinking of language-systems coincide.

FURTHER READING

Generally, as for Chapter 1. In addition, Crystal (1971), chapters 2–3; Lyons (1974).

Of the textbooks asterisked in the Bibliography, Robins (1979a) is the most comprehensive, and also the most neutral in its presentation of controversial issues; Lyons (1968) emphasizes the continuity between traditional grammar and modern linguistics, is restricted to synchronic microlinguistics, and is slanted towards (a now outdated version of) transformational grammar; Martinet (1960) is in the tradition of European structuralism; Gleason (1961), Hill (1958) and Hockett (1958), together with Joos (1966), give a good account of the field from the point of view of so-called post-Bloomfieldian linguistics; Southworth & Daswani (1974) is particularly good on linguistics in relation to sociology and anthropology, and also on applied linguistics; so too though less comprehensive is Falk (1973); Akmajian, Demers & Harnish (1979), Fromkin & Rodman (1974) and Smith & Wilson (1979) are all consistently Chomskyan in inspiration and, generally speaking, stress the biological, rather than the cultural, in language. For discussion of the various trends and schools in modern linguistics, and for further references, cf. Chapter 7.

Historical (i.e. diachronic) linguistics is dealt with later (Chapter 6). So too are most branches of macrolinguistics (Chapters 8–10).

On applied linguistics, see Corder (1973) and for more detailed discussion Allen & Corder (1975a, b, c).

QUESTIONS AND EXERCISES

1. In what sense is linguistics a science? Does this imply that it is not one of the humanities?

2. "since every branch of knowledge makes use of language, linguistics may, in some respects, be said to lie at the centre of them all, as being the study of the tool that they must use" (Robins, 1979a: 7). Discuss.

3. "The only useful generalizations about language are inductive generalizations" (Bloomfield, 1935: 20). Discuss.

4. Why do linguists tend to be so critical of traditional grammar?

5. "It is often felt, by both philosophers and linguists, that . . . intuitions

are 'unscientific', not amenable to direct observation, variable and untrustworthy. It seems to us that this is not a valid objection . . .'' (Smith & Wilson, 1979: 40). Discuss.

6. Devise an appropriate context for the Standard English utterance *I didn't do nothing* (with the appropriate prosodic structure).

7. What, if anything, is wrong with (a) *between you and I* and (b) *You and me will go together*? Can logic or traditional Latin-based principles help us to decide?

8. What is the difference between the **descriptive** and the **prescriptive** (or normative) approach to the investigation of language?

9. Exemplify, from your experience if you can, the phenomenon of **hyper-correction**.

10. "The word 'alibi' is commonly misused these days: it is a legal term which comes from the Latin word meaning "somewhere else" and should not be used as if it was synonymous with the everyday noun 'excuse'." Discuss.

11. Explain what is meant by the priority of the **synchronic** over the **diachronic** point of view in linguistics.

12. Give a critical account of Saussure's famous comparison between a language and a game of chess.

13. A naive view of **literal translation** might be that it consists in the one-for-one substitution of the word-forms of the target language for the word-forms of the source-language. Is this what is normally meant by the term 'literal translation'? Can you identify some of the reasons why the naive view is unrealistic as far as natural languages are concerned?

14. "The language-system itself . . . is a purely abstract structure" (p. 60). Consider this statement with reference to the use of simple codes and ciphers based on the principle of (a) letter-for-letter and (b) word-for-word substitution in written messages. Do such cryptographic techniques necessarily preserve or destroy **isomorphism**?

15. Can you devise a simple code or cipher which exploits the independence of the two levels of structure in a language-system and changes the one without affecting the other?

3
The sounds of language

3.1 *The phonic medium*

Although language-systems are, to a very considerable extent, independent of the medium in which they are manifest, the natural or primary medium of human language is sound. For this reason, the study of sound is of more central importance in linguistics than is the study of writing, of gestures, or of any other language-medium, whether actual or potential. But it is not sound as such, and not the full range of sound, that is of concern to the linguist. He is interested in the sounds that are produced by the human speech-organs in so far as these sounds have a role in language. Let us refer to this limited range of sounds as the **phonic medium** and to individual sounds within that range as **speech-sounds**. We may now define **phonetics** as the study of the phonic medium.

Phonetics, it must be emphasized, is not phonology; and speech-sounds are not to be identified with phonological elements, to which reference has been made in previous sections. Phonology, as we have seen, is one part of the study and description of language-systems, another being syntax, and yet another semantics. Phonology draws upon the findings of phonetics (though differently according to different theories of phonology); but, unlike phonetics, it does not deal with the phonic medium as such. The first three sections of this chapter deal, as simply as possible, with such basic concepts and categories of phonetics as are essential for the understanding of points made elsewhere in this book and of the notation that is employed in making them. They are not intended to serve as a satisfactory introduction to what has become, in recent years, a very broad and highly specialized branch of linguistics.

The phonic medium can be studied from at least three points of view: the **articulatory**, the **acoustic** and the **auditory**. Articulatory phonetics investigates and classifies speech-sounds in terms of the way they are produced by the speech-organs; acoustic phonetics, in terms of the physical properties of the sound-waves that are created by the activity of the speech-organs and travel through the air from speaker to hearer; auditory phonetics, in terms of the way speech-sounds are perceived and identified by the hearer's ear and brain. Of these three branches of phonetics, the longest established, and until recently the most highly developed, is articulatory phonetics. For this reason, most of the terms used by linguists to refer to speech-sounds are articulatory in origin. We will adopt the articulatory viewpoint in the account that is given of them in this book.

There are, however, several facts that have been either discovered or confirmed by acoustic and auditory phonetics – and more especially by the former, which has made great progress in the last twenty-five or thirty years – of which no one with a serious interest in language can afford to be ignorant. Most important of these perhaps is the fact that repetitions of what might be heard as the same utterance are only coincidentally, if ever, physically (i.e. acoustically) identical. Phonetic identity (unlike phonological identity, as we shall see in the following section) is a theoretical ideal: in practice, the speech-sounds produced by human beings – even by highly trained phoneticians – do no more than approximate to this ideal to a greater or less degree. Phonetic similarity, not phonetic identity, is the criterion with which we operate in the phonological analysis of languages. And phonetic similarity, considered from an articulatory, an acoustic or an auditory point of view is multidimensional. Given three speech-sounds, x, y, and z: x may be more similar to y than it is to z on one dimension, but more similar to z than it is to y on another dimension.

Acoustic phonetics has also confirmed what had already been established by articulatory phonetics: the fact that spoken utterances, considered as physical signals transmitted through the air, are not sequences of separate sounds. Speech is made up of continuous bursts of sound. Not only are there no breaks between the sounds of which spoken words are composed; the words themselves are not usually separated by pauses (except of course when the speaker hesitates momentarily or adopts a special style of delivery for dictation or some other purpose). Continuous speech is segmented into sequences of speech-sounds in terms of the more or less grossly discernible transitions between one relatively steady state of the signal and a preceding or following relatively steady state. This point will be exemplified below from the articulatory point of view. It is important to note, however, that segmentation on the basis of purely acoustic criteria would frequently give quite different results from segmentation carried out on the basis of purely articulatory (or auditory) criteria.

The integration of the three branches of phonetics is no simple matter. One of the most important, and initially most surprising, findings of acoustic phonetics was that no straightforward correlation can be established between some of the most prominent articulatory dimensions of speech and such acoustic parameters as the frequency and amplitude of sound-waves. To make the point more generally, in relation to all three branches of phonetics: the categories of articulatory, acoustic and auditory phonetics do not necessarily coincide. For example, what might seem to be obvious articulatory and auditory differences between different kinds of consonants, let us say between *p*-sounds and *t*-sounds or *k*-sounds, do not show up as any single identifiable feature, or set of features, in an acoustic analysis of signals containing them. The auditory dimensions of pitch and loudness correlate with the acoustic parameters of frequency and intensity; but the correlation between pitch and frequency, on the one hand, and between loudness and intensity on the other, is not stateable in terms of a fixed ratio valid for the whole range of speech-sounds varying along the relevant dimensions.

This does not mean that the categories of one branch of phonetics are more or less reliable, or intrinsically more or less scientific, than the categories of any other branch of phonetics. Speaking and hearing, it must be remembered, are not independent activities. Each involves feedback from the other. It is a matter of common observation that when someone goes deaf his speech also tends to deteriorate. This is because we normally monitor our production of speech as we are producing it and, for the most part unconsciously, make the necessary adjustments to the settings of what we may think of as the articulatory apparatus, as and when feedback from this monitoring process tells the brain that the auditory norms are not being met. The acoustic signal contains all the information that is linguistically relevant, but it also contains a lot of information that is not. Furthermore, the acoustic information that is linguistically relevant must be interpreted by the human speaker–hearer mechanisms controlled by the human brain. The new-born baby seems to be endowed with a predisposition to concentrate upon certain kinds of acoustic information and to neglect others. In the acquisition of language he perfects the ability to produce and to identify the sounds that occur in the speech that he hears around him; and he refines both his articulatory and his auditory performance by monitoring the acoustic signals that he himself produces. There is a sense, therefore, in which the child, in the normal process of language-acquisition, is, and must be, without the aid of scientific instruments or specialized training and over a limited range of the phonic medium, a competent practitioner in all three branches of phonetics, and, more especially, in the integration of the quite disparate information that the three branches operate with. So far, the professional phoneticians can give only an incomplete description and explanation of the highly skilled integrative ability that the vast majority of human beings acquire in childhood and practise throughout their speaking lives.

3.2   Phonetic and orthographic representation

Towards the end of the nineteenth century, by which time articulatory phonetics was beginning to make real progress in the Western world (on the basis, it is only fair to add, of the centuries-old Indian tradition), scholars began to feel the need for a standardized and internationally acceptable system of phonetic transcription. Although there was, and still is, much to be said for non-alphabetic systems of representation, it is the International Phonetic Alphabet (IPA), developed and promulgated by the International Phonetic Association since 1888, which, with or without minor modifications, is now most widely used by linguists. The basic principle upon which the IPA is constructed is that of having a different letter for each distinguishable speech-sound. Since there is in fact no limit to the number of distinguishable speech-sounds that can be produced by the human speech organs (or, at least, no typographically reasonable upper limit) this principle cannot be consistently applied. The IPA, therefore, provides its users with a set of **diacritics** of various kinds which can be added to the **letter-symbols** in order to make finer distinctions than the letters alone make possible. By making a correct and judicious employment of diacritics the trained phonetician can represent as much of the fine detail as is necessary for the purpose in hand. He cannot faithfully represent all the phonetic detail that distinguishes one individual utterance from another; and there is no reason, generally, why he should wish to. For some purposes a relatively **broad** transcription is perfectly adequate; for others, a relatively **narrow** transcription is necessary.[1]

We shall make use of the IPA, from now on, whenever we have occasion to refer to speech-sounds or phonetically transcribed forms. And we shall respect the standard convention according to which phonetic transcriptions are enclosed in square brackets. Thus, instead of referring to *p*-sounds, *k*-sounds, etc., as we did earlier, we shall refer to [p] and [k]: I have deliberately chosen IPA letter-symbols here which have the same phonetic value, broadly interpreted, as the letters *p* and *k* have in the writing-systems of most European languages, including English. Most of the IPA letter-symbols come from the Latin or Greek alphabets. But as anyone who knows, say, English, French, Italian and Spanish is well aware, the same letters are far from having the same phonetic value in all the languages that use essentially the same alphabet. Indeed, the same letter does not necessarily have a constant phonetic value within the writing-system of a single language. It is one of the advantages of having a standard and internationally accepted phonetic alphabet that one does not have to relativize the interpretation of one's symbols to particular languages or even particular words: "*a* as in Italian", "*u* as in the French word *lu*", etc. The price that must be paid for this very considerable advantage is that users of the IPA are required to abandon any assumptions that they might have, for whatever reason, about the way in which a particular letter-symbol ought to be pronounced. For example, [c] is a very different sound from any of the sounds represented by the letter *c* in English, French, Italian or Spanish. In what follows, only a minority of the IPA letter-symbols will be introduced, and very few diacritics.

---

[1] The difference between a broad and a narrow transcription (which, in the nature of things, is relative, rather than absolute) is that the former gives less detail than the latter. A broad transcription is not necessarily phonemic (cf. 3.4).

Once we have furnished ourselves with a system of phonetic transcription, we shall have two ways of referring to forms: (a) in italics in their conventional spelling (or transliteration thereof) without square brackets, e.g. the English forms *led* and *lead*; (b) in a broad IPA transcription, in square brackets, e.g. [lɛd] and [li:d].[2] We can now add to this a third: (c) in italics, enclosed within angle brackets, e.g. <*led*> and <*lead*>. Only sparing use will be made of (c). But its availability enables us to distinguish written forms, (c), from phonetically transcribed spoken forms, (b), and each of these from forms whose spoken or written form is not of immediate concern to us, (a). It also enables us to make such statements as the following: the written form <*lead*> corresponds to two spoken forms, [li:d] and [lɛd]; conversely, the spoken form [lɛd] corresponds to two written forms <*led*> and <*lead*>.

Many-to-one correspondence, of this kind, between written and spoken forms is traditionally described as **homophony** ("sameness of sound"): cf. *rode* and *road*, *father* and *farther*, *court* and *caught*, in the so-called Received Pronunciation (RP) of British English.[3] In certain Scottish accents, none of these pairs of forms are homophones; as *father* : *farther* and *court* : *caught* are not, though *caught* and *cot* are, in many American accents. It is an important fact about Standard English that it is pronounced differently by different groups and that what are homophones for one group of speakers may not be for another. The converse of homophony, to which less attention was given by traditional grammarians, is **homography** ("sameness of spelling"): cf. the homographs *import*$_1$ and *import*$_2$, whose spoken correlates differ in respect of the position of the word-stress.

It is because there are in English and in many other languages

---

[2] The colon indicates lengthening of the sound denoted by the preceding letter-symbol.

[3] RP is the pronunciation of English, based originally on the speech of educated people in London and the South-East, which by the nineteenth century had come to be thought of as the only socially acceptable pronunciation in polite English society. In particular, it was the pronunciation of those received at Court. Propagated by the public (fee-paying) schools and adopted in the 1930s by the BBC for their announcers, it is less regionally based nowadays than any other accent of English in any part of the world, though it no longer enjoys quite the same prestige, especially among the young, as it once did. All phonetically transcribed English forms in this book are assumed to be pronounced with an RP accent.

with a conservative spelling-system both homophones that are not homographs, on the one hand, and homographs that are not homophones, on the other, that homophony and homography force themselves upon our attention in the description of such languages. But, as we shall see later, there may be grammatical or semantic reasons for distinguishing forms that are identical in both the phonic and the graphic medium. For example, *found*$_1$ (the past-tense form of 'find') and *found*$_2$ (one of the present-tense forms of 'found') are both homophones and homographs: the words of which they are forms, 'find' and 'found' are (partial) **homonyms**.

3.3 *Articulatory phonetics*

It has already been pointed out that the so-called **speech-organs** have other functions, unconnected with speech and even with the production of sound, and that these other functions are biologically primary. The lungs supply oxygen to the blood; the vocal cords (situated in the larynx, or Adam's apple) serve, when brought together, to close off the trachea, or windpipe, and prevent food from entering; the tongue and teeth are used for eating; and so on. Nevertheless, the speech-organs do constitute what might be reasonably described as a secondary biological system, and there is some evidence of their evolutionary adaptation to the production of speech. In articulatory phonetics, speech-sounds are classified in terms of the speech-organs that produce them and the manner in which they are produced.

Most speech-sounds in all languages are produced by modifying, in some way, the airstream that is expelled by the lungs up the windpipe, through the **glottis** (the space between the **vocal cords**) and along the **vocal tract**. The vocal tract runs from the larynx, at one end, to the lips and nostrils at the other.

If the vocal cords are kept close together and made to vibrate as the air passes through the glottis the sound thus produced is **voiced**; if the air passes through without vibration of the vocal cords, the resultant sound is **voiceless**. This yields one of the major articulatory variables. Most vowels in all languages, and all vowels in English (except in whispered speech), are voiced. But both voiced and voiceless consonants are common throughout the languages of the world, even though the distinction between voiced and voiceless

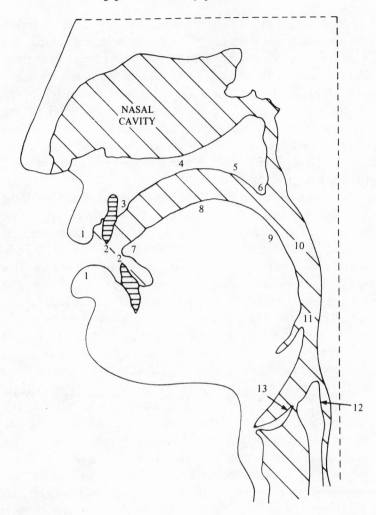

Figure 1. The speech organs. 1. Lips, 2. Teeth, 3. Teeth-ridge (alveolar ridge), 4. Hard palate, 5. Soft palate (velum), 6. Uvula, 7. Tip of tongue, 8. Blade of tongue, 9. Back of tongue, 10. Pharynx, 11. Epiglottis, 12. Food passage, 13. Vocal cords

consonants does not always serve, as it does in English, to distinguish one form from another in the phonic medium. Voiceless consonants include [p], [t], [k], [s], [f]; the corresponding voiced sounds are [b], [d], [g], [z], [v]. When the IPA does not provide two different letter-symbols for corresponding voiced and voiceless speech sounds, diacritics can be used to draw the distinction. The diacritic for voicelessness is a small circle below the letter-symbol. For example, the IPA makes the assumption that vowels are voiced unless they are explicitly marked as voiceless, so that [ḁ], [e̥], [i̥], etc. are the voiceless counterparts of the voiced vowels [a], [e], [i], etc. It is important to note that, despite the fact that diacritics are used in the one case, but not in the other, the phonetic relationship between [a] and [ḁ], or [e] and [e̥], is exactly the same as that between [b] and [p], or [d] and [t].

Another important articulatory variable is that of nasality. If the **velum**, or soft palate, is lowered at the back of the throat to keep open the passage into the nasal cavity, air can escape through the nose at the same time as it also emerges from the mouth. Speech-sounds produced in this way are **nasal**, in contrast with **non-nasal** (or **oral**) sounds, in the production of which there is no emission of air through the nose. Possible nasal consonants include [m], [n] and [ŋ], all of which occur in English, [ŋ] as the final sound in forms like *wrong*, *sing* (in the RP pronunciation of them). Nasal consonants are assumed to be voiced unless they are marked as voiceless with the appropriate diacritic:[m̥], [n̥], [ŋ̥], etc. As [b] contrasts with [p] and [m] with [m̥] on the dimension of voice, so [m] contrasts with [b] and [m̥] with [p] on the dimension of nasality. Similarly for [d] : [t] : :[n]:[n̥], and for [g]:[k]::[ŋ]:[ŋ̥]. Vowels are assumed to be oral unless they are explicitly marked as nasal by means of a so-called tilde [˜] above the appropriate letter-symbol. Thus, [ã], [ẽ], etc. are the (voiced) nasal counterparts of [a], [e], etc. Once again, it is important to realize that [b], [p] and [m], [d], [t] and [n], and [g], [k] and [ŋ] are related to one another phonetically in precisely the same way as [a], [ḁ] and [ã].

A third articulatory dimension is that of aspiration. **Aspirated** sounds differ from the corresponding **unaspirated** sounds in that the former are produced with an accompanying small puff of breath. (Actually, aspiration is more properly treated as an aspect of the voice/voiceless distinction rather than as being a completely independent variable. It depends upon the timing of the switching on and off of voice relative to concomitant articulatory processes. There are other secondary articulations that we shall not go into

here: glottalization, palatalization, labialization, velarization, etc.)
Aspirated consonants, usually voiceless, occur in many languages,
including English, as we shall see later. Instead of using the IPA
diacritic for aspiration, we shall follow what is the more common
practice nowadays and put a raised letter aitch immediately after the
appropriate IPA letter-symbol. Thus [pʰ] is the aspirated counterpart of [p].

So far we have used the traditional terms 'consonant' and 'vowel'
without explaining them. As far as their articulation is concerned,
consonants differ from **vowels** in that consonants are produced by
temporarily obstructing or restricting the airstream as it passes
through the mouth, whereas vowels are produced without any
obstruction or restriction of the airstream. The phonetic difference
between consonants and vowels is not, in fact, absolute; and there
are certain speech-sounds which have an intermediate status. In the
brief and simplified exposition of the main concepts of articulatory
phonetics that is being given here we need not go into such details.

Consonants may be subdivided into several groups according to
the nature of the obstruction of the airstream. The obstruction may
be total, resulting in a **stop** (or **occlusive**), or partial; if it is partial,
but such as to cause audible friction, the resultant sound is classified
as a **fricative**. Typical stops are [p], [t] and [k]; typical fricatives are
[f] and [s]. Consonants are also classified, on another articulatory
dimension, in terms of their **place of articulation**: i.e. according to
the place in the mouth where the obstruction occurs. There are
indefinitely many points along the vocal tract at which the breath
can be obstructed by the **articulators**: vocal cords, tongue, teeth,
lips, etc. No language makes use of more than a small number of
these. The following places of articulation are among those used in
English and other familiar languages (with or without secondary
articulations of various kinds):

bilabial (or simply **labial**), the lips being brought together, e.g. [p],
[b], [m].

labiodental, the lower lip being brought into contact with the upper
teeth, e.g. [f], [v]. Whereas [p], [b], [m] are stops, [f], [v] are
fricatives. (Bilabial fricatives and labiodental stops, both oral and
nasal, are less common, but do occur.)

dental, the tip of the tongue being brought into contact with the upper teeth, e.g. [t], [d], [n], [θ], [ð].

alveolar, the tip of the tongue being brought into contact with the alveolar ridge (the upper teeth-ridge), e.g. [t], [d], [n], [s], [z]. It should be noted that the same symbols may be used, in a broad transcription, for both dental and alveolar stops, though the IPA provides diacritics to distinguish the one class from the other, if it is necessary to do so. The initial consonants of English *thick* and *this* are dental fricatives, voiceless and voiced respectively, transcribable as [θ] and [ð], whereas the [t]-, [d]- and [n]-sounds of most accents of English (in most positions of a word) are alveolar (unlike the [t]-, [d]- and [n]-sounds of French, Spanish or Russian or, for [t] and [d] at least, Italian).

palatal, the back of the tongue being brought in contact with the hard palate, e.g. the stops [c] and [ɟ] and the fricatives [ç] and [j].

velar, the back of the tongue being brought into contact with the velum, or soft palate, e.g. the stops [k] and [g] and the fricatives, [x] and [ɣ]. The difference between palatals and velars, like the difference between dentals and alveolars, is a matter of degree (more so than, for example, the difference between labials and dentals, or between dentals and palatals). Though palatals are not common in most positions of a word in English, the voiceless palatal fricative, [ç] is found in German (in most dialects), Castilian, Spanish and Modern Greek, as well as being one of the possible RP pronunciations of the initial consonant of an English form like *hue* (the letter ⟨h⟩ in English covers a range of sounds the quality of which is largely determined by the accompanying vowel). The sounds that correspond in the English writing-system to the letters ⟨k⟩ and ⟨c⟩ are, in most phonetic environments, varieties of velars, but in certain positions (as is also the case for many languages) they come close to being palatals, e.g. in *key* and *cue*. The voiceless velar fricative [x] does not occur in RP, but is found as the final consonant in a Scottish pronunciation of *loch* and is common in German and some dialects of Spanish.[4] The voiced velar fricative [ɣ] is rarer in Euro-

---

[4] In Castilian Spanish, however, the so-called jota-sound in forms like **hija** "daughter" is commonly pronounced as a post-velar, or uvular, fricative; IPA [χ].

pean languages than its voiceless counterpart, but it does occur in Modern Greek (and in some dialects of Russian).

glottal, the vocal cords being brought momentarily together, e.g. the stop [ʔ] and the fricatives [h] and [ɦ], voiceless and voiced respectively. Since the vocal cords cannot be vibrating when fully closed, there is no voiced glottal stop, though both voiceless and voiceless glottal fricatives exist. The glottal stop occurs as what is often perceived as a socially stigmatized variant of a [t]-sound between vowels, in forms like *city, united, butter*, in many urban accents of England and Scotland including those of London (Cockney), Manchester, Birmingham and Glasgow (as well as occurring, unnoticed as such, in other phonetic environments, even in RP). It is important to emphasize, therefore, that it is from a phonetic point of view a perfectly respectable, independent consonant, not to be confused with [t], and is widespread in the languages of the world.

Many other places of articulation are recognized by the IPA for the classification of consonants, and some of them need to be referred to in a complete phonetic description of English. For the purpose of illustrating the general principles of the articulatory classification of consonants the above will suffice. The symbols introduced so far (and a few others) are given in Table 1. It will be noted that whereas the vertical dimension of the table represents what may be regarded as a single articulatory parameter (if we neglect co-articulation and secondary articulations), the horizontal dimension of the table does not. There is a hierarchical arrangement of stops vs. fricatives, with stops being further subclassified as oral vs. nasal and both stops and fricatives being subclassified as voiceless vs. voiced. The multidimensionality of what is called **manner of articulation**, in contrast with the essential unidimensionality of place of articulation, would be even more obvious if we were to go more fully into the classification of consonants (distinguishing such classes as rolls, flaps, liquids, etc.). Let us keep this point in mind.

We turn now to the articulatory analysis of vowels. Since vowels (in so far as they can be sharply distinguished from consonants) are characterized by the absence of obstruction of the airstream in the mouth, they do not have a place of articulation in the same sense as

Table 1. *Selected consonants in IPA notation. (Aspiration is not represented since it is in all cases symbolized by a diacritic. The symbols for voiceless nasals are similarly constructed by adding a diacritic to the appropriate letter-symbol)*

Manner of articulation / Place of articulation	Stops			Fricatives	
	Oral		Nasal		
	Voiceless	Voiced	Voiced	Voiceless	Voiced
bilabial	p	b	m	Φ	β
labiodental	π	b	ɱ	f	v
dental	t̪	d̪	n̪	θ	ð
alveolar	t	d	n	s	z
palatal	c	ɟ	ɲ	ç	j
velar	k	g	ŋ	x	ɣ
glottal	ʔ			h	ɦ

consonants. We have to consider the total configuration of the oral cavity. This is infinitely variable in three phonetically relevant dimensions, labelled by convention as close : open (alternatively, high : low), front : back and rounded : unrounded.

A **close** (or **high**) vowel is one in the production of which the jaws are held close together (because the tongue is high in the mouth); in contrast, the production of an **open** (or **low**) vowel involves the opening of the mouth more widely (because of the lowering of the tongue). Both [i] and [u] are close (high), and both [a] and [ɑ] open (low).

A **front** vowel is one produced by holding the tongue (more precisely, the highest point of the tongue, since it is of course fixed at its root in the back of the mouth) towards the front of the mouth; a **back** vowel involves retraction of the tongue. Both [i] and [a] are front, and both [u] and [ɑ] back.

A **rounded** vowel is produced with the lips rounded; an **unrounded** vowel is produced without lip-rounding. [u], [o] and [ɔ] are rounded; [i], [e], [ɛ] and [a] are unrounded. Cardinal vowel no. 5, [ɑ], being maximally open, is also unrounded.

Several points may now be made briefly about this three-dimensional classification of vowels. First, since each of these dimensions is continuous, the difference between any two vowels in terms of openness, backness and rounding is always a matter of more or less. However, for purposes of standardizing their reference to vowels, phoneticians make use of the system of **cardinal vowels**. These must not be identified with the vowels of any actual language: they are theoretical points with reference to which the trained phonetician can plot the vowel-sounds of particular languages. He can make such statements as: the vowel in the French form *pie*, which we may transcribe as [pi], approximates more closely to cardinal [i] than does the first part of the vowel in the RP pronunciation of the English word *pea*, which we may also transcribe, broadly, as [pi], or more narrowly (indicating both the aspiration of the consonant and the length, but not the non-uniform, diphthongal, quality of the vowel) as [pʰiː]. The eight primary cardinal vowels are given in Figure 2: we shall come to the secondary cardinal vowels presently. It will be observed that cardinal vowels 1, 4, 5 and 8 – viz. [i], [a], [ɑ] and [u] – are the theoretical extremes on the dimensions of openness and backness. At intermediate points between [i] and [a] and between [u] and [ɑ], at what are judged to be auditorily equal intervals, we find the **half-close** vowels [e] and [o] and the half-open vowels [ɛ] and [ɔ].

The next point to note is that whereas all the front vowels in Figure 2 are unrounded, all the back vowels (except for cardinal vowel no. 5) are rounded. This does not mean that rounded front vowels or unrounded back vowels do not occur. They certainly do. But they are less commonly found – especially unrounded back vowels – in European languages; and both the IPA and the subsequently developed cardinal-vowel system have a certain bias towards European languages. But each of the primary cardinal vowels has its counterpart among the **secondary cardinal vowels** (front rounded and back unrounded), numbered from 9 to 16. For example, the secondary counterpart of [i] is no. 9, the front rounded [y], to which the vowel of the French word *tu* approximates; the

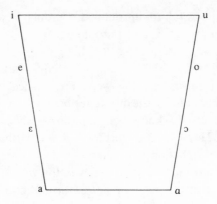

Figure 2. The primary cardinal vowels

secondary counterpart of [u] is no. 16, the back unrounded [ɯ]: Japanese has vowels approximating to cardinal [ɯ].

It will further be noted that the vowels of Figure 2 are arranged along the sides of a quadrilateral, whose base is much shorter than its top. This diagram schematically represents the fact that, for physiological reasons, there is from both an articulatory and auditory point of view less difference along the front–back dimension with open vowels than with close vowels: less difference, for example, between [a] and [ɑ] than there is between [i] and [u]. The same holds true with respect to rounding. So [i] differs from [u] more than [a] differs from [ɑ] in two of the three dimensions (rounding being completely irrelevant in the case of maximally open vowels). It is not surprising, therefore, that languages tend to have asymmetrical vowel systems in which fewer distinctions are made among open vowels than among close vowels.

Finally, it must be once again emphasized that the vowel quadrilateral represents a three-dimensional continuum, within which, except in the theoretical ideal, the IPA vowel-symbols denote regions rather than points. Furthermore, there are regions especially in the centre of the continuum that are not at all well-served by the IPA or the cardinal-vowel system.

So much, then, for the articulation of consonants and vowels. What has been said, brief and selective though our treatment of the question has been, will have made one point abundantly clear. Both consonants and vowels, considered as **segments** of speech, are bundles of articulatory **features**, each of which can be treated as the value of a variable on a particular dimension. For example, [m] is a voiced, bilabial, nasal stop: i.e. it has the value [voiced] on the dimension of voice, the value [labial] on the dimension of (primary) place of articulation, [nasal] on the dimension of nasality, and [stop] on the dimension of occlusion or obstruction.

The square brackets enclosing the terms 'voiced', 'labial', etc., in the previous paragraph indicate that these terms are labels for phonetic features. Tables 2 and 3 now reclassify some of the consonants and vowels introduced above as sets of features. These features, it will be appreciated, are simultaneous, not sequential (in any relevant sense). It will also be appreciated that a distinction must be drawn between features that are independently variable and those that are not. Thus, a speech-sound cannot be, at any one point in time, both voiced and voiceless, or both nasal and oral. Tables 2 and 3 use plus-signs and minus-signs to incorporate this fact: [voiced], [nasal], etc., have been chosen as the positive, and [voiceless], [oral], etc., as the negative, members of correlated pairs of features. As far as the place of articulation of consonants is concerned, the situation is different. True, if a consonant is (primarily) labial it cannot also be (primarily) dental or velar. But we cannot treat either [dental] or [velar] as negative in relation to [labial]. This being so, if a consonant is marked positively with a plus-sign for one of the values along the dimension of place of articulation, it is shown in Table 2 as neutral, rather than negative, for the other values. Similarly as far as the difference between stops and fricatives are concerned. Table 3 represents only the three dimensions of the articulatory classification of vowels that have to do with the configuration of the mouth: it is an easy matter to extend Table 3, in the light of earlier discussion, to incorporate the voiced : voiceless and the oral : nasal distinctions for vowels too. Tables 2 and 3 will be useful for future reference.

But we must now raise the question of segmentation itself. How do we decide that a given burst of speech, analysed from the point of view of articulatory phonetics, consists of such and such a number of sequentially ordered segments? The determining principle of phonetic segmentation is very simple to state, but far from simple to

The sounds of language

Table 2. *Selected consonants analysed into their component articulatory features. (Aspirated voiceless oral stops are exemplified, but not aspirated voiced stops, oral or nasal; nor are voiceless nasals. Places of articulation are restricted, for the purpose of illustration, to three: labial, dental, velar. The table can be readily expanded to include all the consonants in Table 1 with their aspirated counterparts)*

Articulatory features \ Phonetic segments	p	pʰ	b	m	Φ	β	t	tʰ	d	n	θ	ð	k	kʰ	g	ŋ	x	ɣ
voiced	−	−	+	+	−	+	−	−	+	+	−	+	−	−	+	+	−	+
aspirated	−	+	−	−	0	0	−	+	−	−	0	0	−	+	−	−	0	0
nasal	−	−	−	+	0	0	−	−	−	+	0	0	−	−	−	+	0	0
stop	+	+	+	+	0	0	+	+	+	+	0	0	+	+	+	+	0	0
fricative	0	0	0	0	+	+	0	0	0	0	+	+	0	0	0	0	+	+
labial	+	+	+	+	+	+	0	0	0	0	0	0	0	0	0	0	0	0
dental	0	0	0	0	0	0	+	+	+	+	+	+	0	0	0	0	0	0
velar	0	0	0	0	0	0	0	0	0	0	0	0	+	+	+	+	+	+

Table 3. *Selected vowels analysed into their components. (This table does not include [ɛ] and [ɔ]. Not having to distinguish between half-open and half-close it treats [e] and [o] as neither open nor close)*

	i	e	a	a	o	u	y	ɯ
open	−	0	+	+	0	−	−	−
back	−	−	−	+	+	+	+	+
rounded	−	−	−	−	+	+	−	−

apply, without a good deal of more or less arbitrary decision in particular instances. We establish a boundary between segments (and thus establish the segments themselves) at those points at which there is a change of value in one or more of the articulatory variables: for example, from [labial] to [dental], from [voiced] to [voiceless], from [back] to [front], from [nasal] to [oral]. The principle is often difficult to apply, because the changes of value are not always sharp and the stretches of sound between successive changes of value are not perfectly steady states.[5] Furthermore, certain feature transitions (e.g. the onset of voice or aspiration in consonants) would not normally be counted for this purpose unless there were phonological reasons for doing so (cf. 3.4). So the question how many speech-sounds there are in a given form – considered without reference to the phonological structure of the particular language-system or of language-systems in general – does not usually admit of a determinate answer. This is something that must be constantly borne in mind when one is referring to phonetically transcribed language-data.

Indeed, it is one of the disadvantages of an alphabetic system of phonetic transcription that it encourages non-specialists to think of speech as being made up of strings of speech-sounds. Anyone who uses a phonetic alphabet must train himself to dealphabetize, as it were, the strings of symbols that represent spoken utterances. For example, seeing [tɛmān] he must not only be able to analyse [t] into its component simultaneous features, [voiceless], [dental], etc., and so for each of the five speech-sounds here represented. He must notice immediately that the feature [voiceless] runs over two segments, that both [voice] and [nasality] run over three segments, and so on. These features are not rapidly switched off and on between [t] and [ɛ]; or between [m] and [ā] and between [ā] and [n]. When two or more segments share a single feature in this way (especially if it is a consonantal feature having to do with place of articulation) they are commonly described as **homorganic** ("produced by the same organ"). More generally, we can say that there is a tendency for successive segments (in so far as they are distinct segments by the criterion mentioned above) to be **assimilated** to one another in either place or manner of articulation, or both. This fact is of considerable importance when it comes to the phonological analysis of languages.

From what has just been said it should be clear that virtually any phonetic feature can run over successive segments and can there-

---

[5] Diphthongs differ phonetically from so-called pure vowels, or monophthongs, in that they are not steady-state sounds.

fore be, in this sense of the term, **suprasegmental**. For example, [voiced] is suprasegmental in [amba]; [nasal] is suprasegmental in [mãn]; and so on. However, the term 'suprasegmental' is usually restricted to such features as are involved in what is classified, phonologically rather than phonetically, as **length, tone** and **stress**. We shall come back to the notion of suprasegmentality, in both senses, in a later section.

It must be emphasized, however, that the treatment both of segments and of suprasegmental features given in this book is highly selective. As far as potential segments are concerned, there are whole classes of speech-sounds of various kinds that have not been mentioned: **liquids, glides, affricates**, etc. It has not been my purpose to give a complete classification, even in broad outline, of the articulatory variables, but merely to illustrate the general principles.

3.4 *Phonemes and allophones*

From now on we shall be concerned with phonetics (the study of the phonic medium) only in so far as it is of relevance to the **phonological** analysis of language-systems. There are several theories of phonology. They may be distinguished as being either phonemic or non-phonemic theories, according to whether they take **phonemes** to be the basic elements of phonological analysis or not. Of phonemic theories of phonology, what may be referred to as **classical American phonemics**, though it has now been abandoned by most linguists, is of considerable importance for an understanding of the development of more modern theories. Furthermore, it has the pedagogical advantage of being conceptually simpler than many others. This section, therefore, will be devoted to an explanation of the key notions of classical American phonemics, as they were elaborated in the period following the Second World War. We shall concentrate upon those notions and terms which will be of use to us later. Much detail will be omitted.

In the theory that we are dealing with here, phonemes are defined with reference to two principal criteria: (a) **phonetic similarity** and (b) **distribution** (subject to the overriding criterion, which finds its application in all theories of phonology, of **functional contrast**: see below). As we saw in the previous section, phonetic similarity is a matter of more or less, and is multidimensional. It follows that a particular speech-sound may be similar to a second speech-sound on one or more dimensions, whilst differing from it and being similar to a third speech-sound on one or more other dimensions. The practical consequence of this fact, as far as phonemic analysis is concerned, is that the analyst is often faced with alternative solutions when it comes to the problem of deciding which phonetically similar speech-sounds should be grouped together as variants, more technically **allophones**, of the same phoneme. At that point, various supplementary criteria may be applied (which we shall neglect). However, there may still be room for disagreement as to how many phonemes there are in a particular language and what their allophones are in their various contexts of occurrence, even when these supplementary criteria have been invoked. Despite the impression that is given in many textbooks of the period, there is little doubt that classical American phonemics fails, with many languages, to yield a unique and universally acceptable analysis of their phonology.

We turn now to the notion of distribution, which, as we shall see in the course of this book, is relevant, not just in phonology, but also in grammar and semantics. Briefly, the distribution of an entity is the set of contexts in which it occurs throughout the sentences of a language. The term 'entity' is to be taken in as general a sense as possible. As far as the present section is concerned, it may be held to include speech-sounds and phonetic features, on the one hand, and phonemes, on the other. The notion of distribution presupposes the notion of well-formedness (cf. 2.6). What this means, as far as phonology is concerned, is that we must operate, not simply with the actual forms of the language-system, but with the set of phonetically and phonologically well-formed forms, both actual and potential. In all natural languages there are actual forms in more or less common use (frequently borrowed from other languages) which do not conform to the more general phonological patterns and there are many non-existent forms which speakers of the language will recognize as being, in the relevant sense, potential forms of their language: i.e. as conforming to the general patterns. To take a now classic example: [brik] is both a potential and an actual word-form of English (in broad phonetic transcription), cf.

brick; [blik] is a potential, but non-actual, form. *[bnik], on the other hand, is not only not an actual word-form of English, it is phonologically ill-formed (hence the asterisk): there are no well-formed forms of English beginning with [bn].[6]

To the extent that languages are rule-governed systems, every linguistic entity that is subject to the rules of a language-system has a characteristic distribution. Two or more entities have the same distribution if and only if they occur in the same environment – i.e. they are substitutable for one another, **intersubstitutable** – in all contexts (subject to the condition of well-formedness). Entities that are intersubstitutable in some, but not all, contexts **overlap** in distribution: distributional identity can therefore be seen as the limiting case of distributional overlap and, if "some" is held to subsume "all", be so defined that it falls within the definition of 'overlap'. Let us henceforth so define it. Entities that are not intersubstitutable in any context are said to be in **complementary distribution**.

We can now apply these notions to the problem of defining phonemes and their allophones. First, it should be noted that two speech-sounds cannot be in functional contrast unless they overlap in distribution: in particular, speech-sounds that do not overlap in distribution cannot have the function of distinguishing one form from another. For example, there are several phonetically different [l]-sounds in the RP pronunciation of English. Most of them fall into two sets, impressionistically referred to as clear and dark (the members of the two sets may have the same primary place of articulation, but differ as to whether the main part of the tongue is towards the front or the back of the mouth), which never occur in the same position in word-forms: the clear [l]'s occur before front vowels within word-forms and the dark [l]'s in all other positions. This being so, the substitution of a clear [l] for the normal dark [l] in, say, *feel* cannot change it into another form (though it might have the effect of making it sound, in this respect, Irish or French); similarly, the substitution of the dark [l] for the normal clear [l] of, say, *leaf* cannot change it into another word-form, actual or potential. More generally, since all the [l]-sounds, whether clear or dark,

---

[6] Except for so-called allegro-forms, which occur as variants in rapid or informal speech (e.g. [bni:θ] as an allegro-variant of [bəni:θ] *beneath* in RP).

are in complementary distribution, they cannot be in functional contrast. They satisfy both of the conditions mentioned above as definitional for the phoneme, phonetic similarity and complementary distribution, and would be universally assigned to a single phoneme as its allophones: its phonetically distinct, positional variants. It is of the essence of phonological elements that they should be in functional contrast at least somewhere in the language-system.

Allophones are subphonemic. Nevertheless, they have a rule-governed distribution: in that respect they belong to the language-system as it is **realized** in the phonic medium. But they are not elements of the language-system. The elements of a language-system (according to phonemic theories of phonology) are its phonemes. Phonemes are, by convention, represented by taking the letter-symbol (with or without diacritics) appropriate to a broad transcription of one of the phonetically distinguishable allophones and putting it between obliques. For example, the English phoneme /l/ has as its allophones a set of phonetically distinct speech-sounds, all of which could be kept apart, if necessary, in a narrow transcription. So, we now have yet another way of referring to forms: phonemically, or more generally, if we generalize the use of oblique strokes (as we shall in this book), phonologically. It is important to realize, as should be obvious from the explanation given above, that a phonemic representation is not simply a broad phonetic transcription.

One other point should be made. All too often, textbooks of linguistics give an imprecise, not to say nonsensical, formulation of the principle of functional contrast. They might say, for example, that the substitution of a clear [l] for a dark [l] in *feel* does not change the meaning of *feel*, whereas the substitution of [r] for [l] in *lamb* changes its meaning. Strictly speaking, this is wrong. What the substitution of [r] for [l] in *lamb* does is to change the form, not the meaning: it changes the form *lamb* into the form *ram*. True, 'lamb' and 'ram' (i.e. the words of which *lamb* and *ram* are forms) differ in meaning, so that utterances containing them will (generally) differ in meaning. But it is not just unmotivated pedantry which leads me to call attention to the frequently imprecise formulation of the principle of functional contrast. Difference of form does not

guarantee difference of meaning (cf. the phenomenon of synonymy). Nor is difference of meaning the sole criterion whereby we
establish difference of form. Whether there can ever be a difference
of form which does not correlate at some point in a language-system
with a difference of meaning is a controversial question, partly
dependent on how we define 'meaning'. But there is no doubt that
what is at issue in the formulation of the principle of functional
contrast is identity and difference of form, not identity and difference of meaning.

Distributional overlap is a necessary, but not a sufficient, condition of functional contrast. It is quite common for phonetically
different speech-sounds to be intersubstitutable in the same context
and yet to be in **free variation**: i.e. not to be in functional contrast.
For example, [ʔ] and [t] are in free variation, for many RP speakers
of English, in forms like *brightness*, [. . . ʔn . . .] vs. [. . . tn . . .]
or *that bloke*, [. . . ʔb . . .] vs. [. . . tb . . .]: i.e. before stop consonants whether oral or nasal. Here the substitution of one speech-
sound for the other does not change *brightness* or *that bloke* into
some other form. Indeed, it might very well pass unnoticed. In
other cases of what is, for the purpose of phonemic analysis, normally regarded as free variation, the choice of one pronunciation
rather than another by speakers might be determined by stylistic
factors of various kinds. As far as phonemic analysis is concerned,
'functional contrast' may be understood as being restricted to **distinctive function**: i.e. the function of distinguishing one form from
another. It is arguable, as the Prague School phonologists insisted,
that phonological description should also take account of stylistic
variation (cf. 7.3).

It was one of the earliest and most important discoveries of
phonology that speech-sounds that are in functional contrast in one
language may be in complementary distribution or free variation in
another. For example, [ð] and [d] are in functional contrast in
English (cf. *there* vs. *dare*), but in complementary distribution (with
perhaps some stylistic variation) in Castilian Spanish (cf. *nada*
[naða] "nothing" vs. *dos* [dɔs] "two"). Examples could be multi-
plied. The important point is that languages differ considerably
with respect to the phonetic distinctions that they put to work, as it
were, in the realization (in the phonic medium) of the forms out of

which sentences are constructed. This point holds independently of the phonological theory within which it is formulated.

3.5 Distinctive features and suprasegmental phonology

According to the theory of classical American phonemics referred to in the previous section, phonemes are the minimal phonological elements of language-systems. A very different view was taken by Trubetzkoy, one of the founder-members of the Prague School of linguistics, which developed its own version of Saussurean structuralism and was very influential, especially in phonology and stylistics, in the 1930s (cf. 7.3). The key notion of Prague School phonology is that phonemes, though still the minimal segments of language-systems, are not their minimal elements: phonemes are bundles (or sets) of simultaneous **distinctive features**. This notion, with certain modifications subsequently introduced, was taken over in the 1960s by the advocates of **generative grammar**, in the formalization of which it has now replaced the notions characteristic of classical American phonemics that were originally associated with generative grammar as part of its **post-Bloomfieldian** inheritance (cf. 7.4). The account of distinctive-feature theory given here makes no attempt to keep apart the different historical phases of its development.

The term 'distinctive' refers to that part of functional contrast in language-systems which has to do with distinguishing one form from another (cf. 3.4): Prague School phonologists also paid a lot of attention to other kinds of phonological function, but this does not concern us at present. The term 'feature' is already familiar from the section dealing with articulatory phonetics (3.3). Indeed, we can immediately proceed to an explanation of the central ideas of distinctive-feature theory on the basis of what has been said in the previous two sections.

Speech-sounds may be represented as sets of phonetic features. The phonetic features used above were articulatory; but they might equally well have been acoustic or, in principle, auditory. The same is true with respect to the phonological features of distinctive-feature theory; and both articulatory and acoustic features have been employed. In so far as phonology, unlike phonetics, can be thought of as making no direct reference to the phonic medium (though distinctive-feature theorists, on the whole, tend not to take this rather abstract view of phonology), one should perhaps operate with phonological features that are neither articulatory nor acoustic, but relatable (though in a rather complex way) equally well to both and, when auditory phonetics is more highly developed than it is at present, to auditory features. For simplicity of exposition, we will employ articulatory labels. To make it clear when we are talking about phonological features, rather than phonetic features, we will put oblique strokes, rather than square brackets, around the articulatory labels. (This is not standard practice, but it makes for conceptual clarity and allows certain theoretical options to be kept open.) Thus, whereas the speech-sound [p] can be described, with reference to Table 2 above, as the set {[+ labial], [+ stop], [− voiced], [− nasal]}, so the English phoneme /p/, let us suppose, is analysable as the set {/+ labial/, /+ stop/, /− voiced/}.

At first sight, it might appear that we have done no more than play a notational trick, substituting oblique strokes for square brackets and calling the result phonology, instead of phonetics. It should be noted, however, that three, not four, features are listed for English /p/ as distinctive. There is no phonemic feature /− nasal/ listed for /p/ because the absence of nasality is predictable in English (though not in all languages) from the absence of voice; /− nasal/ would be listed for /b/ in order to account for its distinctive function in *ban* vs. *man*, *cub* vs. *come*, etc. Also, the articulatory description of [p] is very incomplete (being restricted to the articulatory features included in Table 2). In general, the set of distinctive features that define and characterize a phoneme will be much smaller than the set of phonetic features that characterize any one of its allophones. For example, the English phoneme /p/ has as one of its allophones an aspirated, voiceless, bilabial, oral stop – viz. [pʰ] – whose fuller articulatory description would involve reference, not only to aspiration, but also to the degree of force with which the air is released after the labial obstruction, to the duration of the obstruction and the aspiration, and to several other features that go to make it a recognizable English [pʰ] (in a particular accent) for the position in which it occurs. But none of these other phonetic features is distinctive: none of them serves to change the phonetic realization of one English form into the phonetic realization of another English form.

As to the three features recognized above as components of /p/: /+ labial/ (which matches [+ labial]) distinguishes (a pronunciation of) *pin* from (a pronunciation of) *tin*, *kin*, etc.; /+ stop/ distinguishes *pat* from *fat* (since English has no labial fricatives, except as allophones of /p/ in other positions, and no labio-dental stops, one can think of /f/ and /v/ as being the /+ fricative/ counterparts of /p/ and /b/), *tick* from *sick* (and *thick*); /− voiced/, according to the conventional view, is the feature which distinguishes *pin* from *bin*, *pat* from *pad*. It is arguable that the feature which distinguishes /p/, /t/, /k/, /s/, /θ/, etc. from /b/, /d/, /g/, /z/, /ð/, etc. in English should not be identified with voicelessness, but with something else, of which either voicelessness or aspiration (or both) are the usual phonetic concomitants. However, whatever view we take on this question, the fact remains that we do not need both /+ aspirate/ and /− voice/ in a distinctive-feature analysis of English.

I have used the term 'allophone' in the account just given of the relation between phonemes and the distinctive features of which they are composed. In fact, the notion of allophonic variation is handled rather differently in distinctive-feature theory, so that the applicability of the term itself is questionable. The crucial point about the distinctive-feature analysis of phonemes is that every phoneme should differ from every other phoneme in the language-system with respect to the presence or absence in the set of features that define it of at least one feature; and its set of defining features remains constant throughout the whole range of its occurrences. What classical American phonemics referred to in terms of allophonic variation is handled in distinctive-feature theory (especially within the framework of generative grammar) by means of rules which (having converted the minimal set of phonological features, sufficient to distinguish each phoneme from every other, into phonetic features: /+ labial/ → [+ labial], /+ voiced/ → [+ voiced], etc.) add contextually appropriate, non-distinctive phonetic features for particular positions of occurrence. For example, the phonetic feature [+ aspirate] would be added for the phonetic realization of English /p/ in word-initial position (e.g. in *pit* or *pot*) but not for its realization when it follows /s/ (e.g. in *spit* or *spot*); and the phonetic feature [− voiced] would be added for all positions of occurrence.

It was pointed out in the previous section that languages differ considerably as to the phonetic features that they make distinctive and the phonetic features which, if they have them at all, they treat as non-distinctive. This remains true, regardless of the theory of phonology within which it is stated. It is after all an empirical fact that [+ aspirated] is distinctive in Hindi and Mandarin Chinese; that French vowels may be simultaneously both distinctively front and distinctively rounded; that in very many Australian languages nasality, but not voice, is distinctive and characterizes more phonemes than it does in any European language; and so on. It will be noticed, however, that in each of these examples I have made use of terms – 'aspirated', 'front', 'back', 'nasality' – that are also used in the description of hundreds, not to say thousands, of other spoken languages. Distinctive-feature theory as such would not be incompatible with the view that there is an unlimited number of possible distinctive features from which particular language-systems make their own unique selection, as it were, and combine in unpredictable ways to construct their own phonemes. But recent formulations of distinctive-feature theory have tended to assume, with a fair amount of evidence to support the assumption, that all existing natural languages can be satisfactorily described, as far as their phonology is concerned, with reference to a master-list of little more than a dozen potentially distinctive features. It is certainly true that there are very many physiologically phonetic features that are not made distinctive, as far as we know, in the phonology of any natural language; and there are many physiologically possible combinations of features that are extremely rare, or not found at all. Chomsky has suggested that this is because the phonology of natural languages, like their syntax and their semantics, is heavily constrained by a specifically human predisposition to operate with certain kinds of distinctions, rather than others (cf. 7.4).

One of the most striking advantages of distinctive-feature theory by comparison with classical American phonemics is that it gives a motivated account of the principles that determine the well-formedness of sequences of phonemes over a wide range of instances in many languages. For example, between initial /s/ and /r/

within the same form in English /p/, /t/ and /k/ can occur, but /b/, /d/ and /g/ cannot (cf. *spray*, *stripe*, *scratch* vs. */sbr—/, */sdr—/, */sgr—/). This is just one of many contexts in which /p/, /t/, /k/ are intersubstitutable whereas /b/, /d/; /g/ are not. This part of the distribution of these two sets of phonemes is accounted for (in a phonetically motivated way) by means of a single rule which makes reference to /— voice/ vs. /+ voice/. Similarly, the assimilation of /n/ to /m/ and /ŋ/ (under certain circumstances) in the context of a following /p/, /b/ or /m/, on the one hand, and /k/ or /g/, on the other can be attributed to the presence of /+ labial/, on the one hand, and /+ velar/, on the other, as components of the phoneme that conditions the assimilation: cf. *unproductive* [mp], *unbeatable* [mb], *unmistakeable* [mm], *uncouth* [ŋk], *unguarded* [ŋg]. (The spelling does not here bear witness to the assimilative process, as it does for /n/ → /m/ in the Latin-derived forms *imponderable*, *imbued*, *immutable*.) It is commonly the case that a particular feature, e.g. /+ labial/, /+ nasal/, /+ voice/, can be seen as being, in certain contexts, **suprasegmental**: i.e. as running over a sequence of two or more (phonemic) segments.

But what about the possibility that a particular distinctive feature should never be other than suprasegmental in a particular language-system? This is not simply a theoretical possibility. Suprasegmental features of this kind are found in many languages. For example, what is referred to as **vowel harmony** is not uncommon. As it operates in Turkish, it involves the contrasting features /+ back/ vs. /— back/ and /+ rounded/ vs. /— rounded/. If we set aside word-forms that do not conform to the general pattern (forms of words that have been for the most part borrowed from other languages), we can say that all vowels in successive positions of a Turkish word must have the same value for the /± back/ contrast and (subject to a further condition, which excludes the combination of /+ rounded/ with the segmental feature /+ open/ in all but the initial syllable) for the /± rounded/ contrast. No matter how long the word is – and by virtue of its grammatical structure Turkish has many long word-forms – /± back/ and /± rounded/ are suprasegmental in the sense explained.

Suprasegmental distinctive features of the kind just exemplified are what the so-called **prosodic theory** of phonology refers to, in a specialized sense of the term, as **prosodies**. The prosodic theory of phonology, characteristic of what has been called the London School of Linguistics, has much that it shares with distinctive-feature theory in its more recent developments. Unfortunately, differences of terminology, not to mention differences of theoretical outlook in respect of more general issues, tend to obscure the similarities. The principal difference between orthodox distinctive-feature theory, as it were, and prosodic theory is that the former is still an essentially phonemic, or segmental, theory, as classical American phonemics was. Prosodic theory, on the other hand, allows that both phonemic (segmental) and prosodic (suprasegmental) elements are to be found and have equal, but complementary, status in the phonological inventories of language-systems. Furthermore, it recognizes that, although there is a tendency (for phonetic reasons) for certain features to be segmental and others suprasegmental in languages, the notion of suprasegmentality is, in principle, relative to particular language-systems.

The term 'suprasegmental', it must now be explained, has been employed here in a non-standard sense. Most linguists, if they employ the term 'suprasegmental' at all, use it to refer to such things as stress, tone and length, which were a problem for classical American phonemics, whose basic assumption was that the structure of words and sentences could be fully accounted for in terms of sequentially ordered phonological elements.

The stress-difference between the noun-form *import* and the verb-form *import* in spoken English (the former being stressed on the first, and the latter on the second, syllable) is not naturally handled as a difference between segmental phonemes. There are two partly independent reasons why it is not: first, stress is essentially a matter of the greater prominence of one syllable in relation to other syllables in the same form (or accompanying forms); second, the phonetic realization of stress, unlike the phonetic realization of segmental phonemes, cannot be said to precede or follow in time the phonetic realization of its neighbouring phonological elements. Obviously, one could represent the stress-difference between forms in a phonemic representation by more or less arbitrarily deciding to put the corresponding stress-phoneme before (or after) the vowel-phoneme which corresponds to the nucleus of the syllable in the phonetic realization. The point is that, although segmentalization can always be carried out in phonology at the price, if necessary, of arbitrary decision, the arbitrariness of the decisions forced upon the linguist in cases like this is itself an indication of the theoretical inadequacy of the framework within which the analysis is being carried out.

What has been said in relation to stress, holds also for tone which, in many languages (so-called **tone languages**), serves to distinguish forms in much the same way that stress does, though not very extensively, in English. As to length, there can be long consonants, just as there can be long vowels, in particular languages; and there can be an interdependence between the length of the one and the length of the other. Even in English (in the RP pronunciation), the length of vowels varies according to the quality of the consonants that follow them in the same syllable. What are traditionally called long vowels and are analysed as such by some phonologists, but not others, are realized as phonetically shortened segments when they are followed by a /− voiced/ stop: thus the vowel segment of *seat* is phonetically shorter than that of either *seed* or *see*. Indeed, it can be shorter, in its phonetic realization, than that of the phonologically short vowel of *sit*. This fact will serve to illustrate, not only the difference between phonological length and phonetic duration, but, more generally, the complexity of the relationship between phonological analysis and phonetic transcription.

3.6 *Phonological structure*

This is a very short section for a very big topic. Its purpose is simply to explain what is meant by 'structure', in this context, and to emphasize that there is a lot more to phonological analysis than establishing inventories of segmental and suprasegmental elements.

Given the existence of an inventory of phonological elements for a particular language, the phonological structure of that language is describable in terms of relations which hold among the elements themselves and relations, of various kinds, holding between sets of phonological elements, on the one hand, and larger phonological complexes or forms or other grammatical units, on the other.

Relations among the elements themselves are of two kinds, commonly referred to in the Saussurean tradition as 'syntagmatic' and 'paradigmatic'. The term 'syntagmatic', etymologically related to 'syntactic', but not to be confused with it, means no more than "combinatorial". Since 'paradigmatic' though historically explicable and widely employed, is potentially misleading, I will use the term 'substitutional' instead. So, both here and later, except when we are dealing specifically with Saussurean structuralism, I will talk of **syntagmatic** and **substitutional** relations. The former are the relations that hold among elements that can occur in combination with one another, in well-formed **syntagms**; the latter are relations that hold among sets of intersubstitutable elements at particular places in syntagms. It was one of Saussure's major achievements, as we shall see in our discussion of structuralism, to have made clear, at the turn of the century, the interdependence of syntagmatic and substitutional relations (cf. 7.2).

As we have seen, language-systems may differ from one another phonologically, not only in respect of the number of phonological elements in their inventories (and in the phonetic realization of these elements), but also in terms of the syntagmatic relations that determine the phonological well-formedness of possible combinations: i.e. phonological syntagms. To talk, for simplicity, as if phonological syntagms could be defined satisfactorily as sequences of phonemes: we know that not all phonemes can precede or follow all other phonemes. There are sequential constraints which prohibit the occurrence of the members of one set of phonemes next to the members of another set of phonemes. The rules which determine phonological well-formedness in particular languages must specify what these sequential constraints are: more generally, they must specify which elements can be put together in well-formed syntagms and in what way.

But that is not all there is to phonological description. The term 'syntagm' that has just been employed carries with it the implication that there are certain larger entities, the syntagms themselves, of which the phonological elements are the component parts. This is certainly the case. What is more controversial is whether there are, in all, or indeed in any, natural languages such purely phonological syntagms as **syllables** (not to mention phonological phrases), which need to be postulated in order to describe the phonological structure of the language in question and are definable without reference to the syntactic structure of the language. It is much easier to formulate the sequential constraints holding among English consonants in terms of their position in the same or successive syllables than it is if we make no reference at all to syllables. But this presupposes a theoretically satisfactory definition of syllables as phonological entities. Linguists are still divided as to the possibility, and further the necessity, of postulating syllables and other purely phonological syntagms in the structure of English and other languages. It may well be, of course, that some languages do have purely phonological syntagms and others do not.

There is far less controversy nowadays about the necessity of making reference to syntactic units in the phonological analysis of languages; or, to make essentially the same point in more recognizably modern terms, of integrating the phonological rules with the syntactic rules of language-systems. In many, and presumably all, natural languages there are **inter-level dependencies** of various kinds which are just as much a part of the language as are the purely phonological or purely syntactic relations. Indeed, we have covertly incorporated this notion of inter-level dependency in earlier sections. Not only did we first introduce the principle of phonological well-formedness in relation to forms (i.e. to phonological syntagms that are also syntactic units – under the simplifying assumptions of 2.6), but we have frequently made reference to the position of phonemes – as initial, medial, final, etc. – in words; and words, in this sense of 'word', are a subclass of forms.

The interdependence of syntax and phonology is much more extensive, however, than anything that has been said above would suggest. There are junctural phenomena, such as what is traditionally referred to as **liaison** in French, whose description necessitates reference, not only to word-boundaries, but also to the syntactic relation, if any, holding across word-boundaries: e.g. the occurrence of [z] in [lezɔm] *les hommes* "the men", and [ʒəlezevy] *Je les ai vu* "I have seen them", in contrast with its absence in [dɔnleamaʀi] *Donne-les à Marie* "Give them to Mary". Many of the phenomena in the non-verbal component of spoken languages which we have referred to as prosodic (cf. 1.5) – of which stress and intonation are the most important – cannot be accounted for properly unless their domain is specified syntactically; and yet they are also phonological phenomena, in that they involve the segmental and suprasegmental elements of the language-system. As we have seen, to the extent that these prosodic elements have no correlate in written language, corresponding written and spoken languages are non-isomorphic. It will now be clear that, in so far as there are syntactically (and semantically) relevant phonological distinctions that are not transferable to the graphic medium, corresponding written and spoken languages will necessarily differ, up to a point, syntactically (and semantically).

FURTHER READING

Most of the general works asterisked in the Bibliography contain chapters on phonetics and phonology. Useful introductory treatments are: Crystal (1971: 167–87); Fudge (1970); Henderson (1971). More comprehensive are:

(a) for phonetics: Abercrombie (1966); Fry (1977); Ladefoged (1974, 1975); Malmberg (1963); and, at a more advanced level, Brosnahan & Malmberg (1970); Catford (1977); Malmberg (1968).

(b) for phonology: Fischer-Jørgensen (1975); Sommerstein (1977).

The following readers exemplify points of theory and practice in phonology: Bolinger (1972); Fudge (1973); Jones & Laver (1973); Makkai (1972); Palmer (1970).

For a selection of exercises in phonological analysis, cf. Langacker (1972), chapter 4; Robinson (1975).

Acoustic phonetics: Fry (1979); Ladefoged (1962).

On the phonetics of English, especially RP: Brown (1977); Gimson (1970); Jones (1975).

Generative phonology: introductory accounts in Akmajian, Demers & Harnish (1979); Fromkin & Rodman (1974); Smith & Wilson (1979). More comprehensive: Hyman (1975); Kenstowicz & Kisseberth (1979); Schane (1973). The classic work is Chomsky & Halle (1968).

Prosodic phonology: Lyons (1962); Palmer (1970); Robins (1979a), section 4.4.

Prague School phonology: the classic work is Trubetzkoy (1939); for background and exemplification cf. Jakobson (1973); Vachek (1964, 1966). Close to the Prague School in many respects is Martinet (1960).

QUESTIONS AND EXERCISES

1. "A medium . . . is not in itself language; it is a vehicle for language" (Abercrombie, 1967: 2). Discuss.

2. How does **phonetics** differ from **phonology**?

3. What are the three principal branches of phonetics?

4. "the child, in the normal process of language-acquisition, is, and must be . . . a competent practitioner in all three branches of phonetics . . ." (p. 69). Explain and discuss.

5. Explain and exemplify (using forms, other than those in the text, from your own variety of English) (a) **homophony** and (b) **homography**.

6. "What we call 'the vocal organs' or 'the organs of speech' . . . are not primarily organs of speech at all" (O'Connor, 1973: 22). Discuss.

7. How do (a) **vowels** differ from **consonants** and (b) **stops** differ from **fricatives** in terms of an articulatory classification of speech sounds?

8. What articulatory feature do the following sets of speech-sounds have in common: (i) [p], [b], [m]; (ii) [p], [t], [k]; (iii) [θ], [f], [s], [ð]; (iv) [m], [n], [ŋ]?

9. What are the eight primary **cardinal vowels**? And what purpose is served by this system of classification?

10. Give the IPA symbols for: (a) a close front rounded vowel; (b) a velar nasal stop; (c) a voiced dental fricative; (d) a voiceless labial oral stop.

11. Give a broad phonetic transcription of your own versions of *asking*, *anguish*, *bathing*, *brother-in-law*, *buses*, *cloth*, *clothes*, *daughters*, *finger*, *found*, *gloves*, *king*, *months*, *operation*, *persuade*, *return*, *theatre*, *upstairs*, *without*.

12. Extract from the following phonetically represented forms (by de-alphabetizing the strings of symbols: cf. p. 83) all the contiguous **homorganic** features in terms of the classification of consonants and vowels used in section 3.3, and specify their domain. (For example, in [amba], the phonetic feature [voice] runs through all four segments, but [labiality] through only [mb].) (i) [indi]; (ii) [mãnɔŋ]; (iii) [pạtẹtị]; (iv) [ʌpti]; (v) [aŋkara].

4
Grammar

4.1 *Syntax, inflection and morphology*

The first thing that must be said in this chapter is that the term
'grammar' will be employed here and throughout this book (except
in the phrases 'traditional grammar' and 'generative grammar') in a
fairly narrow sense, in contrast with 'phonology', on the one hand,
and with 'semantics', on the other. This is one of its traditional
senses, and the one which is closest to the ordinary sense of 'grammatical'. Nowadays, many linguists subsume 'phonology', and even
'semantics', under 'grammar'. This can lead to confusion.

So far we have been operating with the assumption that
languages have two levels of structure: their phonology and their
syntax. This assumption will not be jettisoned in what follows. But it
will need to be modified, unless we are prepared either to broaden
our concept of phonology or to extend the term 'syntax' beyond the
bounds of its traditional interpretation. We have already seen that
there are in some, and presumably in all, natural languages inter-
level dependencies which make it impossible to make a rigid separa-
tion between phonological and syntactic structure. We shall now
see that, in certain languages at least, there is a gap, as it were,
between the syntax (as the term 'syntax' is traditionally understood)
and the phonology. This gap is covered in traditional grammar by
the term 'inflection'.[1]

---

[1] Contrary to what is implied in many textbooks of linguistics, it is 'inflection', not
'morphology', that opposes 'syntax' in traditional grammar. Not only is the term
'morphology' of relatively recent origin, but when it is put in contrast with 'syntax'
– especially if it is defined in terms of the even more recent term 'morpheme' – its
use implies a very untraditional view of the grammatical structure of languages.
Despite its undoubted faults, traditional grammar was not necessarily wrong on
this particular issue. Properly explained and precisely formulated, the traditional
view is at least as satisfactory as any alternative that has yet been proposed by
linguists.

All the standard dictionaries of European languages, ancient and
modern, presuppose the distinction between syntax and inflection.
So too does the way we have all learned to talk about language at
school. Even though the actual terms 'syntax' and 'inflection' may
be new to us, there is a sense in which we all know what they mean.
We are accustomed to operating with the term 'word' and using it,
as was the practice in traditional grammar, with two quite different
meanings, which depend ultimately on our practical understanding
of what falls within the scope of the term 'inflection'. Let us start
therefore with 'word'.

How many words are there in English? This question is ambiguous. Under one interpretation, *sing, sings, singing, sang* and *sung*
count as distinct words. Under the other, they are regarded as
different **forms** of the same word, viz. 'sing'. Generally speaking, if
asked how many words there are in a particular dictionary we take
the term 'word' in the second sense. On the other hand, if we are
asked to write a 2000-word essay on some topic, we take it in the
first sense and, furthermore, count each separate occurrence of
sing, of *sings*, of *singing*, etc., towards the total.

Let us now introduce some terminology which we can use, when
necessary, to keep apart the two senses of 'word'. We will say that
sing, sings, sang, etc. are **word-forms** (i.e. they are forms which are
also words): we have occasionally employed the term 'word-form'
in previous sections. And we will say that 'sing' (note: 'sing', not
sing) is a **lexeme**, or vocabulary-word, whose forms are *sing, sings,
sang*, etc. They are, in fact, what would be traditionally described as
its **inflectional forms**. But *sing* occupies a privileged position among
the forms of 'sing': it is both the standard **citation-form** and also
what many linguists would regard as the **base-form**. And it is no less
important to distinguish the citation-form from the base-form than
it is to distinguish each of them from the lexeme itself. The citation-
form of the lexeme is the form that is employed to refer to the
lexeme; it is also the form that is used for the alphabetical listing of
lexemes in a conventional dictionary. The base-form is that form, if
any, from which all the other forms of the lexeme can be derived by
the **morphological** rules of the language. The citation-form of the
lexeme is distinct from the base-form, as far as verbs are concerned,
in French, German, Russian and most modern European

languages, and for all verbs and for most nouns and adjectives in Latin and Greek.

As we can refer to lexemes, so we can refer to any one of their forms. Indeed, we have been doing so and shall continue to do so, normally in italics (without angle brackets: cf. 3.2), but occasionally in phonetic or phonemic notation, throughout this book. Forms themselves can vary, in certain respects, according to the context in which they occur – the degree and nature of their phonetic variation in the spoken language being determined by the phonological rules. But they too have a citation-form with which they can be referred to; and the term 'citation-form' is frequently used by linguists, and more especially by phoneticians, with respect to the citation-forms of phonetically variable forms. For example, both *come* and *came* (forms of the lexeme 'come') will be pronounced with a bilabial nasal [m] in the final position of their citation-forms, but may well be pronounced with a labio-dental nasal [ɱ], in normal usage, immediately before another labio-dental consonant, [f] or [v].

This kind of variation is subphonemic, since the bilabial vs. labio-dental distinction is not one of the phonologically distinctive contrasts of English; but there is also a certain amount of contextually determined variation which, within the framework of classical American phonemics, would be said to involve the substitution of one phoneme for another. In both cases, it is common nowadays, especially in generative phonology, to talk of deriving, or generating, all the phonetically variable forms from a common **underlying form**, which will be either identical with the citation-form of the phonetically variable form in question or more similar to the citation-form than it is to any of the other phonetic variants.

On the basis of the distinction between a lexeme (more precisely, a word-lexeme) and its forms, we can now formulate the traditional distinction between **syntax** and **inflection** as follows. Taken together, syntax and inflection are complementary and constitute the principal part, if not the whole, of what we are calling grammar. Jointly, they determine the grammaticality (i.e. the grammatical well-formedness) of sentences: the syntax, by specifying how lexemes combine with one another in particular **constructions**; the inflectional rules (in so far as traditional grammar had rules, rather than paradigms), by specifying which of the forms of the lexeme should occur in one construction rather than another. Intermediate between syntax and inflection there is a level, or sublevel, of description at which one makes use of such phrases as 'the third-person singular, present-tense (form) of (the lexeme) SING', 'the possessive singular (form) of (the lexeme) BOY'. I have deliberately introduced at this point an alternative notation for lexemes, which is employed in several recent works: 'sing' and SING are notational variants, referring to exactly the same entity.[2]

The modern (and more particularly post-Bloomfieldian) distinction of **syntax** vs. **morphology**, according to which syntax deals with the distribution of words (i.e. word-forms) and morphology with their internal grammatical structure is, at first sight, very similar to the traditional distinction of syntax vs. inflection. But it differs from it in two respects: (a) morphology includes not only inflection, but also **derivation**; (b) it handles both inflection and derivation by means of rules operating upon the same basic units – morphemes. For example, as the inflectional form *singing* is made up of the two more basic units (morphemes) *sing* and *ing*, so the derivational form *singer* is made up of the two more basic units *sing* and *er*. Furthermore, it is the same process of **affixation**: i.e. of adding an **affix** to a base-form in each case. Looked at from this point of view, **morphemes** – minimal forms – are seen as the basic units of grammatical structure; and a good deal of morphology can be brought within the scope of syntax by demoting the word from its traditional position of centrality in grammatical theory.

There are arguments in favour of morpheme-based grammar and there are arguments against it. The same is true of the more traditional word-based grammar. The problem is to preserve the advantages of each within a coherent and, in other respects, well-motivated theory of the grammatical structure of human languages. Greater progress has been made towards this general goal in the last twenty years or so than in any previous period in the long history of linguistics. Most of this progress can be attributed, directly or indirectly, to the formalization of a particular theory of syntax,

[2] Strictly speaking, it is not words in the sense of lexemes, nor yet words in the sense of word-forms whose distribution is accounted for by the syntactic rules of traditional grammar, but words in the sense of these intermediate entities: morpho-syntactic words. But we need not be concerned in this book with such further refinements of terminology (cf. Matthews, 1974).

within the framework of generative grammar, by Chomsky. More will be said about this later. Here it is sufficient to note that, although Chomsky's theory of syntax is morpheme-based, rather than word-based, it has come to adopt, in its most recent development, a rather more traditional view of the complementarity of syntax and inflection than it did in its earlier versions. In particular, it now treats derivational morphology as something which is not handled by the central syntactic component of the grammar, but as relating to the structure of the vocabulary (or **lexicon**). Whatever theory of grammar we currently operate with, it is clear that we can no longer simply say, as we did in our earlier formulation of the principle of duality, that the units of the primary level are composed of elements of the secondary level (1.5). The relation between the two levels is far more complex than this formulation suggests. However, this complexity is rule-governed. Furthermore, despite the very considerable differences of grammatical and phonological structure among human languages, there are equally striking similarities, which would suggest that at least some of the rules that determine and integrate the two levels – rules that children master in a relatively short period during the acquisition of language – are common to all human languages.

4.2 *Grammaticality, productivity and arbitrariness*

Sentences are, by definition, **grammatical** (i.e. grammatically well-formed: cf. 2.6). For present purposes, they may be regarded as well-formed **word-strings** (i.e. sequences of word-forms), such that, for example,

(1) This morning he got up late

and

(2) He got up late this morning

are, by definition, different sentences of English. From a theoretically more general, and more traditional, point of view, sentences may be defined as classes of strings of word-forms, each member of the class having the same syntactic structure. This definition would allow, but not oblige, us to treat (1) and (2) as being, not different sentences, but alternative versions of the same sentence.

It must also be remembered that every sentence of spoken language will have, superimposed upon the string of word-forms, a characteristic **prosodic contour** (notably a particular intonation-pattern) without which it is not a sentence. Just how much of the prosodic structure of spoken utterances is to be attributed to the structure of sentences is a matter of controversy within linguistics. Most linguists would say that at least that part of the prosodic structure of utterances which distinguishes statements from questions and commands should be attributed to sentence-structure. We will tacitly accept this viewpoint. This leaves open the possibility that both (1) and (2) are in correspondence, not with single sentences, but with sets of different sentences of spoken English. It follows, in view of what was said in the preceding paragraph, that, if difference of word-order and difference of prosodic contour are given equal weight as potential indicators of grammatical structure, the difference between two intonationally distinct versions of either (1) or (2) counts, in principle, as much as the difference between (1) and (2). This point should be borne in mind, even though we shall be talking, throughout much of this book, as if sentences of spoken languages are satisfactorily represented as strings of words.

What is the difference between a grammatical and an ungrammatical string of words? The answer is simple, but of itself unilluminating. An ungrammatical string of words is one in the formation of which the grammatical rules of the language-system are not respected. This statement covers not only sentences, but also phrases: e.g. *morning this*, *late got up* are ungrammatical (hence the asterisk: cf. 2.6). Let us see what it implies, and – no less important – what it does not imply, as far as sentences are concerned.

It does not of course, imply a normative, or prescriptive, attitude towards language: we are concerned with the immanent rules which, in default of any linguistically irrelevant inhibiting or distorting factors, native speakers of a language unconsciously apply. Nor does it imply any very direct connection between grammaticality and probability of occurrence. Finally, it does not imply any identification of grammaticality with meaningfulness; on the other hand, it allows that there may be a close and essential connection between at least some part of the grammaticality of sentences and the meaningfulness of actual or potential utterances.

The way in which meaning, of various kinds, is conveyed by natural languages will occupy us more fully in Chapter 5. The point being made here is simply that, whatever the connection between grammaticality and meaningfulness, the two properties must be distinguished. Chomsky's now classic example,

(3) Colourless green ideas sleep furiously

is a perfectly well-formed sentence of English, though it cannot be given a coherent literal interpretation. Conversely,

(4) *Late got this morning he up

is undoubtedly ungrammatical, though it is, arguably, no less readily interpretable than (1) or (2), once we make allowances for its violation of those rules of English which control the position of words of various classes relative to one another in sentences. There are indefinitely many trickier cases than those exemplified by (3) and (4): there is, undoubtedly, a very large, and theoretically interesting, area of interdependence between grammaticality and meaningfulness. But these two properties of sentences are not to be identified.

Traditional grammar gave only a very partial and often highly inexplicit account of grammaticality. It succeeded in establishing many of the more specific principles with which linguists still operate and, for certain well-studied languages, it codified a large number of different grammatical constructions, as well as noting an even larger number of disparate facts which, though held to be sanctioned by usage and thus to be in a certain sense grammatical, fell outside the scope of the rules of the language-system as such. Modern grammatical theory sets out to be more explicit and more comprehensive, especially in respect of the formulation of the syntactic rules of language-systems, than traditional grammar ever aspired to be. One reason for this was that, since Latin and Greek were highly inflected languages and most of what is obviously a matter of grammaticality can be stated, directly or indirectly, in terms of inflectional categories (gender, number, case, tense, mood, etc.), 'grammar', as traditionally interpreted, was heavily biased towards the study of inflection. Hence the not uncommon belief that non-inflecting languages, such as Classical Chinese, have no grammar and that English, which has relatively little inflectional morphology, has less grammar than Latin and Greek, or even French and German. Modern grammatical theory operates with a notion of 'grammar' which is not biased towards inflecting languages.

Another reason why traditional grammar not only failed, but did not even try, to provide a comprehensive and fully explicit account of the syntax of the languages that it dealt with, was that much of syntax was held, explicitly or implicitly, to be determined by common sense or, to use a more grandiloquent term, the laws of thought. The fact that one says *This morning he got up late* or *He got up late this morning*, rather than *Late got this morning he up*, in English was not held to stand in need of any other explanation than that the order of the words reflects the order of thought. This view becomes more and more difficult to uphold when a sufficiently wide and representative sample of the world's languages is seriously investigated. Word-order is, within limits, very largely a matter of stylistic variation in Latin and Greek. There are many languages, including English, in which the stylistic role of word-order is far smaller and its syntactic function proportionately more important.

A fairly good case can be made for the view that stylistically variable word-order, as exemplified in (1) and (2), is determined by psychological factors and logical principles that may be referred to, loosely, as the laws of thought. But how do we account for the fact that in stylistically neutral declarative sentences of English the subject precedes the verb, whereas in comparable sentences of Irish it is the verb that comes first? Or again, for the fact that in noun phrases the adjective normally precedes the noun in English (*red coat*), but (for most adjectives) normally follows it in French (*manteau rouge*)? Chauvinistic explanations to the effect that one word-order is more in accord with the laws of thought than another and that one nation's language is consequently more logical than that of another soon break down. So too does the even more desperate hypothesis that each nation has its own logic, different perhaps from that of other nations, and that a particular nation's logic determines the principles of syntactically functioning word-order in a particular national language. If an Englishman and a Frenchman are asked to describe a red coat, does the former think first of all that it is red and only then that it is a coat, and does the Frenchman perform these mental operations in reverse order? It seems unlikely.

Syntactically functioning word-order is but one of the many aspects of grammatical structure that are, to some considerable extent, **arbitrary** in the sense that they cannot be accounted for in terms of more general logical and psychological principles (cf. 1.5).

And yet the young child, in the normal course of language-acquisition, succeeds in learning, without being taught, the grammatical rules of his native language. This is all the more astonishing in that natural languages, by virtue of their grammatical structure, also have the property of **productivity** (cf. 1.5). The task that confronts the young child during the period of language-acquisition is that of inferring from a large, but finite, sample of utterances, those largely arbitrary grammatical principles by virtue of which an indefinitely large, and perhaps infinite, set of word-strings are grammatical and another, even larger, set of word-strings are grammatically ill-formed.

It was Chomsky who, in the mid-1950s, first appreciated the significance of the child's mastery of the syntactic determinants of grammaticality. It was he, too, who put forward what has proved to be the most influential theory of syntax so far developed in any period of linguistics, ancient or modern. Chomskyan syntax is formalized within the framework of generative grammar and, especially in its more recent versions, integrates syntax with phonology and semantics in a comprehensive theory of the structure of language. We cannot, in a book of this nature, go into the more technical details of generative grammar. However, we shall devote one section of this chapter to a non-technical account of the main principles of Chomskyan **generative grammar** (4.6) and, in a later chapter, look at what I will call **generativism** in its historical context (cf. 7.4).

Generativism, in contrast with structuralism, functionalism, historicism, etc., is what most people have in mind when they refer, correctly, to the Chomskyan revolution. Like all revolutions, it takes over from the past and leaves intact much more than is realized by the revolutionaries themselves and the majority of their contemporaries. As Aristotelian philosophy cannot be understood except in the context of Platonism, and as Descartes cannot be understood without reference to the scholastic tradition against which he reacted and from which he unquestioningly accepted as much as he rejected, so it is with Chomsky in relation to the ideas with which he was most familiar, by virtue of his own training in linguistics, psychology and philosophy: Chomskyan generativism is very much conditioned by the very particular intellectual and cultural context in which it developed. These more general issues we shall, for the present, leave on one side.

4.3 *Parts of speech, form-classes and grammatical categories*

What are traditionally, and rather misleadingly, referred to as parts of speech – nouns, verbs, adjectives, prepositions, etc. – play a crucial role in the formulation of the grammatical rules of languages. It is important to realize, however, that the traditional list of ten or so parts of speech is very heterogeneous in composition and reflects, in many of the details of the definitions that accompany it, specific features of the grammatical structure of Greek and Latin that are far from being universal. Furthermore, the definitions themselves are often logically defective. Some of them are circular; and most of them combine inflectional, syntactic and semantic criteria which yield conflicting results when they are applied to a wide range of particular instances in several languages. In fact, taken at their face value, the traditional definitions do not work perfectly even for Greek and Latin. Like most of the definitions in traditional grammar, they rely heavily upon the good sense and tolerance of those who apply and interpret them.

It is easy enough to pick holes in the traditional definitions: "A noun is the name of any person, place or thing", "A verb is a word which denotes an action", "An adjective modifies a noun", "A pronoun stands for a noun", etc. Nevertheless, most linguists still operate with the terms 'noun', 'verb', 'adjective', etc., and interpret them, explicitly or implicitly, in a fairly traditional way. And they are right to do so. It is an important fact about the structure of natural languages that linguists are able to make empirically verifiable statements to the effect that some languages have a syntactic distinction between adjectives and verbs (English, French, Russian, etc.), whereas others (Chinese, Malay, Japanese, etc.) arguably do not; that most languages have a syntactic distinction between nouns and verbs (English, French, Russian, Chinese, Malay, Japanese, Turkish, etc.) but that a few (notably, the American-Indian language Nootka, as described by Sapir) arguably do not; that in some languages (Latin, Turkish, etc.) adjectives are grammatically more similar to nouns and less similar to verbs than they are in other languages (English, Chinese, Japanese, etc.).

But there is another aspect of the traditional theory of the parts of speech that must be clarified at this point. The terms 'noun', 'verb', 'adjective', etc., are employed in traditional grammar with the same ambiguity that 'word' is; and this ambiguity has been carried over into many otherwise untraditional modern treatments of syntax, which prefer to talk of word-classes, rather than parts of speech. If we decide to restrict the term 'part of speech' to classes of lexemes, saying that 'boy' is a noun, that 'come' is a verb, and so on, we can say that *boy*, *boys* and *boy's* are **noun-forms**, that *come*, *comes*, *coming*, *came* are **verb-forms**, and so on.

There is more to this question than simply a desire for terminological consistency. One of the problems with the traditional theory of the parts of speech is that, by failing to draw the distinction that has just been drawn, it found itself obliged to recognize that certain words (I deliberately equivocate here with 'word') belonged simultaneously to two parts of speech. This is most notoriously the case with participles (whose traditional label reflects their dual status). Looked at from one point of view, that of inflectional morphology, they are verb-forms; looked at from another point of view, in terms of their syntactic function, they are adjectives (cf. *dancing* in *the dancing girls*, construed as "the girls who dance/are dancing"). Similarly, what are traditionally called gerunds (or, more revealingly, verbal nouns) are verb-forms whose syntactic function is characteristically that of nouns (cf. *dancing* in *shoes for dancing* and, at one further remove, as a noun used adjectivally in *dancing shoes*).

More interesting, if only because it is not so widely acknowledged either in traditional grammar or in modern grammatical theory, is the fact that certain noun-forms are, from a syntactic point of view, characteristically adjectival or adverbial. For example, the possessive *bishop's* in *the bishop's mitre* (construed as "the mitre of the kind that bishops wear") is syntactically an adjective: cf. *the episcopal mitre*. We cannot make coherent statements about facts such as these unless we draw the distinction between the assignment of a lexeme to a particular part of speech and the identification of the syntactic functions of its forms in different contexts.

Many modern works talk about **form-classes** rather than parts of speech. Having reserved 'part of speech' for lexeme-classes, we can conveniently appropriate the term 'form-class' (in one of the senses in which it has been defined) for classes of forms having the same syntactic function. We can then give what is called a distributional interpretation to 'syntactic function': two forms have the same syntactic function if, and only if, they have the same distribution (i.e. are intersubstitutable: cf. 3.4) throughout the grammatical (though not necessarily meaningful) sentences of the language. Distributional definitions of this kind played a crucial role in the later period of post-Bloomfieldian linguistics and prepared the way for the development of Chomskyan generative grammar.

It will be immediately apparent that inflectionally variant forms of the same lexeme do not, in general, have the same distribution; and this is why syntax and inflection are complementary parts of grammar. For example, *boy* and *boys* differ distributionally in various ways, but most notably in that the former, but not the latter, can occur in a range of contexts including

(1) The —— is here

and the latter, but not the former, in a range of contexts including

(2) The —— are here.

By virtue of the semantic function of the distinction between *boy* and *boys*, in most contexts, we refer to *boy* as the singular form and *boys* as the plural form of 'boy'. If this distinction of meaning did not correlate with a difference of distribution (i.e. if the singular and plural forms of lexemes were intersubstitutable throughout the sentences of English without consequential changes elsewhere in the same sentences), there would be no syntactic rule of English dependent upon it. Though there is an intrinsic connection between the meaning of forms and their distribution, it is their distribution alone that is of direct concern to the grammarian. Anyone who wishes to understand modern grammatical theory, in its most distinctive and most interesting developments, must be able to think of the distribution of forms independently of their meaning.

Since the term 'form' is broader than, but subsumes, 'word-form', the term 'form-class' is correspondingly broader than either 'word-class' or 'part of speech'. Morphemes (i.e. minimal forms) can be grouped into form-classes on the basis of the criterion of intersubstitutability; so too can phrases composed of several words. In a morpheme-based grammar, the part of speech label, which we have assigned to lexemes, would be attributed, primarily, to what are traditionally referred to as **stems**, or even **roots**. (The difference between stems and roots is that roots are morphologically unanalysable, whereas stems may include, in addition to their root, one or more derivational affixes.) For example, the form *boy* would be classified as a noun by virtue of its being the stem of a whole set of inflected word-forms, including *boy*, *boys* and *boy's*. It is, however, a purely contingent fact of English grammatical structure that noun-stems, verb-stems, adjective-stems, etc. are always word-forms (and citation-forms: cf. 4.1). It is also a purely contingent fact that in English (as in, say, Chinese, but not Turkish) very many forms can serve as either noun-stems or verb-stems (cf. *walk, turn, man, table*, etc.). In both of these respects English is far from being representative of the languages of the world. Current versions of generative grammar, being morpheme-based, operate with definitions of 'noun', 'verb', 'adjective', etc., which apply, primarily, to lexeme-stems and secondarily to larger forms containing them or syntactically equivalent with them.

In traditional word-based grammar, as inflection is complementary to syntax, so the inflectional, or grammatical, **categories** are complementary to the parts of speech. For example, 'singular' and 'plural' are terms in the category of **number**; 'present', 'past' and 'future', terms in the category of **tense**; 'indicative', 'subjunctive', 'imperative', etc., terms in the category of **mood**; 'nominative', 'accusative', 'dative', 'genitive', etc., terms in the category of **case**; and so on. Such traditional labels as 'first-person singular of the present-tense indicative of the verb BE' exemplify the way in which, to use the traditional terminology, particular parts of speech are said to be inflected for a particular set of grammatical categories.

Two points may be made in connection with the inflectional categories of traditional grammar. The first is that none of them is truly universal, in the sense that it is found in all languages. There are languages without tense; languages without case; languages without gender; and so, without exception, for every one of the traditional categories. On the other hand, there are many categories not recognized in traditional grammar that exist in languages that have been investigated, in more recent times, by linguists.

The second point is that what are traditionally described as grammatical categories would be commonly treated, in morpheme-based grammar, as sets of **grammatical morphemes** (in contrast with the **lexical morphemes** listed as noun-stems, verb-stems, etc., in the vocabulary). And their distribution would be handled directly by syntactic rules. This is, in essence, the treatment that is adopted in current versions of generative grammar.

4.4 *Some additional grammatical concepts*

It is the function of the grammatical rules of a language to specify the determinants of grammaticality for that language (cf. 4.2). As we shall see later, a generative grammar does this by generating (in a sense to be explained) all and only the sentences of a language and assigning to each, in the very process of its generation, a **structural description**. In this section, a number of grammatical notions will be listed, and briefly explained, which have been elaborated by linguists in their attempts to formulate, for particular languages and for language in general, the determinants of grammaticality and the kind of information that should be included in the structural descriptions of sentences.

It cannot be too strongly emphasized that the linguist – nowadays at least – is not interested in classification and pigeon-holing for its own sake. He is concerned, as we saw at the outset, with the question "What is language?" and, whether directly or indirectly, with the native speaker's ability to produce and understand an indefinitely large, and potentially infinite, number of utterances that differ fron one another in form and meaning. An explication of the concept of grammaticality is central to the task of accounting for the native speaker's ability to do this (and for the child's acquisition of this ability), and it is one of the central issues involved in any intellectually satisfying answer that might be offered to the question "What is language?"

The list of grammatical concepts that follows, though fairly lengthy, is far from exhaustive. Many of them originate in traditional grammar; others have been developed more recently. Not all of them will be invoked in later sections of this book. This is partly because the account that will be given here of grammatical structure and of generative grammar is, inevitably, both very elementary and highly selective. But there is a more important reason. In the present state of grammatical theory, it is unclear just how many logically independent, or primitive, notions are required for the specification of the determinants of grammaticality in any particular language, let alone in all languages. If one set of notions is selected as primitive, in this logical sense of the term, others can be defined in terms of them. But there are many options open to the linguist in deciding what is primitive and what is derived. Current versions of generative grammar have, often for purely historical reasons, made one selection of primitives rather than another. It may not prove to be the right selection. Indeed, it must be regarded as an open question whether there is a right selection – right, that is to say, for all human languages.

It does not matter much if the reader to whom the following list of grammatical notions is unfamiliar fails to remember most of them. Anyone embarking upon the study of linguistics at a more specialized level should, of course, not only understand them, but be able to exemplify them and, no less important, be able to add to the list and show how one notion shades into, or is definable in terms of, another. The reason why I present this reasonably long list of grammatical concepts in what is intended to be an elementary, and very general, book on language and linguistics is that most comparable works fail to make the point that was made in the preceding paragraph. Even an elementary book should give its readers some sense of the range and complexity of the subject it deals with. And no treatment of grammatical theory should fail to state clearly that, although great progress has been made recently, we are far from having a satisfactory general theory of grammatical structure.

Sentences may be classified (and are so classified in traditional grammar) along the intersecting dimensions of (a) structure and (b) function: as (a) **simple** vs. non-simple, with non-simple sentences being subdivided into **complex** vs. **compound**; and (b) **declarative, interrogative, imperative**, etc. A simple sentence consists of a single **clause** (with the appropriate prosodic contour); a minimal complex sentence consists of two clauses, one of which is subordinate to the other; a minimal compound sentence consists of two or more clauses, both of which are co-ordinate. (For convenience of exposition, I will here introduce the term **composite** to cover both compound and complex sentences.) The notions of subordination and co-ordination invoked here are, as we shall see, very general notions, applicable not just to the classification of sentences, but within sentences.

As to the functional classification of sentences, two points may be made. The first is that, if we draw a distinction between declarative sentences and statements, between interrogative sentences and questions, between imperative sentences and commands, requests, etc., we can say that a declarative sentence is one whose grammatical structure is that of sentences that are used, characteristically, to make statements, and so on. This enables us to keep distinct, but to interrelate, the grammatical structure of sentences and the communicative function of utterances (cf. 5.5). We shall draw upon this distinction in the chapter on semantics. The second point is that 'imperative', unlike 'declarative', and 'interrogative' is traditionally employed, with 'indicative', 'subjunctive', etc., to label one of the terms in the grammatical category of mood. This double employment of 'imperative' should be noted, if only because it has led to a lot of confusion in modern grammatical theory.

Within sentences, whether simple or non-simple, there are various kinds of part–whole relations: relations of **constituency**. For example, all the clauses of a complex or compound sentence are **constituents** of the sentence as a whole; in a simple sentence all the word-forms (let us assume) are constituents, and groups of words may constitute **phrases** which are also constituents, of the sentence (the words being, in turn, constituents of the phrases, and thus only indirectly of the sentences of which the phrases are constituents). As we shall see in the following sections, this notion of constituency, coupled with a somewhat more general version of the traditional concept of the phrase, is at the very heart of the formalization of grammatical structure in Chomskyan generative grammar.

Another kind of syntactic relation – one to which traditional grammar attached particular importance – is that of **dependency**. This is an asymmetrical relation that holds (to use modern terminology) between a **governor**, or **controller**, and one or more **dependents**. For example, the verb is said to **govern** its object (if it has one) in one form rather than another, as the verb 'see', like all transitive verbs in English, governs its object in what would be traditionally described as the accusative case (cf. *I saw him* vs. **I saw he*; the category of case, *he* vs. *him*, etc., is an inflectional category of pronouns, but not of nouns, in English). More generally, we can establish a relation of dependency within a particular construction whenever the occurrence of one unit, the controller, is a precondition for the occurrence, in the appropriate form, of one or more other units, its dependents. What is traditionally referred to as **government**, exemplified above, can be brought within the scope of the broader concept of dependency which does not presuppose the existence of inflectional variation. In so far as the clustering of a controller with its dependents establishes, implicitly, a part–whole relation between each of the units and the cluster itself, constituency and dependency are not wholly independent variables. Chomskyan generative grammar has opted for constituency, in this respect following Bloomfield and his successors. Traditional grammar laid more emphasis on dependency.

Reference was made, in the preceding paragraph, to transitive verbs. The traditional distinction between **transitive** and **intransitive** verbs can be generalized in two directions: first of all, by including verbs within the broader class of **predicators**; then by subclassifying predicators in terms of their **valency**: i.e. in terms of the number and nature of their dependent units. Counting, not only the direct and indirect object, but also the subject, of a verb among its dependents, we can say that an intransitive verb like 'die' has a valency of 1, a transitive verb like 'eat' has a valency of 2, verbs like 'give' or 'put' have a valency of 3, and so on.

This notion of valency does not presuppose, it should be noted, that the dependents of a predicator are necessarily noun phrases. What are traditionally referred to as adverbial complements of time, place, etc., also fall within the scope of the definition of valency. We must also allow for the existence of predicators with zero-valency. For example, the verbs 'rain', 'snow', etc., in English are arguably of this kind, the form *it* of *It is raining/snowing*, etc., being no more than a dummy subject.

The term 'valency' (borrowed from chemistry) is not, so far, very widely employed in British and American works on linguistics. But the notion is latent in a good deal of grammatical theory that does not actually employ the term. The most controversial, and untraditional, aspect of the notion of valency, as it has just been presented, is its demotion, as it were, of the traditional distinctions of **subject** and **predicate** (of the clause), on the one hand, and of **subject** and **object** (of the verb), on the other. These two distinctions, it should be noted, are logically independent. The former rests upon the division of the clause (in accordance with traditional assumptions) into two complementary parts; the latter does not. The subject of the verb is that unit which, though dependent upon the verb just as much as the object is, determines the form of the verb in what is commonly called **subject–verb agreement** (cf. *The boy is running* vs. **The boy are running*, and *The boys are running* vs. **The boys is running*). Other criteria can be, and have been, proposed for the identification of a more general notion of syntactic subject applicable to all languages. But the question of the universality of either kind of syntactic subject (or of some more general notion of subject which subsumes both) is as controversial today as it was when it was hotly debated by linguists in the late nineteenth century.

4.5   *Constituent-structure*

In this section we shall concentrate upon that aspect of grammatical structure which can be handled in terms of the notion of constituency. We shall do so within the framework of morpheme-based grammar and from the distributionalist point of view characteristic of the later period of post-Bloomfieldian linguistics (cf. 7.4). By adopting this point of view, we can kill two birds with one stone: we can further illustrate the application of important notions that have been introduced above – those associated with the terms 'morpheme', 'morphology', 'inflection', 'derivation', 'form-class', 'distribution', not to mention 'constituency' itself; and we can prepare the way for our treatment of generative grammar in the following section.

Though the Bloomfieldian concept of constituent-structure is primarily a syntactic concept, we shall begin by showing how it applies within word-forms. It will be recalled that in post-Bloomfieldian linguistics grammar was divided into morphology and syntax (cf. 4.1). Morphology dealt with the internal structure of word-forms; syntax dealt with the distribution of word-forms throughout the well-formed sentences of a language. But post-Bloomfieldian morphology was itself a kind of syntactic morphology. It applied the same principles to the grammatical analysis of word-forms as it did to the syntactic analysis of such larger units as phrases and sentences. Indeed, post-Bloomfieldian linguists, in principle, if not always consistently in practice, eventually came to abandon the distinction between morphology and syntax, with a consequential broadening of the definition of 'syntax'. Syntax became the study of the distribution of morphemes (rather than of word-forms); and word-forms were recognized, not as purely syntactic units, but as units that could serve (with the appropriate prosodic contour) as minimal utterances and, in certain languages, as the domain of certain suprasegmental phonological features (cf. 3.6). This is, in essence, the point of view adopted, as part of its post-Bloomfieldian inheritance, by Chomskyan generative grammar.

Throughout this section, and the next, the term 'word' is to be understood as referring to word-forms. Words, in this sense, can be represented as strings of (one or more) morphemes: morphemes being minimal forms; and words being, in Bloomfield's classic (though only partially satisfactory) definition, **minimum free forms** (i.e. forms not consisting wholly of smaller free forms). A **free** form, in contrast with a **bound** form, is one that could occur, with the appropriate prosodic contour, as an utterance (though not necessarily as a full sentence) in some normal context of use. Not all the forms traditionally recognized as words in English, and separated, by spaces in the written medium, satisfy this definition. We shall use as examples only those that do. Thus: *cat* is both a morpheme (being a minimal form) and a word (being a free form); *cats* is not a morpheme since it is composed of two minimal forms, *cat* and *s*, but it is a word (though *cat* is a free form, *s* is not); *unfriendliness* is a word composed of four morphemes, *un-friend-ly-ness*, all of which, except *friend*, are bound forms. Bound forms that are constituents of words are affixes: prefixes, if they precede the base-form to which they are attached, or affixed; suffixes, if they follow it.

But there is more to the constituent-structure of words than can be fully accounted for in terms of their constituent morphemes. Many of the words of English, and other languages, have an internal **hierarchical structure**, which can be represented, formally, by means of the mathematical notion of **bracketing**. For example, the constituent structure of the word *unfriendliness* can be represented as

(1) [[*un-*[*friend-ly*]]*-ness*]

or equivalently, by means of a **tree-diagram**, as in (2).

(2)
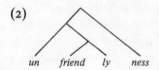

un   friend   ly   ness

It is important to appreciate that (1) and (2) are formally equivalent. Each tells us no more and no less than the following: that the **immediate constituents** (ICs) of *unfriendliness* are *unfriendly* and *ness*; that the ICs of *unfriendly* are *un* and *friendly*; that the ICs of *friendly* are *friend* and *ly*; and, no further analysis being possible at the grammatical level of description, that the **ultimate constituents** of the whole syntagm are *un*, *friend*, *ly* and *ness*. Alternatively, they tell us that *friend* and *ly* may be combined (in sequence) to form an intermediate constituent, *friendly*, to which *un* may be prefixed to form a larger intermediate constituent, *unfriendly*, to which *ness* may be suffixed to form the whole word-form. Both methods of representation, (1) and (2), are neutral as between the analysis and the synthesis of syntagms.

I do not propose to justify, in detail, the particular bracketing of *unfriendliness* assigned to it in (1) and (2). In principle, it rests (according to the postulates of post-Bloomfieldian distributionalism) upon the criteria of substitutability and generality. The form *unfriendliness* belongs to a form-class (i.e. a set of intersubstitutable forms) which we will call, using traditional terminology, abstract nouns and symbolize as N_a. Very many of these are formed in English by adding the suffix *ness* to what are traditionally called adjectives (more precisely, to the base-forms of adjectives). Similarly, the prefixation of *un* to an adjective-form (A) is a highly productive morphological process in English. In contrast the prefixation of *un* to noun-forms (of subclass N_a) is not a productive process. It follows that even though there is a word 'friendliness' in English, we do not wish to recognize [[*friend-ly*]-*ness*], not to mention [*friend*-[*ly-ness*]], as a constituent of *unfriendliness*. As for the innermost bracketing of [*friend-ly*], this is justified by a moderately productive morphological process, whereby adjectives are formed out of nouns, of let us say subclass N_c, by the suffixation of *ly* (cf. *man-ly*, etc.).

The distributional justification of the constituent-structure assigned to the word-form *unfriendliness* is fairly straightforward. This is far from being the case in respect of all the word-forms of English, especially if the distributional criteria are converted into mechanical discovery procedures (cf. 7.4). However, we are not concerned to argue for distributionalism as such, but merely to illustrate what is meant by constituent-structure. The point is that, whether a particular analysis is validated by purely distributional criteria or not, the use of a particular term or symbol, e.g. 'noun' or N_c, to **label** a form-class implies that the members of the form-class are intersubstitutable in all the contexts covered by any rule that uses the label in question. For example, let us arbitrarily assign the label A_x to that particular set of forms which results from the suffixation of *ly* to the members of the form-class N_c. We can now express what has just been said by means of the following rule:

(3) $N_c + ly \rightarrow A_x$

This tells us, in effect, that all forms of subclass N_c are intersubstitutable in at least the range of contexts covered by (3). It further implies that all the members of subclass A_x are intersubstitutable in contexts covered by other rules, such as

(4) $A_x + ness \rightarrow N_a$

and

(5) $un + A_x \rightarrow A_x$

The fact that distributionalism, in the form in which it was developed by the post-Bloomfieldians, has been discredited does not mean that the notion of distribution itself is no longer relevant in grammatical analysis. On the contrary, it is the crucial notion in the formalization of grammar.

Before we proceed, one point may be noted. Rule (5), in contrast with rules (3) and (4), is potentially **recursive**: i.e. if it is allowed to apply to its own output (A_x), it will yield indefinitely many syntagms of increasing complexity – [*un-friendly*], [*un-[un-friendly]*], [*un-[un-[un-friendly]]*], etc. Presumably, we should not wish to regard *ununfriendly*, still less *unununfriendly*, etc., as being grammatically well-formed. Therefore, rule (5) is technically faulty; for *friendly* and *unfriendly* are not members of exactly the same form-class. On the other hand, there are many syntactic, if not morphological, constructions in English, and possibly in all natural languages, that are fully recursive. It is for this reason that the sentences of a language, though each finite in length, may be infinite in number (cf. Chomsky's definition of 'language' quoted in 1.2 and 2.6).

Exactly the same notion of constituent-structure applies to sequences of words – **phrases** in both the traditional and the everyday sense of this term – as applies (according to the Bloomfieldian and post-Bloomfieldian conception of morphology) within words. For example, *on the wooden table* is what is traditionally called a **prepositional phrase**; which is composed of a **preposition** (*on*) and what is traditionally called a **noun phrase** (*the wooden table*); which is composed of the **definite article** (*the*) and the phrase *wooden table*; which is composed of an adjective (*wooden*) and a noun (*table*). What has just been said can be expressed, without the traditional labels that were employed, by means of

(6) [*on*[*the*[*wooden table*]]]

or, equivalently, the tree-diagram in (7).

(7)

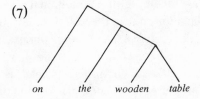

Both (6) and (7), like (1) and (2), are **unlabelled** representations of constituent-structure.

It is customary, however, to operate with the notion of **labelled** representations – the labels, as above, being used to indicate form-class membership. Let us therefore convert (6) and (7) into a **labelled bracketing** and a **labelled tree**, (8) and (9) respectively, using standard mnemonic symbols for the labels: NP for 'noun phrase', P for 'preposition', PP for 'prepositional phrase', A for 'adjective', Art for '(definite) article'. It will be noted that (8)

(8) $[_{PP}[_{P}on]$ $[_{NP}[_{Art}the]$ $[_{N}[_{A}wooden]$ $[_{N}table]]]]$

and (9) are formally equivalent. Since labelled bracketings, though more compact, are difficult to read, linguists commonly operate with labelled trees.

(9)

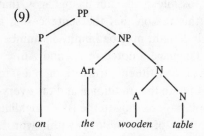

Two general points may be made in relation to (8) and (9). The first is that they represent the phrase *wooden table* as being of the same form-class as *table* (N). This is distributionally justifiable; and, although there are certain principles which determine the relative sequence of adjectives that precede nouns within the same phrase in English, there is no finite limit to the number of adjectives that may occur in that position. However, there is room for doubt about the internal structure of strings of adjectives in such positions.

A second point has to do with the terms 'noun phrase' and 'prepositional phrase'. These are taken over from traditional grammar; and they find their explanation, not in the notion of constituency, but in that of dependency (cf. 4.4). A noun phrase in traditional grammar is a phrase whose controller, or **head**, is a noun; a prepositional phrase, one whose controller, or head, is a preposition. The constituent-structure representation in (8) and (9) says nothing about dependency. The terms 'noun phrase' and 'prepositional phrase' are, in this respect, unmotivated. If they are understood, instead, to imply that noun phrases and prepositional phrases have the same distribution as nouns and prepositions respectively, this is obviously not so, as far as prepositional phrases are concerned. It might seem, at first sight, that the term 'noun phrase' is more appropriate from this point of view. For some languages it is. They include Latin and Russian, which have no definite article and, unlike English, can use so-called common nouns in the singular without a definite or indefinite article or any other member of the class of forms nowadays referred to as **determiners**. But a little reflection will show that, although *the wooden table* and *the table* have much the same distribution as proper names and pronouns, they do not have the same distribution as common nouns, like *table*.

The examples that have been used here to illustrate the notion of constituent-structure are straightforward enough and, apart from one or two details, uncontroversial. When it comes to the analysis of a representative set of the sentences of English and other languages from the point of view adopted in this section all sorts of problems arise. In particular, it is difficult to integrate the constituent-structure of word-forms with the constituent-structure of the larger syntagms in which the word-forms themselves occur as constituents. Few linguists, if any, would nowadays think it either possible or desirable to describe the syntax of a language within the framework outlined here without invoking additional notions. At the same time, it is clear that there is such a thing as constituent-structure in some, and presumably all, natural languages. Theoretical syntax was considerably advanced by the post-Bloomfieldian attempt to formalize the notion of constituent-structure in distributional terms.

In conclusion, mention should be made, on the one hand, of what are commonly (though perhaps inappropriately) referred to as **discontinuous constituents** and, on the other, of the question of sequential order. Many languages yield instances of either ultimate or intermediate constituents whose component parts are separated by a string of one or more forms. For example, the past participles of most German verbs are formed by prefixing *ge-* and suffixing either *-t* or *-en* to the appropriate base-form: *ge-lob-t* "praised", *ge-sproch-en* "spoken". Discontinuity within the word is not uncommon in inflecting languages. It is very common indeed in larger syntagms. For example, *looked . . . up* in *He looked the word up in the dictionary*, *he . . . doesn't like bananas* in *He evidently doesn't like bananas*, *has . . . en* and *be . . . ing* in *has been singing*.

Discontinuity violates the principle of **adjacency**: the principle that units (or component parts of units) which are syntactically connected should be placed next to one another in sentences. In some languages, this principle is no more than a stylistic tendency; in others, adjacency itself is used as a way of showing syntactic connectedness. For example, *walking down the road* is shown by adjacency, or proximity, to go with *John* rather than *Mary* in both *Walking down the road, John met Mary* and *John, walking down the road, met Mary* (when they are pronounced with normal stress and intonation). It is important to realize that the notion of constituent-structure does not of itself imply the adjacency of co-constituents.

Nor does it imply that co-constituents must appear in a fixed **sequential order**. It so happens that much, though by no means all, of the sequential ordering of forms in English is a matter of grammatical rule, rather than of stylistic tendency: neither word-forms like **friend-un-ness-ly*, **ness-friend-un-ly*, etc., nor phrases like **wooden the table on*, **on table the wooden*, etc., are well-formed. It is no doubt the case that in most words in all natural languages the sequential order of the constituent morphemes is fixed by rule. But there is considerable variation among languages in respect of the use they make of sequential order within larger syntagms. As we shall see, Chomsky's formalization of constituent structure, and of grammatical structure in general, takes both adjacency and sequential order to be necessarily a matter of rule.

4.6 *Generative grammar*

The term 'generative grammar', which was introduced into linguistics by Chomsky in the mid-1950s, is nowadays employed in two rather different senses. In its original, narrower and more technical, sense, it refers to sets of rules which define various kinds of language-systems. This is what is meant by 'generative grammar' in this section.

In its second, broader sense – for which we will use the term 'generativism' – it refers to a whole body of theoretical and methodological assumptions about language-structure, the discussion of which will be postponed until Chapter 7. Not only was Chomsky the originator of the version of generative grammar most widely used in linguistics, but he has also been the leading proponent of generativism; and it is in this role that he has been most influential, not only in linguistics, but also in other disciplines. This being so, it is important to make the point that, although one can hardly be a generativist without being interested in generative grammar, it is quite possible to be interested in generative grammar without subscribing to those tenets of linguistic theory and methodology most characteristic of generativism.

A **generative grammar** is a set of rules which, operating upon a finite vocabulary of units, **generates** a set (finite or infinite) of syntagms (each syntagm being composed of a finite number of units) and thereby defines each syntagm to be well-formed in the language that is **characterized** by the grammar. Generative grammars that are of interest to linguists will also assign to each well-formed syntagm (and more particularly to each sentence) that they generate an appropriate **structural description**. The definition of 'generative grammar' given here is more general in one respect than Chomsky's. It uses the term 'syntagm', where Chomsky would use 'string' or 'sequence'. A syntagm, as we have seen, is a combination of grammatical units (or, in phonology, of elements) which are not necessarily ordered sequentially. Though Chomsky defines sentences and phrases as (structured) strings, it is quite reasonable, and indeed it is in accord with traditional conceptions, to think of them as syntagms: i.e. as sets of units brought together in a particular construction. What traditional grammar called a difference of construction will be identified in generative grammar by means of a difference in the associated structural description.

The term 'generate', used in the definition, is to be understood in exactly the sense in which it is used in mathematics. To illustrate: given that x can take as its value any one of the natural numbers $\{1, 2, 3, \ldots\}$, the function $x^2 + x + 1$ (which we can think of as a set of rules, or operations) generates the set {3, 7, 13, . . .}. It is in this abstract, or static, sense of the term that the rules of a generative grammar are said to generate the sentences of a language. We do not need to go into the mathematics. The important point is that 'generate', in this sense, does not relate to any process of sentence-production in real time by speakers (or machines). A generative grammar is a mathematically precise specification of the grammatical structure of the sentences that it generates.

The definition given above does not restrict the applicability of generative grammar to natural languages. In fact, it does not imply that generative grammar has any relevance at all to the description of natural languages. The sets of syntagms characterized as languages by generative grammars are what logicians call **formal languages**. Every possible syntagm is either well-formed or it is not; there are no syntagms of indeterminate status. Furthermore, every well-formed syntagm has a fully determinate structure, as defined by the structural description assigned to it by the grammar. It is not clear that natural languages are formal languages in this sense. Many linguists would say that they are not.

But this does not mean that formal languages cannot serve as models of natural languages. It suffices that the property of grammaticality, if not fully determinate, should be empirically determinable within reasonable limits, and also that such structural properties as are built into the model should be identifiable in any natural language for which the formal language in question serves as a model. The word 'model' is here being used in the sense in which an economist might talk of a model of, let us say, imperfect competition; or a chemist, of a model of molecular structure. In each case, the construction of the model involves abstraction and idealization. So too in linguistics. Theoretical synchronic micro-linguistics, being concerned with what it takes to be the essential properties of language-systems, can afford to neglect much of the detail and indeterminacy that other branches of linguistics would need to include (cf. 2.1). So the fact that natural languages may not be formal languages does not of itself invalidate the applicability of generative grammar in linguistics.

Another important point to note about the definition of generative grammar given above is that it allows for the existence of many different kinds of generative grammars. The question for theoretical linguistics is this: which, if any, of the indefinitely many different kinds of generative grammars will best serve as a model for the grammatical structure of natural languages? Put like this, the question presupposes that all natural languages can be modelled by grammars of the same kind. This assumption is commonly made these days in theoretical linguistics. One reason why generativists make it is that all human beings are apparently capable of acquiring any natural language. It is in principle possible that very different kinds of generative grammars should be appropriate for the description of different kinds of natural languages. But so far there is no reason to believe that this is so.

Chomsky demonstrated, in his earliest work, that some kinds of generative grammars are intrinsically more **powerful** than others: they can generate all the formal languages that less powerful grammars can generate and others that less powerful grammars cannot generate. In particular, he proved that **finite-state grammars** are less powerful than **phrase-structure grammars** (of various kinds) and that phrase-structure grammars are less powerful than **transformational grammars**. The difference between these three types of generative grammars (which Chomsky, in a somewhat different sense of 'model', referred to as three models of linguistic description) is something that we shall not go into here: there are many readily accessible accounts at different levels of technicality. All that needs to be said about finite-state grammars is that, under certain reasonable assumptions about the syntactic structure of English and other natural languages, the formal languages that they generate were shown by Chomsky to be inappropriate as models of at least some natural languages. Finite-state grammars are not powerful enough in principle; it is largely because finite-state models were being constructed in the 1950s by behaviourist psychologists that Chomsky was concerned to demonstrate their inappropriateness as models of the grammatical structure of language.

Transformational grammars, on the other hand, are certainly powerful enough in principle to serve as models for the grammatical description of natural language-systems. But there are all sorts of transformational grammars. Paradoxical though it may appear at first sight, some – and perhaps all – are too powerful. They permit the formulation of rules which are never required, as far as we know, in the description of any natural languages. Ideally, and this is at the very heart of generativism, one wants a type of generative grammar which is just powerful enough to reflect, directly and perspicuously, those properties of the grammatical structure of natural languages which are, by common consent, essential to them. Though a particular type of transformational grammar, formalized by Chomsky in the mid-1950s and modified several times since then, has dominated theoretical syntax for over twenty years, the role of the transformational rules themselves has been continually restricted. And the future of transformational grammar as such (though not of generative grammar) is currently in doubt.

Chomsky drew particular attention, at the outset, to two properties of English and other natural languages which must be taken into account in the search for the right kind of generative grammar: recursiveness and constituent-structure (cf. 4.5). Both of these are reflected, directly and perspicuously, in a phrase-structure grammar. (They are also reflected in a Chomskyan transformational grammar, which can be described, loosely, as a phrase-structure grammar with a transformational extension.) In fact, rules (3)–(5) in 4.5 are cast in the format of phrase-structure rules, whose function it is to generate strings of symbols and to assign to each a labelled bracketing of the kind that has already been illustrated: cf. (6) and (8) in 4.5. Such labelled bracketings are referred to as **phrase-markers**. Since phrase-structure grammars are formalized within the more general framework of **concatenation grammars** (i.e. grammars which generate **strings** of units), the phrase-marker represents, not only the constituent-structure of the syntagm and the form-class of each constituent, but also their sequential ordering relative to one another.

As, in an elementary book of this nature, we will not go into the technical differences between one kind of generative grammar and another, so I will not develop further the formalism and mode of operation of phrase-structure grammars. What needs to be emphasized here is the fact that one kind of generative grammar may have advantages that another kind of generative grammar does not have and that, so far at least, it is unclear which, if any, of the many different kinds of generative grammar that have now been constructed and investigated will best serve as a model for the grammatical description of natural languages. Although it has been a widely held view for many years that some version of transformational grammar will best serve this purpose (so that the terms 'generative grammar' and 'transformational grammar' are quite frequently treated as synonyms), recent work has called into question the validity of the arguments that led Chomsky and others to this conclusion.

FURTHER READING

In addition to the relevant chapters of the general introductions listed for Chapters 1 and 2, Palmer (1971) is especially useful as a point of departure: it has both the advantages and disadvantages of theoretical neutrality. Most of the more specialized works on grammatical theory may be classified in terms of particular schools or movements: generativist, functionalist, systemic, etc. (cf. Chapter 7). Allerton (1979) and Brown & Miller (1980) are valuable exceptions. So among the standard textbooks of general linguistics is Robins (1979a), chapters 5–6.

On morphology (including inflection), the best general account currently available in English is Matthews (1974). Also recommended, for those who read German, is Bergenholtz & Mugdan (1979): it is up-to-date and has a wealth of illustrative material and exercises. Nida (1949) is the classic discussion (with exercises) in the post-Bloomfieldian framework.

On syntax (which for many linguists also includes inflectional morphology), a critical discussion of basic concepts, with full references, is Matthews (1981). Householder (1972) contains many classic articles and has a good editorial introduction on the historical development of syntactic theory. From particular points of view:

Generative syntax: most presentations of generative syntax also depend, on or presuppose, generativism (cf. 7.4). There are now many reliable textbooks, which rapidly become obsolete on particular issues (e.g. the status of deep structures) but provide a good introduction to the technical concepts and the formalism. For a relatively non-technical exposition: Lyons (1970), chapter 6, and (1977a). Textbook accounts include Akmajian & Heny (1975); Bach (1974); Baker (1978); Culicover (1976); Huddleston (1976); Keyser and Postal (1976); Stockwell (1977). Many of these include problems and exercises. Especially useful in this respect are Koutsoudas (1966); Langacker (1972). Readers include Fodor & Katz (1964); Jacobs & Rosenbaum (1970); Reibel & Schane (1969).

Functional syntax: Dik (1978); Martinet (1960, 1962).

Systemic grammar: Berry (1975, 1977); Halliday, McIntosh & Strevens (1964); Hudson (1971); Sinclair (1972).

Tagmemic grammar: Cook (1969); Elson & Pickett (1962); Longacre (1964).

Stratificational grammar: Gleason (1965); Lockwood (1972); Makkai & Lockwood (1973).

These distinctive labels for distinguishable points of view, though useful, can be misleading. The points of view themselves, which give rise to the labels, are not necessarily incompatible. For example, functional syntax is not necessarily non-generative (cf. Dik, 1978); systemic grammar, too, can be formulated, in principle, as a generative system (cf. Hudson, 1976) and, in particular developments, is strongly associated with functionalism (cf. Halliday, 1976). On points of detail systemic grammar has much in common with tagmemic grammar, on the one hand, and with stratificational grammar, on the other. Differences of terminology and notation frequently obscure these similarities.

English grammar: some classic works of reference are Curme (1935); Jespersen (1909–49); Poutsma (1926–9). The most comprehensive recent work, dealing with both written and spoken English (in purely synchronic terms), is Quirk, Greenbaum, Leech & Svartvik (1972): it is theoretically eclectic, drawing upon contributions from most of the identifiable schools of linguistics, but in general reliable as far as facts of usage are concerned. Many of the questions and exercises for this chapter that relate to the grammatical structure of English can be answered, in part, on the basis of information given in Quirk, Greenbaum, Leech & Svartvik (1972).

On the English verbal system, in addition to the treatments given in works listed above for particular points of view, see Leech (1976); Palmer (1974).

On grammaticality in relation to meaningfulness: additionally Lyons (1977b), chapter 10; Sampson (1975), chapter 7.

On words and morphemes: Matthews (1974); Robins (1979a), chapter 5 – both with full references to the relevant literature.

On parts of speech and form-classes: additionally Lyons (1977b), chapter 11.

On the distributional approach to grammatical analysis, the classic work is Harris (1951). Fries (1952) exemplifies this approach, on a limited scale, in relation to English.

On grammatical categories: Lyons (1968), chapter 7.

On dependency grammar and the notion of valency there is much more available in French (the classic work is Tesnière, 1959), German (e.g. Helbig, 1971) and Russian (e.g. Apresjan, 1974) than in English; but see Fink (1977).

So-called case-grammar, referred to in many recent textbooks and introductions to grammatical theory, is rooted in the same tradition, as well as being strongly influenced by Chomskyan generative grammar.

For a thorough discussion of dependency in relation to constituency, see Matthews (1981).

QUESTIONS AND EXERCISES

1. What is **grammar** (a) in its broadest sense and (b) in the sense in which it is used in this book?

2. How does **syntax** differ (a) from **inflection** and (b) from **morphology**?

3. Distinguish clearly between the **base-form** and the **citation-form** of a lexeme.

4. **Morphemes** are sometimes defined as minimal meaningful units. How does this definition differ from the one given in the text?

5. What distinction, if any, would you draw between **parts of speech** and **form-classes**?

6. "*boy* and *boys* differ distributionally in various ways . . ." (p. 111). Identify as many of these distributional differences as you can (a) for the written forms *boy* and *boys* and (b) for the spoken [boi] and [boiz]. Can you justify on **distributional** grounds the recognition of the three homophonous, but non-homographic, forms *boys*, *boy's*, *boys'*?

7. The definitions of **complex** and **compound** sentences given above are for minimal (two-clause) composite sentences. (a) Exemplify each such class of sentences in English. (b) Consider whether there are any systematic restrictions upon the combination of declarative, interrogative and imperative clauses (i.e. a declarative with another declarative, a declarative with an imperative, etc.) in minimal composite sentences. (c) How can we extend the definitions to cover non-minimal composite sentences (containing more than two clauses)? (d) Is it possible to have a compound clause as a constituent of a complex sentence, and vice versa? Or a compound/complex clause as a constituent of another compound/complex sentence? (e) Can you diagram the several possibilities? (f) What implications do these have for the distinction of clauses from sentences?

8. "Chomskyan generative grammar has opted for constituency . . . Traditional grammar laid more emphasis on dependency" (p. 116). Explain what is meant by **constituency** and **dependency** in this context.

9. "A free form which consists entirely of two or more lesser free forms . . . is a **phrase**. A free form which is not a phrase is a **word**. A word, then, . . . is a **minimum free form**" (Bloomfield, 1935: 178). (a) The term 'word' is ambiguous (cf. 4.1). What kind of words is Bloomfield's definition intended to cover? (b) Are there any traditionally recognized words of English (in the appropriate sense of 'word') that fail to satisfy Bloomfield's definition? (c) What other criteria have been involved in the definition of the word?

10. Do all languages have (a) **words**, (b) **morphemes**, (c) **sentences**?

11. Make a list of fifty English lexemes whose base-forms end in *-able* (including 'acceptable', 'edible', 'honourable', 'marriageable', 'payable', 'reasonable'). (b) Write a rule of the form X + *able* → Y (substituting for X and Y appropriate form-class labels) to generate as many of the fifty base-forms as possible. (b) For how many of the list is the rule **semantically** satisfactory?

12. How do proper nouns differ **syntactically** from common nouns and pronouns in English? How do countable nouns differ syntactically from mass nouns?

13. "There are rules of order which govern the occurrence of the words of which the phrase *all the ten fine old stone houses* is made up. Some of these rules are absolute . . ." (Hill, 1958: 175). (a) Which rules of order relevant to this example are absolute? (b) How many different phrases can you construct by substituting other word-forms in each position? (c) Can you extend it by adding other adjectives between the article and the noun? (d) What, if any, are the principles determining the order of distributionally distinct subclasses of adjectives? (cf. Crystal, 1971: 128–41). (e) What relevance has stress and intonation to the formulation of these principles?

14. Explain what is meant by **generative grammar**. What are its principal aims?

15. Do you think that natural languages are **formal languages**? Give reasons for your answer.

16. On the basis of some of the relevant additional reading, explain the difference between **finite-state grammars** and **phrase-structure grammars**.

17. A **transformational grammar** "can be described, loosely, as a phrase-structure grammar with a transformational extension" (p. 128). Explain.

18. Generally speaking, every **declarative sentence** of English (e.g. 'John is at home', 'His brother played football for Ireland') can be matched with a corresponding **interrogative sentence** ('Is John at home?', 'Did his brother play football for Ireland?'), and vice versa. Similarly, every **affirmative sentence** (e.g. 'He likes fish and chips', 'The man in the moon is smiling at me', 'Did his brother play football for Ireland?') with a corresponding **negative sentence** ('He doesn't like fish and chips', 'The man in the moon isn't smiling at me', 'Didn't his brother play football for Ireland?'), and vice versa. Can you formulate a rule which will relate declaratives to interrogatives and another rule which will relate affirmative to negative sentences? What do the two rules have in common? What is the corresponding declarative for 'Did anyone

call?'? And the corresponding affirmative sentence for 'He didn't see anybody?'? Is 'Nobody called' affirmative or negative in terms of your rule?

19. Various proposals have been made for the generation of the full range of verb-forms in English in the base-component of a transformational grammar. Chomsky's now classic treatment (1957), slightly modified, included the following rules:

    Verb → Aux V
    Aux → Tense (M) (*have en*) (*be ing*)
    Tense → {Present, Past}
    M → {*will, can, may, shall, must*}
    V → {*open, see, come, . . .*}

    In these rules 'Aux' stands, mnemonically, for 'auxiliary (verb)', 'M' for 'modal verb' and 'V' for '(lexical) verb'. Parentheses (i.e. round brackets) enclose optional items. Curly brackets enclose sets of items, only one of which is to be selected by the rewriting rules. (For further details cf. Lyons (1977a) or standard textbooks.)

    (a) List five strings generated by the above rules, each with its associated **phrase-marker**.

    (b) How many different strings do the rules generate for each lexical verb?

    (c) What further operations are required in order to generate such verb-forms as *opened, will see, have seen, could be opening, may have been coming*, etc.? Why do you think that *have* and *en*, and also *be* and *ing*, have been associated within the same parentheses in the rules? And why is Tense made the first constituent of Aux?

    (d) Are there any other auxiliary verbs in English not covered by the above rules?

    (e) Why is it that no provision is made in the rules for distinctions of number (singular/plural: e.g. *opens/open, has/have*) and voice (active/passive: e.g. *opens/is opened*)?

20. Explain and exemplify the notion of **syntactic ambiguity**. Show how some kinds of syntactic ambiguity can be accounted for by phrase-structure grammars.

21. Many textbooks contain problems in the grammatical analysis of real or hypothetical languages. For the most part, these concentrate upon isolated fragments of each language. The version of what I have called Bongo-Bongo, which follows, was deliberately constructed in order to give students the opportunity of working on a plausible hypothetical language, different from English in many respects but similar to a variety of other natural languages in one or other of its structural characteristics. The sentences are given in a broad phonetic transcription. You should begin by phonemicizing the data on the basis of

phonetic similarity and complementary distribution. Then see how much of the morphology and syntax you can work out, paying particular attention to the categories of **case**, **gender**, **number** and **tense/aspect**. You will find it helpful to consult some textbooks of general linguistics on the definition and coverage of these terms. (The translation into English is free rather than literal.)

Bongo-Bongo

1. iwampi isulpin.
(He beats his wife (regularly).)

2. tixawampixep?
(Have you finished hitting me?)

3. jem tiwampusu ivand?
(Why were you beating that drum?)

4. pul ap tiwampi isulpiθin?
(Since when have you stopped beating your husband?)

5. ap piwampi issulpifin.
(We do not beat our wives.)

6. iwampusi isulpin.
(She was beating her husband.)

7. iðilpixet.
(She is falling in love with you.)

8. ixaðilpusip.
(They had fallen in love with us.)

9. ixaðilpixe.
(They are in love with her.)

10. spurje iðilpu zjelt.
(Children love books.)

11. pixaðilpixo ijelt.
(We love this book.)

12. iðungosu ujelt.
(She was reading that book.)

13. uθimbi iðungexo jelt.
(That girl is reading a book.)

14. izeltu uxaxarpik pu iðamp.
(The books are on the table.)

15. ispurje ixaxarpus.
(The children were in bed.)

16. pixaxarpixe ifurj.
(I am putting baby to bed.)

17. zgoldifini isurgo zalp.
(Some of our friends are pipe-smokers.)

18. pirdi isurgexo zalp.
(Fred is smoking a pipe.)

19. uholdifini ixayimkik.
(That friend of mine is here now.)

20. iharti ixayiyimkosi izgoldin.
(The farmer brought his friends.)

21. uθimbi ixajarcexe pird.
(The girl over there is Fred's fiancée.)

22. ixacengosu uwing usark.
(She was wearing that expensive dress.)

23. icengo pirt sark.
(She always dresses beautifully.)

24. pul tixazimjek?
(How long have you been up?)

    uzgoldiθini bump bump ixazazimjexep.
(Those friends of yours got me up very early.)

25. uzgarti ihoncos: iharti ixahoncek.
(Those farmers were getting rich: this farmer is rich (already).)

26. zdarbu ufirt: iðarbu pirt uxafirtik.
(Roses are beautiful: this rose is really beautiful now.)

27. kansi iðiðilpi stimb: korti
iðanti pirt stimb.

(Hans is a lady-killer: Kurt is a wolf.)

28. pinge iðanti skuld.

(Ping is a fisherman.)

29. uwunt usturpi iðantusi
uhart isulpin.

(Those blind mice you see over there were chasing that farmer's wife.)

30. ifirt istimbi iðilpi gonc
zgart.

(These pretty girls are always falling in love with rich farmers.)

5
Semantics

5.1 *The diversity of meaning*

Semantics is the study of meaning. But what is meaning? Philosophers have debated the question, with particular reference to language, for well over 2000 years. No one has yet produced a satisfactory answer to it. One reason may be that the question, in the form in which it is posed, is unanswerable. It makes two presuppositions which are, to say the least, problematical: (a) that what we refer to, in English, with the word 'meaning' has some kind of existence or reality; (b) that everything referred to as meaning is similar, if not identical, in nature. We may call these, respectively: (a) the presupposition of existence and (b) the presupposition of homogeneity.

I am not saying that these two presuppositions are false, but simply that they are philosophically controversial. Too many introductions to semantics ride roughshod over this fact. In what follows, we shall be careful not to commit ourselves to either presupposition. In particular, we shall avoid saying, as several textbooks of linguistics do, that language throws a bridge between sound and meaning. Statements like this can, it is true, be given a rather sophisticated interpretation, which makes them more acceptable than they appear to be at first sight. Taken at their face value, however, they are misleading and philosophically tendentious. They encourage us to think that meaning, like sound, exists independently of language and is homogeneous in nature.

It is of course traditional enough to think of meaning in this way. According to what has long been the most widely accepted theory of semantics, meanings are ideas or concepts, which can be transferred from the mind of the speaker to the mind of the hearer by embodying them, as it were, in the forms of one language or another.

The identification of meanings with concepts will not help us to answer the question "What is meaning?", unless and until the term 'concept' is clearly defined. As it is commonly employed, it is too vague, or too general, to support the weight that is required by its role as the foundation-stone in the traditional conceptualist theory of meaning. What is there in common among the concepts associated with the following words (selected from the first page of a list of the most frequently occurring words in English): 'the', 'for', 'I', 'first', 'year', 'little', 'write', 'three', 'school', 'boy', 'development', 'name', 'anything'? In some cases we might reasonably say that the associated concept is a visual image of some kind. But we cannot surely maintain this view in respect of words like 'the', 'for', 'anything' or even 'name'. Even for the cases for which it is plausible to think of concepts as visual images, this creates more problems than it solves. Mental images associated with a word, e.g. 'school', by different people are variable and full of detail. Very often there is little or nothing that is common to these detailed and very personal mental images. And yet we still wish to say that, in general, people use words with more or less the same meaning. There is no evidence to suggest that the visual images that we can undoubtedly call up, voluntarily or involuntarily, in association with particular words are an essential part of the meaning of those words or necessary to their everyday employment.

In fact, there is no evidence to suggest that concepts, in any clearly defined sense of the term 'concept', are relevant to the construction of an empirically justifiable theory of linguistic semantics. Obviously nothing is gained by using the very vagueness of the term 'concept', as it is ordinarily interpreted, to protect a theory of semantics that is based upon it from refutation. We shall make no appeal to concepts in our discussion of meaning.

Instead of asking "What is meaning?", we shall pose the rather different question: "What is the meaning of 'meaning'?" This shift of focus, from talking about meaning to talking about 'meaning', has several advantages. First of all, it does not commit us to the same two presuppositions of existence and homogeneity with respect to what 'meaning' refers to. It does, of course, commit us to the presupposition of existence with respect to the English word 'meaning'. But that is harmless enough. It is a further advantage of the move from talking about things to talking about words (if I may formulate the distinction, rather crudely, in terms of words and things) that it brings us up sharply against the possibility that the English word 'meaning' may not have the same range of application as any single word in other languages. This is so. For example, there are contexts in which 'meaning' can be translated into French with 'signification' or 'sens', and there are contexts in which it cannot. Similarly, the distinction between 'Bedeutung' and 'Sinn' in German, in ordinary usage, does not match either the French distinction between 'signification' and 'sens' or the English distinction between 'meaning' and 'sense'. It is at least conceivable that by formulating our question "What is the meaning of 'meaning'?" in English rather than in some other language we are influencing, however slightly, the construction of a theory of semantics. For semantics, we have said, is the study of meaning: i.e. of what is covered by the word 'meaning'. We have no reason to suppose that an everyday word like 'meaning', any more than an everyday word like 'force' or 'energy', can be taken over without refinement or redefinition for scientific purposes.

I have said that the question "What is the meaning of 'meaning'?" does not commit us to the presupposition of homogeneity. It is an important fact about most everyday words that they do not have a single clearcut meaning or even a set of meanings, each sharply distinguishable from the others. The word 'meaning' itself is no exception. It is not surprising, therefore, that there is little agreement among linguists and philosophers as to the boundaries of semantics. There are those who take a broad view of semantics, as I shall do here; there are others who circumscribe the field of semantics much more narrowly.

This is not simply a matter of opting, whether arbitrarily or not, for a relatively broad or a relatively narrow interpretation of 'meaning'. As I have just said, the distinguishable senses of the word 'meaning' can be seen as shading into one another. Everyone will agree that certain uses of the term 'meaning' are of more central concern in linguistic semantics than others are. For example, that

(1) What is the meaning of 'life'?

illustrates a more central use of 'meaning' than

(2) What is the meaning of life?

Or again, that from the point of view of linguistic semantics the use
of the verb 'mean' that is found in

(3) The French word 'fenêtre' means "window"

or

(4) The French word 'fenêtre' means the same as the English
     word 'window'

is more central than that found in

(5) He is clumsy, but he means well

The trouble is that there are intermediate uses of both 'meaning'
and 'mean' about which there is room for disagreement. And some
philosophers have argued that the more obviously linguistic uses,
having to do with the meaning of words, sentences and utterances,
cannot be satisfactorily explained otherwise than by deriving these
obviously linguistic uses, or senses, from intermediate uses that
seem to apply not only to language, but to other kinds of **semiotic**
behaviour (cf. 1.5).

I cannot go into this question in the present brief and selective
introduction to linguistic semantics. However, it is important for
anyone who is at all concerned with the structure and functions of
language to realize that there is a rich and complex philosophical
tradition which bears, at several points, on issues that are central to
the study of meaning by linguists. I will continue to use the term
'meaning' throughout this book, without definition, as a non-
technical word of everyday English. But I will concentrate upon
certain kinds of meaning or certain aspects of meaning which are
commonly taken to be of particular importance in linguistics and we
shall introduce some more technical terms in order to refer to these,
as the occasion arises.

One obvious distinction to be drawn is between the meaning of
words – more precisely, of lexemes – and the meaning of sentences:
between **lexical meaning** and **sentence-meaning**. Until recently,
linguists have paid much more attention to lexical meaning than
they have to sentence-meaning. This is no longer so. It is now

generally recognized that one cannot account for the one without accounting for the other. The meaning of a sentence depends upon the meaning of its constituent lexemes (including its phrasal lexemes if it contains any: cf. 5.2); and the meaning of some, if not all, lexemes depends upon the meaning of the sentences in which they occur. But the grammatical structure of sentences, as is intuitively obvious and will be demonstrated below, is also relevant to the determination of their meaning: so we must also reckon with **grammatical meaning** as a further component of sentence-meaning (cf. 5.3). In so far as linguistics is concerned primarily with the description of language-systems (cf. 2.6), lexical meaning, grammatical meaning and sentence-meaning clearly fall within the scope of linguistic semantics.

Somewhat more controversial is the status of **utterance-meaning**. We have not so far drawn upon the distinction between sentences and utterances, though it was mentioned in the preceding chapter (cf. 4.4). The meaning of an utterance includes, but is not exhausted by, the meaning of the sentence that is uttered. The rest of the meaning is contributed by a variety of factors that may be referred to, loosely, as contextual. Many scholars would say that utterance-meaning falls outside the province of linguistic semantics, as such, and within that of what has come to be called **pragmatics** (cf. 5.6). This is controversial, as we shall see later, because the notion of sentence-meaning is arguably dependent, both logically and methodologically, upon the notion of utterance-meaning, so that one cannot give a full account of sentence-meaning without relating sentences, in principle, to their possible contexts of utterance.

Another set of distinctions has to do with the variety of semiotic, or communicative, functions that languages are used for. Not everyone would agree with the proposal made by Wittgenstein, one of the most influential philosophers of language of his day, that the meaning of a word or an utterance could frequently be identified with its use. But there is clearly some kind of connection between meaning and use. And Wittgenstein's emphasis upon this connection and upon the multiplicity of purposes that languages fulfil had the salutary effect of encouraging both philosophers and linguists, in the 1950s and 1960s, to question, if not always to abandon, the traditional assumption that the role or basic function of language is that of communicating **propositional**, or factual, information. It is of course undeniable that languages do have what I will refer to as a **descriptive** function. It may also be the case that no other semiotic systems can be used in this way – for making statements that are either true or false according to whether the situation that they purport to describe does or does not obtain. Nevertheless, languages also have other semiotic functions.

Some of these are systematically related to the descriptive, or statement-making, function, and correlate, up to a point, with structural differences among sentences. For example, as has already been mentioned, the functional differences between statements, questions and commands correlates in many languages with the structural difference between declarative, interrogative and imperative sentences. This has long been recognized by philosophers and grammarians. Recently, however, much more attention has been given to the nature of this correlation. Moreover, it has been realized that statements, questions and commands are only a few of the many functionally distinguishable **speech-acts**, which are systematically interrelated in various ways. One of the liveliest controversies of recent years, in both philosophical and linguistic semantics, has been centred on the question whether statements are but one class of speech-acts among many, to which no kind of logical primacy should be accorded, or, alternatively, constitute that special, and logically basic, class from which all other speech-acts can, in some sense, be derived. This controversy is still unresolved; and we shall look at it later (5.4, 5.6).

We can draw a distinction, then, between the **descriptive meaning** of statements and the **non-descriptive meaning** of other kinds of speech-acts. We can also, for the present at least, identify the descriptive meaning of an utterance with the **proposition** that is asserted in statements and may be presented, though is not asserted, in other speech-acts, notably in questions. For example, the following utterances, intended and understood as a statement and a question respectively:

(6) *John gets up late*
(7) *Does John get up late?*

can be said to present, or contain, the same proposition, though only (6) asserts it and thereby describes, or purports to describe, a particular situation. It is the defining property of propositions that they have a definite **truth-value**: i.e. they are either true or false. There is therefore an intrinsic connection between descriptive meaning and truth. It is this connection, as we shall see later, which is at the very heart of **truth-conditional semantics**. Truth-conditional semantics, in effect, restricts the scope of the term 'semantics' so that it covers only descriptive meaning (cf. 5.6).

From what has been said, it will be clear that some utterances at least may have both a descriptive and a non-descriptive meaning. In fact, it is arguable that the vast majority of everyday utterances, whether they are statements or not and, if they are not statements, whether they have descriptive meaning or not, convey that kind of non-descriptive meaning which is commonly referred to as **express-ive**. The differences between descriptive and expressive meaning is that the latter, unlike the former, is non-propositional in character and cannot be explicated in terms of truth. For example, if someone exclaims *Good heavens!*, with the stress and intonation indicating surprise, we can reasonably say that he is (or is not) surprised and therefore that *John is surprised* (on the assumption that 'John' is his name) is a true (or false) statement. But it would be absurd to maintain that *Good heavens!* describes the speaker's emotions or state of mind, as *John is surprised* does. To do so would be to commit what some philosophers have referred to as the naturalistic or descriptivist fallacy. Of course, *Good heavens!* is a clear case of what traditional grammar recognized as an exclamation and frequently treated as belonging to a class of utterances distinct from statements, questions and commands. Furthermore, it is an exclamation which cannot be related to a corresponding statement with descriptive meaning, unlike, say, *Oh Granny, what big teeth you've got!*. But there can be exclamatory statements, exclamatory questions, exclamatory commands, and so on. In fact, exclamation is but one way in which a speaker (or writer) **expresses**, or reveals, his feelings, attitudes, beliefs and personality. In so far as we cannot, in the last resort, draw a distinction between a person and his personality or feelings, it is legitimate to interpret the term 'self-expression' literally. Expressive meaning relates to everything that falls within the scope of 'self-expression' and can be subdivided, and has been for particular purposes, in various ways. One kind of expressive meaning to which both literary critics and moral philosophers have paid particular attention is **emotive** (or **affective**) meaning.

Somewhat different from expressive meaning – though, as we shall see, the one merges with the other and they can be seen as interdependent – is **social meaning**. This has to do with the use of language to establish and maintain social roles and social relations. Much of our everyday discourse has this as its principal purpose and can be subsumed under the term **phatic communion** (i.e. "communion by means of speech"). This felicitous expression, coined by the anthropologist Malinowski in the 1920s and widely employed by linguists since then, emphasizes the notions of fellowship and participation in common social rituals: hence 'communion' rather than 'communication'.

It is not only the most obviously ritualized utterances – greetings, apologies, toasts, etc. – that have as their primary function that of oiling the wheels of social intercourse. Looked at from one point of view, this might be correctly identified as the most basic function of language, to which all others – including its descriptive function – are subordinate. Language-behaviour is normally purposive. Even coldly dispassionate scientific statements, whose associated expressive meaning is minimal, usually have as one of their aims that of winning friends and influencing people. In general, both what is said and the way in which it is said are determined, most obviously in everyday conversation, but in any context in which language is used, by the social relations obtaining among the participants and their social purposes. We shall look at social meaning more closely in Chapters 9 and 10. But the point that has just been made should be borne in mind throughout the present chapter. Languages vary as to the degree in which social meaning can or must be conveyed in sentences of various kinds. It must not be thought, therefore, that social meaning can be left to the sociolinguist and is of no concern to the microlinguist whose horizons are fixed by his deliberately restricted definition of the language-system as a set of sentences (cf. 2.6).

Many other kinds of meaning can be, and have been, recognized. Some of these will be mentioned later in this chapter. The trichotomy of descriptive, expressive and social meaning will suffice for the present. It remains to make two general observations in relation to it. The first is that, since man is a social animal and the structure of language is determined and maintained by its use in society, self-expression in general and self-expression by means of language in particular is very largely controlled by socially imposed and socially recognized norms of behaviour and categorization. Most of our attitudes, feelings and beliefs – most of what we think of as the personality or the self – are the product of our socialization. To this extent expressive meaning is dependent upon social relations and social roles. At the same time, what we can identify as self-expression also serves to establish, maintain or modify these social roles and relations. This is what I meant when I said earlier that expressive and social meaning were interdependent.

The second observation is that, whereas descriptive meaning may well be unique to language, expressive and social meaning certainly are not. They are found in other natural semiotic systems, both human and non-human. It is interesting, at this point, to refer back to our discussion of the structure of language from a semiotic point of view (cf. 1.5). We saw there that it is the verbal component of language-signals that separate them most clearly from other kinds of human and non-human signals. It may now be pointed out that expressive and social meaning is conveyed, characteristically though not exclusively, in the non-verbal component of language, whereas descriptive meaning is restricted to the verbal component. However, the functions of languages are no less closely integrated than are their distinguishable structural components. This reinforces what was said earlier about the relation between language and non-language: whether one stresses the similarities or the differences depends very much upon one's personal or professional point of view. In this chapter we are concerned with linguistic semantics – i.e. the study of meaning in natural languages, subject to the further restriction that is involved in the postulation of the language-system (cf. 2.6). It would be possible to adopt a broader viewpoint.

5.2 *Lexical meaning: homonymy, polysemy, synonymy*

Every language contains a vocabulary, or lexicon, which is complementary to the grammar in that the vocabulary not only lists the lexemes of the language (indexed by means of their citation-forms or stem-forms or, in principle, in any other way that distinguishes one lexeme from another), but associates with each lexeme all the information that is required by the rules of the grammar. This grammatical information is of two kinds: (a) syntactic; and (b) morphological. For example, the English lexeme 'go' would have associated with it in its **lexical entry**: (a) the information that it belongs to one or more subclasses of intransitive verbs; and (b) all the information that is needed, including the stem or stems, for the selection or construction of its forms (*go*, *goes*, *going*, *went*, *gone*).

Not all lexemes are word-lexemes (i.e. lexemes whose forms are word-forms). Many of them will be phrasal lexemes (i.e. lexemes whose forms are phrases, in the traditional sense of this term). For example, among the phrasal lexemes of English, which we should expect to find listed in any dictionary of the language are: 'put up with', 'pig in a poke', 'red herring', 'draw a bow at a venture', 'go for a song', etc. Phrasal lexemes tend to be either grammatically or semantically **idiomatic**, or both: i.e. either their distribution throughout the sentences of the language or their meaning is unpredictable from the syntactic and semantic properties of their constituents. Commonly, as is illustrated by 'red herring', and possibly by 'pig in a poke' and 'draw a bow at a venture', phrasal lexemes can be matched with non-idiomatic phrasal expressions (some or all of whose forms are identical with those of the corresponding phrasal lexemes). Such non-idiomatic phrasal expressions are not lexemes: they are not part of the vocabulary of the language. When a semantically idiomatic phrasal lexeme can be put into correspondence with a non-idiomatic phrasal expression, it is traditional to say that the latter has a **literal meaning**, in contrast with the idiomatic, metaphorical or **figurative meaning** of the former.

Nothing further will be said about phrasal lexemes as such or about the various kinds and degrees of idiomaticity that are found in language. But we shall come back to the distinction between literal and figurative meaning, which is sometimes drawn in relation to the distinguishable meanings of word-lexemes, as well as to those of corresponding non-lexemic and lexemic phrases. It should be emphasized here that, although we talk loosely of the vocabulary of

a language as consisting of the words (i.e. word-lexemes) of that
language, the word-lexemes constitute only a part of the vocabulary
in any natural language. The term 'lexical meaning', which is used
as the heading for this section, is to be interpreted as "the meaning
of lexemes". It may also be mentioned here that, although there are
plenty of clear cases of phrasal lexemes in any language, there are
likely to be at least as many phrasal expressions whose status as
lexemic or non-lexemic is debatable. There is no generally accepted
criterion which would enable us to draw a sharp distinction between
phrasal lexemes, on the one hand, and **clichés** or **fixed collocations**,
on the other. This is but one reason why the vocabulary of any
natural language, though finite, is of indeterminate size.

Another reason has to do with the difficulty of distinguishing
between **homonymy** and **polysemy**. Traditionally, homonyms are
said to be different words (i.e. lexemes) with the same form. Since
lexemes may have more than one form and it is not uncommon for
lexemes to share one or more, but not all, of their forms (the shared
forms not necessarily including either the citation-form or the base-
form), the traditional definition of homonymy obviously needs
refinement to allow for various kinds of partial homonymy. Any
such refinement would require us to take into account the possibility of non-coincidence between the units of spoken and written
language: i.e. the possibility of there being homophones that are
not homographs, and vice versa (cf. 3.2). However, it is not difficult
to make the necessary adjustments to the traditional definition of
homonymy on the basis of what has been said in earlier chapters;
and I will assume that the reader can do so and supply appropriate
examples from English to illustrate various subtypes of absolute
and partial homonymy. We are not concerned with this aspect of
the problem of distinguishing homonymy from polysemy.

Polysemy (or multiple meaning) is a property of single lexemes;
and this is what differentiates it, in principle, from homonymy. For
example, 'bank$_1$' and 'bank$_2$' (meaning, respectively, "side of a
river" and "financial institution") are normally regarded as
homonyms, whereas the noun 'neck' is treated in standard dictionaries of English as a single lexeme with several distinguishable
meanings: i.e. as being **polysemous**. Our notation captures this
distinction between homonymy and polysemy: cf. 'bank$_1$' : 'bank$_2$',

each of which may in fact be polysemous; but 'neck', whose meanings are roughly "neck$_1$" = "part of the body", "neck$_2$" = "part of shirt or other garment", "neck$_3$" = "part of bottle", "neck$_4$" = "narrow strip of land", etc. All standard dictionaries respect the distinction between homonymy and polysemy. But how do they draw the line between the two?

One criterion is **etymological**. For example, 'meal$_1$', meaning "repast", and 'meal$_2$', meaning "flour", are treated as different lexemes in most dictionaries primarily, if not solely, because they derive historically from what were non-homonymous lexemes in Old English. The etymological criterion is irrelevant, as we have already seen, in synchronic linguistics (cf. 2.5). In any case, though it may be held by lexicographers to constitute a sufficient condition for homonymy, difference of origin has never been taken to be a necessary, or even the most important, condition distinguishing homonymy from polysemy.

The principal consideration is relatedness of meaning. The several meanings of a single polysemous lexeme (e.g. "neck$_1$", "neck$_2$", "neck$_3$", etc.) are judged to be related; if this condition were not met, the lexicographer would talk of homonymy, rather than polysemy, and put several different lexical entries in the dictionary ('neck$_1$', 'neck$_2$', 'neck$_3$', etc.). There is a historical dimension to relatedness of meaning; and this complicates the issue. For example, it can be shown that the meaning of 'pupil$_1$' ("schoolchild") and 'pupil$_2$' ("part of the eyeball") are historically connected, though they have diverged through time to the point that no speaker of English would think of them as being synchronically related. It is synchronic relatedness that we are after.

It is easy to see that, whereas identity of form is a matter of yes or no, relatedness of meaning is a matter of more or less. For this reason, the distinction between homonymy and polysemy, though easy enough to formulate, is difficult to apply with consistency and reliability.

Some modern treatments of semantics have proposed that one should simply cut the Gordian knot and postulate homonymy, rather than polysemy, in every instance. However attractive this proposal may appear at first sight, it does not really solve the day-to-day problems that confront the lexicographer. More important, it misses the theoretical point. Lexemes do not have a determinate number of distinct meanings. Discreteness in language is a property of form, not meaning (cf. 1.5). It is of the essence of natural languages that lexical meanings shade into one another and are indefinitely extensible. The only way of solving, or perhaps circumventing, the traditional problem of homonymy and polysemy is by abandoning semantic criteria entirely when it comes to the definition of the lexeme and relying solely upon syntactic and morphological criteria. This would have the effect of making "bank$_1$" and "bank$_2$" into two (readily distinguishable) meanings of the same synchronically polysemous lexeme. Most linguists would not favour such a radical solution. And yet it is both theoretically and practically more defensible than the alternative. Perhaps we should rest content with the fact that the problem of distinguishing between homonymy and polysemy is, in principle, insoluble.

Meaning, as we saw in the preceding section, can be descriptive, expressive and social; and many lexemes combine two of these or all three. If **synonymy** is defined as identity of meaning, then lexemes can be said to be **completely synonymous** (in a certain range of contexts) if and only if they have the same descriptive, expressive and social meaning (in the range of contexts in question). They may be described as **absolutely synonymous** if and only if they have the same distribution and are completely synonymous in all their meanings and in all their contexts of occurrence. It is generally recognized that complete synonymy of lexemes is relatively rare in natural languages and that absolute synonymy, as it is here defined, is almost non-existent. In fact, absolute synonymy is probably restricted to highly specialized vocabulary that is purely descriptive. A standard example is 'caecitis' : 'typhlitis' (meaning "inflammation of the blind gut"). But how many native speakers of English are familiar with either of these two words? What tends to happen in cases like this is that, although a pair, or set, of terms may co-exist among specialists for a short time, one of them comes to be accepted as the standard term with the meaning in question. Any rival that it had either disappears or develops a new meaning. The same process can be observed in the everyday language with respect to the vocabulary created for new inventions or institutions: 'radio' has almost ousted 'wireless', though they co-existed for a while as alternatives for many speakers of British English; 'aerodrome' (and 'airfield') and 'airport', on the other hand, now differ in their descriptive meaning.

It will be noticed that (unlike most writers on semantics) I have drawn a distinction between absolute and complete synonymy. In my view, it is important to do so. Context-restricted synonymy may be relatively rare, but it certainly exists. For example, 'broad' and 'wide' are not absolutely synonymous, since there are contexts in which only one is normally used and the substitution of one for the other, if acceptable, might reasonably be held to involve some difference of meaning (cf. *He has broad shoulders, She has a lovely broad smile, The door was three feet wide*). But there are also contexts in which they appear to be completely synonymous (cf. *They painted a wide/broad stripe right across the wall*). The reader is invited to think of similar examples, in English and other languages, and to reflect upon them. He will find, I think, that, even when some difference of meaning definitely exists, it is very difficult to be sure what that difference is. He will also find that it is not always clear when there is and when there is not a difference of meaning; and he may be tempted, as semanticists and prescriptive writers on correct usage undoubtedly are, to postulate the existence of subtle nuances differentiating one word from another.

These discoveries are salutary. They reinforce the point made earlier about the partial indeterminacy of lexical meaning. At the same time, they also show that much of one's knowledge of language, in so far as the language-system is determinate, is beyond the scope of reliable introspection. As with the grammatical rules of a language, so with the rules or principles that determine – to the extent that lexical meaning is determinate – the meaning of words and phrases. In one sense, we demonstrate that we know them by our use of the language: they are manifest in language-behaviour and we can, up to a point reliably, recognize violations of them. In another sense, we obviously do not know what these rules and principles are: when asked to identify them, we are hard put to do so and usually get them wrong.

The problem is complicated by the undoubted existence of what are popularly referred to as the **connotations** of lexemes. (There is also a more technical use of 'connotation' in semantics. This does not concern us here.) The frequent use of a word or phrase in one range of contexts rather than another tends to create a set of associations between that word or phrase and whatever is distinctive about its typical contexts of occurrence. For example, there are differences of connotation, over and above their difference of descriptive meaning, between 'church' and 'chapel' in England and Wales. When the difference is as clear as this, a question like *Are they church or chapel?* has a fairly straightforward interpretation. Very often, however, the connotations are less readily identifiable. And yet they are real enough, for particular groups of speakers at least; and they are exploited, notably by orators and poets, but by all of us at times in pursuit of our everyday purposes. Whether we say that the contextually determined connotations of a lexeme are part of its meaning depends very largely upon how broad an interpretation we are prepared to assign to 'meaning'. Frequently, but not always, what are referred to as the connotations of a lexeme would fall within the scope of expressive or social meaning.

Incomplete synonymy is by no means rare. In particular – and this is perhaps the only such case of identity of one kind of meaning, but not of others, that is clearly and usefully recognizable as such – lexemes may be descriptively synonymous without having the same expressive or social meaning. **Descriptive synonymy** (commonly called **cognitive** or **referential** synonymy) is what many semanticists would regard as synonymy properly so called. Examples of descriptive synonyms in English are: 'father', 'dad', 'daddy', 'pop', etc.; 'lavatory', 'toilet', 'loo', 'WC', etc. Both of these sets of descriptive synonyms exemplify the fact that not all speakers of a language will necessarily use, though they may well understand, all members of a set of synonyms; and the second example, more strikingly than the first, illustrates the further fact that there may be social **taboos** operative within the language-community, such that the use of particular words indicates membership of particular groups within the community. Some years ago the distinction between so-called U and non-U vocabulary ('U' standing for 'upper-class') was the subject of everyday conversation in Britain – the distinction having been popularized, though not invented, by Nancy Mitford. It was, and still is (though the terms 'U' and 'non-U' are now dated) a sensitive issue, especially for the members of the genteel middle classes.

The role played by social taboos in language-behaviour is something that falls within the scope of sociolinguistics. It is mentioned here because they do affect the expressive and social meanings of lexemes. One may no longer lay oneself open to the risk of prosecution if one uses one of the so-called four-letter words, but there are still differences of social and expressive meaning which distinguish, say, 'prick' or 'cock' from 'penis'; and 'breast' or 'tit' from 'bosom' or 'bust'. Diachronic investigations of the vocabulary have shown how important a factor **euphemism** – the avoidance of tabooed words – has been in changing the descriptive meaning of words. This implies synchronic interdependence, for a time, of both descriptive and non-descriptive meaning.

Finally, a word should be said about synonymy between lexemes belonging to different languages. Even descriptive synonymy across languages is far less common, except in the more or less specialized subparts of their vocabularies, than bilingual dictionaries encourage us to believe. It would be absurd to maintain that there is no such thing as inter-language (or indeed inter-dialect) synonymy. On the other hand, we must recognize that word-for-word translation is generally impossible between any two natural languages. The theoretical importance of this fact is something that will occupy us later.

5.3 *Lexical meaning: sense and denotation*

In this section we shall be concerned solely with descriptive meaning. This involves at least two distinguishable components: sense and denotation. The terms are taken from philosophy, rather than linguistics. Until recently, linguists have tended not to be concerned with the philosophical issues that have led to a recognition of the distinctions that are to be explained here. Philosophers, for their part, have not always been concerned, as linguists must be, with the full range of human languages and with structural differences among them which are relevant to the formulation of the distinctions in question. It must also be acknowledged that the terms 'sense' and 'denotation' have been used differently by other linguists and philosophers. I will not go into these differences, but will simply present my own view of the issues involved. This is in certain respects controversial. So too is every alternative – and there are many – represented in the long history of philosophical semantics.

It is obvious that some lexemes, if not all, are related both to other lexemes in the same language (e.g. 'cow' is related to 'animal', 'bull', 'calf', etc.) and to entities, properties, situations, relations, etc., in the outside world (e.g. 'cow' is related to a particular class of animals). We will say that a lexeme which is related (in the relevant way) to other lexemes is related to them in **sense**; and that a lexeme which is related (in the relevant way) to the outside world is related by means of **denotation**. For example, 'cow', 'animal', 'bull', 'calf', etc., and 'red', 'green', 'blue', etc., and 'get', 'obtain', 'borrow', 'buy', 'steal', etc., constitute sets of lexemes within which there hold sense-relations of various kinds. 'Cow' denotes a class of entities which is a proper subclass of the class of entities denoted by 'animal'; which differ from the class of entities denoted by 'bull' (or 'horse', or 'tree', or 'gate'); which intersects with the class denoted by 'calf'; and so on.

It is clear that sense and denotation are interdependent. And if the relationship between words and things – or between language and the world – were as direct and as uniform as it has often been supposed to be, we could readily take either sense or denotation to be basic and define the other in terms of it. For example, we might take the view that denotation is basic: that words are names, or labels, for classes of entities (such as cows, or animals) which exist in the world, external to language and independently of it; and that learning the descriptive meaning of lexemes is simply a matter of learning what labels to assign to each class of entities. This view was made explicit in the traditional realist doctrine of **natural kinds** (i.e. natural classes and natural substances), and it lies behind much modern philosophical semantics in the empiricist vein. Alternatively, we might take the view that sense is basic: we might argue that, whether or not there are any natural kinds (i.e. language-independent groupings of entities), the denotation of a lexeme is determined by its sense and that it is, in principle, possible to know the sense of a lexeme without knowing its denotation. This view might commend itself to a **rationalist** – i.e. to someone who, in contrast with the **empiricist**, holds that reason, rather than sensory experience is the source of knowledge (cf. 2.2). It could be justified, philosophically, by means of the traditional identification of the meaning (i.e. the sense) of a word with the associated idea, or mental concept (cf. 5.1).

All that needs to be said here is that each of the simple, clearcut alternatives presented in the preceding paragraph runs into insuperable philosophical difficulties. There are more sophisticated ways of defending the logical or psychological priority of either sense or denotation. But they need not concern us. What the linguist must emphasize are the following two facts: first, that most lexemes in all human languages do not denote natural kinds; second, that human languages are, to a very considerable extent, lexically non-isomorphic (i.e. they differ in lexical structure) with respect to sense and denotation. Let us take each point in turn.

Some lexemes, in English and other languages, do indeed denote natural kinds (e.g. biological species and physical substances): 'cow', 'man', 'gold', 'lemon', etc. The vast majority do not. Furthermore, and this is the crucial point, lexemes that denote natural kinds do so incidentally and indirectly, as it were. It is in general the culturally important distinctions among classes of entities and more or less homogeneous aggregates of matter, such as water, rock or gold, that determine the lexical structure of languages; and these may or may not coincide with natural boundaries. For example, according to Bloomfield, who had strong empiricist prejudices, the English word 'salt' ordinarily denotes sodium chloride ($NaCl$). Granted that this is its denotation, if not the whole of its meaning, and that sodium chloride is a naturally occurring substance, it is only because salt has a distinctive role to play in our culture (and because we frequently have occasion to refer to it) that the word 'salt' has the denotation that it does have. The fact that 'salt' denotes a natural substance is a linguistically irrelevant consideration.

As to lexical non-isomorphism: the most superficial examination of the vocabularies of human languages quickly reveals that lexemes in one language tend not to have the same denotation as lexemes in another language. For example, the Latin word 'mus' denotes both rats and mice (not to mention some other species of rodents); the French word 'singe' denotes both apes and monkeys;

and so on. There are, of course, many examples of denotational equivalence between languages. Some of these result, diachronically, from cultural diffusion. Others are to be explained by the constancy, across cultures, of certain human needs and interests. Relatively few can be attributed to the structure of the physical world as such. We shall have more to say on this topic in Chapter 10.

Many linguists have been attracted, in recent years, by the so-called **componential analysis** of sense and, more particularly, by the view that the senses of all lexemes in all languages are complexes of universal atomic concepts, comparable with the allegedly universal features of phonology (cf. 3.5). It is now apparent, however, that very few of the sense-components that are commonly invoked in this connection are truly universal; and furthermore that relatively few lexemes are plausible candidates for componential analysis. At most, we can represent some of the sense of some lexemes in terms of what might well be universal sense-components. For example, on the reasonable assumption that [HUMAN], [FEMALE] and perhaps also [ADULT] are universal components of sense, "woman" can be analysed as the set {[HUMAN], [FEMALE], [ADULT]}, "man" as {[HUMAN], [NON-FEMALE], [ADULT]}, "girl" as {[HUMAN], [FEMALE], [NON-ADULT]} and "boy" as {[HUMAN], [NON-FEMALE], [NON-ADULT]}. A little reflection will show that this analysis leaves unexplained the fact that the relation between "girl" and "woman", in most contexts, differs from the relation that holds between "boy" and "man".

It was pointed out earlier, in the discussion of polysemy, that relatedness of meaning is a matter of degree. This holds true with respect to that part of descriptive meaning which is here called sense. But we can none the less usefully recognize different kinds of **sense-relations** in the vocabularies of all human languages. In particular, we can recognize what is traditionally called **antonymy** (or oppositeness of sense) and what is nowadays commonly referred to as **hyponymy**. Actually, there are several distinguishable kinds of oppositeness of sense (cf. 'single' : 'married', 'good' : 'bad', 'husband' : 'wife', 'above' : 'below', etc.): 'antonymy' can be given a broader or narrower interpretation. Some authors have even extended it to cover all kinds of **incompatibility** of sense, saying that, for example, 'red', 'blue', 'white', etc., are antonyms. Whatever

terms we use and however broadly or narrowly we define 'antonymy', the theoretically important point is that incompatibility, and
more especially oppositeness of sense, is one of the basic structural
relations in the vocabularies of human languages. Equally basic is
hyponymy (the term is recent, but what it refers to has long been
recognized by lexicographers, logicians and linguists): the relation
that holds between a more specific and a more general lexeme
(between 'tulip', 'rose', etc., and 'flower'; between 'honesty',
'chastity', etc., and 'virtue'; and so on).

Antonymy and hyponymy are substitutional relations of sense.
No less important are the many syntagmatic relations that hold
between lexemes (cf. 3.6): between 'eat' and 'food'; between
'blond' and 'hair'; between 'kick' and 'foot'; and so on. Taken
together, the substitutional and syntagmatic sense-relations (of
various kinds) give to particular **lexical fields** their particular semantic structure. It is often possible to identify lexical fields across
languages (e.g. the field of colour, of kinship, of furniture, of food)
and to demonstrate that the fields are non-isomorphic. A very
considerable amount of semantic research in recent years has been
guided by the principle that the sense of a lexeme is determined by
the network of substitutional and syntagmatic relations that hold
between the lexeme in question and its neighbours in the same
lexical field. The theoretical pronouncements of the so-called field-
theorists (like those of the practitioners of componential analysis)
have often been highly implausible or philosophically controversial.
But the empirical results that they and their followers have obtained have immeasurably improved our understanding of lexical
structure.

Especially important was their insistence upon the logical priority
of structural relations in the determination of the sense of a lexeme.
Instead of saying that two lexemes are (descriptively) synonymous
because each has such and such a sense and the two senses happen
to be identical, they would say that the synonymy of lexemes is part
of their sense. Similarly for antonymy and hyponymy; and for the
whole set of relevant substitutional and syntagmatic sense-
relations. To know the sense of a lexeme is to know what these
several sense-relations are.

This statement, as we shall see in the following sections, requires supplementation. Not only lexemes, but larger expressions composed of more than one lexeme, may have sense. Exactly the same substitutional and syntagmatic relations may hold between a lexeme and a more complex, non-lexemic, expression, or between two more complex expressions, as hold between lexemes. It seems reasonable to say that knowing the sense of a lexeme also involves knowing how it is related to the relevant non-lexemic expressions: knowing, for example, that 'spinster' has the same sense as 'unmarried woman' (or perhaps 'woman who has never been married'). Obviously, one cannot have this additional knowledge without also knowing the grammatical rules of the language and what contribution, if any, they make to the sense of syntactically complex expressions. It was one of the deficiencies of much earlier work in semantics that it not only restricted itself to lexical structure but failed to appreciate that the sense of lexemes could not be properly described without also accounting for the sense-relations that hold between lexemes and more complex expressions.

5.4 *Semantics and grammar*

The meaning of a sentence is the product of both lexical and grammatical meaning: i.e. of the meaning of the constituent lexemes and of the grammatical constructions that relate one lexeme, syntagmatically, to another (cf. 5.1). The terms 'grammar' and 'grammatical', it will be recalled, are being employed in the narrow sense throughout this book (cf. 4.1).

That there is such a thing as grammatical meaning becomes clear if we compare pairs of sentences such as the following:

(1) The dog bit the postman

(2) The postman bit the dog

These two sentences differ in meaning. But this difference cannot be attributed to any of the constituent lexemes, as can the difference between (1) and

(3) The dog bit the journalist

or between (2) and

(4) The postman pacified the dog

The semantic difference between (1) and (2) is traditionally explained by saying that in (1) 'the dog' is the **subject** and 'the postman' is the **object**, whereas in (2) these grammatical roles are reversed.

The semantic difference between (1) and (2) is a difference of descriptive meaning: it can be accounted for, as we shall see later, in terms of their **truth-conditions** (cf. 5.6). Grammatical meaning, however, is not necessarily descriptive. Corresponding declarative and interrogative sentences, such as (1) and

(5) Did the dog bite the postman?

might reasonably be said to have the same descriptive meaning, but to differ on some other dimension. What this other dimension is we will discuss in the section devoted to the relation between sentences and utterances (5.5). A case can be made for subsuming it under expressive and social meaning. And there are many other grammatical differences between sentences which correlate with differences of non-descriptive meaning.

For example, word-order serves an expressive function in many languages. So too, in certain circumstances, does the selection of one **mood** rather than another (e.g. a subjunctive rather than an indicative in particular constructions, in French, German and Spanish). As for social meaning, it is well-known that most European languages, though not Standard English, impose upon their users a distinction between two pronouns of address (French 'tu' : 'vous'; German 'du' : 'Sie'; Spanish 'tú' : 'usted'; Russian 'ty' : 'vy'; etc.) and that the use of one or the other is determined, in part, by social roles and relationships (cf. 10.4). The use of one pronoun rather than another correlates in each case with a difference of either **number** (singular vs. plural) or **person** (second vs. third); and this grammatical difference may be the sole difference between two sentences with the same descriptive meaning. There is also, in many languages, the so-called royal first-person plural. This is exemplified, in English, by

(6) We have enjoyed ourself

which differs in descriptive meaning from

(7) We have enjoyed ourselves

and, as Queen Victoria has made us all aware (cf. *We are not amused*), from

(8) I have enjoyed myself

in either social or expressive meaning. More will be said about the conveyance of social and expressive meaning in later chapters. Here I am concerned to make the general point that the difference between lexical and grammatical meaning does not coincide with the difference between descriptive and non-descriptive meaning.

The difference between lexical and grammatical meaning depends, in principle, upon the difference between the vocabulary (or lexicon) and the grammar. So far we have been operating under the assumption that this difference is clearcut. But it is not. Linguists sometimes draw a distinction between full words, belonging to the major parts of speech (nouns, verbs, adjectives and adverbs), and so-called function words of various kinds, including the definite article (*the*), prepositions (*of, at, for*, etc.), conjunctions (*and, but*, etc.), the negative particle (*not*) – to illustrate the distinction from English. It is the characteristic of such function words that they belong to classes of small membership and that their distribution tends to be very strongly determined by the syntactic rules of the language. And very often they play the same role as inflectional variation does in other languages. For example, *for* in *for three days*, in contrast with *in* in *in three days*, is semantically comparable with the use of the accusative rather than the ablative case in Latin (*tres dies* : *tribus diebus*). It is generally accepted that the function words are less fully lexical than are nouns, verbs, adjectives and most adverbs, and furthermore that some function words are more lexical in character than others. In the limiting case, where a function word cannot but occur in a given syntactic construction, it has no lexical meaning at all: cf. *to* in *He wants to go*, or *of* in *three pounds of butter*. But between the limiting case of purely grammatical words, without lexical meaning, and full lexemes at the other extreme, there are many subclasses of function words, which, without being full lexemes, contribute some measure of lexical meaning to the sentences in which they occur. What is referred to here as the difference between full words and function words is matched in a morpheme-based grammar by the difference between lexical and grammatical morphemes (cf. 4.3).

Subject to what has just been said about the difficulty of drawing a sharp distinction between the grammar of a language and its vocabulary, it may be affirmed, as an important theoretical point, that what is **lexicalized** in one language may be **grammaticalized** in another language. For example, the lexical distinction between 'kill' and 'die' in English (which also correlates with a grammatical difference of valency: cf. 4.4) is matched in many other languages by the grammatical distinction between a **causative** verb and a corresponding non-causative verb. Or again, what some languages can convey by means of the grammatical category of tense (e.g. past vs. present) other languages, without tense, must convey by means of lexemes meaning, say, "in the past" vs. "now". These two examples, however, illustrate a further point that must be made in qualification of the principle that the same semantic distinction may be either lexicalized or grammaticalized.

As we have already seen, the meaning of lexemes tends to be, to a greater or less degree, indeterminate (cf. 5.2). But the meaning associated with distinctions within such grammatical categories as causativity, tense, mood, etc., is even more indeterminate. Consequently, it is often very difficult to decide whether a lexical distinction in one language is the exact semantic equivalent of a grammatical distinction in a different language. The causative forms of the Turkish verb 'ölmek' ("to die") would commonly be used to translate the English verb 'kill'. But one might argue that they do not have exactly the same meaning, as one might argue that the lexically complex English expression 'cause to die' differs in meaning from the lexeme 'kill'. As for tense, it is significant that no one has yet succeeded in giving a satisfactory account of the meaning of the tenses (traditionally identified by means of such terms as 'past', 'present', 'future') in English or any well-studied language. And tense is, of all the traditional grammatical categories, the one which seems to be, at first sight, the most easily definable from a semantic point of view. It was mentioned earlier that there is undoubtedly a semantic basis for the distinction between the parts of speech and the grammatical categories (cf. 4.3).

In accepting that this is so, we must also acknowledge that the nature of the correlation between grammatical structure and semantic structure is, in this respect, extremely difficult to make precise. Generally speaking, the more a particular language is studied, the more complex this correlation appears to be. It is well to bear this point in mind when one is reading accounts of the meaning of grammatical categories in less well-studied languages. Almost all the traditional labels for the grammatical categories in familiar European languages are misleadingly precise: the past tense does not necessarily refer to past time; the singular is used much more widely than the term suggests; the imperative is employed in many constructions that have nothing to do with giving orders; and so on. There is no reason to believe that the situation is any different with respect to the labels employed by linguists in the grammatical description of other languages.

Let us now turn briefly to another aspect of the relation between semantics and grammar: the question of meaningfulness and grammaticality. It has already been said that these two properties of sentences must not be identified (cf. 4.2). As often, it is far easier to proclaim a general principle than it is to apply it. There are several complicating factors. One is that not everything is a matter of grammatical rule that appears to be such at first sight. For example, English, contrary to what is usually said to be the case, does not have the grammatical category of gender. What is commonly described as gender agreement in English depends solely, as far as reference to adult human beings is concerned, upon the sex that is ascribed to the **referent** (i.e. to the entity being referred to: cf. 5.5) at the time of utterance by the speaker. (The actual, real-life sex of the referent is, in principle, irrelevant. If I mistake a man for a woman, or vice versa, and use the wrong pronoun in referring to him, or her, I do not thereby violate any rules of English.) Sentences like

(9) My brother had a pain in her stomach

might seem to run counter to what has just been said about so-called gender agreement. But (9) is neither syntactically nor semantically anomalous. For example, if X is known (or, strictly speaking, believed) by Y to be a girl and is playing the role of Y's brother on stage, then (9) would be a perfectly acceptable sentence for Y to utter. (Arguably, it would differ in meaning from *My brother had a pain in his stomach* said in similar circumstances. But that is another matter.) It might also be appropriate for Y to utter (9) if X had changed sex: questions of tact, of Y's acceptance of the situation, etc., would presumably determine the appropriateness or non-appropriateness of (9) and differently for different people. On the other hand,

(10) He had a pain in her stomach

is undoubtedly anomalous. But it violates none of the purely syntactic rules of English. Indeed, one might reasonably argue that it is also a semantically well-formed sentence; and that what is odd about (10) is that, on the assumption that *he* and *her* refer to the same person, its utterance would imply inconsistency (or a change of mind in the course of utterance) on the part of the speaker. There is a further important issue that comes up here – the difference between semantic well-formedness and contextual appropriateness: we shall come back to this in our discussion of the relation between sentence-meaning and utterance-meaning. Only one example has been given to illustrate the point that word-strings which are commonly said to violate the grammatical rules of a language may be, in fact, both grammatically and semantically well-formed sentences. Indefinitely many other examples could be given, including several taken from recent works on semantics and grammar, whose authors have been rather hasty in their assignment of the label 'ungrammatical' to the word-strings they cite.

Another complicating factor has to do with the problem of deciding whether a particular anomalous **collocation** (i.e. grammatically connected combination of lexemes) is anomalous by virtue of the meaning of the constituent lexemes and of the grammatical construction which brings them together or for some other reason. For example, 'the blond(-haired) boy' and 'the bay(-coloured) horse' are normal collocations, whereas 'the blond horse' and 'the bay(-haired, -coloured) boy' are not. Is this because of the meaning – more particularly, of the sense and denotation – of 'bay' and 'blond'? Even if a person's hair were of exactly the same reddish-brown colour as the coat of a bay horse, we would surely not use the lexeme 'bay' descriptively either of him or of his hair. Conversely, if a horse's head-hair or coat exactly matched the colour of a blond person's hair, we would still be reluctant to predicate the adjective 'blond' of the horse in question. The point is that there are very many lexemes in all languages whose meaning cannot be considered to be totally independent of the collocations in which they most characteristically occur. In the last resort, the distinction between a collocational tendency and a grammatical rule is impossible to draw other than arbitrarily.

Finally, there is the general problem, which has much exercised linguists recently and has puzzled philosophers for far longer, of drawing the boundary between the linguistic and non-linguistic determinants of grammaticality. This problem is often formulated, by those who subscribe to the tenets of generativism, in terms of drawing a boundary between knowledge of the language and knowledge of the world or, in what is arguably a misuse of the useful technical distinction, between **competence** and **performance** (cf. 7.4). For example, we may assume that the following word-string (with an appropriate prosodic contour superimposed upon it)

(11) The President of the United States has just elapsed

would be judged to be nonsensical by the vast majority of speakers of English. But is it grammatically ill-formed? If so, its ungrammaticality is readily explicated in terms of the valency of 'elapse'. The verb 'elapse', we might say, is one of a particular subclass of intransitive verbs whose subject must contain a noun belonging to the set {'year', 'month', 'day', 'century', . . .}.

And yet if (11) violates this putative syntactic rule and is therefore not a grammatical sentence of English,

(12) Three presidents have elapsed and nothing has changed

must also be a non-sentence. But (12) is surely not uninterpretable. Of course, it might be argued that in order to interpret it – to make sense of it – we have to take either 'president' or 'elapse' in some non-literal, or transferred, meaning. The most obvious interpretation, perhaps, is that which involves taking 'president' as meaning "presidency" (cf. *three presidents later*, etc.). This would be referred to as either synecdoche or metonymy by a traditionally minded grammarian. The terms are little used nowadays; and the elaborate framework of the so-called **figures of speech** (like the traditional classification of the parts of speech) is open to all sorts of detailed criticism. The point is that the very fact that we can so readily interpret (12) depends upon our understanding of the interdependence of the meaning of 'elapse' and its grammatical valency. Whether (11) and (12) are grammatical or ungrammatical is not so much a matter of fact as of theoretical or methodological decision. If we decide to count them as grammatical, we can still explain their anomalous status and the possibility of interpreting (12) more readily than (11) on semantic grounds.

The way in which the grammatical structure of particular languages and of language in general relates to the world is a genuinely troublesome philosophical question. We will come back to it in Chapter 10. It has been mentioned here because of its implications for the relation between semantics and grammar. Generally speaking, linguists have been inclined to talk rather too confidently in recent years about the distinction between linguistic and non-linguistic knowledge. Many word-strings are classified as ungrammatical whose status is, to say the least, debatable. Others are said to be, like (11) and (12), literally meaningless and perhaps also ungrammatical: these are the theoretically interesting examples. But very many word-strings have been cited in articles and textbooks which, despite what is said about them by their authors, are unquestionably both grammatical and semantically well-formed.

We started this section by saying that the meaning of a sentence is the product of both lexical and grammatical meaning. We have now seen that, although there is a distinction between these two kinds of meaning in clear cases, the boundary between them is not always as easy to identify as we might like it to be. We have also seen that the distinction between the meaningfulness and the grammaticality of sentences is, for various reasons, far from sharp. Let us now look more closely at the notion of sentence-meaning.

5.5 *Sentence-meaning and utterance-meaning*

The first thing that must be done is to draw a distinction between the meaning of sentences and the meaning of utterances. Many linguists and logicians, who operate with a narrower interpretation of 'semantics' than is traditional in linguistics and has been adopted in this book, would say that, whereas sentence-meaning falls within the scope of semantics, the investigation of utterance-meaning is part of **pragmatics** (cf. 5.6). Chomskyan generativists tend to identify both the sentence/utterance distinction and the semantics/pragmatics distinction with competence/performance (cf. 7.4).

It is generally agreed by those who distinguish sentences and utterances that the former, unlike the latter, are abstract entities which are context-independent, in the sense that they are not tied to any particular time and place: they are units of the language-system to which they belong. As far as it goes, this is unobjectionable. Unfortunately, the term 'utterance' (like many other grammatically comparable words of English) is ambiguous: it can be used to refer to an act or to the product of that act: i.e. to a bit of language-behaviour or to the interpretable signal that is produced by the bit of behaviour in question and passes from sender to receiver along some channel of communication (cf. 1.5). No one would confuse sentences with acts of utterance. But it is quite easy to identify sentences, whether inadvertently or not, with what is uttered. Indeed, there is a perfectly normal sense of the term 'sentence' in which we do this regularly in our everyday references to language. For example, we might say that the first paragraph of this section is composed of three sentences. In this sense of 'sentence', sentences are either utterances (the term 'utterance' is intended to cover both spoken and written language) or connected parts of a single utterance. And in this sense of 'sentence' – i.e. the sense in which a sentence is what is uttered – sentences are obviously to a greater or less degree, context-dependent. But they are also repeatable at different times and in different places. Context-dependence does not therefore imply spatio-temporal uniqueness; and abstractness, in the sense of not being tied to any particular time and place, does not imply complete contextual independence.

There is the further point that many, and perhaps most, utterances (i.e. utterance-products) of everyday conversation are not full sentences, but are in one way or another **elliptical**. For example,

(1) Next Friday, if I can manage it
(2) How about Peter's?

(3) You'll just have to, won't you?

are typical of what most linguists, like the traditional grammarian, would describe as incomplete, or elliptical, sentences. And their meaning is the same as that of the full sentences from which they can be said to be derived on particular occasions of utterance.

We shall not go into the problems of relating the sentences of a language-system to actual and potential utterances. Due allowances being made for the complexities mentioned above, we can say that utterance-meaning is the product of sentence-meaning and context. In general, the meaning of an utterance will be richer than the meaning of the sentence (or sentences) from which it is derived.

At the same time, it must be appreciated that the native speakers of a language have no access, as far as we know, to the meaning of the decontextualized, abstract, units of the language-system that the linguist calls sentences. Indeed, sentences, in this sense of the term, may have no psychological validity at all; they are theoretical constructs of linguistics, and more specifically of general grammatical theory. When we put to native speakers what we call sentences and test their reactions ("Is the following sentence acceptable?", "Does this (sentence) mean the same as that (sentence)?", etc.), what we are really doing is asking them to give judgement, intuitive or reasoned, on potential utterances. We can, as linguists, draw a distinction between sentence-meaning and utterance-meaning by abstracting from the former, and attributing to the non-sentential part of the latter, everything that has to do with particular contexts of utterance: the beliefs and attitudes of particular persons, reference to particular entities in the environment, conventions of politeness operative among particular groups, and so on. But there is no reason to suppose that speakers of a language can do this by virtue of their linguistic competence. Linguistic competence – in either of the two senses: "competence in a language" and "competence for language" – is always performance-orientated.

We have already seen that particular kinds of sentences are related to particular kinds of utterances: declarative sentences to statements, interrogative sentences to questions, etc. The nature of this relationship was explained by invoking the notion of **characteristic use**. It was, and must be, acknowledged that on any given occasion a speaker may use a sentence, uncharacteristically, to mean something different from, or in addition to, what it is characteristically used to mean. There is, however, an intrinsic connection between the meaning of a sentence and its characteristic use. For example, some declarative sentences may be used, **indirectly**, to ask questions, to issue commands, to make promises, to express the speaker's feelings, etc. But if sentences with the particular grammatical structure that we call declarative were not felt to be associated by speakers of the language with the speech-act of making statements – this associative link between grammatical form and communicative function being established and maintained by regular use – the sentences in question would not be called declarative. Furthermore, an uncharacteristic use of a sentence is generally explicable on the basis of its characteristic use. To take a famous example:

(4) It's cold in here

has the grammatical form of a declarative sentence but might well be used, in the appropriate circumstances, uncharacteristically and indirectly, instead of

(5) Close the window (please)!

in order to get the addressee to do something: i.e. as a directive. It is because (4) is characteristically uséd to make a statement, which the addressee can interpret and from which, in the light of the relevant contextual factors, he can draw conclusions, that it can also be used, on occasion, uncharacteristically and indirectly.

It must be emphasized that 'characteristically' does not mean "most frequently"; also that the notion of characteristic use relates, in principle, not to individual sentences, but to whole classes of sentences with the same grammatical structure. Very many sentences are used uncharacteristically and indirectly with great frequency in everyday language-behaviour. For example,

(6) Can you tell me the time?

is more likely to be uttered as a request than a question. If the addressee responded by saying *Yes* without proceeding to comply with the request and then tried to defend himself against the charge of rudeness or unco-operative behaviour by arguing that he had answered the question, he could reasonably be accused of **literalism**. He has taken the utterance, inappropriately, in its literal meaning: i.e. in the meaning that is determined by the characteristic use of sentences with a certain grammatical structure (thereby defined to be interrogative).

The very fact that literalism exists as an identifiable (and socially reprehensible) phenomenon – linguists and philosophers being occupationally prone to it! – is justification for the postulation of the theoretically defined notions of characteristic and uncharacteristic use, on the one hand, and of direct and indirect speech-acts, on the other. But these are theoretical notions. It is not to be supposed that on each and every occasion of what is, in this specialized sense, an uncharacteristic use of a sentence the addressee must perform a step-by-step deduction of its intended indirect, or non-literal, meaning on the basis of its direct, or literal, meaning. There are degrees of indirectness: e.g. (4) is more indirect than (6) as a request and would require more contextual support to be taken as such. And many sentences are, in whole or in part, conventionalized in their intended indirect meaning. For example, *Can you . . . ?* and *Would you mind . . . ?* (in contrast with the more or less synonymous *Are you able to . . . ?* and *Would it trouble you to . . . ?*) are highly conventionalized in their use in requests.

The point that has been made about the intrinsic connection between the meaning of a sentence and its characteristic use in utterances may be generalized. A distinction is commonly drawn between the inherent meaning of an expression and what the speaker uses the expression to mean. (In fact, there are several related distinctions involving interconnected senses of the term 'meaning' that have been discussed by philosophers. But this one will suffice for the present purpose.) On any given occasion, a speaker might use an expression to mean something different from the meaning that it has by virtue of its lexical and grammatical meaning. But he cannot always do this. Nor is he free to use an expression with any meaning that he chooses to give to it. Unless he has come to some prior agreement with the addressee about the intended interpretation of an expression, what he means by it must be systematically related to its inherent meaning. And its inherent meaning is determined by its characteristic use. Although we may reject the straightforward identification of meaning and use, for the same reason that we reject the identification of sentence-meaning and utterance-meaning, we may yet wish to maintain that the meaning of expressions and sentences is anchored by their characteristic use. This being so, semantics in the narrow sense is not logically prior to pragmatics. The two are interdependent.

To conclude this section, something must be said about **reference** and **deixis**, and about their contribution to utterance-meaning. Reference, like denotation, is a relation which holds between expressions and entities, properties or situations in the outside world (cf. 5.3). But there is an important difference between denotation and reference: the latter, unlike the former, is bound to the context of utterance. For example, the expression 'that cow' may be used, in the appropriate context, to **refer** to a particular cow – its **referent**. It may be used in different contexts to refer to different cows, its reference on any particular occasion being determined partly by its inherent meaning (including the denotation of 'cow') and partly by the context in which it is uttered. The vast majority of **referring expressions** in natural languages are context-dependent in one way or another. Not even proper names have a unique, context-independent reference; and this fact is all too often forgotten.

The context-dependence of most referring expressions has the semantically important consequence that the proposition conveyed by the utterance of a sentence tends to vary with the context of utterance. For example,

(7) My friend has just arrived

can be used to make a statement about indefinitely many different individuals according to the reference of 'my friend' on particular occasions of utterance. When we talk of semantic relations holding between sentences by virtue of their propositional content, we do so under the tacit or explicit assumption that the reference of all referring expressions is held constant.

Not only may the same expression refer to different entities on different occasions; different expressions may refer to the same entity. For instance, the pronoun 'he', the proper name 'John' and any one of indefinitely many descriptive phrases, 'the man drinking a martini', 'the milkman', 'Mary's husband', etc., could have the same reference as one another, or as 'my friend', in the appropriate circumstances. This fact also must be borne in mind.

Up to a point, the potential reference of expressions is determined, not only by their inherent meaning and such contextual factors as the shared assumptions of speaker and addressee, but also by grammatical rules, on the one hand, and stylistic conventions or tendencies, on the other, operative within sentences and over longer stretches of text or discourse. In particular, such rules or tendencies (and it is not always clear whether it is a matter of grammar or style) control what has come to be called **co-reference**: reference to the same entity (or set of entities) by different expressions or by different occurrences of the same expression. For example, in

(8) My friend missed the train and he has just arrived

and

(9) Since he missed the train, my friend has just arrived

'my friend' and 'he' may be, but are not necessarily, co-referential. But they would not normally be taken to be co-referential (without rather special prosodic and paralinguistic features) in

(10) He missed the train and my friend has just arrived

This is usually, and perhaps rightly, said to be a matter of grammatical rule, relating to the difference between co-ordination and subordination. On the other hand, there is no grammatical rule of English (although some linguists have said that there is) prohibiting the construction of sentences like

(11) John loves John

There is at most a stylistic tendency which favours either

(12) John loves himself

or

(13) John loves him

according to whether or not the subject and the object are

co-referential. The phenomenon of potential co-referentiality has been extensively studied within the framework of generative grammar in recent years.

Deixis is like reference, with which it overlaps, in that it relates to their context of occurrence. But deixis is both broader and narrower than reference. Reference can be either **deictic** or non-deictic; and deixis does not necessarily involve reference. The essential property of deixis (the term comes from the Greek word meaning "pointing" or "showing") is that it determines the structure and interpretation of utterances in relation to the time and place of their occurrence, the identity of the speaker and addressee, and objects and events in the actual situation of utterance. For example, the referent of 'that man over there' cannot be identified except in relation to the use of the expression by someone who is in a particular place on a particular occasion. So too for 'yesterday' and many other **deictic expressions**. Deixis is grammaticalized in many languages in the categories of person and tense: in English, for example, the selection and interpretation (in this case the reference) of 'I' or 'you' is determined by the speaker's adoption of that role and by his assignment to another of the role of addressee; and the use of a particular tense is determined (let us assume – it is far more complicated than this) in relation to the moment of utterance. The demonstrative pronouns 'this' and 'that' and, in some of its uses at least, the definite article 'the' are also deictic. So too are such temporal and locative adverbs as 'now', 'then', 'tomorrow', 'here', 'there'. These are but the most immediately obvious examples of deictic categories and deictic lexemes. In fact, deixis is all-pervasive in the grammar and vocabulary of natural languages.

5.6 *Formal semantics*

Although the term 'formal semantics' might be used, in a very general sense, to refer to a whole set of different approaches to the study of meaning, it is commonly employed nowadays with particular reference to a certain version of **truth-conditional semantics**, which originated in the investigation of specially constructed formal languages by logicians and has recently been applied to the investigation of natural languages. This is what we are concerned with here. Formal semantics, in this sense, is generally taken to be complementary with **pragmatics** – variously defined as the study of actual utterances; the study of use rather than meaning; the study of that part of meaning which is not purely truth-conditional; the study of performance rather than competence; etc.

Let us start by distinguishing the truth-value of a **proposition** from the truth-conditions of a sentence. All that needs to be said about propositions is that they can be asserted or denied; that they can be known, doubted or believed; that they can be held constant under paraphrase and translation; and that each proposition is either true or false. The truth or falsity of a proposition is its truth-value; and this is invariable. We may change our mind about the truth of a proposition: for example, at one time believing that the earth is flat and later, whether rightly or wrongly, coming to believe that it is not. But this does not imply that a once-true proposition has become false. It is important to grasp this point.[1]

Most sentences, as such, do not have a truth-value. As we saw in the previous section, the proposition that they convey will generally depend upon the reference of the deictic and non-deictic referring expressions that they contain. For example, the sentence

(1) My friend has just arrived

may be used to assert indefinitely many true or false propositions by virtue of the variable reference of 'my friend' (which includes the deictic expression 'my') and the deictic character of 'just' and of the past tense. But sentences may have **truth-conditions**: i.e. a precisely specifiable account of the conditions which determine the truth-value of the propositions conveyed by sentences when they are used to make statements. To use the standard classic example (originating with the Polish-born logician Tarski):

(2) 'Snow is white' is true if and only if snow is white

What we have in (2) is a statement made in English about English, but we can in principle use any language (a **metalanguage**) to talk about either itself or any other language (the **object-language**), provided that the metalanguage contains the necessary theoretical

---

[1] What is said here about propositions depends, in part, upon a particular view. Alternative definitions of 'proposition' would not, however, affect the substance of the points made in this section.

vocabulary, including such terms as 'true', 'meaning', etc. What is enclosed in quotation-marks in (2) is a declarative sentence of English; and (2) tells us under what conditions this sentence of the object-language may be used to make a true statement about the world – what conditions the world must meet, as it were, for the proposition conveyed by 'Snow is white' to be true. What (2) or any similar example does is to bring out and make explicit the intuitively obvious connection between truth and reality. Formal semantics accepts that this connection holds. It also accepts the further principle that to know the meaning of a sentence is to know its truth-conditions.

But this does not take us very far. We clearly do not learn the truth-conditions of sentences by matching each sentence with some state of the world. Apart from anything else, both the sentences of natural languages and states of the world constitute indefinitely large, and perhaps infinite, sets. What formal semantics does is to define the meaning of lexemes in terms of the contribution that they make to the truth-conditions of sentences and to provide a precisely formulated procedure for the computation of the truth-conditions of any arbitrary sentence on the basis of the meaning of its constituent lexemes and grammatical structure. It will be clear that formal semantics is most naturally associated with some version or another of generative grammar (cf. 7.4).

That there is an intrinsic connection between descriptive meaning and truth is beyond dispute. It may also be accepted that, if a sentence has truth-conditions, to know the meaning of the sentence is to know what state of the world it purports to describe (on the assumption that the sentence is being used to make a statement). But it by no means follows that all sentences have truth-conditions and that the whole of their meaning is truth-conditional.

As we saw in the last section, a distinction must be drawn between sentence-meaning and utterance-meaning – the former being determined, ultimately, by the latter in terms of the notion of characteristic use. At first sight at least, it would seem that only declarative sentences have truth-conditions (by virtue of their characteristic use to make descriptive statements). Non-declarative sentences of various kinds – notably imperative and interrogative sentences – do not have as their characteristic use that of making statements. And yet, unless we are prepared to accept an absurdly restricted notion of meaning, we must say that they are no less meaningful than declarative sentences, and furthermore that the difference in meaning between corresponding declarative and non-declarative sentences, where such a correspondence exists (e.g. between 'My friend has just arrived' and 'Has my friend just arrived?') is systematic and constant. Various solutions to this problem have been proposed within the framework of formal semantics.

One of these solutions involves treating non-declaratives as being logically equivalent to declaratives of the rather special kind that the philosopher J. L. Austin called explicit **performatives**: i.e. sentences like

(3) I promise to pay you £5
(4) I name this ship the 'Mary Jane'

whose primary function is not to describe some external and independent event, but to be a constitutive and effective component of the action in which they are embedded. Austin's notion of performatives was the starting-point for the theory of speech-acts (which was mentioned, though not explained, in 5.5). Adopting the proposal that non-declarative sentences should be given the same logical status as explicit performatives, we might say that 'Is the door open?' is logically equivalent to (i.e. has the same truth-conditions as)

(5) I ask whether the door is open

that 'Open the door' is logically equivalent to

(6) I order you to open the door

and so on. But Austin said that sentences like (3) and (4) do not have truth-conditions, when they are being used as performatives. (Obviously, they can also be used to make straightforward descriptive statements.) Austin's view has been challenged by a number of formal semanticists. However, whether we say that they have truth-conditions or not, their status still distinguishes them from what we may refer to, loosely, as ordinary declaratives. And many linguists and philosophers have argued that it is perverse to attempt to treat (5) and (6) as being more basic than 'Is the door open?' and 'Open the door.'

Other problems are posed by deictic expressions (often called **indexicals**). All the declarative sentences of English (as well as many non-declaratives) have tense, and most of them contain context-dependent expressions of various kinds whose reference is determined by deixis. Even Tarski's example, (2), is deceptively simple in this respect, as well as being highly unrepresentative of the declarative sentences of English. It trades upon our assumptions about the intended interpretation of both the object-language sentence 'Snow is white' and the metalanguage clause 'if and only if snow is white'. But each of these can have a deictic interpretation ("Snow is (contingently) white at the time and in the place of utterance") as well as the non-deictic (or generic) interpretation ("Snow is (of its nature) always and everywhere white") which is presumably what Tarski intended. The existence of deixis – and its prevalence in natural languages – does not invalidate the application of the truth-conditional theory of semantics in linguistics. But it certainly introduces very considerable technical complications.

So too does the fact that very many of the lexemes of natural languages are, to a greater or less extent, either vague or indeterminate in meaning. For example, we might insist that, in a given context of utterance, (1) conveys a proposition which is either true or false. But how recent must be the arrival of the referent of 'my friend' for it to be true to say that he has just arrived? The word 'just' is not untypical.

These are but some of the problems that complicate, if they do not ultimately invalidate, the application of the theory of formal semantics to the analysis of meaning in natural languages. My own bias in favour of a more comprehensive notion of meaning and one which does not take descriptive meaning to be theoretically more basic than non-descriptive meaning has already been revealed (cf. 5.1). That being so, I must emphasize that the very attempt to extend the notions of formal semantics to natural-language data for which they do not seem to be well adapted, whether it succeeds or fails, sharpens our understanding of the data. This has been demonstrated time and time again in recent years.

Furthermore, even though we may decide that there is more to meaning than can be captured in truth-conditional semantics, this does not of course alter the fact that the sense and denotation of lexemic and non-lexemic expressions can be formalized in terms of truth-conditions, due allowance being made for the indeterminacy of many lexemes (cf. 5.3). If two sentences have the same truth-conditions (in all possible worlds) they have the same descriptive meaning: cf. 'John opened the door' and 'The door was opened by John.' If two expressions are intersubstitutable in sentences that have the same truth-conditions, the expressions in question are descriptively synonymous: they have the same sense. Formal semantics has made precise much that was imprecisely expressed or simply taken for granted in more traditional approaches to the study of meaning. No less important, it is making a serious attempt to give content to what was stated rather programmatically at the beginning of an earlier section (5.4): the meaning of a sentence is the product of both lexical and grammatical meaning. It is doing so by trying to formulate precisely the way in which the two kinds of meaning interact.

FURTHER READING

Most of the older general textbooks and introductions to linguistics are weak on semantics. The more recent works are better, but tend to be superficial in their discussion of theoretical issues, and to give excessive attention to currently fashionable research topics. They also differ among themselves in what they subsume under 'semantics'; and on whether they draw a distinction between 'semantics' and 'pragmatics' (and if so, how they draw it).

Of the many works devoted exclusively to semantics, the following are recommended.

(a) *Elementary*: Leech (1971), chapters 1–7; Lyons (1981); Palmer (1976); Waldron (1979). Of these, Palmer (1976) is the most comprehensive and the most eclectic; Leech (1971), in its later chapters, makes extensive use of a somewhat idiosyncratic notation; Lyons (1981) relates most directly to the present work and to the more comprehensive Lyons (1977b). Ullmann (1962) is still unsurpassed for its treatment of lexical semantics from a traditional and European structuralist point of view. Dillon (1977) gives a relatively non-technical outline of semantics from the viewpoint of generativism.

(b) *More advanced*: Fodor (1977); Kempson (1977); Levinson (1981); Lyons (1977b). Of these, Kempson (1977) and Levinson (1981) are, broadly speaking, complementary (though they differ on particular issues); Fodor (1977) gives the best and most accessible account of work done in semantics within the framework of Chomskyan generative grammar and contains a good general chapter on philosophical semantics, but it takes for granted a technical knowledge of generative grammar and is difficult to understand without this requisite background; Lyons (1977b) is the most comprehensive treatment of semantics so far published, though it requires supplementation, notably for historical semantics, by works referred to in Ullmann (1962) and presents an avowedly personal and somewhat controversial view of particular topics.

All the works recommended above under the rubric 'More advanced' contain detailed references for the topics that they deal with or mention. So do Leech (1976) and Ullmann (1962). Taken together, they provide ample material for the questions and exercises appended to this chapter.

Most of the work in formal semantics is too technical to be referred to here: Allwood, Andersson & Dahl (1977) gives a clear account of the basic concepts and notation.

Two readers which, together, provide the necessary philosophical background are Olshewsky (1969) and Zabeeh, Klemke & Jacobson (1974).

QUESTIONS AND EXERCISES

1. Explain and exemplify some of the principal kinds of meaning that are encoded in natural languages.

2. " "When I use a word", Humpty Dumpty said in a rather scornful tone, "it means what I choose it to mean – neither more nor less" " (Lewis Carroll, *Through the Looking Glass*: cf. Palmer, 1976: 4). Does a speaker always and necessarily mean what his utterance means? Does he always and necessarily mean what he says? Is what he says the same as what his utterance means? Note that Humpty Dumpty appears to be concerned solely with the meaning of words. Is there more to the question than this? And does Humpty Dumpty, on this occasion, (a) say what he means and (b) mean what he says (n.b. "in a rather scornful tone")? (Cf. "Speaker-meaning is what a speaker means in producing an utterance. Now, if we are speaking *literally* and mean what our words mean, there will be no important difference between the linguistic meaning and the speaker-meaning. But if we are speaking *nonliterally*, then we will mean something different from what our words mean" (cf. Akmajian, Demers & Harnish, 1979: 230).)

3. Discuss the connection between the propositional meaning of utterances and the descriptive function of language in relation to the notion of truth.

4. "The competence–performance distinction . . . implies as a special case a distinction between the meaning of a sentence and the interpretation of an utterance" (Smith & Wilson, 1979: 148). Discuss.

5. Explain and exemplify the distinction drawn in the text between absolute and partial **homonymy**.

6. What distinction, if any, would you draw between **homonymy** and **polysemy**?

7. It has been suggested that the English words 'almost' and 'nearly' are **absolutely synonymous**. Is this true (a) in your own everyday colloquial usage and (b) in what you recognize to be a more formal style of Standard English? If they are not absolutely synonymous, are they completely synonymous? Are they descriptively synonymous?

8. Consider the effect of substituting (a) 'handsome' for 'pretty' (and, independently and separately, 'woman' for 'girl') in 'She is a (very) pretty girl' and (b) 'pretty' for 'handsome' (and, independently and separately, 'lad' and 'man' for 'boy') in 'He is a (very) handsome boy.' Is 'handsome' synonymous with 'pretty' (cf. also Leech, 1971: 20)? Is 'boy' synonymous with 'lad'?

9. "Examples of descriptive synonyms in English are: 'father', 'dad', 'daddy', 'pop', etc." (p. 150). Can you extend this list? Construct a similar list starting with 'mother'. Can you identify any social or expressive factors which determine your own usage of particular expressions or the usage of other speakers of English known to you? Are the sex and social class of speakers relevant variables?

10. What distinction, if any, would you draw between **sense** and **denotation**?

11. Give a critical account of **componential analysis** (otherwise referred to as **lexical decomposition**).

12. Explain and exemplify (with examples other than those given in the text) **antonymy** and **hyponymy**.

13. Do the propositions "X is a tulip/rose" **entail** "X is a flower"? Do the propositions "X is honest/chaste" similarly entail "X is virtuous"? If not, or alternatively if the second question is more difficult to answer than the first, is what is said in the text invalidated (cf. p. 155)?

14. Did "as Queen Victoria has made us all aware . . ." on p. 158 strike you as abnormal when you were reading the text? Does it so strike you now? What are the effects of substituting *made* for *has made* in respect of acceptability and meaning? On the assumption that 'Socrates' is being used to refer to the famous Greek philosopher of the fifth century B.C., what differences of meaning and acceptability, if any, hold among the following:

    (1) Socrates says that no one does wrong intentionally
    (2) Socrates said that no one does wrong intentionally
    (3) Socrates said that no one did wrong intentionally
    (4) Socrates has said that no one does wrong intentionally

In answering this question, did you consider (1)–(4) as sentences or utterances?

15. Can you contextualize 'He had a pain in her stomach?' so that its utterance would be explicable and the proposition it expresses non-contradictory (cf. p. 161)? Must *he* and *her* necessarily refer to the same person?

16. Explain what is meant by the **truth-conditions** of a sentence.

17. It has been said of 'You are the cream in my coffee' that it is "a sentence which is necessarily false" (Kempson, 1977: 71). Do you agree? Justify your answer in relation to: (a) a particular interpretation of 'necessarily'; (b) the meaning of 'you'; (c) the distinction between sentences and utterances; (d) the author's view of the interdependence of truth-conditionality and the literal interpretation of sentences.

18. Discuss the validity of the notion of **characteristic use** and its relevance to the analysis of **indirect speech-acts**.

19. What distinction, if any, would you draw between **reference** and **denotation**?

20. "deixis is all-pervasive in the grammar and vocabulary of natural languages" (p. 170). Discuss.

6
Language-change

6.1 *Historical linguistics*

What is now called historical linguistics was developed, in its main lines at least, in the course of the nineteenth century (cf. 2.1).

Scholars had long been aware that languages change with time. They also knew that many of the modern languages of Europe were descended, in some sense, from more ancient languages. For example, it was known that English had developed out of Anglo-Saxon, and that what we now refer to as the Romance languages – French, Spanish, Italian, etc. – all had their origin in Latin. However, until the principles of historical linguistics were established it was not generally realized that language-change is **universal, continuous** and, to a very considerable degree, **regular.**

Each of these three aspects of language-change will be discussed in some detail later. Here it may be noted that the universality and continuity of the process of language-change – the fact that all living languages are subject to it and that the process itself is going on all the time – was obscured, for most people, by the conservatism of the standard literary languages of Europe and by the prescriptive attitudes of traditional grammar (cf. 2.4). The status of Latin is particularly important in this respect. It had been used for centuries in Western Europe as the language of scholarship, administration and international diplomacy. Since the Renaissance, it had gradually yielded ground, in these functions, to the emergent Romance languages, as well as to others that were not derived from Latin: English, German, Dutch, Swedish, Danish, etc. By the nineteenth century Latin was close to being a dead language, but it still enjoyed a prestige that set it apart from most other languages. And it does so to this day for traditionally minded grammarians. The importance of the special position of Latin in the present context is that until well after the Renaissance scholars could think of it as having existed as a living language, more or less unchanged, for some 2000 years and as having been preserved from corruption, throughout this period, by the usage of the educated and by the rules and precepts of the grammarians. As we have seen, similar attitudes were adopted in respect of the modern literary languages of Europe when they came into being – or, more precisely, when they came to be recognized as languages that could be used for literary purposes – in the post-Renaissance period.

Literary languages were more highly regarded than non-literary languages and dialects; and any differences that were noted by grammarians between the literary and the colloquial, or between the standard language and non-standard dialects, tended to be condemned and attributed to slovenliness or a lack of education. Few, if any, realized the significance of the fact that the transmission of the literary languages of Europe from generation to generation is highly untypical of the way in which people acquire, as children, their native language. Nor was sufficient attention paid to the fact that in the case of many modern languages, notably English and French, the spelling-system, which is still based on the pronunciation of centuries ago, conceals most of the phonetic and phonological changes that have taken place in them. If we are literate in English or French we have relatively little difficulty in reading Shakespeare or Ronsard; we would find their works more or less incomprehensible if we heard them spoken as they were spoken by their authors. It was only after a great deal of detailed work had been done during the nineteenth century, in what we may now think of as the classical period of historical linguistics, from the 1820s to the 1870s, that scholars came to a better understanding of the relation between written and spoken languages, on the one hand, and between standard and non-standard languages, on the other.

On the basis of this detailed research and by applying the so-called **comparative method** (which will be explained in 6.3), it was demonstrated beyond doubt, not only that all the great literary languages of Europe had originated as spoken dialects, but also that their origin and development could only be explained in terms of principles which determine the acquisition and use of the associated spoken language. Such is the force of traditional attitudes and of the habits of literacy that most of us still find it difficult, without special training, to think in these terms.

We often find it difficult, for example, to appreciate the full significance of the fact that, although languages may become extinct at a particular point in time, so that, speaking metaphorically, we can talk of them as dying, there is no sense in which it is reasonable, making use of the same organic or biological metaphor, to talk of languages as being born.[1] The point is worth making because, as we shall see, the terminology of historical linguistics is consistently metaphorical. We group languages into **families** by virtue of their **common descent** from an earlier **parent-language**; and we say that languages that can be traced back to a common **ancestral** language – as the Romance languages can all be traced back to Latin – are **genetically related**. When these terms were introduced into linguistics in the nineteenth century, they were frequently given a more literal interpretation – under the influence of German romanticism, on the one hand, and of Darwinian evolutionism, on the other – than is generally the case nowadays. It must be appreciated that there is no point at which, say, Anglo-Saxon suddenly was transformed into, or gave birth to, English; and no point at which Latin gave birth to the Romance languages, whilst continuing to exist itself as a scholarly language for several centuries. And yet this is how the origin of languages is commonly conceived by non-linguists.

The truth of the matter is that the transformation of one language into another is not sudden, but gradual. It is largely a matter of convention and arbitrary decision that leads us to divide the history of English into three periods – Old English (or Anglo-Saxon), Middle English and Modern English – and to consider these alternatively as three different languages or as three stages of the same language. There are both linguistic and non-linguistic reasons for making the divisions where we do. What is now Standard English is, in the essential features of its phonology and grammar and in much of its vocabulary, a descendant of the dialect of London, which

---

[1] Pidgins and creoles might perhaps be said to be born of the union of two parent-languages, each of which continues to exist during the life-time of their offspring (cf. 9.3). But this more or less acceptably metaphorical interpretation of 'parentage' and 'birth' is not what is at issue here.

being close to the point where three of the four major Anglo-Saxon dialects came into contact – Mercian, West Saxon, and Kentish – contains features from all three. It also contains a few more isolated features which derive from the fourth major dialect, Northumbrian – notably the forms *they*, *their*, *them* and most of the words written with initial *sk-* ('skill', 'sky', 'skin', 'skirt', etc.) – which was strongly influenced, from the ninth century, by the language of the Vikings.

For about a century and a half after the Norman Conquest in 1066, the language of the ruling classes was French, as far as literature and administration were concerned; and when English came to be used again as a literary language at the beginning of the thirteenth century, it was very noticeably different from Anglo-Saxon of the earlier period. Apart from other developments that had taken place, what we now refer to as Middle English had come under the influence of Norman French and been deeply affected by it in vocabulary and grammar. Chaucer, for example, wrote in the London dialect of Middle English, which, by virtue of the political and economic importance of the capital, was now beginning to emerge as a standard national language. By the end of the Hundred Years' War in the fifteenth century, England had become very conscious of its own independent national identity and had been transformed from a feudal state to one with an educated, wealthy and increasingly powerful bourgeoisie. This was an important factor in the formation and increasing standardization of literary Middle English.

The period of Middle English is separated from that of Modern English by the Renaissance, which reached England in the late fifteenth century. One of the most important consequences in the sphere of education and culture was the revival of Latin as a literary language. But this was a relatively short-lived phenomenon. Although Latin continued to enjoy great cultural prestige until well into the nineteenth century, the greatest literary works of the Elizabethan and post-Elizabethan period, including the plays of Shakespeare and Milton's *Paradise Lost*, were written in English. Meanwhile, Britain was beginning to play an increasingly important role in world affairs. English-speaking colonies were established in North America in the seventeenth century. And by the nineteenth century English was the language of administration, higher education and business, not only in the United States, Canada, Australia and New Zealand, where it was now the first language of most of the politically and economically dominant settlers and their descendants, but also in India and other Asian and African countries within the British Empire. English in the post-Renaissance period has become a world language in much the same way that Latin had become a world language (in the so-called old world of Europe, North Africa and parts of Asia) almost 2000 years earlier; and for much the same reasons. But both Latin and English were in origin nothing other than the local dialects of small tribes, Italic in the one case and Germanic in the other, and did not differ in any linguistically relevant detail from the related Italic and Germanic dialects of neighbouring tribes.

The brief and highly oversimplified account of the evolution and expansion of English that has just been given will serve to illustrate the general point that, although there may be good reason to divide both the external and the internal history of a language into more or less distinct periods, the process of language-change itself is continuous. What produces the illusion of discontinuity between, for example, Anglo-Saxon and Middle English or, to a lesser degree, between Middle English and Modern English, is the coincidence of several factors, including, on the one hand, gaps in the historical record between identifiable periods and, on the other, the relative stability of literary languages over quite long stretches of time. We have very little in the way of non-literary written records for the various dialects of Anglo-Saxon and Middle English. But we can be sure of two things: first, that from the earliest times the dialects of spoken English were less homogeneous and less neatly separable one from another than traditional accounts of the history of English based on the evidence of literary texts represent them as being; and, second, that, if we had a full historical record of any one spoken dialect, whether it was the dialect of London or of some small village in a remoter part of the country, we should be unable to identify any definite time at which the dialect in question suddenly changed from being that of one period to being that of another. Languages change more rapidly in certain periods than they do in others. Even literary languages change in the course of time; and spoken languages acquired in childhood and employed throughout life in a variety of situations – living languages in the full sense of the term – change far more obviously than literary languages do. Furthermore no living language is completely uniform (cf. 1.6). And this fact, as we shall see later, is crucial for the explanation of language-change.

In what follows, I will begin by giving an account of historical linguistics of the kind that might have been given (except in respect of details that have come to light more recently or relate specifically to the present day) by one of the so-called Neogrammarians or their successors. The Neogrammarians (Junggrammatiker, in German) were a group of scholars, based at the University of Leipzig in the late nineteenth century, who were largely responsible for formulating the principles and methods of historical linguistics that have since governed most work in the subject. These principles and methods were controversial when they were first proclaimed; and much of the criticism that was directed against them we now know to have been justified. However, they have reigned supreme for almost a century; and they underlie much of the linguist's everyday thinking about language-change, as well as being the basis for all the standard treatments of language-families in encyclopaedias and other works of reference. In later sections of this chapter one or two of the Neogrammarian principles will be called into question and reformulated in the light of recent work.

6.2 *Language-families*

To say that two or more languages belong to the same family – that they are genetically related – is to say that they are divergent variants, descendants, of a common ancestral language, or **proto-language**.

In most cases we have no direct knowledge of the proto-language from which the members of a particular family, or subfamily, are descended. The Romance languages are in this respect highly untypical: although the dialect of Latin from which they are descended must have differed in many details of grammar and vocabulary from that of even the more colloquial texts that have come down to us, we have a much better idea of the structure of what we might call **Proto-Romance** than we have of most other proto-languages.

Generally speaking, proto-languages are hypothetical constructs, for whose existence there is no direct evidence, but which are postulated as having existed and as being of such-and-such a structure, in order to account for the genetic relatedness of two or more attested languages. For example, **Proto-Germanic** is postulated as the ancestor of the Germanic languages (English, German, Dutch, Danish, Icelandic, Norwegian, Swedish, etc.); and **Proto-Slavonic** as the ancestor of the Slavonic languages (Russian, Polish, Czech, Slovak, Serbo-Croatian, Bulgarian, etc.). In each case, we have documentary evidence relating to the earlier history of the family. For Germanic, apart from a number of earlier fragmentary inscriptions, we have the fourth-century A.D. translation of the bible in Gothic (as spoken by the Visigoths who were settled at the time on the lower Danube); quite extensive literary texts in the various dialects of Anglo-Saxon (or Old English) covering the period from the sixth to the eleventh century A.D.; the texts of the Old Icelandic (or Old Norse) sagas of the twelfth century A.D.; Old High German texts dating from the second half of the eighth century A.D.; and so on. For Slavonic, the earliest evidence that we have to go on is that of the ninth-century A.D. texts written in Old Church Slavonic. In neither case do we have anything as close to the postulated ancestral proto-language as the language of the Latin texts which have come down to us must have been to that presumably more popular dialect of Latin (often referred to as Vulgar Latin) which we are calling Proto-Romance.

On the basis of all the available evidence, and by applying the principles which were elaborated in the course of the nineteenth century and formulated in their essentials by the Neogrammarians, scholars can **reconstruct** with a fair degree of confidence much of the sound-system and some of the grammatical structure of both Proto-Germanic and Proto-Slavonic. They can also reconstruct intermediate stages in the development of the attested members of a particular language-family from their assumed common ancestor. For example, Figure 3 gives a schematic representation of the development of the officially recognized Germanic languages spoken today and of Gothic, which went into decline in the early Middle Ages and finally died out (yielding to one or other of the Slavonic dialects) some centuries later. It will be noted that English which, as we saw in the preceding section, was already dialectically

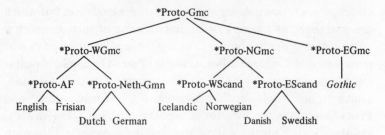

Figure 3. The Germanic languages. Reconstructed proto-languages are indicated by means of a preceding asterisk; the names of extinct languages are italicized. Gmc = Germanic; WGmc = West Germanic; NGmc = North Germanic; EGmc = East Germanic; AF = Anglo-Frisian; Neth-Gmn = Netherlandic German; WScand = West Scandinavian; EScand = East Scandinavian. (Much of the detail is omitted: e.g. High German is not distinguished from Low German, and older attested ancestors of modern languages – Anglo-Saxon, Old High German, etc. – are not included.)

differentiated at the time of our earliest surviving records, is shown as being more closely related to Frisian than it is to Dutch or German, and as being more closely related to both of them than it is to the Scandinavian languages. Frisian was once far more widely spoken than it is today. Although it is not a national language in the sense that all the other modern Germanic languages shown in Figure 3 are, it has official status in the province of Friesland in the northern part of the Netherlands, where it is being heavily influenced, however, in vocabulary at least, by Standard Dutch. Not only English, but all the modern languages shown in Figure 3 exist in several dialects; and very often the transition between one dialect and another is not sharp, but gradual. As we shall see later, the conventional **family-tree-diagram** of language-relatedness tends to oversimplify the facts, if not to distort them completely, by failing to give recognition to the phenomena of convergence and diffusion and by representing language-relatedness as being the result of necessary and continuous divergence.

Going further back and taking a wider range of evidence into account, including that of the Hittite inscriptions of Asia Minor (deciphered in 1915), the Mycenaean Greek tablets (deciphered in 1952) and, for the earliest Sanskrit, the Vedic hymns – all of which evidence can be dated to about the middle of the second millennium B.C. – we can partially reconstruct the phonology and some of the grammatical characteristics and vocabulary of **Proto-Indo-European**, the hypothetical ancestor of Proto-Germanic, Proto-Slavonic, Proto-Celtic, Proto-Italic, Proto-Indo-Iranian, etc., and ultimately of all the Indo-European languages, ancient and modern.

We can even locate Proto-Indo-European, more or less confidently, in space and time – to the plains of South Russia in the fourth millennium B.C. – and, by combining the linguistic and archaeological evidence, say something about the culture of those who spoke it. For example, most of the earliest-attested Indo-European languages have words that can be traced back to hypothetical source-words meaning "horse", "dog", "cow", "sheep", etc. That the reconstructed vocabulary of Proto-Indo-European contains these words, as well as words relating to spinning, weaving, ploughing and other agricultural and pastoral occupations, indicates fairly clearly that the speakers of Proto-Indo-European led a relatively settled existence. Words denoting flora and fauna, climatic conditions, etc., enable us to identify, within limits, their geographical habitat, whilst common vocabulary relating to social and religious institutions makes it possible to draw inferences about the more abstract features of their culture. It is quite clear, for example, that their society was patriarchal and that they worshipped a sky-god and other deified natural phenomena. As to the archaeological evidence, it has recently been suggested that this points to the Proto-Indo-European speakers being the bearers of the so-called Kurgan culture, a Bronze Age culture which spread westwards from South Russia in the earlier half of the fourth millennium B.C. and eastward into Iran somewhat later. This hypothesis, though perhaps the most plausible one so far produced, is not universally accepted; and many scholars are sceptical about the possibility of saying anything very definite, on present evidence, about the habitat and culture of the speakers of Proto-Indo-European.

The reason why I have mentioned this question at all is that the Indo-European family of languages occupies a rather special place in historical linguistics. This is in part due to the fact that many of

the Indo-European languages, as we have seen, have written records going back hundreds, if not thousands, of years. Although
many of the relationships that hold within the Indo-European
family could undoubtedly be established on the basis of modern
spoken languages, the details of these relationships could not be
worked out – and Proto-Indo-European could not be reconstructed
to the degree that it has been reconstructed – without the evidence
of the older texts.

But to say that it would be possible to group many, if not all, the
modern Indo-European languages into a single family even if we
had no records of the earlier stages of these languages is to presuppose that the idea of grouping languages into families should
already have occurred to us, and furthermore that we should have
at our disposal a reliable method for comparing languages and
demonstrating genetic relatedness. This brings us to the second
reason why the Indo-European family of languages has pride of
place in historical linguistics: it was the reconstruction of Proto-Indo-
European, and of the intermediate proto-languages for the subfamilies of Indo-European (notably for the Germanic subfamily),
which provided the motivation and ultimately the methodology upon
which historical linguistics, as we know it, now depends. It is arguable
that, not only historical linguistics, but linguistics itself as an independent and scientific discipline, originated in what might be described,
somewhat romantically, as the nineteenth-century quest for
Proto-Indo-European.

It is customary to date the beginning of Indo-European scholarship with the statement made in 1786 by Sir William Jones (1746–
94) about Sanskrit, the ancient sacred and literary language of
India, and its relatedness to Greek, Latin and other languages:

"The *Sanscrit* language, whatever be its antiquity, is of a wonder-
ful structure; more perfect than the *Greek*, more copious than the
Latin, and more exquisitely refined than either, yet bearing to both
of them a stronger affinity both in the roots of verbs and in the forms
of grammar, than could possibly have been produced by accident;
so strong indeed, that no philologer could examine them all three,
without believing them to have sprung from a common source
which, perhaps, no longer exists: there is a similar reason, though
not quite so forcible for supposing that both the *Gothick* and the

Celtick, though blended with a very different idiom, had the same origin with the *Sanscrit*; and the old *Persian* might be added to the same family."

There is much in this famous quotation that is worth noting. However, the point that must be given particular emphasis is that what seemed so obvious an explanation to Jones, at the end of the eighteenth century, of the remarkable similarity that he observed between the classical languages of Europe and Sanskrit – the hypothesis of family-relationship – might not have seemed so obvious in another age, or indeed to someone of different educational background and a less liberal outlook. Evolutionary ideas were in the air and from the mid-eighteenth century had been applied to language by such scholars as Condillac (1715–80), Rousseau (1712–78) and Herder (1744–1803), not to mention James Burnett (1714–99) with whom Sir William Jones was in correspondence at the time. By the end of the eighteenth century, as a consequence of the post-Renaissance expansion of Europe, a lot more was known about the diversity of the languages of the world. It was no longer possible to maintain with the same degree of plausibility as previous generations of classically trained scholars had done that all languages must be similar in structure. The resemblances between Greek and Latin had been taken for granted for centuries. But in the context of what was known about language-diversity the fact that Sanskrit was strikingly similar to Greek and Latin cried out for explanation; and the explanation that seemed so natural to Sir William Jones, and to his contemporaries once he proposed it, was the one that general movements in European thought at that time made available to him.

Something should also be said about the importance of the new spirit of romanticism, which was particularly strong in Germany, and its connection with nationalism. Herder had maintained that there was an intimate connection between language and national character. This idea took deep root in Germany and contributed to the development of a climate of opinion in which the study of earlier stages of the German language was seen as being an integral part of the assertion and authentication of the national identity of the German-speaking peoples.

In this connection it is important to emphasize the difference between language and race. Terms like 'Germanic' and 'Indo-European' apply primarily to language-families. They do not apply to anything that a physical anthropologist would regard as genetically distinct races. There is no such thing, and never has been, as a Germanic or Indo-European race. In so far as the use of these terms in historical linguistics implies the existence of a language-community speaking Proto-Germanic or Proto-Indo-European at some time and in some place in the past, it is reasonable to assume that the members of these language-communities may have thought of themselves as belonging to the same cultural and ethnic groups. The possession of a common language is, and presumably always has been, an important mark of cultural identity and ethnicity. But there is no connection, other than partial and coincidental, between race, genetically defined, and either culture or ethnicity.

This point is worth emphasizing for two reasons. The first is that terms like 'Germanic' and 'Indo-European' – or alternatively 'Nordic' and 'Aryan' – have often been given a racial, and indeed racist, interpretation. It is up to the linguist and the anthropologist to correct the misconception upon which this particular kind of racism is based. There is no warrant at all for belief in the racial distinctiveness of the speakers of Indo-European languages; still less for the use that was made of the assumption of racial superiority by Nazi propagandists in the 1930s. The same holds true in respect of terms like 'Celtic', 'Slavonic', or 'English'; or indeed of any terms that apply primarily to language-families and languages.

The second reason for emphasizing the fact that there is no intrinsic connection between race and language – and it reinforces the first – is that it gives us a better understanding of how language-families are formed and therefore of the nature of language. We do not know whether there was once a single proto-language from which all human languages are descended, in the way that the Germanic languages are descended from Proto-Germanic, and Proto-Germanic in turn from Proto-Indo-European. We cannot even relate the Indo-European languages with certainty to any of the other major language-families so far established. It is quite possible that all languages go back in the far distant past – perhaps half a million years ago – to a single ancestral language and are thus, in the technical sense of the term, members of the same language-family. On the other hand, the several quite striking structural correspondences among the languages of the world, which at first sight would seem to support the hypothesis of monogenesis, are no less readily accounted for in terms of diffusion and convergence.

The transmission of language from one generation to the next is partly a matter of biology and partly a matter of culture. We may be genetically programmed, as human beings, to acquire language; but we are not genetically programmed to acquire a particular language. It follows that, given the right social and cultural conditions, not only individuals, but whole communities, can acquire a language or dialect which differs from that of their parents. The great nineteenth-century founders of historical linguistics, to whom we are indebted for the notion of language-families with which we still operate, did not give to this fact the theoretical importance that we now know it should have. All too often the spread of languages over a large area was assumed to imply great movements of people. This is, to say the least, an unnecessary assumption. We shall see later that cultural diffusion and convergence are no less important for the explanation of language-change than are migration of peoples and divergence. The traditional family-tree model of language-relatedness does not allow for anything other than the continuous divergence of languages from a common ancestor.

The Indo-European family of languages is but one of very many different language-families so far identified. Some scholars have argued for a classification of all the languages of the world into about thirty major families, of which a number of the more generally accepted families would be subfamilies. But much of this more comprehensive genetic classification and subclassification of languages is still controversial. For example, something like a thousand different languages are spoken in Africa. All of these (except for English, French, Spanish, Afrikaans, etc., which were brought to Africa in the period of European colonization) have recently been grouped into four large families, one of which, **Hamito-Semitic** (or Afro-Asiatic), comprising all the indigenous languages spoken north of the Sahara, contains the traditionally recognized **Semitic** family, whose best known members are Arabic, Hebrew and Amharic. Similarly, the **Bantu** languages (including

Swahili, Xhosa, Zulu, etc.) are now generally, though not universally, regarded as a subfamily of the **Niger–Congo** family. Much the same situation obtains in respect of the languages spoken elsewhere in the world. Progress is gradually being made in the grouping of a larger number of subfamilies into a smaller number of what might be called super-families (or language-phyla). Since the evidence for the larger groupings is frequently very scanty, the resulting genetic classification which depends upon it is correspondingly tentative, and must be treated as such. Not all the language-families identified and named by linguists are equally well established.

6.3 *The comparative method*

The standard way of demonstrating the genetic relatedness of languages is by means of the so-called comparative method. This was developed and refined in what was referred to earlier as the classical period of historical linguistics: between the 1820s and the 1870s (cf. 6.1). It rests upon the fact that many of the most obviously related words across languages can be put into systematic correspondence in terms of their phonological and morphological structure. By the 1870s scholars had achieved such a high degree of success in the application of the comparative method to the more obvious instances of genetic relatedness that they felt confident of its reliability in the case of languages whose relatedness was far from obvious.

I will exemplify the principle of systematic correspondence, in the first instance, from the Romance languages. This has the advantage, not only that the fact of their relatedness is beyond dispute, but also that we have direct evidence of the proto-language from which they are derived, Latin. However, as we shall see, there are instances where the Proto-Romance forms which, given evidence from the Romance languages themselves, can be reconstructed by means of the comparative method differ from the attested Latin forms.

Table 4 brings together for comparison several sets of obviously related words (in their normal orthographic citation-forms) from Latin and three of the Romance languages: French, Italian and Spanish. The table could be extended both horizontally, by including the appropriate words from other Romance languages and dialects (Rumanian, Portuguese, Catalan, Sardinian, Ladino, etc.),

Table 4. *Some systematic correspondences of form in Latin and three Romance languages*

		Latin (L)	French (Fr)	Italian (It)	Spanish (Sp)
(1)	"thing"	causa	chose	cosa	cosa
	"head"	caput	chef	capo	cabo
	"horse"	caballus	cheval	cavallo	caballo
	"sing"	cantare	chanter	cantare	cantar
	"dog"	canis	chien	cane	
	"goat"	capra	chèvre	capra	cabra
(2)	"plant"	planta	plante	pianta	llanta
	"key"	clavis	clef	chiave	llave
	"rain"	pluvia	pluie	pioggia	lluvia
(3)	"eight"	octo	huit	otto	ocho
	"night"	nox/noctis	nuit	notte	noche
	"fact"	factum	fait	fatto	hecho
	"milk"	lacte	lait	latte	leche
(4)	"daughter"	filia	fille	figlia	hija
	"beautiful"	formosus			hermoso

and vertically, by adding many more sets of related words. Limited though it is, the information given in Table 4 will serve to illustrate what is meant by the principle of systematic correspondence.

The first point to note is that the words brought together in each row of Table 4 are related, not only in form – to which the principle of systematic correspondence applies – but also in meaning. Now, words can change their meaning in the course of time. For example, the ordinary Classical Latin for "horse" was not 'caballus', which had the more specific meaning of "pack-horse" and was also used pejoratively to mean "nag" or "hack", but 'equus'. However, 'caballus' and 'equus' are obviously related in terms of meaning; and it is plausible to suppose that 'caballus' lost both its specific meaning and its pejorative overtones in late Latin (i.e. in Proto-Romance) and became the general and stylistically neutral word in place of 'equus'. Conversely, the descendants of the Latin word 'caput' shown in the table have all acquired a set of narrower or metaphorical senses: e.g. Fr. 'chef' means "head" in the sense of "chief" or "boss", as does It. 'capo'; and Sp. 'cabo' means "cape" (i.e. "headland"), "corporal", "end", etc. But once again there is an intuitively obvious connection between the meaning of L. 'caput' and the meanings of its descendants.

None of the words listed in Table 4 causes any problems as far as the fact of their being semantically related is concerned, even though there may be room for disagreement, in particular instances, about the nature of their relationship. Very often, however, it is not clear – especially in the case of languages for which we have far less evidence than we do in the case of the Romance languages – whether two words are semantically related or not. It is for this reason that the comparative method gives priority to relatedness of form. It should also be noted that words may not only change their meaning in time, but also, for various reasons, fall into disuse and be replaced. This explains the gaps in Table 4. Modern Spanish has replaced the word derived from L. 'canis' with 'perro'; and neither Italian nor French preserves in its vocabulary any descendants of L. 'formosus'.

To turn then to the correspondences of form exemplified in the table. The words are all given in their written citation-form. It must be remembered, therefore, that we are concerned, in principle, not with letters, but with sounds. As far as Latin, Spanish and Italian are concerned, there is relatively little discrepancy between spelling and pronunciation. We have to keep in mind the fact that in Modern Spanish there is no phoneme in correspondence with the letter <*h*>; that in both Spanish and Italian the letter <*c*> is pronounced differently in different positions; that <*ch*> is pronounced [k] in Italian, but [tʃ] in Spanish; and so on. But these are minor discrepancies; and we can operate, without doing too much violence to the facts, on the assumption that there is a one-to-one correspondence between single letters (or, in certain instances, groups of letters: Sp. <*ll*>, <*ch*>; It. <*ch*>, <*ggi*>) and phonemes. The situation is very different for French. For example, there is no way of knowing on the basis of the orthographic conventions of French that *clef* is pronounced [kle], but *chef* is pronounced [ʃɛf]; or that *huit* is generally pronounced with a final [t], whereas *nuit* and *lait* are not (except in certain fixed expressions), and that there are alternative pronunciations for *fait*. However, in so far as French orthographic practice is based on the pronunciation that was current some centuries ago (as is also the English spelling-system), we can take the French written forms, for present purposes, at their face value. Nor need we be concerned with the fact that it is not usually the Latin citation-form of a lexeme that is the source of the diachronically related forms of French, Spanish and Italian: it is almost always the accusative form of nouns and adjectives, rather than their nominative form, which provides the source of the Romance stem-forms – *canem*, *caballum*, etc. (the final [m] being lost in late Latin, or Proto-Romance).

If the words in the different sections of Table 4 are compared, it will be observed that there are regular correspondences holding among related forms (i.e. among the forms of related lexemes). These correspondences are indicated in bold type and may be represented, in terms of sounds rather than letters, but, as explained above, taking the orthography at face value, as:

(1) L. [k] = Fr. [ʃ] = It. [k] = Sp. [k]
(2) L. [pl], [kl] = Fr. [pl], [kl] = It. [pi̯], [ki̯] = Sp. [ʎ]
(3) L. [kt] = Fr. [it] = It. [tt] = Sp. [tʃ]
(4) L. [f] = Fr. [f] = It. [f] = Sp. [h]

Both Fr. <it> and Sp. <h> are here given a phonetic value which we know to be appropriate for earlier periods: this is what I mean by taking the orthography at face value. We could just as well operate with phonetic transcriptions (or with phonological representations) of the modern spoken forms. The systematic correspondences of form could still be formulated. But they would be less immediately obvious. It will be noted that, in addition to (1)–(4), other correspondences can be extracted from the words given in Table 4:

(5) L. [b] = Fr. [v] = It. [v] = Sp. [b]
(6) L. [a] = Fr. [ɛ] = It. [a] = Sp. [a]

and so on. How do we explain these systematic correspondences?

The answer given by the nineteenth-century inventors of the comparative method was that the sound-changes which take place in a language in the course of its history are **regular**. The principle of the regularity of sound-change was not emphasized, however, until

the mid-1870s, when the Neogrammarians proclaimed it in its
strongest and most uncompromising form: "The sound changes
which we can observe in documented linguistic history proceed
according to fixed laws which suffer no disturbance save in accordance with other laws." At first sight, the thesis that **sound-laws** (as
they had now come to be called) operated without exception was
patently false. There were many instances of obviously related
words which did not exhibit the expected correspondences. Let us
take a famous example – one which turned out to be no more than
an apparent exception when the problem that it gave rise to was
brilliantly resolved by the Danish scholar, Karl Verner, in 1875.

In 1822, Jacob Grimm (one of the two brothers who are more
widely known for their interest in Germanic folklore) pointed out
that there is a systematic correspondence holding between the
consonants of the Germanic languages, on the one hand, and of the
other Indo-European languages, on the other. He was not the first
to notice this correspondence: the credit for the original observation must go to the Danish scholar, Rasmus Rask. But Grimm's
work, being written in German, was more readily accessible to
international scholarship; and the sound-law that was postulated to
account for the observed correspondences is generally known as
Grimm's Law. Reformulated in the terms of modern articulatory
phonetics (and simplified in certain respects), Grimm's Law says
that:

(a) Proto-Indo-European (PIE) voiced aspirates [*bʰ, *dʰ, *gʰ]
    became voiced stops [*b, *d, *g] – or possibly voiced frica-
    tives [*β, *ð, *ɣ] – in Proto-Germanic (PGmc);
(b) PIE voiced stops [*b, *d, *g] became voiceless stops [*p, *t,
    *k] in PGmc;
(c) PIE voiceless stops [*p, *t, *k] became voiceless fricatives
    [*f, *θ, *h] in PGmc.

The asterisks indicate, according to the convention that has long
been established in historical linguistics, that the sounds in question
are reconstructed, rather than being directly attested. We shall take
up the notion of reconstruction presently. Both Proto-Indo-
European and Proto-Germanic are, of course, hypothetical constructs (cf. 6.2).

Now Grimm's Law, thus formulated, covers a large number of observed correspondences. For example, it accounts for the fact that English (E.) has [f] where Latin (L.), Greek (Gk), Sanskrit (Skt), etc., have [p]: cf. E. *father*: L. *pater*, Gk *pater*, Skt *pitar-*; E. *foot*: L. *pes/pedis*, Gk *pous/podus*, Skt *pāt/padas*. It also accounts for the initial and medial consonants of Gothic *taíhun*: L. *decem*, Gk *deka*, Skt *daśa* – E. *ten* preserves no trace of the medial consonant, but cf. Modern German *zehn*, as well as Old High German *zehan* and Old Saxon *tehan* (the initial [tˢ] of German represented by the letter <z> in the orthography results from the so-called High German Sound-Shift, which probably took place about the sixth century A.D.). The [ʃ]-sound of Skt *daśa*, represented here by <ś>, results from a palatalization of PIE [*k], which, at a very early prehistoric time, affected many of the eastern subfamilies of the Indo-European languages, including all the Indo-Iranian, Baltic and Slavonic languages, as well as Armenian and Albanian: there are certain complications attaching to the reconstruction of what I have, for simplicity, taken to be velar stops, [*gʰ, *g, *k], in PIE; but they do not bear upon the general formulation or validity of Grimm s Law. Due allowance being made for subsequent developments in particular languages, or intermediate proto-languages, Grimm's Law, as summarized in the previous paragraph, is supported by an impressively large number of instances of systematic correspondences.

But there were many apparent exceptions. Of some of these, Grimm himself had commented: "The sound-shift succeeds in the majority of cases, but never works itself out completely in every individual case; some words remain in the form they had in the older period; the current of innovation has passed them by." For example, the [p] of E. *spit*, *spew* corresponds to a [p] in other languages, in apparent violation of Grimm's Law: L. *spuo*, etc. Similarly, for Gmc [t] = L. [t], Gk [t], Skt [t]: cf. E. *stand*: L. *sto/stare*, etc. Here indeed, as Grimm said, the current of innovation has left the Germanic consonants unchanged. It will be noticed, however, that in each case the voiceless stops, [*p, *t, *k], occur as the second segments of two-segment consonantal clusters. All that we need to do, therefore, is to modify the formulation of Grimm's Law given above, so that it is assumed not to have applied to the Germanic **reflexes** (i.e. descendants) of PIE [*p, *t, *k] in this kind of phonetic (or phonological) environment. In effect, we are saying – to introduce some modern terminology – that what Grimm's Law accounts for was a **phonetically conditioned** sound-change. Provided that it is so formulated, the preservation of a voiceless stop in words like E. *spit/spew, stand, eight*, etc., can be seen as a regular development.

More interesting is another class of apparent exceptions. If we take the words for "father" and "brother" in various Germanic languages other than English, we see that they differ in respect of the medial consonant: Go. *fadar* : *brōθar*, G. *Vater* : *Bruder*, etc. And Old English shows the same difference: OE *faeder* : *brōþor*. The fact that German, like its ancestor Old High German (*fater* : *bruodar*), has a voiceless stop in the word for "father" and a voiced stop in the word for "brother", can be explained, once again, as being the consequence of the High German Sound-Shift. Let us grant that, on the basis of all the evidence, we can reconstruct as the Proto-Germanic sources of the words in question, **fader-* and **brōθar-*, what is represented by means of <d> being either a stop [d] or a fricative [ð], but in either case voiced and thus different from the voiceless fricative [θ] of the word for "brother". Since the corresponding words of the non-Germanic Indo-European languages show no such difference (L. *pater* : *frater*, Skt *pitar-* : *bhrātar-*, etc.) and, according to Grimm's Law, PIE [*t] should yield PGmc. [*θ], the word for "father" appears to be irregular as far as its medial, but not its initial, consonant is concerned.

It was this problem that was solved by Verner. He demonstrated that, on the assumption that the PIE words for "father" and "brother" had differed with respect to the place of the word-stress, as they do in Sanskrit (*pitár-* : *bhrắtar-*), the apparent exceptional status of PGmc **fader* could be satisfactorily explained in terms of what is now called **Verner's Law**: intervocalic voiceless fricatives, e.g. [θ], become voiced unless they are immediately preceded by the word-stress. What is assumed is a sequence of stages that can be represented as follows:

(i) PIE　　**pətér-* : **bʰrắter-*
(ii)　　　　**faθér-* : **brōθar-*

(iii)   *$faðér$-: *$bróθar$-
(iv) PGmc *$fáder$-: *$bróθar$-

Grimm's Law is traditionally held to account for the transition from
(i) to (ii), and Verner's Law for the transition from (ii) to (iii). Both
laws, it will be noted, are held to have operated prior to the period
which we identify as that of Proto-Germanic, which is characterized
by having the word-stress on the initial syllable of all words. The
sound-changes that are accounted for by Grimm's Law and Verner's
Law taken together might be explained somewhat differently
nowadays. This is of no consequence in the present connection. The
point is that a whole class of apparent exceptions to Grimm's Law
were shown by Verner to fall within the scope of a supplementary
generalization: another sound-law.

Several other so-called sound-laws were formulated about the
same time as Verner's Law. Taken together, they gave scholars a
much better idea of the relative chronology of developments within
the different branches of the Indo-European family of languages.
More important, they made the famous Neogrammarian principle
of the absolute regularity of sound-change far more plausible than it
would have seemed to an earlier generation of historical linguists.
This principle was highly controversial when it was put forward in
the 1870s. However, it soon came to be accepted, by most of those
in what we may think of as the mainstream of scholarship, as the
very basis, not only of the comparative method, but of the whole
discipline of historical linguistics. We shall have occasion to look
more critically later at the principle of the regularity of sound-
change, and at the use that the Neogrammarians made of the term
'law' in connection with it. But nothing that is said in qualification
of it should be taken as detracting from its methodological
significance. It forced those who subscribed to it to draw a
distinction between conditioned and unconditioned sound-change
and to formulate as precisely as possible the conditions under
which a particular conditioned sound-change took place. And it
laid upon them the onus of providing an explanation for the forms
which had not developed in accordance with the sound-laws
whose conditions they appeared to fulfil. Two explanatory factors
to which the Neogrammarians and their followers appealed in

this connection, as we shall see, were analogy and borrowing (cf. 6.4).

We are concerned in this section with the technique of historical reconstruction by means of the comparative method. It is fitting that the reader should now be cautioned against misinterpreting the so-called **starred forms** (i.e. the hypothetical forms to which an asterisk is prefixed: e.g. PIE *pətér-* or PGmc *fader-*) which result from the application of the technique of reconstruction. They must not be identified with the actual forms of Proto-Indo-European or of any other proto-language. There are several reasons why this is so.

First of all, the comparative method tends to exaggerate the degree of regularity in a reconstructed language-system. This point may be illustrated with reference to the differences between certain attested Latin forms and what we take to be the Proto-Romance forms from which the corresponding forms in French, Italian, Spanish, etc., are derived. The attested Latin word for "head" had *caput* as its citation-form and *capit-* as its stem-form. None of the Romance languages preserves any evidence of the stem-final [t]. They indicate, instead, that the Proto-Romance form was *capu(m)*: see Table 4 above. Now it is quite likely that the irregular noun 'caput' was regularized in late Latin. But we have no direct evidence that it was. It may have been regularized independently, but at a relatively early date, in different branches of the Romance family. The point is that irregularities tend to disappear in the course of time and, generally speaking, the comparative method is unable to reconstruct them.

Secondly, the comparative method operates on the assumption that each member of a family of related languages is in a direct line of descent from the proto-language and has been unaffected, throughout this time, by contact with other related languages and dialects. This is, to say the least, an unrealistic assumption. All languages are, to a greater or less degree, dialectally differentiated. There is no reason to believe that Proto-Indo-European, Proto-Germanic, Proto-Slavonic and the other proto-languages that we hypothesize as the source of families and subfamilies of attested language were dialectally undifferentiated. Wherever possible, the comparative method will reconstruct a single protoform for all the attested forms. It follows that the reconstructed language-system is likely to be, not only morphologically more regular, but also dialectically more uniform than any actual language-system. Furthermore, we have no way of knowing whether all the sounds that occur in a starred form did in fact co-occur at the same time and in the same dialect of the proto-language.

For these and other reasons, reconstructed proto-languages must be taken as hypothetical constructs, whose relation to actual spoken languages of the past is rather indirect. We cannot go further into the technicalities of this question – or into the several criteria that must be weighed in the process of reconstruction. It suffices, for our purposes, to have drawn attention to the fact that all historical reconstruction tends to idealize and oversimplify the facts. As far as particular starred forms are concerned, some parts of the reconstruction may be more soundly based than others; and no part can be sounder than the evidence that supports it. The evidence is highly variable.

In conclusion, it should be mentioned that, although we have been concerned throughout this section with lexical reconstruction, it is possible, in favourable cases, to reconstruct features of the grammatical structure of proto-languages. It was of course the morphological correspondences between related languages that so impressed the first generation of historical linguists, since such grammatical features as inflectional endings, they felt, were unlikely to spread from one language to another by borrowing (cf. 6.4).

6.4 *Analogy and borrowing*

The concept of **analogy** goes back to antiquity. The term itself is from the Greek word 'analogia', which meant "regularity" and more especially, in the usage of mathematicians and grammarians, "proportional regularity". For example, the proportional regularity that holds between 6 and 3, on the one hand, and 4 and 2, on the other, is an analogy, in the intended sense of this term: it is a relation of four quantities (6, 3, 4, 2) such that the first divided by the second is equal to the third divided by the fourth ($6 : 3 = 4 : 2$). Analogical reasoning was used widely by Plato and Aristotle, and

by their followers, not only in mathematics, but also in the development of other branches of science and philosophy, including grammar. Unless this fact is appreciated, it is impossible to understand
one of the basic principles of traditional grammar: that of the
paradigm. Given, let us say, the paradigm *jump*, *jumps*, *jumping*
and *jumped* (i.e. the forms of the model English verb 'jump': the
term 'paradigm' comes from the Greek word meaning "model" or
"example"), we can construct such proportional equations as the
following: *jump* : *jumps* = *help* : *x*; *jump* : *jumped* = *help* : *y*; etc.
And we can solve these equations, assigning to the unknown quantities (*x*, *y*, etc.) their appropriate values (*helps*, *helped*, etc.).

This, then, is what is meant by 'analogy' in traditional grammar,
and more particularly in the controversy between the analogists and
the anomalists, which arose in the second century B.C. and was to
endure, in one form or another, until modern times, exerting a
profound influence upon the development of linguistic theory.
Roughly speaking, we can say that the analogists took the view that
the relation between form and meaning was governed by the principle of proportional regularity, and that the anomalists adopted
the contrary view. We have no need to go into the details of this at
times confused, and confusing, controversy. It is important to realize, however, that it is all part of the background against which the
Neogrammarians established their own notion of analogy and its
role in the historical development of languages.

Let us take an example. English, like German, draws a distinction between what are conveniently referred to as weak and strong
verbs. The former, which constitute the majority of all the verbs in
the language, form their past tense by adding a suffix to the present-
tense stem (cf. E. *jump-s*, *jump-ed*; G. *lieb-t*, *lieb-te*); the latter
exhibit a difference, of one kind or another, in the vowels of
corresponding present-tense and past-tense stems, and usually lack
the past-tense suffix characteristic of the weak verbs (cf. E. *ride-s*,
rode; *sing-s*, *sang*; G. *reit-et*, *ritt*; *sing-t*, *sang*). The strong verbs fall
into several subclasses according to the nature of the vowel alterna-
tion which distinguishes their present-tense and past-tense forms;
and they are commonly regarded as irregular. They are certainly
less regular than the weak verbs, which have been on the increase
for many centuries and which conform to what has long been the

synchronically productive rule. Evidence for the synchronic productivity of the rule in question comes partly from language-
acquisition by children and partly from the adult speaker's ability to
construct the past-tense form of new verbs that he first meets in
their present-tense (or present-participle) form. As far as language-
acquisition is concerned, the fact that the child has mastered the
rule for the formation of regular past-tense forms by suffixation is
proved by his production, not only of a large number of correct
forms (e.g. *jumped*, *walked*, *loved*), but also of the occasional
incorrect form such as *rided* or *goed*. In fact, paradoxical though it
may appear at first sight, the production of such incorrect forms by
analogy with some typical member of the regular class of weak
verbs (*jump* : *jumped* = *ride* : *x*; therefore *x* = *rided*) constitutes a
more convincing proof that the child is applying a rule than does his
production of any number of correct past-tense forms, all of which
might, in principle, have been remembered and imitated as un-
analysed wholes (cf. 8.4).

There are a few instances of weak verbs having been made into
strong verbs by the force of analogy in the history of English. For
example, in some American dialects the past-tense form of 'dive' is
dove, rather than *dived*; and, contrary to what one might suppose, it
is *dove* that is the result of innovation. In the vast majority of cases,
however, analogy has operated in the reverse direction, increasing
the weak verbs at the expense of the strong: e.g. Middle English
holp (cf. *got*) was replaced with Modern English *helped*. It should
be noted that *dived → dove* is just as much a result of analogical
pressure as *holp → helped* is. The language exhibits two patterns of
formation, either of which might serve as the paradigm for analogical extension.

It is worth observing at this point that the fact that many obviously
related verbs of English and German show the same phenomenon
of vowel-alternation is a particularly striking piece of evidence
in favour of the hypothesis that these two languages are, in fact,
genetically related: cf. E. *begin-s*, *began*, *begun* : G. *beginn-t*,
begann, *begonn-en*; E. *bring-s*, *brought* : G. *bring-t*, *brach-te*, *ge-
brach-t*; E. *find-s*, *found* : G. *find-et*, *fand*, *ge-fund-en*; E. *give*,
gave, *giv-en* : G. *gib-t*, *gab*, *ge-geb-en*. (I have added the past-
participle form, for both German and English, when it differs from

the past-tense form, as it almost always does in German.) Analogy has operated independently in both English and German, for several hundred years, to reduce the incidence of vowel-alternation: so that, for example, whereas 'help' is weak in Modern English, the related verb 'hilfen' in German is strong (*hilf-t, half, ge-holf-en*). Sound-changes that have taken place independently in the several Germanic languages have also had their effect, increasing the number of distinct sets of vowel-alternations and making the correspondence between the forms of individual verbs less systematic, in detail, than it was in earlier periods. But there are still dozens of verbs which exhibit a similar vowel-alternation. The same is true of Dutch, which, as we saw earlier (cf. 6.2), is more closely related to German than it is to English: cf. *begin-t, begon, begonn-en*; *breng-t, brach-t, ge-brach-t* ("bring"); *vind-t, vond, ge-vond-en* ("find"); etc. Even the North Germanic languages have strong verbs whose past-tense and past-participle forms can be related to the present-tense forms in terms of more or less regular vowel-alternations: cf. Swedish *skriver, skrev, skrivit* ("write"); *kryper, krop, krupit* ("creep"). Indeed, this pattern of vowel-alternation goes back ultimately to the Proto-Indo-European period: cf. Greek *peith-ō, pe-poith-a, e-pith-on* ("persuade"); *leip-ō, le-loip-a, e-lip-on* ("leave"); etc. As was mentioned at the end of the preceding section, it was this kind of correspondence – what Sir William Jones referred to as "a stronger affinity both in the roots of verbs and in the forms of grammar than could possibly have been produced by accident" (cf. 6.2) – that so much impressed the founding fathers of comparative philology. But we are here concerned with analogy; and in this connection there are two points to be made.

The first is the one that was given particular emphasis by the Neogrammarians: that analogy often inhibits (or subsequently reverses the effect of) otherwise regular sound-changes. For example, after the operation of Verner's Law (cf. 6.3), but prior to our earlier texts, intervocalic [s] became [r] in Germanic. It is this sound-change which accounts for the letter <r> – still pronounced as [r] in some dialects – in the plural of the past-tense of the verb 'to be' in English, in contrast with what the orthography shows was once an [s] in the singular: *were* : *was*. Dutch shows the same contrast (but without a difference in the vowels): *ik was* "I was" : *wij waren* "we were". German, on the other hand, has remodelled the singular stem by analogy with that of the plural: *ich war*: *wir waren*. In this instance the historically regular final [s] of the singular has been replaced with the historically irregular [r]. Interestingly enough, in very early Latin intervocalic [s] also became [r]. Hence the contrast in Classical Latin between the nominative singular form *honos* "honour" and the other forms of the same noun: *honorem, honoris*, etc. (from *honosem*, *honosis*, etc.). And in later Latin *honos* was replaced by *honor*, so that *honor-* was generalized as the stem throughout the whole set of inflectional forms. It is also worth adding that analogy is responsible for the fact that the verb 'to be' is the only verb in Modern Standard English in which there is a difference between a singular stem and a plural stem in the past tense. In Middle English, many of the strong verbs showed a similar difference. Analogy has, once again, generalized either one stem or the other (or, in some instances, the past-participle form); and this accounts for the very considerable fluctuation that there is across English dialects and even in the spontaneous usage of individual speakers.

The second point to be made about analogy is that it is a much more potent factor in language-change than the Neogrammarians held it to be. In fact, the Neogrammarians were inclined to invoke the influence of analogy only when it enabled them to explain away apparent exceptions to one of their postulated sound-laws. Furthermore, some of them drew a distinction between sound-change as a physiologically explicable process and analogy as something that resulted from the sporadic and unpredictable intervention of the human mind. For those who took this view, the sound-laws were seen as being comparable with the so-called laws of nature. It is now more clearly realized, first of all, that no such sharp distinction can be drawn, as far as language is concerned, between the physical and the psychological; and secondly that analogy – provided that the traditional term is interpreted according to the spirit, rather than the letter, of the tradition – operates on both the phonological and the grammatical levels of language-structure. What was traditionally described in terms of proportional regularity can be subsumed under the more general principle of regularization on the basis of existing patterns of correspondence between form and meaning.

Indeed, it would not be unreasonable to identify both the Saussurean notion of structure and the generativist's notion of rule-governed creativity with an appropriately modernized version of the traditional concept of analogy. But this is a bigger, and more controversial, question (cf. 7.4).

Another phenomenon to which the Neogrammarians appealed in order to explain some of the apparent exceptions to the sound-laws was **borrowing**. For example, in addition to the word 'chef', which we identified above as the French descendant of the Latin 'caput', whose Proto-Romance citation-form may in fact have been *capu(m)* (see Table 4), we also find, in Modern French, the word 'cap' (cf. 'de pied en cap', literally "from foot to head"). The form *cap* quite clearly violates all three of the sound-laws (apart from the loss of the final vowel) required to derive *chef* from *capu*. The explanation is that it was borrowed into French (at a fairly early date) from Provençal, to which the sound-laws in question did not apply. Similarly, there are many words in English that begin with *sk-* in their written form (cf. *sky*, *skill*, *skirt*, etc.) which are apparent exceptions to the sound-law that changes [sk] to [ʃ] before front vowels in English (cf. *shirt*, *ship*, *shed*, etc.). Such words were borrowed from one or other of the Scandinavian dialects, which were brought to England at the time of the Viking invasions and had a considerable influence on the speech of the Danelaw region. (To this day, much of the vocabulary of the local dialects of Northern England and Southern Scotland is of identifiably Scandinavian origin; but we are here concerned with what may be regarded as borrowings into Standard English.) Pairs of co-existent cognate native and borrowed words, like English 'skirt' and 'shirt' or French 'cap' and 'chef', are often called **doublets**. Lexical doublets, it may be noted, are very rarely even descriptively synonymous (cf. 'skirt' : 'shirt', 'skipper' : 'shipper', etc.).

The same point can be made about borrowing as was made about analogy: that it is a far more important factor in language-change than the Neogrammarians (and many of their successors) have taken it to be. In particular, like analogy, it should not be seen as merely providing an explanation for apparent exceptions to the sound-laws. If English is considered to be a purely West Germanic language – and it is conventionally so regarded (cf. 6.2) – we have to say that, in the course of its history, it has borrowed enormously, not only in its vocabulary, but also in grammar and phonology, from other languages and dialects.

But does it make sense to talk as if a sharp distinction can always be drawn between native and non-native forms? It has long been evident that the conventional family-tree-diagrams of language-development and language-relatedness can be seriously misleading if they are taken to be realistic models of historical processes. More recent work in dialectology and sociolinguistics has made clear the importance of synchronic dialectal and stylistic variation within a language-community as a causal factor in language-change. In conditions of synchronic variation – and more especially of bilingualism and diglossia (cf. 9.4) – the traditional concept of borrowing is perhaps inapplicable.

However that may be, it is certainly the case that the Neogrammarians drew too sharp a distinction between what could be handled in terms of sound-laws and what was to be explained by means of analogy and borrowing. Nevertheless, most general accounts of the historical development of languages still follow the Neogrammarians in this respect.

6.5   *The causes of language-change*

Why do languages change in the course of time? There is no generally accepted answer to this question. Several theories of language-change have been put forward. But none of them covers all the facts. The most that can be done here is to mention, and to comment briefly upon, some of the main factors that scholars have referred to in the explanation of language-change.

It is customary, in discussions of this question, to operate with two separate distinctions: (a) between sound-change, on the one hand, and grammatical and lexical changes, on the other; (b) between internal and external factors. But neither of these two distinctions should be pressed too hard. As we have seen, the Neogrammarians' view that sound-change is radically different from other kinds of language-change is, at best, no more than a half-truth. Even such more or less physiologically explicable processes as **assimilation** (which results in successive sounds being made identical, or more similar, to one another in terms of place or manner of articulation: cf. Italian, *otto, notte*, etc., in Table 4 of section 6.3), or **haplology** (the loss of one of two phonetically similar syllables in sequence: e.g. Old English *Engla-land* "country of the Angles" > *England*) require the support of other more general factors, if they are to produce permanent changes in the sound-system of a language. As for the distinction between external and internal factors, which depends upon the abstraction of the language-system, as such, from the cultural and social matrix in which it operates, this too breaks down, in the last resort: the communicative function of language, which interrelates form and meaning within a language-system, also relates that language-system to the culture and society whose needs it serves.

Two of the most general factors of language-change were mentioned in the preceding section: analogy and borrowing. It may now be emphasized that much of what the Neogrammarians accounted for in terms of sound-laws can be brought within the scope of the joint action of these other two factors. The sound-laws themselves have no explanatory value: they are no more than summaries of what happened in a particular area (more precisely, in a particular language-community) between two points in time. Considered in retrospect, and macroscopically, the change that has taken place may appear to be regular enough (in the sense in which the principle of regularity was understood by the Neogrammarians and their followers). However, the investigation of sound-changes that are taking place at the present time has shown that they can originate in one or more borrowed words and can then spread by analogy into others over a period of time.

One of the symptoms of this process of language-change is what is commonly called **hypercorrection**. An example of this is the analogical extension of the Southern English vowel of *butter* into words like *butcher* by speakers from the north of England who have acquired (i.e. borrowed) the RP pronunciation of the former class of words. Phonetic hypercorrection of this kind does not differ, as far as its causation is concerned, from the hypercorrection which has resulted in middle-class, and often educated, speakers of Standard Southern English saying *between you and I*. It will be readily appreciated that the former, though not the latter, kind of hypercorrection could eventually lead to what might well be described, macroscopically and in retrospect, as a regular sound-change.

It is not being suggested, of course, that all sound-change can be explained in this way. We must still allow for the possibility of gradual and imperceptible **phonetic drift** over time throughout all the words in which a particular sound occurs. The point being made is simply that a variety of causal factors may interact to produce the same kind of end-result: something that is usually regarded as regular sound-change and, in the Neogrammarian tradition at least, contrasted with such allegedly sporadic phenomena as analogy and borrowing.

Scholars who emphasize the distinction between internal and external factors – and more especially those subscribing to the tenets of structuralism and functionalism (cf. 7.2, 7.3) – tend to attribute as much language-change as they can to what are classified as internal factors: especially to the continual readjustments that are made by a language-system as it moves from one state of equilibrium (or near-equilibrium) to another. One of the most influential proponents of this point of view has been the French scholar, André Martinet, who has tried to account for language-change, and more particularly sound-change, with reference to his conception of languages as self-regulating semiotic systems, governed by the complementary principles of least effort and communicative clarity. The former principle (under which one can subsume such physiologically explicable phenomena as assimilation and haplology, referred to above, and also the tendency to shorten forms of high predictability) will have the effect of reducing the number of phonological distinctions and of maximizing the work that each of them does. It will be held in check, however, by the necessity of maintaining a sufficient number of distinctions for the purpose of keeping apart utterances that might otherwise be confused in the acoustic conditions under which spoken languages are normally used. This notion has a good deal of intuitive appeal and a certain number of sound-changes have been explained in terms of it. So far, however, it has not been convincingly shown to have all the explanatory power its proponents claim for it.

The main contribution that the structuralists and functionalists have made to historical linguistics comes from their insistence that each postulated change in a language-system must be evaluated in terms of its implications for the system as a whole. For example, they have made it clear that the several parts of Grimm's Law (or of the Great Vowel Shift, which took place in the transition from Middle English to Early Modern English) must be considered together. And they have raised interesting questions about the kinds of **chain-reactions** that seem to take place at certain periods in the historical development of languages. To take Grimm's Law as our example: did the PIE voiced aspirates, [*bʰ, *dʰ, *gʰ], in losing their aspiration, cause the PIE voiced unaspirated stops, [*b, *d, *g], to lose their voice and this in turn cause the PIE voiceless stops [*p, *t, *k], to become fricatives? Or was it rather that the PIE voiceless stops initiated the process, pulling the others behind them, as it were, into the place that they were leaving vacant? These questions may not be answerable. But they do at least give recognition to the fact that the several changes summarized in Grimm's Law may be causally connected.

What is now referred to as **internal reconstruction** (in contrast with reconstruction by means of the comparative method) may also be set to the credit of structuralism. This is based on the conviction that synchronically observable partial regularities and asymmetries can be explained with reference to what were fully regular, productive processes at an earlier period. For example, even if we had no comparative evidence to go on and no records of earlier stages in the development of English, we might infer that the partial regularities evident in the English strong verbs (cf. *drive* : *drove* : *driven*, *ride* : *rode* : *ridden*; *sing* : *sang* : *sung*, *ring* : *rang* : *rung*; etc.) were the relics, as it were, of an earlier more fully regular system of verb-inflection. Internal reconstruction is now a recognized part of the methodology of historical linguistics and it has proved its worth on several occasions.

As we shall see later, generativism develops out of, and in part continues, a particular version of structuralism. It is characteristic of generativism that it should see language-change in terms of the addition, loss or reordering of the rules that determine a speaker's linguistic competence. In so far as the competence/performance distinction can be identified with the langue/parole distinction of Saussurean structuralism (cf. 7.2), the contribution made to the theory and methodology of historical linguistics by generativists can be seen as a refinement and development of the structuralists' conception of language-change. Preference is given in both cases to what are classified as internal factors. The structuralists' notion of self-regulation has been replaced with that of the restructuring of the rules of the language-system and a tendency towards simplification. It is difficult to see any fundamental differences between these two notions.

However, one difference between the Chomskyan competence/performance distinction and the Saussurean distinction of langue/parole is that the former lends itself more readily than the latter to a psychological interpretation. Generativists, as we shall see, have been much concerned, for various reasons, with the problem of language-acquisition by children. They have emphasized the fact that the child, as he begins to acquire his native language, is not taught the rules of the underlying system, but must infer these from the patterns of correspondence between form and meaning which he detects in the utterances that he hears around him. What is traditionally regarded as false analogy (e.g. the child's tendency to say *goed* rather than *went*) is seen by the generativist as part of the more general process of the acquisition of rules.

Generativists are not the first to have sought an explanation of language-change in the transmission of language from one generation to another. But they have looked more carefully than others at the process of language-acquisition in terms of the nature of the rules that are required at identifiable stages in this process. Furthermore, they have begun to investigate in detail syntactic, as well as phonological and morphological, change: syntactic change was hardly dealt with at all, other than occasionally and unsystematically, until recently. Most important of all, however, is the fact that generativism has provided historical linguistics with a more precise conception of formal and substantive **universals**, in relation to which postulated changes in prehistoric and unattested stages of a language can be evaluated as more or less probable.

On the debit side, both structuralism and generativism have been inclined to pay insufficient attention to the importance of synchronic variation as a factor in language-change. Apart from anything else, this has given rise to such pseudo-questions as the following: Is sound-change sudden or gradual? Does language-change originate in competence or performance? As far as the first of these two questions is concerned, it is now over a hundred years since Johannes Schmidt challenged the family-tree concept of language-relatedness favoured by the Neogrammarians, and pointed out that innovations of all kinds, and more particularly sound-changes, can spread out from a centre of influence, like waves on a lake, losing force as they reach points further and further from the centre. In the decades that followed, it was demonstrated, especially by scholars working on the history of the Romance languages, where there was abundant evidence, both synchronic and diachronic, that what has come to be called the **wave theory** of language-change provided a more satisfactory account of the facts, in many cases at least, than did the more orthodox **family-tree theory**, with its inbuilt assumptions of sudden and thereafter continuous divergence between related dialects. It was also shown, by dialectologists, that, far from applying simultaneously to all words in which they were applicable, sound-changes might originate in just one or two words and then spread to other words and, along the lines of communication, to other areas. If this is generally the case, it is clear that the question whether sound-change is gradual or sudden loses much of its point. Since it also turns out to be the case that individuals may fluctuate in their usage, between an older and a newer form, so too does the question whether language-changes originate in competence or performance.

More recently, sociolinguists have shown that what is true of the geographical diffusion of phonological, grammatical or lexical variants also holds true of their diffusion through the socially distinguishable classes of a given community. In general, it has become clear that social factors (of the kind that we shall consider in Chapter 9) are far more important in language-change than was previously realized. After all, it is not only geographical, or even political, boundaries that set limits to the degree of intercommunication among people living in the same area. Social dialects may be as distinct from one another as geographically based dialects. On the other hand, given the right social conditions (breakdown in a traditionally stratified society, the imitation of upper-class forms or expressions, etc.), one social dialect may be modified by contact with another. Indeed, it is now coming to be accepted that **bilingualism** and **diglossia** – and even **pidginization** and **creolization** – may have played a much more extensive role in the formation of the language-families of the world than was once thought to be the case (cf. 9.3, 9.4).

We began this section with the question: Why do languages change in the course of time? We may conclude it by repeating what was said in an earlier chapter (cf. 2.5): the ubiquity and continuity of language-change is far less puzzling once it is realized that no natural language is ever stable or uniform and that much of what is describable, macroscopically, as language-change is the product of socially conditioned synchronic variation. This is not to say that all language-change is to be accounted for in this way, but only that social factors are undoubtedly far more important than they were once thought to be.

FURTHER READING

Most general textbooks and introductions to linguistics have chapters on language-change. In particular, Bloomfield (1935), chapters 18–27, is still well worth reading for an essentially Neogrammarian view, with many now classic examples from English and other languages.

Recent introductions to historical linguistics as such include Aitchison (1981); Bynon (1977); Lehmann (1973). Bynon (1977: 281–2) gives additional references, by topic, for everything dealt with in this chapter; Aitchison (1981) emphasizes the role of social factors in language-change.

On the history of English (at various levels of detail and technicality): Barber (1972); Baugh (1965); Francis (1967); Lass (1969); Potter (1950); Strang (1970); Traugott (1972). For other languages and language-families, the *Encyclopaedia Britannica*, 15th edn (1974) is the most convenient work of reference.

QUESTIONS AND EXERCISES

1. What grounds are there for recognizing three different periods in the history of English: Old English (Anglo-Saxon), Middle English and Modern English?
2. On the basis of information to be found in encyclopaedias or other works of reference, list the principal extant members of the Germanic, Romance and Slavonic families of languages.
3. What is a **proto-language**?
4. Explain the purpose of **reconstruction** in historical linguistics.

5. English, like French, Russian, Hindi, etc., is said to be an **Indo-European** language. What does this mean and is it true? How about Finnish, Hungarian, Basque, Turkish, Tamil?

6. Why do you think Sir William Jones attached so much importance to what he called "the roots of verbs" and the "forms of grammar" (cf. p. 188)?

7. "One of the strongest reasons for adopting the assumption of regular phonetic change is the fact that the constitution of the residues . . . throws a good deal of light upon the origin of new forms" (Bloomfield, 1935: 405). Discuss.

8. Give an account of **Grimm's Law** (using examples other than those in the text) and show how **Verner's Law** relates to it.

9. Explain what is meant by the **analogical** regularization of synchronically irregular forms.

10. What inferences can be drawn about the history of a language from the existence of **lexical doublets**? Make a list of ten such pairs of lexemes in Modern English other than those used as examples in the text. What distinction, if any, would you draw between lexical doublets and co-existent grammatically equivalent forms of the same lexeme (*got* : *gotten*, *learnt* : *learned*, *dived* : *dove*)? How would you classify *brothers* : *brethren*, *mediums* : *media*, *struck* : *stricken* in relation to such a distinction?

11. Comment upon the following more or less fossilized forms and constructions: *Rest in peace!*, *Bless you!*, *If it please your Majesty* . . . (cf. also *If your Majesty pleases* . . .), *methinks* (vs. *I think*). What light do they throw on earlier stages of English?

12. Such fixed expressions in Modern English as 'meat and drink' and 'neither flesh nor fowl (nor good red herring)' preserve older meanings of some or all the constituents. Can you think of similar examples?

13. Show how **borrowing** can account for apparent exceptions to the regular operation of a sound-law.

14. "Language change, then, offers important evidence about the nature of human language – namely that it is rule-governed" (Akmajian, Demers & Harnish, 1979: 226). Discuss this statement in relation to the generativists' notion of **restructuring**.

15. "What is perhaps the most important contribution towards an understanding of the actual mechanism of language change has come from the detailed sociolinguistic investigation of living speech communities" (Bynon, 1977: 198). Discuss.

16. Explain and exemplify the notion of **internal reconstruction**.

17. Compare and contrast the **family-tree theory** and the **wave theory** (Wellentheorie) of language-development.

18. Evaluate the contribution that structuralism and generativism have made to the theory and methodology of historical linguistics.

19. What contribution can the study of (a) **language-acquisition** and (b) **pidgins** and **creoles** make to historical linguistics? (This question is best tackled after reading Chapters 8 and 9.)

7
Some modern schools and movements

7.1 *Historicism*

In this chapter, I will discuss a number of twentieth-century movements in linguistics which have shaped current attitudes and
assumptions. The first of these, to which I will give the label **historicism**, is usually thought of as being characteristic of an earlier
period of linguistic thought. It is of importance in the present
connection in that it prepared the way for structuralism.

Writing in 1922, the great Danish linguist, Otto Jespersen, began
one of the most interesting and controversial of his general books
on language with the following sentence: "The distinctive feature of
the science of language as conceived nowadays is its historical
character." Jespersen was here expressing the same point of view as
Hermann Paul had done in his *Prinzipien der Sprachgeschichte*
(*Principles of Language History*), first published in 1880 and commonly described as the bible of Neogrammarian orthodoxy: the
view that (to quote from the fifth edition of Paul's book, which
appeared in 1920) "as soon as one goes beyond the mere statement
of individual facts, as soon as one tried to grasp their interconnec-
tion [den Zusammenhang], to understand the phenomena [die
Erscheinungen], one enters upon the domain of history, albeit
perhaps unconsciously". Both Jespersen's book and the fifth edition of Paul's *Prinzipien*, it will be noted, were published several
years after Saussure's posthumous *Cours de linguistique générale*,
which inaugurated the movement now known as structuralism, and
only a few years before the foundation of the Prague Linguistic
Circle, in which structuralism was combined with functionalism and
some of the ideas of present-day generativism had their origin.
Structuralism, functionalism and generativism are the principal
movements, or attitudes, with which we shall be concerned in this
chapter.

It is interesting to observe, in passing, that Bloomfield, in *Language* (1935), whilst recognizing the great merits of Paul's *Prinzipien*, criticized it, not only for its historicism, but also for its mentalism and its substitution of what Bloomfield regarded as "philosophical and psychological pseudo-explanations" for inductive generalization on the basis of "descriptive language study". The wheel has now come full circle! For, as we shall see later, Bloomfieldian **descriptivism** (which may be regarded as a peculiarly American version of structuralism) provided the environment in which Chomskyan generativism was born and against which it reacted. It is impossible, in a book of this nature, to do justice to the complexity of the relations that hold among twentieth-century schools of linguistics and of the influence that one school has exerted upon another. What follows, in this chapter, is highly selective and, of necessity, involves a certain amount of personal interpretation. It is, of course, a truism that one cannot achieve a genuinely historical perspective in relation to contemporary ideas and attitudes. Even to try to do so may be itself a kind of historicism!

But what, precisely, is historicism – in the sense in which the term is being employed here? It is the view, expressed most forcefully by Paul in the passage from which just one sentence was quoted above, that linguistics, in so far as it is, or aspires to be, scientific, is necessarily historical in character. More particularly, the historicist takes the view that the only kind of explanation valid in linguistics is the kind of explanation which a historian might give: languages are as they are because, in the course of time, they have been subject to a variety of internal and external causal forces – such forces as were mentioned in the final section (6.5) of the chapter on historical linguistics. In taking this view, the great nineteenth-century linguists were reacting against the ideas of the philosophers of the French Enlightenment and their predecessors in a long tradition, which goes back, ultimately, to Plato, Aristotle and the Stoics, whose aim it was to deduce the universal properties of language from what were known, or assumed, to be universal properties of the human mind.

Historicism, in the sense in which the term is being used here, does not necessarily imply **evolutionism**: the view that there is directionality in the historical development of languages.

Evolutionism was, in fact, quite influential in linguistics in the late nineteenth century; and Jespersen, in the book referred to above, defends a particular version of it. Other versions have been put forward by idealists of various schools; and also, of course, within the framework of dialectical materialism, by Marxists. It is probably true to say, however, that, with a few notable exceptions, most linguists in the twentieth century have rejected evolutionism (cf. 1.4). Historicism, as we shall see in the following section, is one of the movements against which structuralism reacted and in relation to which it may be defined.

7.2 *Structuralism*

What is commonly referred to as **structuralism**, especially in Europe, is of multiple origin. It is both conventional and convenient to date its birth as an identifiable movement in linguistics from the publication of Saussure's *Cours de linguistique générale* in 1916. Many of the ideas that Saussure brought together in the lectures that he delivered at the University of Geneva between 1907 and 1911 (upon which the *Cours* is based) can be traced back into the nineteenth century and beyond.

Several of the constitutive distinctions of Saussurean structuralism have been introduced already (though not always in Saussurean terminology). It suffices to remind the reader of them and to show how they fit together. Since we have just been discussing historicism, it is natural to begin with the distinction between the synchronic and diachronic point of view in the study of languages (cf. 2.5).

As we have seen, the Neogrammarians took the view that linguistics, in so far as it is scientific and explanatory, must necessarily be historical. Against this view, Saussure argued that the synchronic description of particular languages could be equally scientific; and also that it could be explanatory. Synchronic explanation differs from diachronic, or historical, explanation in being **structural**, rather than causal: it gives a different kind of answer to the question, "Why are things as they are?" Instead of tracing the historical development of particular forms or meanings, it demonstrates how all the forms and meanings are interrelated at a particular point in time in a particular language-system. It is important to realize that, in opposing the Neogrammarian view, Saussure was not denying the validity of historical explanation. He had made his reputation, as a very young man, with a brilliant reconstruction of the Proto-Indo-European vowel-system; and he never abandoned his interest in historical linguistics. What he was saying in his Geneva lectures on general linguistics was that the synchronic and the diachronic modes of explanation were complementary; and that the latter was logically dependent upon the former.

It is as if we were asked to explain why, let us say, a Rolls Royce car-engine of such-and-such a model and such-and-such a year was as it is. We could give a diachronic explanation in terms of the changes that had taken place, over the years, in the design of the carburettor, the crankshaft, etc.; and this would be a perfectly appropriate answer to the question. Alternatively, we could describe the role that each component plays in the synchronic system; and in doing so we should be explaining how the engine fits together and how it works. This would be a non-historical, structural (and functional) explanation of the facts. Since languages are not designed and, in Saussure's view at least, do not evolve through time according to some external or internal purpose, we must be careful not to press this analogy of the car-engine too hard (just as we must not press too hard Saussure's own analogy of the game of chess: cf. 2.5). Due allowance being made for the absence of a controlling designer and the difference between a machine and a social institution, we can say, quite legitimately, though metaphorically, that a structural description of a language tells us how all the components fit together.

There are certain aspects of Saussure's distinction between the diachronic and the synchronic point of view that are controversial, not to say paradoxical: in particular, his assertion that structuralism has no place in historical linguistics. This is paradoxical in view of the fact that Saussure's own early work on the Proto-Indo-European vowel-system in 1879 can be seen as foreshadowing what would be later described as internal reconstruction; and, as we have seen, this method of reconstruction was subsequently refined and adopted by scholars who called themselves structuralists and drew their inspiration, at least partly, from Saussure (cf. 6.5). However, it would seem that Saussure himself believed, rightly or wrongly, that all changes originated outside the language-system itself and did not take account of what were later to be identified as structural pressures within the system operating as internal causal factors of language-change. No more need be said about this.

Little need be said either about Saussure's dichotomy between **langue** and **parole**: between the **language-system** and **language-behaviour** (cf. 1.3, 2.6). What must be emphasized, at this point, is the abstractness of Saussure's conception of the language-system. A language (langue), says Saussure, is a form, not a substance. The term 'form' is well established in this sense in philosophy and relates, on the one hand, to Wilhelm von Humboldt's notion of the inner form of a language (innere Sprachform) and, on the other, to the Russian formalists' notion of form as opposed to content in literary analysis. But it is potentially misleading (cf. 2.6). We are not doing violence to Saussure's thought if we say that a language is a **structure**, implying by the use of this term that it is independent of the physical substance, or medium, in which it is realized. 'Structure', in this sense, is more or less equivalent to 'system': a language is a two-level system of **syntagmatic** and **substitutional** (or **paradigmatic**) relations (cf. 3.6). It is this sense of 'structure' – the sense in which particular emphasis is given to the internal combinatorial and contrastive relations within a language-system – that makes the term 'structuralism' appropriate to several different twentieth-century schools of linguistics, which might differ, one from another, in various respects, including the abstractness of their conception of language-systems and their attitudes to the fiction of homogeneity (cf. 1.6). As we shall see later, generativism is also a particular version of structuralism in this very general sense.

But there are other features of Saussurean structuralism that are more distinctive of it. One is the assertion that "the one and only true object of linguistics is the language-system [la langue] envisaged in itself and for itself". Actually, this famous quotation from the last sentence of the *Cours* may not accurately represent Saussure's view, since the sentence appears to have been added by the editors without warrant in the lectures themselves. There is some doubt, too, as to what exactly is meant by "in itself and for itself" ("en elle-même et pour elle-même"). However, in the Saussurean tradition it has usually been taken to imply that a language-system is a structure that can be abstracted, not only from the historical forces that have brought it into being, but also from the social matrix in which it operates and the psychological process by which it is acquired and made available for use in language-behaviour. Thus interpreted, the Saussurean slogan, whether it originated with the master himself or not, has often been used to justify the principle of the **autonomy** of linguistics (i.e. its independence of other disciplines) and a methodological distinction of the kind that was drawn in an earlier chapter between **microlinguistics** and **macrolinguistics** (cf. 2.1). It has also been identified, at times, with the somewhat different, but no less characteristically structuralist, slogan that every language-system is unique and should be described on its own terms. We shall come back to this point (cf. 10.2).

There might seem to be some conflict between Saussure's view (if indeed it was his view) that the language-system should be studied in abstraction from the society in which it operates and the view (which he certainly did hold) that languages are social facts. The conflict is only apparent. For even if they are social facts – in the sense in which the term 'social fact' was employed by the great French sociologist, Émile Durkheim (1858–1917), Saussure's contemporary – they have their own unique constitutive principles. As we have seen, a structural analysis of a language-system is not to be confused with a causal account of how the system came to be as it is. In saying that language-systems are social facts, Saussure was asserting several things: that they are different from, though no less real than, material objects; that they are external to the individual and make him subject to their constraining force; that they are systems of values maintained by social convention.

More particularly, he took the view that they are semiotic systems in which that which is signified (**le signifié**) is arbitrarily associated with that which signifies (**le signifiant**). This is Saussure's famous principle of the arbitrariness of the linguistic sign (l'arbitraire du signe) – a principle which was discussed, independently of the role it fulfils in Saussurean structuralism, in an earlier chapter (cf. 1.5). The important point to note here, and it is essential for the understanding of Saussurean structuralism, is that the sign is not a meaningful form: it is a composite entity which results from the imposition of structure on two kinds of substance by the combinatorial and contrastive relations of the language-system. Meanings

cannot exist independently of the forms with which they are associated; and vice versa. We must not think of a language as a nomen-
clature, says Saussure: that is, as a set of names, or labels, for
pre-existing concepts, or meanings. The meaning of a word – or
rather, that aspect of its meaning which Saussure called the 'signifié'
(that aspect of meaning which is wholly internal to the language-
system; its sense, rather than its reference or denotation: cf. 5.3) – is
the product of the semantic relations which hold between that word
and others in the same language-system. To invoke the traditional
philosophical distinction between essence and existence, it derives
not only its essence (what it is), but also its existence (the fact that it
is) from the relational structure that is imposed by the language-
system upon the otherwise unstructured substance of thought.
Similarly, what Saussure calls the 'signifiant' of a word – its phonological shape, as it were – results ultimately from the network of
contrasts and equivalences that a particular language-system
imposes upon the continuum of sound.

We need proceed no further with our investigation of Saussurean
structuralism as such. What has just been said is no doubt difficult to
comprehend when it is formulated in such general terms, as it has
been here. It should be comprehensible, however, as far as the
imposition of structure on the substance of sound is concerned, in
the light of the distinction drawn earlier between phonetics and
phonology (cf. 3.5). Whether we can legitimately talk of the imposition of structure upon the substance of thought in the same sort of
way is, to say the least, problematical.

The Saussurean view of the uniqueness of language-systems and
of the relation between structure and substance leads naturally,
though by no means inevitably, to the thesis of **linguistic relativity**:
the thesis that there are no universal properties of human languages
(other than such very general semiotic properties as arbitrariness,
productivity, duality and discreteness: cf. 1.5); the thesis that every
language is, as it were, a law unto itself. Any movement or attitude
in linguistics which accepts this point of view may be referred to
conveniently, as **relativism** and contrasted with **universalism**. Relativism, in a stronger or weaker form, has been associated with most
kinds of twentieth-century structuralism. In part, it can be seen as a
methodologically healthy reaction to the tendency to describe the

indigenous languages of the New World in terms of the categories of Western traditional grammar. But relativism has also been defended by its proponents, in association with structuralism, in the more controversial context of the discussion of such traditional philosophical issues as the relation between language and mind and the role played by language in the acquisition and representation of knowledge (cf. 10.2). Both philosophical and methodological relativism have been rejected, by Chomsky and his followers, as we shall see, in their formulation of the principles of generativism (cf. 7.4). What needs to be emphasized here is the fact that, although there is a strong historical connection between structuralism and relativism, there have been many structuralists – notably Roman Jakobson and other members of the Prague School (cf. 7.3) – who never accepted the more extreme forms of relativism. This holds not only within linguistics, but also in other disciplines, such as social anthropology, in which structuralism has been an important twentieth-century influence.

We cannot go into the relation between structural linguistics and structuralism in other fields of investigation. It must be appreciated, however, that structuralism is very much an interdisciplinary movement. Saussurean structuralism, in particular, has been a powerful force in the development of a characteristically French approach to semiotics (or semiology) and its application to literary criticism, on the one hand, and to the analysis of society and culture, on the other. Taking 'structuralism' in a more general sense, we can say, as the philosopher Ernst Cassirer did in 1945: "Structuralism is no isolated phenomenon; it is, rather, the expression of a general tendency of thought that, in these last decades, has become more and more prominent in almost all fields of scientific research." What characterizes structuralism, in this more general sense, is a greater concern with the relations which hold among entities than with the entities themselves. There is a natural affinity, in this respect, between structuralism and mathematics; and one of the criticisms most commonly made of structuralism is that it exaggerates the orderliness, elegance and generality of the relational patterns in the data that it investigates.

7.3 *Functionalism*

The terms 'functionalism' and 'structuralism' are often employed in anthropology and sociology to refer to contrasting theories or methods of analysis. In linguistics, however, **functionalism** is best seen as a particular movement within structuralism. It is characterized by the belief that the phonological, grammatical and semantic structure of languages is determined by the functions that they have to perform in the societies in which they operate. The best-known representatives of functionalism, in this sense of the term, are the members of the **Prague School**, which had its origin in the Prague Linguistic Circle, founded in 1926 and particularly influential in European linguistics in the period preceding the Second World War. Not all the members of the Prague Linguistic Circle, incidentally, were based in Prague; nor were they all Czech. Two of its most influential members Roman Jakobson and Nikolaj Trubetzkoy, were émigré Russians, the former teaching in Brno and the latter in Vienna. From 1928, when the Prague School manifesto (as one might call it) was presented to the First International Congress of Linguists held at The Hague, scholars from many other European countries began to associate themselves, more or less closely, with the movement. The Prague School has always acknowledged its debt to Saussurean structuralism, although it has tended to reject Saussure's point of view on certain issues, especially on the sharpness of the distinction between synchronic and diachronic linguistics and on the homogeneity of the language-system.

It was in phonology that the Prague School first made its impact. In fact, the notion of functional contrast, which was invoked above in drawing the distinction between phonetics and phonology, is essentially that of Trubetzkoy, whose concept of **distinctive features**, as modified by Jakobson and later by Halle (working in collaboration with Chomsky), has been incorporated within the theory of generative phonology (cf. 3.5). But the **distinctive function** of phonetic features is only one kind of linguistically relevant function recognized by Trubetzkoy and his followers. Also to be noted are **demarcative function**, on the one hand, and **expressive function**, on the other.

Many of the suprasegmental features referred to above – stress, tone, length, etc. (cf. 3.5) – have a demarcative, rather than a distinctive, function in particular language-systems: they are what Trubetzkoy called boundary-signals (Grenzsignale). They do not serve to distinguish one form from another on the substitutional (or, in Saussurean terms, paradigmatic) dimension of contrast; they reinforce the phonological cohesion of forms and help to identify them syntagmatically as units by marking the boundary between one form and another in the chain of speech. For example, in many languages, including English, there is no more than one primary stress associated with each word-form. Since the position of the primary stress on English word-forms is only partly predictable, its association with one syllable rather than another does not identify word-boundaries quite so clearly as it does in languages (such as Polish, Czech or Finnish) with so-called fixed stress. Nevertheless, word-stress does have an important demarcative function in English. So too does the occurrence of particular sequences of phonemes. For example, /h/ rarely occurs in English (otherwise than in proper names) except at the beginning of a morpheme, and /ŋ/ never occurs without a following consonant except at the end. The occurrence of either of these phonemes can serve therefore to indicate the position of a morpheme-boundary. It is not just prosodic features that have demarcative function in a language-system; and this is something that phonologists have often failed to appreciate. The fact that not all sequences of phonemes are possible word-forms of a language is of importance for the identification of those forms that do occur in utterances.

By the expressive function of a phonological feature is meant its indication of the speaker's feelings or attitude. For example, word-stress is not distinctive in French; and it does not play a demarcative role, as it does in many languages. There is, however, a particular kind of emphatic pronunciation of the beginning of the word which has an acknowledged expressive function. It is probably true to say that every language puts a rich set of phonological resources at the disposal of its users for the expression of feeling. Unless the notion of linguistic meaning is restricted to that which is relevant to the making of true and false statements, it is surely right to treat the expressive function of language on equal terms with its descriptive function (cf. 5.1).

It is not only in phonology that members of the Prague School demonstrated their functionalism, and more especially their readiness to take full account of the expressive and interpersonal functions of language. From the outset, they have opposed, not only the historicism and positivism of the Neogrammarian approach to language, but also the intellectualism of the pre-nineteenth-century Western philosophical tradition, according to which language is the externalization or expression of thought (and 'thought' is understood to mean propositional thought). Intellectualism, as we shall see, is one of the components of that complex and heterogeneous movement in modern linguistics to which we are giving the label 'generativism' (cf. 7.4). There is no logical contradiction between functionalism and intellectualism. After all, one might as an intellectualist take the view that the sole or primary function of language is the expression of propositional thought and yet as a functionalist maintain that the structure of language-systems is determined by their teleological adaptation to this their sole or primary function. In practice, however, not only Prague School linguists, but also others who have called themselves functionalists, have tended to emphasize the **multifunctionality** of language and the importance of its expressive, social and conative functions, in contrast with or in addition to its descriptive function.

One of the enduring interests of the Prague School, as far as the grammatical structure of languages is concerned, has been **functional sentence perspective** (to use the term which emphasizes the functionalist motivation of research on this topic). It was pointed out in an earlier chapter that

(1) This morning he got up late

and

(2) He got up late this morning

might be regarded as different versions of the same sentence or, alternatively, as different sentences (cf. 4.2). Whichever point of view we adopt, two things are clear: first, that (1) and (2) are truth-conditionally equivalent and therefore, on a narrow interpretation of 'meaning', can be said to have the same meaning (cf. 5.1); second, that the contexts in which (1) would be uttered differ systematically from the contexts in which (2) would be uttered. In so far as word-order is held to be a matter of syntax, we can say that, in some languages at least, the syntactic structure of utterances (or of sentences, under a definition of 'sentence' which would make (1) and (2) different sentences) is determined by the communicative setting of the utterance, and in particular by what is taken for granted, or **given** as background information and what is presented against this background as being **new** to the hearer and thus genuinely informative. Considerations of this kind are involved in the definition of what Prague School linguists have called functional sentence perspective. There are differences of terminology and of interpretation which make it difficult to compare the various functionalist treatments of the communicative settings of utterances within a common theoretical framework. What they all share is the conviction that the structure of utterances is determined by the use to which they are put and the communicative context in which they occur.

In general, we can say that functionalism in linguistics has tended to emphasize the instrumental character of language. There is a natural affinity, therefore, between the functionalist viewpoint and that of the sociolinguist or of such philosophers of language as have subsumed language-behaviour under the more embracing notion of social interaction. Functionalism is, in this respect and in others, firmly opposed to generativism (cf. 7.4).

But is it true, as the functionalist maintains, that the structure of natural languages is determined by the several interdependent semiotic functions – expressive, social and descriptive – that they fulfil? If it were, their structure would be in this respect non-arbitrary; and in so far as different language-systems fulfilled the same semiotic functions, they could be expected to be similar, if not identical, in structure. Now it is possible that linguists have at times exaggerated the arbitrariness of grammatical processes and have failed to give due weight to functional considerations in the description of particular phenomena. It is also possible that functional explanations will ultimately be found for many facts which at present seem to be quite arbitrary: for example, the fact that the adjective regularly precedes the noun in noun phrases in English, but usually follows its noun in French; the fact that the verb is put at the end of subordinate clauses in German; and so on. In certain instances it has been noted that the presence of one such apparently arbitrary property in a language tends to imply the presence or absence of another apparently arbitrary property. But so far at least **implicational universals** of this kind have not been satisfactorily explained in functional terms. It would seem that there is indeed a good deal of arbitrariness in the non-verbal components of language-systems, and more particularly in their grammatical structure (cf. 7.4); and that functionalism, as defined above, is untenable. It does not follow, of course, that weaker versions of functionalism, according to which the structure of language-systems is partly, though not wholly, determined by function are equally untenable. And linguists who call themselves functionalists tend to adopt one of the weaker versions.

7.4 *Generativism*

The term 'generativism' is being used here to refer to the theory of language that has been developed, over the last twenty years or so, by Chomsky and his followers. Generativism, in this sense, has been enormously influential, not only in linguistics, but also in philosophy, psychology and other disciplines concerned with language.

Generativism carries with it a commitment to the usefulness and feasibility of describing human languages by means of generative grammars of one type or another. But there is much more to generativism than this. As has already been pointed out, although a commitment to the tenets of generativism necessarily implies an interest in generative grammar, the converse does not hold true (cf. 4.6). Indeed, relatively few of the linguists who were impressed by the technical advantages and heuristic value of Chomsky's system of transformational-generative grammar when he first put this forward in the late 1950s have ever explicitly associated themselves with the body of assumptions and doctrines that is now identifiable as generativism. It is also worth emphasizing that these assumptions and doctrines are, for the most part, logically unconnected. Some of them, as I shall indicate below, are more widely accepted than others. However, the influence of Chomskyan generativism upon all modern linguistic theory has been so deep and so pervasive that even those who reject this or that aspect of it tend to do so in terms that Chomsky has made available to them.

Generativism is usually presented as having developed out of, and in reaction to, the previously dominant school of post-Bloomfieldian American descriptivism: a particular version of structuralism. Up to a point, it is historically justifiable to see the origin of generativism within linguistics in this light. But, as Chomsky himself came to realize later, there are many respects in which generativism constitutes a return to older and more traditional views about language. There are others in which generativism simply takes over, without due criticism, features of post-Bloomfieldian structuralism which have never found much favour in other schools of linguistics. It is impossible to deal satisfactorily with the historical connections between Chomskyan generativism and the views of his predecessors in this book; and, for present purposes, it is unnecessary to attempt to do so. I will merely pick out, and comment briefly upon, the most important of the recognizably Chomskyan components of present-day generativism.

As was noted in Chapter 1, language-systems are productive, in the sense that they allow for the construction and comprehension of indefinitely many utterances that have never previously occurred in the experience of any of their users (cf. 1.5). In fact, from the assumption that human languages have the property of **recursiveness** – and this appears to be a valid assumption (cf. 4.5) – it follows that the set of potential utterances in any given language is, quite literally, infinite in number. Chomsky drew attention to this fact, in his earliest work, in his criticism of the widely held view that children learn their native language by reproducing, in whole or in part, the utterances of adult speakers. Obviously, if children, from a fairly early age, are able to produce novel utterances which a competent speaker of the language will recognize as grammatically well-formed, there must be something other than imitation involved. They must have inferred, learned, or otherwise acquired the grammatical rules by virtue of which the utterances that they produce are judged to be well-formed. We shall be looking further at the question of language-acquisition in a later chapter (cf. 8.4). Here, it is sufficient to note that, whether Chomsky is right or wrong about other issues that he has raised in this connection, there can be no doubt that children do not learn language-utterances by rote and then simply reproduce them in response to environmental stimuli.

I have deliberately used the words 'stimulus' and 'response' at this point. They are key-terms of the school of psychology known as **behaviourism**, which was very influential in America before and after the Second World War. According to the behaviourists everything that is commonly described as being the product of the human mind – including language – can be satisfactorily accounted for in terms of the reinforcement and conditioning of purely physiological reflexes: ultimately, in terms of habits, or **stimulus–response** patterns, built up by the same kind of conditioning as that which enables experimental psychologists to train laboratory rats to run through a maze. Since Bloomfield himself had come to accept the principles of behaviourism and had explicitly advocated them as a basis for the scientific study of language in his classic textbook (1935), these principles were widely accepted in America, not only by psychologists, but also by linguists, throughout the so-called post-Bloomfieldian period.

Chomsky has done more than anyone else to demonstrate the sterility of the behaviourists' theory of language. He has pointed out that much of the technical vocabulary of behaviourism ('stimulus', 'response', 'conditioning', 'reinforcement', etc.), if taken seriously, cannot be shown to have any relevance to the acquisition and the use of human language. He has shown that the behaviourists' refusal to countenance the existence of anything other than observable physical objects and processes is based on an outdated pseudo-scientific prejudice. He has asserted – and, as far as the evidence goes, correctly – that language is **free from stimulus-control**. This is what he means when he talks of **creativity**: the utterance that someone produces on any particular occasion is, in principle, unpredictable and cannot be properly described, in the technical sense of these terms, as a response to some identifiable linguistic or non-linguistic stimulus.

Creativity is, in Chomsky's view, a peculiarly human attribute, which distinguishes men from machines and, as far as we know, from other animals. But it is **rule-governed** creativity. And this is where generative grammar comes into its own. The utterances that we produce have a certain grammatical structure: they conform to identifiable rules of well-formedness. To the extent that we succeed in specifying these rules of well-formedness, or grammaticality, we shall have provided a scientifically satisfying account of that property of language – its productivity (cf. 1.5) – which makes possible the exercise of creativity. Productivity, it should be noted, is not to be identified with creativity: but there is an intrinsic connection between them. Our creativity in the use of language – our freedom from stimulus-control – manifests itself within the limits set by the productivity of the language-system. Furthermore, it is Chomsky's view – and this is a very central component in Chomskyan generativism – that the rules which determine the productivity of human languages have the formal properties that they do have by virtue of the structure of the human mind.

This brings us to **mentalism**. Not only the behaviourists, but psychologists and philosophers of many different persuasions, have rejected the distinction that is commonly drawn between body and mind. Chomsky takes the view that it is a valid distinction (although he would not necessarily accept the terms in which it has been formulated in the past). And it is his contention that linguistics has an important role to play in the investigation of the nature of the mind. We will return to this question presently (cf. 8.2). Meanwhile, it is worth noting that there is far less difference between Bloomfield's and Chomsky's views of the nature and scope of linguistics than one might expect. Bloomfield's commitment to behaviourism had little practical effect upon the techniques of linguistic description that he and his followers developed; and Chomsky's mentalism, as we shall see, is not of the kind that (to quote Bloomfield) "supposes that the variability of human conduct is due to the interference of some non-physical factor". Chomsky's mentalism transcends the more old-fashioned opposition between the physical and the non-physical that Bloomfield here invokes. Chomsky, no less than Bloomfield did, wishes to study language within the framework of concepts and assumptions provided by the natural sciences.

Nevertheless, there are significant differences between Chomskyan generativism and both Bloomfieldian and post-Bloomfieldian structuralism. One of these has to do with their attitudes towards **linguistic universals**. Bloomfield and his followers emphasized the structural diversity of languages (as did the majority of post-Saussurean structuralists: cf. 7.2). Generativists, in contrast, are more interested in what languages have in common. In this respect, generativism represents a return to the older tradition of universal grammar – as exemplified, most notably, by the Port-Royal grammar of 1660 and a large number of eighteenth-century treatises on language – which both Bloomfield and Saussure condemned as speculative and unscientific. But Chomsky's position is interestingly different from that of his predecessors in the same tradition. Whereas they tended to deduce the essential properties of language from what they held to be the universally valid categories of logic or reality, Chomsky is far more impressed with such universal properties of language as cannot be so accounted for: in short, with what is universal, but **arbitrary** (cf. 1.5). Another difference is that he attaches more importance to the formal properties of languages and to the nature of the rules that their description requires than he does to the relations that hold between language and the world.

The reason for this change of emphasis is that Chomsky is looking for evidence to support his view that the human language-faculty is **innate** and **species-specific**: i.e. genetically transmitted and unique to the species. Any universal property of language that can be accounted for in terms of its functional utility or its reflection of the structure of the physical world or of the categories of logic can be discounted from this point of view. According to Chomsky, there are several complex formal properties which are found in all languages, and yet are arbitrary in the sense that they serve no known purpose and cannot be deduced from anything else that we know of human beings or of the world in which they live.

Whether there are indeed such universal formal properties in language, of the kind that the generativists have postulated, is as yet uncertain. But the search for them and the attempt to construct a general theory of language-structure within which they would find their place has been responsible for some of the most interesting work in both theoretical and descriptive linguistics in recent years. And many of the results that have been obtained are independently valuable, regardless of whether they lend support to Chomsky's hypothesis about the innateness and species-specificity of the language-faculty or not.

A further difference between generativism and Bloomfieldian and post-Bloomfieldian structuralism – though in this respect generativism is closer to Saussurean structuralism – relates to the distinction that Chomsky draws between **competence** and **performance**. A speaker's linguistic competence is that part of his knowledge – his knowledge of the language-system as such – by virtue of which he is able to produce the indefinitely large set of sentences that constitutes his language (in Chomsky's definition of a language as a set of sentences: cf. 2.6). Performance, on the other hand, is language-behaviour; and this is said to be determined, not only by the speaker's linguistic competence, but also by a variety of non-linguistic factors including, on the one hand, social conventions, beliefs about the world, the speaker's emotional attitudes towards what he is saying, his assumption about his interlocutor's attitudes, etc. and, on the other hand, the operation of the psychological and physiological mechanisms involved in the production of utterances.

The competence–performance distinction, thus drawn, is at the very heart of generativism. As presented in recent years, it relates to mentalism and universalism in the following way. A speaker's linguistic competence is a set of rules which he has constructed in his mind by virtue of his application of his innate capacity for language-acquisition to the language-data that he has heard around him in childhood. The grammar that the linguist constructs for the language-system in question can be seen as a model of the native speaker's competence. To the extent that it successfully models such properties of linguistic competence as the ability to produce and understand an indefinitely large number of sentences, it will serve as a model of one of the faculties, or organs, of the mind. To the extent that the theory of generative grammar can identify, and construct a model for, that part of linguistic competence which, being universal (and arbitrary) is held to be innate, it can be regarded as falling within the province of cognitive psychology and as making its own unique contribution to the study of man. It is, of course, this aspect of generativism, with its reinterpretation and revitalization of the traditional notion of universal grammar, which has excited the attention of psychologists and philosophers.

The distinction between competence and performance, as drawn by Chomsky, is similar to Saussure's distinction between langue and parole. Both of them rest upon the feasibility of separating what is linguistic from what is non-linguistic; and they both subscribe to the fiction of the homogeneity of the language-system (cf. 1.6). As for the differences between the two distinctions, it is arguable that Saussure's has less of a psychological slant to it than Chomsky's: though Saussure himself is far from clear on this point, many of his followers have taken the language-system to be something quite abstract and other than even the idealized speaker's knowledge of it. A more clearly identifiable difference has to do with the role that is assigned to the rules of syntax. Saussure gives the impression that the sentences of a language are instances of **parole**; both he and his followers talk of a **langue** as a system of relations and say little or nothing about the rules that are required to generate sentences. Chomsky, on the other hand, has insisted from the out- set that the capacity to produce and understand syntactically well- formed sentences is a central part – indeed, the central part – of a speaker's linquistic competence. In this respect, Chomskyan generativism undoubtedly constitutes an advance upon Saussurean structuralism.

Chomsky's competence–performance distinction has come in for a lot of criticism. Some of this has to do with the validity of what I have called the fiction of homogeneity: provided that 'validity' is interpreted in terms of fruitfulness for the purpose of describing and comparing languages, this line of criticism may be discounted. With the same proviso we may also discount the criticism that Chomsky draws too sharp a distinction between linguistic competence and the other kinds of knowledge and cognitive ability that are involved in the use of language as far as grammatical and phonological struc- ture is concerned: semantic analysis is more problematical (cf. 5.6, 8.6). At the same time, it must be recognized that the terms 'com- petence' and 'performance' are inappropriate and misleading as far as the distinction between what is linguistic and what is non- linguistic is concerned. Granted that language-behaviour, in so far as it is systematic, presupposes various kinds of cognitive ability, or competence, and that one kind is the speaker's knowledge of the rules and vocabulary of the language-system, it is confusing, to say the least, to restrict the term 'competence', as Chomskyan gener- ativists do, to what is assumed to pertain to the language-system, lumping everything else under the catch-all term 'performance'. It would have been preferable to talk about linguistic and non-linguistic competence, on the one hand, and about performance, or actual language-behaviour, on the other. And it is worth noting that in his most recent work Chomsky himself distinguishes grammatical competence from what he calls pragmatic competence.

By far the most controversial aspects of generativism are its association with mentalism and its reassertion of the traditional philosophical doctrine of innate knowledge (cf. 8.2). As far as the more narrowly linguistic part of generativism is concerned (the microlinguistic part: cf. 2.1), there is also much that is controversial. But most of this it shares with post-Bloomfieldian structuralism, out of which it emerged, or with other schools of linguistics, including Saussurean structuralism and the Prague School, with which, in one respect or another, it has now associated itself. For example, it continues the post-Bloomfieldian tradition in syntax, by making the morpheme the basic unit of analysis and by attaching more importance to constituency-relations than it does to dependency (cf. 4.4). Its commitment to the autonomy of syntax (i.e. to the view that the syntactic structure of languages can be described without recourse to semantic considerations) may also be attributed to its post-Bloomfieldian heritage, though many other linguists, outside the post-Bloomfieldian tradition, have taken the same view. As we have seen, Chomskyan generativism is closer to Saussurean, and post-Saussurean, structuralism on the necessity of drawing a distinction between the language-system and the use of that system in particular contexts of utterance. It is also closer to Saussurean structuralism and some of its European developments in its attitude towards semantics. Finally, it has drawn heavily upon Prague School notions in phonology, without however accepting the principles of functionalism. Generativism is all too often presented as an integrated whole in which the technical details of formalization are on a par with a number of logically unconnected ideas about language and the philosophy of science. These need to be disentangled and evaluated on their merits.

FURTHER READING

On the recent history of linguistics: Ivić (1965); Leroy (1963); Malmberg

(1964); Mohrmann, Sommerfelt & Whatmough (1961); Norman & Sommerfelt (1963); Robins (1979b).

On Saussurean and post-Saussurean structuralism: additionally Culler (1976); Ehrmann (1970); Hawkes (1977); Lane (1970); Lepschy (1970). For those who read French, Sanders (1979) provides an excellent introduction to Saussure's *Cours*, and to the more specialized critical editions and commentaries.

On Prague School structuralism and functionalism: additionally Garvin (1964); Jakobson (1973); Vachek (1964, 1966). See also Halliday (1970, 1976) for a partly independent approach.

On Chomskyan generativism, the literature both popular and scholarly is by now immense. Much of it is controversial, misleading or outdated. Lyons (1977a) will serve as a relatively straightforward introduction to Chomsky's own views and writings, and provides a bibliography and suggestions for further reading. To the works listed there, one may now add: Matthews (1979), a lively critique of the central tenets of generativism; Piattelli-Palmarini (1979), which is particularly interesting for Chomsky's own comments on the biological and psychological aspects of generativism; Sampson (1980), which develops and in part modifies Sampson (1975); Smith & Wilson (1979), a spirited and readable account of linguistics from a Chomskyan point of view. Chomsky's own most recent publications have tended to be rather technical, but Chomsky (1979) will bring the reader more or less up to date.

QUESTIONS AND EXERCISES

1. What is **historicism**? How does it differ from **evolutionism**? What role have they both played in the formation of twentieth-century linguistics?

2. What do you take to be the most important features of Saussurean structuralism?

3. Distinguish clearly between 'structuralism' in its more general sense and in the sense in which it is opposed to 'generativism'.

4. "structuralism is based, in the first instance, on the realization that if human actions or productions have a meaning there must be an underlying system of conventions which make this meaning possible" (Culler, 1973: 21–2). Discuss.

5. Explain what is meant by **functionalism** in linguistics with particular reference to the work of the Prague School.

6. "Chomsky has done more than anyone else to demonstrate the sterility of the behaviourists' theory of language" (p. 230). Discuss.

7. "The term 'deep structure' has, unfortunately, proved to be very misleading. It has led a number of people to suppose that it is the deep structures and their properties that are truly 'deep' in the non-technical

sense of the word, while the rest is superficial, unimportant, variable across languages, and so on. This was never intended" (Chomsky, 1976: 82). How did Chomsky draw the **deep/surface** distinction in *Aspects* (1965)? What is its status today in Chomsky's own work and that of other generativists?

8. Why does Chomsky attach so much importance to the notion of **formal universals**?

9. "there is far less difference between Bloomfield's and Chomsky's views of the nature and scope of linguistics than one might expect" (p. 231). Discuss.

10. "We have plenty of our own problems to mind. And if we mind those we will rediscover the genuine virtues of generative grammar, as one technique of linguistic description, which is especially appropriate for syntax, and not as a model of competence" (Matthews, 1979: 106). Is this fair comment? Do the author's arguments justify his conclusions?

8
Language and mind

8.1 *Universal grammar and its relevance*

From the earliest times there has been a close connection between the philosophy of language and such traditionally recognized branches of philosophy as logic (the study of reasoning) and epistemology (the theory of knowledge). As far as logic is concerned, the very name of what has now become a highly technical and more or less independent discipline proclaims the connection: the Greek word 'logos' is related to the verb meaning "to speak" or "to say" and can be translated, according to context, as either "reasoning" or "discourse". That there should be this kind of historical connection is hardly surprising. Common sense and introspection support the view that thought is a kind of inner speech; and various more sophisticated versions of this view have been put forward, over the centuries, by philosophers. In fact, throughout most of the 2000 years or so during which Western traditional grammar held sway in the various centres of scholarship, no clear distinction was drawn, at the theoretical level, between grammar and logic. In particular periods – most notably in the thirteenth century and again in the eighteenth – systems of what came to be called **universal grammar** were developed, in which the connection between logic and grammar was made explicit and given some kind of philosophical justification. In all such cases it was grammar that was subordinated to logic, since the principles of logic were held to be of universal validity.

Nineteenth-century linguists tended to be sceptical of philosophically based universal grammar. On the one hand, it was by now apparent that there was a much greater diversity of grammatical structure among the languages of the world than previous generations of scholars had supposed. On the other, both the spirit of the age and the very solid achievements of the new discipline of diachronic linguistics favoured historical, rather than philosophical, explanation (cf. 7.1). There were those, too, who began to wonder whether the categories of traditional, Aristotelian, logic were truly universal. Writing in the 1860s, the German classicist and philosopher A. Trendelenburg (1802–72) had put forward the view that, if Aristotle had spoken Chinese or Dakotan, rather than Greek, the categories of Aristotelian logic would have been radically different. This point of view was very much in keeping with that of Herder (1744–1803) and Wilhelm von Humboldt (1762–1835), who had emphasized both the diversity of language-structure and the influence of language-structure upon the categorization of thought and experience. We shall come back to this in our discussion of the so-called Whorfian hypothesis (cf. 10.2). But here it should perhaps be noted that historicism – not to mention Darwinian evolutionism – also had its effect, in the late nineteenth century, on the emergent disciplines of anthropology and psychology. Not only was it common to talk of the evolution of culture from barbarism to civilization, but such scholars as Levy-Bruhl were prepared to argue that the mind of the so-called savage operated differently from that of civilized man.

For various reasons, then, universal grammar, in the traditional sense, went out of favour in the course of the nineteenth century. It has been revived in the last twenty years, as part of what I have called generativism, by Chomsky and his followers (cf. 7.4). Chomsky's version of universal grammar makes the same assumption as earlier versions do about the universality of logic and about the interdependence of language and thought. It is Chomsky's view, however, that the empirical study of language has more to contribute to the philosophy of mind than traditional logic and the philosophy of language have to contribute to linguistics. This makes a profound difference to the way in which the argument is conducted even when the point at issue is recognizably traditional: for example, whether the language-faculty is innate or not. Chomsky's originality, in this respect, has been neatly summarized in a recent introduction to his theory of language and of linguistics: "he was probably the first to provide detailed arguments from the nature of language to the nature of mind, rather than vice versa" (Smith & Wilson, 1979: 9).

Much of what was traditionally held to fall within the scope of the philosophy of mind – including epistemology – is now studied jointly, though often from different points of view, by both philosophers and psychologists. In so far as it is language that is being investigated, rather than some other faculty or mode of operation of the human mind, a whole new subdiscipline has developed in recent years called **psycholinguistics**. As the term implies, this can be seen as the intersection of psychology and linguistics, drawing equally upon both; it also draws, in its more theoretical aspects, upon work done in logic and the philosophy of language; and it links up, at one end, with **neurolinguistics** (the study of the neurological basis for language) and **cognitive science** (cf. 8.6) and, at the other, with **sociolinguistics**. The field of investigation is vast; and so far at least there is no generally accepted framework of assumptions within which it is possible to formulate a coherent interdisciplinary programme of research. Nevertheless, progress has been made in certain areas: notably in the study of speech-perception and language-acquisition. It is the purpose of this chapter to give a brief and non-technical account of the principal theoretical issues connected with the study of language and mind and to introduce the reader to some of the empirical work that has been done recently in the fields of neurolinguistics, language-acquisition and what has come to be called cognitive science.

But first a brief comment about the use of the word 'mind'. It is of course an everyday word of English. At the same time, it is a word which has long been employed to refer to the subject-matter of a particular branch of philosophy, on the one hand, and of psychology, on the other. Its sense, in everyday English, is narrower – being close to that of 'intellect', 'reason', 'understanding' and 'judgement' – than the more or less technical sense that it bears in the philosophy of mind and (for those psychologists who use the term) in psychology. In this latter, more technical, sense it covers not only man's reasoning faculty, but also his feelings, memory, emotions and will. This is an important point – the more so as there has been a tendency in recent work in theoretical linguistics and in the philosophy of language, as we shall see, to give too narrow an interpretation to 'mind' (and to 'mentalism').

It is also worth pointing out that the existence of the mind and its relation to the body which it inhabits, or with which it is in some way associated, constitute a long-standing and controversial philosophical problem. Of the several recognized attempts to formulate and, in some cases, to solve the so-called mind–body problem the following may be mentioned here: dualism, materialism, idealism and monism.

As a philosophical doctrine **dualism** is associated notably with Plato and Descartes. But, arguably, by virtue of its religious underpinning in the Christian tradition, it is also the tacitly accepted creed of the unreflecting European man-in-the-street. The dualist holds, not only that mind exists, but that it differs from matter in being non-physical. In the traditional Christian teaching, the mind is usually described as a faculty of the soul. For Plato and the Greeks, no clear distinction was drawn between the mind and the soul, the word 'psyche' covering both. Various theories have been put forward by dualists to account for the interdependence that appears to hold between bodily and mental phenomena.

Materialism, which is less common nowadays than it was in the late nineteenth and early twentieth centuries, holds that nothing exists but matter; that what are commonly regarded as mental phenomena are explicable, ultimately, in terms of the purely physical properties of material bodies. One version of materialism is **behaviourism**, according to which there is no such entity as the mind and such mentalistic terms as 'mind', 'thought', 'emotion', 'will' and 'desire' should be construed as referring to particular kinds of behaviour or, alternatively, as dispositions to behave in a particular way. It has already been noted that behaviourism was an important movement, not only in American psychology, but also, by virtue of Bloomfield's explicit espousal of it, in pre-Chomskyan American linguistics (cf. 7.4); it never had much impact on European linguistics, though it had some influence in philosophy (cf. Ryle, 1949).

As materialism denies the existence of mind, so **idealism** denies the existence of matter and holds that everything that exists is mental. An alternative term for 'idealism' is 'mentalism'. Recently, however, the term 'mentalism' has come to be used, especially by linguists, in an untraditional and rather confusing sense (cf. 8.2).

Finally, **monism**, in contrast with dualism, proclaims that reality is one. Both materialism and idealism can, therefore, be regarded as different versions of monism. However, it is more usual to reserve the term 'monism' for the view that neither the physical nor the mental is the ultimate reality: that they are both different aspects of something more neutral and more fundamental.

It is obviously impossible to convey the full import of a philosophical term by defining it in so general a manner as I have done here. Inadequate though they are from a philosophical point of view, the definitions just given will help us to evaluate some of the more recent work in linguistics, psychology and cognitive science that bears upon the investigation of what is traditionally referred to as language and mind.

8.2 *Mentalism, rationalism and innateness*

Chomsky and those who subscribe, with him, to the principles of generativism have claimed that language provides evidence for **mentalism**: i.e. for a belief in the existence of mind. This has been widely misunderstood. 'Mentalism' is often equated with either 'idealism' or 'dualism'. This is the sense in which Bloomfield used the term (cf. 7.4). But Chomsky and those who share his views are certainly not idealists, and not necessarily dualists. What they are saying is that the acquisition and use of language cannot be explained without making an appeal to principles which are currently beyond the scope of any purely physiological account of human beings. They are not committed to the view that the mind is some non-physical entity distinct from the brain or any other part of the body. On the other hand, they refuse to be bound by the methodological prejudices of those psychologists, notably the behaviourists, who insist that everything that is traditionally described as mental is the product of simple physical processes.

Chomskyan mentalism has both a negative and a positive aspect, the latter being more interesting, and more controversial, than the former. Its negative, or critical, aspect is its anti-physicalism or anti-materialism, and more particularly, in the context of what were previously dominant ideas in American linguistics and psychology, its anti-behaviourism. Behaviourism, as we have seen, is simply a particular version of materialism: one which restricts the subject-matter of psychology to human behaviour and sets out to explain all kinds of behaviour, including speech – thought being defined as internalized speech – on the basis of deterministic physiological and biochemical processes (cf. 7.4). It is possible to exaggerate the importance of behaviourism in Bloomfieldian and post-Bloomfieldian linguistics. But there is no doubt that it exerted a powerful influence in American psychology and that it discouraged many linguists from engaging in any serious work in semantics and from collaborating with psychologists and philosophers in the discussion of what is traditionally subsumed under the rubric of language and mind. There are more sophisticated versions of behaviourism, which may or may not be defensible. The kind of behaviourism advocated by Bloomfield, as well as that attacked by Chomsky in his famous review of B. F. Skinner's *Verbal Behavior* (1957), is, to say the least, unpromising. And Chomsky can take much of the credit for the fact that it has lost much of the support that it had, in linguistics and psychology, a generation ago.

What I have described as the negative aspect of mentalism should not be decried or underestimated. As we saw in an earlier chapter, linguists have been much concerned, in earlier decades of this century, with the status of linguistics as a science (cf. 2.2). Very often they have assumed that any discipline with scientific pretensions must necessarily model itself upon the so-called hard sciences, physics and chemistry. And this assumption has sometimes been coupled, as it was in the case of Bloomfield, with the philosophical doctrine known as **reductionism**: the doctrine that some sciences are more basic than others, in the sense that the theoretical concepts of a less basic science are to be defined, ultimately, in terms of the theoretical concepts of a more basic science. For example, given that physics is more basic than chemistry, chemistry more basic than biology, biology more basic than psychology, and so on, the reductionist would argue that the theoretical terms with which psychologists operate must be defined ultimately by biology, that the theoretical terms of biology must find their definition within chemistry, and so on.

It will be obvious how this view might be associated with materialism and with what is now widely regarded as an essentially nineteenth-century view of the physical sciences. Very few philosophers of science would nowadays wish to defend the doctrine of

reductionism. Nevertheless, there are many practitioners and
theorists of the social sciences who seem to feel, quite wrongly, that
there is something unscientific about the postulation of entities and
processes that cannot be described in physical terms. Thanks
largely to Chomsky, this feeling is now less common than it once
was among linguists; and linguistics is, in consequence, a richer and
more interesting discipline.

So much, then, for the critical, or negative, aspect of the reassertion of mentalism by Chomsky and those who have been influenced
by him in linguistics, psychology and philosophy. It is his positive
proposals which constitute both the most original and the most
controversial part of what I am calling Chomskyan mentalism. One
of the central problems in the philosophy of mind has to do with the
acquisition of knowledge, and more particularly with the part
played in this process by the mind, or reason, on the one hand, and
by the experience of the senses, on the other. Those who emphasize
the role of reason, as did Plato or Descartes, are traditionally
referred to as **rationalists**; those, such as Locke or Hume, who stress
the overriding importance of experience, or sense-data, are called
empiricists. Chomsky sides with the rationalists. Furthermore, he
takes the view – as most rationalists have done – that the principles
whereby the mind acquires knowledge are **innate**: that the mind is
not simply a blank slate ('tabula rasa' is the traditional Latin term)
upon which experience leaves its imprint, but should be thought of,
as Leibniz put it, on the analogy of a block of marble, which can be
hewn into several different shapes, but whose structure imposes
constraints upon the sculptor's creativity.

The acquisition of language is a particular instance of the more
general process of the acquisition of knowledge. At the same time,
that part of the acquisition of one's native language which consists
in learning the meaning of words has seemed to many to be an
integral part of the acquisition of all other kinds of knowledge. For
the acquisition of knowledge, according to the traditional view,
involves being made aware of concepts of which one was not previously aware; and there is clearly some kind of connection between
the discovery or formation of new concepts (on the assumption that
this is possible) and learning the meaning of words. Is the possession of the appropriate concepts a precondition of the acquisition

and correct use of the vocabulary of one's native language? Alternatively, is the connection between language and thought such that one cannot draw even a logical distinction between being in possession of a particular concept and knowing the meaning of some word which identifies and, as it were, stabilizes the concept for us? In view of such considerations it is hardly surprising that the acquisition of language has played a prominent role, throughout the centuries, in the debates between rationalists and empiricists.

Like his predecessors in the rationalist tradition, Chomsky takes the view that language serves for the expression of thought; that human beings are innately (i.e. genetically) endowed with the capacity to form some concepts rather than others; and that concept-formation is a precondition of one's acquisition of the meaning of words. But Chomsky's concern with language differs from that of his rationalist predecessors in two respects; and this is what makes his contribution to the philosophical discussion of this issue both original and important. First of all, he has made it clear that learning (or, to use the more neutral term, acquiring) the grammatical structure of one's native language stands as much in need of explanation as does the process of matching the meaning of a word with its form; and his formalization of different kinds of generative grammar has set new standards of precision for those who wish to evaluate the structural complexity of human languages in relation to other systems of communication (cf. 1.5). Second, he has argued that the nature of language and the process of language-acquisition are such that they are inexplicable otherwise than on the assumption that there is an innate language-acquisition faculty.

These two points are connected. As we saw earlier, Chomsky rests his case for the innateness and species-specificity of the language-faculty upon the universality of certain arbitrary formal properties of language-structure (cf. 7.4). These formal properties are commonly subsumed under the general heading of **structure-dependency** which, though it is perhaps also to be found in phonology and morphology, is most obviously characteristic of syntax. To say that a rule, or principle, is structure-dependent is to imply that the set or sequence of objects to which it applies has an internal structure and that the rule, or principle, makes essential reference to this structure as a condition of applicability or a determinant of its manner of application. For example, given that the sentences of a language have the kind of syntactic structure that is nowadays described by linguists in terms of the notion of constituency, they can be generated by means of a phrase-structure grammar, the rules of which are structure-dependent in the required sense (cf. 4.6). Furthermore, relations between corresponding sentences of different types (e.g. 'John wrote the book' and 'Did John write the book?'; 'John wrote the book', and 'Was the book written by John?'; etc.) can be made precise, with reference to the phrase-markers that formalize their phrase-structure (at a certain level of description), by means of transformational rules, which are more powerful than phrase-structure rules and involve a more complex notion of structure-dependency.

The technical details of structure-dependency and of its formalization by means of one kind of generative grammar or another do not concern us here. The point is that Chomsky's positive contribution to the philosophy of the mind, on the one hand, and to the psychology of language-acquisition, on the other, rests upon his recognition of the importance of structure-dependency as an apparently universal property of human languages and of the necessity of showing how children can come to acquire the mastery of this property in the acquisition and use of language. Chomsky's view is that what we call the mind can be best described in terms of a set of abstract structures whose physical basis is as yet relatively unknown, but which are like such bodily organs as the heart or the liver in that they mature according to a genetically determined programme of development in interaction with the environment. What we have been calling the language-faculty (in the sense in which the term 'faculty' is traditionally employed) is one of many such mental structures, each of which is highly specialized with respect to the function that it performs.

Is he right? The immediate, and totally unsatisfying, response to this question is that he may or may not be. The available evidence – from the investigation of language-acquisition; from case-studies of language-disorders of various kinds; from experiments with other primates, notably chimpanzees; from advances that are being made in our understanding of the neurophysiology of the brain; and from several other fields – does not seem to be conclusive. It is important to emphasize, however, that the stock of relevant evidence is continually increasing. It is not beyond the bounds of possibility that what has been conducted for centuries as a purely philosophical debate will eventually be settled by interdisciplinary empirical research. And 'empirical', it must be remembered, does not imply any commitment to empiricism!

Chomsky's particular version of mentalism is by no means the only kind of mentalism to have been developed in recent years and invoked with reference to language-acquisition. No less influential has been the theory of the Swiss psychologist, Piaget. According to Piaget, there are four stages in the development of the child's mental processes. Crucial for language-acquisition, in Piaget's view, is the transition from the **sensori-motor** stage, which lasts until the child is about two years old and during which he experiments with concrete objects in his environment, to the so-called **pre-operational** stage, which lasts until he reaches what was traditionally referred to as the age of reason (about seven years old) and during which he comes to manipulate words and phrases on the basis of his prior understanding of the way in which concrete objects can be compared, moved around and transformed. What many psycholinguists find attractive in Piaget's work is its obvious connections with functionalism (cf. 7.3) and also its attempt to account for language-acquisition in terms of more general principles of mental development. But, as we have seen, Chomsky has argued that the evidence does not support Piaget here: that syntactic structure in particular cannot be accounted for in functionalist terms; and that language-acquisition appears to be unaffected by differences in children's intellectual ability. It is only fair to add, however, that there are many linguists and psychologists who would say that this evidence, in both respects, is unclear.

Piaget's theory of mental development is usually thought of as falling between the traditional extremes of rationalism and empiricism. On the one hand, he stresses the importance of experience – and in particular sensori-motor experience; on the other, he takes the several stages of cognitive development to be species-specific and genetically preprogrammed (i.e. determined by what might be described, in a modern sense of the old rationalist term, as innate ideas). Similarly, though Chomsky calls himself a rationalist, he does not dispute the essential role of experience in the acquisition of knowledge; or, indeed, of what he is quite happy to identify (in terms more characteristic of empiricist, and even behaviourist, psychology) as the processes of triggering and shaping. Perhaps the most judicious concluding comment for this section should be that the traditional debate between rationalism and empiricism has been transformed by modern developments in genetics, neurophysiology and psychology to the point that it is no longer possible to use either of the two traditional terms, without extended qualification, in order to classify any currently defensible position on the issues that divide one group of philosophers or psychologists from another. This should be seen as progress. For it implies that current versions of what their authors themselves may describe, in a general way, as either empiricism or rationalism have to take account of a range of evidence that was not available to the great philosophers of the past. The originally very general issues that served to label, let us say, Descartes as a rationalist and Locke as an empiricist have been split into a variety of much more specific questions answerable to multi-disciplinary empirical research.

8.3 *Language and the brain*

No one these days, whatever might be his view of the celebrated mind–body problem (cf. 8.1), is likely to deny that, of all the bodily organs, it is the brain that plays the most significant role in the operations that we normally describe as mental.

The human brain is very complex; and the way in which it performs its various functions is only partly understood. But considerable progress has been made in recent years in this respect, and some of what is now known is relevant to the subject-matter of this chapter.

The brain – more particularly the **cerebrum** – is divided into two halves, or **hemispheres**, linked (in normal circumstances) by the **corpus callosum**. The outer layer of both hemispheres consists of grey matter – the **cortex** – containing something like 10^{10} neurons, or nerve cells; and these are interconnected by means of an equally numerous set of fibres in the white matter that lies below the cortex. The right hemisphere controls (and responds to signals from) the left side of the body, whereas the left hemisphere controls the right side. It is for this reason that brain damage or blood-clotting in one hemisphere may be accompanied by paralysis of the limbs on the opposite side of the body. And signals that are received on one side of the body – tactile, auditory or visual – must go first to the appropriate hemisphere before they are passed for processing to the other hemisphere along the corpus callosum. It follows that, if the corpus callosum is severed by means of surgery – this surgical technique was sometimes employed until quite recently, when its undesirable consequences were discovered, in the treatment of epilepsy – signals from the right side of the body can be processed only by the left hemisphere, and vice versa.

For well over a hundred years it has been known that there is a special relationship (for all those who are right-handed and for most, but not all, left-handers) between language and the left hemisphere, such that, speaking very generally, we can say that (for most people) language is controlled by the left hemisphere. The process whereby one hemisphere of the brain is specialized for the performance of certain functions is known as **lateralization**. (In the small minority of cases, among left-handers, in which the left hemisphere is not specialized for language, it is the right hemisphere that is: i.e. lateralization still takes place.) The process of lateralization is maturational, in the sense that it is genetically preprogrammed, but takes time to develop. There are, of course, many maturational processes of this kind in the biological development of all species. But lateralization appears to be specific to human beings. It is generally thought to begin when the child is about two years old and to be complete at some time between the age of five and the onset of puberty.

Lateralization for language is not the only kind of specialization of function that develops in human beings with respect to one hemisphere of the brain rather than another; and lateralization in general is commonly held to be an evolutionary precondition of man's development of superior intelligence. It is also a widely held view nowadays that lateralization is a precondition (both phylogenetically and ontogenetically) of the acquisition of language. In support of this view we may note the fact that language-acquisition begins at about the same time as lateralization does and is normally complete, as far as the essentials are concerned, by the time that the process of lateralization comes to an end. Further support comes from the fact that it becomes progressively more difficult to acquire language after the age at which lateralization is complete. In fact there seems to be what is frequently referred to as a **critical age** for language-acquisition in the sense that language will not be acquired at all, or at least not with full mastery of its resources, unless it is acquired by the time the child reaches the age in question.

Although the notion that there is a critical age for language-acquisition is not universally accepted, it gets some support from the striking, but sad, case of the young girl known in the literature as Genie. Genie was discovered by social workers in Los Angeles in 1970. At that time she was thirteen years old and had been brought up by her parents in total isolation from them and from others, being beaten whenever she made a noise, as well as being made the victim of virtually every other kind of emotional and sensory deprivation. One of the consequences, of course, was that she could not speak. Having been taken into care, she embarked upon the process of language-acquisition, under the guidance of psychologists and linguists, and at first made quite rapid progress. Furthermore, she went through the same stages in the acquisition of English as normal children do at the normal age. At first sight she would seem to have refuted the critical-age hypothesis. However, it is reported that, although her memory for vocabulary is very good and her general intellectual development is satisfactory, she has difficulty with all but the simplest aspects of the grammatical structure of English. It has been claimed, therefore, that Genie's case, not only confirms the critical-age hypothesis, but also the view that the language-acquisition faculty is independent of other intellectual abilities.

Until recently it was thought that, despite the genetic determinants of lateralization, there was sufficient plasticity, as it were, for the other hemisphere to take over the functions for which it would not normally be specialized – for example, in the event of brain damage or surgery – provided that the necessity for this arose before the end of the process of lateralization. However, it has now been suggested, on the basis of the more careful study of the language-behaviour of those whose left hemisphere had been removed in early childhood, that, although this is not immediately

apparent, they have difficulty with certain grammatical constructions.

So far we have been talking about the lateralization of language
at a very general level. It should now be mentioned – though we
cannot go into much detail – that different aspects of language-
processing appear to be more characteristic of the left hemisphere
than others. For example, the right hemisphere can interpret single
words denoting physical entities without difficulty; it is not so good
at the interpretation of grammatically complex phrases. Similarly,
though non-speech-sounds are processed directly and efficiently by
the right hemisphere, speech-sounds are generally passed to the left
hemisphere, which is more highly specialized for this purpose. It
may also be relevant that, whereas the left hemisphere is said to be
better at associative thinking and analytic reasoning, the right is
more efficient not only for visuo-spatial processing, but also for the
recognition of intonation-patterns and, interestingly enough, for
the interpretation of music. What this suggests is that language-
behaviour involves the integration of several neurophysiologically
distinct processes. Generally speaking, we can say that what one
would, on other grounds, recognize as the most distinctively linguistic part of language is associated with the left hemisphere (cf. 1.5).
It is this component perhaps which must be acquired, if it is acquired at all, before the critical age is reached; and it is this component perhaps which cannot be acquired by, let us say, chimpanzees
or other primates.

What has been said in this section is certainly consistent with the
Chomskyan hypothesis that the language-faculty is a uniquely
human and genetically transmitted capacity which is distinct from,
but operates in collaboration with, other mental faculties. It must be
emphasized, however, that the neurophysiological evidence is so
far relatively meagre (though it is being continually increased) and
that it is far from conclusive. Psychologists and philosophers are
therefore still divided on the question whether there is a genetically
transmitted language-faculty.

8.4   *Language-acquisition*

Let me start this section by making a purely terminological point.
Why do many psychologists and linguists nowadays prefer to talk

about the **acquisition**, rather than the learning, of language? The reason is simply that 'acquisition' is neutral with respect to some of the implications that have come to be associated with the term 'learning' in psychology. There are those who would say that, although 'acquisition' is more neutral than 'learning' in the relevant respects, it is still misleading, in that it implies coming to have something that one did not previously have. If language is innate, it is not acquired: it grows or matures naturally – or, as Chomsky might say, organically. However, 'acquisition' is now the standard term, and we shall continue to use it.

A further point must be made which is not purely terminological. What is commonly referred to as the acquisition of language manifests itself, in all normal circumstances, in the knowledge and use of particular languages. This is what was meant when it was said, in the very first section of this book, that one cannot possess (or use) language without possessing (or using) some particular language (cf. 1.1). Although this statement might well be challenged on philosophical grounds, it has now been reformulated in such a way (especially with the qualification 'in all normal circumstances') that it is surely correct. The term 'language-acquisition' can be interpreted as meaning either "the acquisition of language" or "the acquisition of a language". Even if we accept that there is some sense in which language (i.e. what Chomsky and others have called the language-faculty) is not acquired, we can reasonably assume that most, if not all, of the structure of English, French, Russian, etc., is acquired (though not necessarily learned) by those who come to use them as native speakers.

The term 'language-acquisition' is normally used without qualification for the process which results in the knowledge of one's native language (or native languages). It is conceivable that the acquisition of a foreign language, whether it is learned systematically at school or not, proceeds in a quite different way. Indeed, as we have seen, the acquisition of one's native language after the alleged 'critical age' for language-acquisition may differ, for neurophysiological reasons, from the normal child's acquisition of his native language (cf. 8.3). And it has been suggested recently, on the basis of clinical observations of brain-damaged bilinguals, that the acquisition of a second language, whether as an adult or as a child, has significant neurophysiological consequences. We must be cautious, therefore, in drawing conclusions of general import from the investigation of the monolingual child's acquisition of his native language in normal circumstances and applying them to the problem of foreign-language teaching. For example, there may or may not be arguments in favour of the so-called direct method of language-teaching in schools; but one argument that is commonly invoked – "that's the way you learned your native language" – is clearly invalid. In what follows we are concerned with language-acquisition in its normal sense.

Let us begin with a few facts – some of them matters of everyday observation; others, the result of painstaking research and experimentation. All normal children acquire the language that they hear spoken around them without special instruction. They start talking at roughly the same age and they go through the same stages of language-development. The progress that they make is, at times at least, so rapid that, as both parents and researchers have noted, it is hard to keep a comprehensive and systematic record of it. Furthermore, their progress is, on the whole, unaffected by differences of intelligence and by differences of social and cultural background.

Although I have just said that children start talking at roughly the same age, it is impossible to say of any child exactly when he has started to talk. First of all, it is not clear what should count as a criterion: the child's ability to use single words appropriately? his ability to construct two-word utterances by means of some productive and regular operation? – these are but two of the several possible criteria, and there is no reason to prefer the one to the other. A second reason is that the transition between one identifiable stage of language-development and another is gradual, rather than abrupt. Though we can recognize a fairly stable sequence of developmental stages – in the child's acquisition of the phonology, grammar and vocabulary of his native language – it may not make sense to think of the child as passing suddenly from one stage to another. There is the further complication that a child's production may not match his comprehension. In fact, it is generally agreed that comprehension always precedes production in the developmental sequence. It follows that a child's spontaneous utterances may not directly reflect his knowledge of the language that he is acquiring.

It is now known that babies in the first few days of postnatal life (if not earlier) are responsive, not only to the human voice as such, but to the difference between corresponding voiced and voiceless consonants. This is sometimes taken to be evidence of the child's innate knowledge of the allegedly universal distinctive features of phonology (cf. 3.5). However, it has recently been shown that very young chimpanzees are also able to respond to the same acoustic distinction. It is arguable, therefore, that, since chimpanzees do not develop speech and children do not make use of the phonetic distinction of voicing, either in comprehension or production, until something like the second year of life, it is not a species-specific phonological distinction, as such, that is innate. Rather it is an ability common to both human beings and the higher primates, but one which only human beings learn to invest with distinctive function by virtue of their exposure to languages in which it is functional. Once again, the evidence is as yet inconclusive. But this does not mean that the innateness and species-specificity issue is beyond the reach of empirical investigation. On the contrary, new evidence is being collected all the time. It is quite possible that this issue will soon be resolved.

In the first six months of postnatal life the child normally passes successively from crying to **cooing** and from cooing to **babbling**. There is little doubt that this developmental sequence is innately determined, since the sounds that are produced in crying and cooing, and in the earlier part of the babbling period, are unaffected by the linguistic environments in which the child is being brought up; and deaf children cry, coo and, initially at least, babble in the same way that hearing children do. Of particular interest is the fact that during the babbling period (which lasts until the average child is about twelve months) many speech-sounds may be produced which are not employed in the language of the child's environment and which he will have great difficulty in acquiring, should he later learn a foreign language. By the end of the babbling period most children will have acquired some of the intonation-patterns of their native language. There is no evidence, however, that the intonation-patterns superimposed upon a babbled utterance have a dis-

tinctive communicative function (though adults frequently interpret them as if they do). Though babbling clearly prepares the way,
in some sense, for speech, it is disputed whether it should be seen as
having this as its primary biological function.

When the child is about nine months old – it must not be forgotten
that we are talking about the average child: there is a considerable
range of variation in the ages of children at different stages of the
developmental sequence; and there is no reason to believe that this
variation correlates with the child's subsequent linguistic competence or with his general intellectual ability – he begins to show
evidence of having embarked upon the construction of the phonological system of his native language. In some cases babbling overlaps
for a considerable time with the process of acquiring and making
use of phonological distinctions; and the difference between babbling and talking is then quite apparent. Most of these phonological
distinctions will have been mastered by the time the child is five
years old. But some of the phonetically more difficult or, in the case
of prosodic structure, functionally more complex distinctions may
not be acquired until the child is much older. As far as the segmental
distinctions are concerned, there is a fairly well established sequence (which partially confirms Roman Jakobson's predictions of
almost forty years ago): for example for consonants, labials precede
dentals/alveolars and velars; stops precede fricatives; oral stops
precede nasals. There are also certain generalizations that can be
made about the combinatorial, or syntagmatic, dimension. Early
speech, regardless of the language to which the child is exposed,
consists of words that lack consonant clusters and tend to be redup-
licative (e.g. [dada], [kiki]), or to have consonants that share the
same place (or manner) of articulation (e.g. [gek], [giŋiŋ] for
English *leg* and *singing*). It must be emphasized, however, that the
child can often distinguish words in adult speech when he hears
them (e.g. *bad*, *bath*, and *back* in an accent of English in which
these words all have the same vowel) even though he may treat
them as homophones in his own speech.

As with phonology, so with grammar: there is evidence, in the
earliest stages at least, of a developmental sequence that is independent of the structure of the language of the child's environment.
First comes the so-called **holophrastic** period, during which the

child produces what are traditionally thought of as one-word sentences (hence the term 'holophrastic'). This may last from the age of about nine to eighteen months and is followed by the so-called **telegraphic** period, initiated by the production of two-word (or perhaps one should say, more neutrally, two-unit) utterances. The term 'telegraphic' derives from the observation that the child's speech throughout this period lacks inflections and what are often referred to as function words (e.g. prepositions, determiners and conjunctions) rather like the language of telegrams. As the child proceeds, during the telegraphic period, from the two-word stage to later stages characterized by the production of longer utterances, his speech will approximate more and more, in terms of word-order, etc., to that of adult speech. If the language that he is acquiring has inflections and so-called function words, he will also gradually come to use these appropriately, so that by the time that he is about four years old his speech, though still defective by comparison with that of adults, is no longer describable as telegraphic. It must be emphasized, however, that the impressionistic term 'telegraphic' has little descriptive value with reference to the acquisition of so-called isolating languages (e.g. Vietnamese), in which there is no morphological variation.

Until the early 1960s there had been little systematic investigation of the acquisition of grammatical structure. The situation changed dramatically with Chomsky's demonstration of the fact that languages are **rule-governed** (and most obviously so in respect of their grammar) and with the realization that existing theories of learning could not adequately account for the acquisition (and creative use) of rule-governed systems with the property of productivity. Throughout the 1960s psycholinguists were concerned almost exclusively with grammar in their study of child-language, but the balance of opinion has since shifted in favour of the view that it is impossible to study the child's developing grammatical competence in isolation from his general cognitive, emotional and social development.

The scope of child-language studies has now been broadened to cover, not only phonology, grammar and vocabulary, but also the semantic structure of utterances, their role in social interaction and their reflection of the child's beliefs about the world. It has also been extended longitudinally, as it were, in both directions. There is currently a good deal of research being carried out into the prelinguistic determinants of the acquisition of grammar in the crying, cooing and babbling stages of the developmental sequence. And it has now become clear that much of the grammatical structure of a language may not be properly mastered (even though the constructions produced by the child may not manifest the more obvious signs of ungrammaticality) until the child is about ten years old or older. This discovery of itself does not invalidate the innateness and species-specificity hypotheses or the associated hypothesis that the language-faculty is separate from man's other mental capacities. But it does complicate the argument.

It is because of its implications for the study of the nature of language in relation to the human mind that language-acquisition has been dealt with in the present chapter. There are of course more practical reasons for being concerned with this topic. Language-related disabilities of children – and, in many cases, of adults – cannot be properly diagnosed and treated by speech therapists except on the basis of a better understanding of both normal and abnormal language-acquisition. Teaching materials for primary-school children can be improved if they are geared, not only in vocabulary, but also in grammar, to the linguistic competence of the children for whom they are intended. Furthermore, in so far as the mental age of a child with which educators work is determined in part by language-related tests, it can be ascertained whether the tests in question are valid and reliable. It is especially important that teachers and all those concerned with the education of children should not, on the one hand, fail to spot the signs of partial deafness or of incipient dyslexia or, on the other, diagnose either mental retardation or a so-called language-deficit on the basis of unreliable evidence. Recent work in the study of language-acquisition has done a lot to make the evidence more reliable, though it may not have resolved, so far, any deep theoretical issues in either linguistics or psychology or in the philosophy of mind.

8.5 *Other areas of psycholinguistics*

Language-acquisition is not the only area of research within the field of psycholinguistics. And it is not the only area to have been revolutionized by the rise of Chomskyan generativism.

As we have seen, Chomsky's general theory of language rests upon his distinction between **competence** and **performance** (cf. 7.4). These terms were not used until the so-called standard theory of transformational grammar was developed in the mid-1960s. However, the distinction between the language-system conceived as a set of rules known to native speakers and the use of those rules in language-behaviour, though expressed in different terms, was clear enough from the outset. Its significance, not only for psycholinguistics, but for the study of human behaviour in general, was recognized, more or less immediately, by the eminent American psychologist George Miller, who generalized Chomsky's ideas and made them familiar to his colleagues (cf. Miller, Galanter & Pribram, 1960) and also collaborated with Chomsky in some of the early theoretical work on performance models. Miller's famous comment on the impact that Chomsky's work had made upon him, and subsequently upon many of his colleagues, is worth quoting at this point: "I now believe that mind is something other than a four-letter word."

Much of the early psycholinguistics research inspired by Chomskyan generativism was directed at the so-called **psychological reality** problem. Actually, this splits into two rather different problems in terms of Chomsky's distinction between competence and performance. (It will be recalled that a good deal of confusion has been caused by Chomsky's definition of 'performance' to include, not only actual behaviour, but also the non-linguistic knowledge, or competence, underlying that behaviour: cf. 7.4.) Do native speakers have in their minds, and thus, presumably, stored neurophysiologically in their brains, sets of rules of the kind that linguists formulate in their generative models of the language-system? To put it crudely (making use of what Chomsky himself refers to as a systematic ambiguity, by virtue of which we can use the term 'grammar' to refer both to the model and to that of which it is a model), have we all got a generative grammar in our heads? This is the first question. The second (which presupposes an affirmative answer to the first) is as follows: What role, if any, do these rules play in the production and comprehension of utterances?

Some of the earliest psycholinguistic research influenced by Chomskyan generativism was addressed to the second of these questions, and was based on the assumption (which Chomsky himself did not make) that all the rules required to generate a sentence were also employed by users of the language in performance – in the production and comprehension of utterances. (Apart from anything else, the distinction between sentences and utterances was not widely appreciated: cf. 5.5.) For example, it was demonstrated experimentally that native speakers reacted more quickly to active sentences than they did to passive sentences and more quickly to affirmative sentences than to negative sentences, and furthermore that the difference between the reaction times for active affirmative sentences and for passive negative sentences could be accounted for by adding together the differences for active and passive sentences, on the one hand, and for positive and negative sentences, on the other. At first this was interpreted as a rather dramatic confirmation of the hypothesis that the mental processing of sentences involved such rules as those of passive formation and negative insertion (formulated as transformational rules in the earliest version of Chomskyan generative grammar). Later it was realized that there were other potentially relevant variables; and when they were controlled for, in so far as they could be, the results were less clear-cut.

In fact, it became apparent in the course of the 1960s that, even if we do have a generative grammar of our native language in our heads, the structure of the linguist's model of that grammar is not likely to reflect the operations involved in language-processing. For the linguist deliberately sets aside all those factors which, though they obviously have a bearing on language-behaviour (limitations of attention and memory, motivation and interest, factual knowledge and ideological bias, etc.), are not directly relevant to the definition of well-formedness for particular languages and the formulation of general statements about the nature of language. Granted that generative grammars are psychologically real in the sense that we do have rule-systems stored neurophysiologically in our brain, it is reasonable to assume that, in the production and comprehension of utterances, other psychological rules or strategies are brought into play which enable us to by-pass some of the grammatical rules as such. It is in any case quite clear (e.g. from the rather trivial fact that we tend not to notice misprints and slips of the tongue) that language-comprehension is based upon sampling, rather than upon a complete processing of the input signal. Similarly, it is a matter of everyday observation, and can be demonstrated experimentally, that we start making predictions about the grammatical structure of utterances (not to mention their phonological structure and their meaning) as soon as our interlocutor starts speaking. Unless these predictions are contradicted – and we are not usually aware of them unless they are contradicted by other information in the signal that we happen to pick up in our sampling – there is no need for us to know everything about the linguistic structure of an utterance in order to understand it.

For these and other reasons the investigation of the so-called psychological reality problem has turned out to be far more complex than it seemed to be to many psychologists in the 1960s. It should also be mentioned that, although Chomsky himself still holds to the view that so far linguists should continue to set aside what is known about psychological mechanisms and processes in their definition of linguistic competence, there are several generative grammarians who disagree with him. At the present time, the movement in favour of what is called psychologically real grammar appears to be gaining strength. Whatever view is taken of the psychological reality problem – in either of its two interpretations – and of its relevance for linguistics, there can be no doubt that the psychological investigation of language-storage and language-processing has made considerable progress in recent years under the influence of Chomskyan generativism. Many of the experimental results, having to do with perceptual strategies, the role of short-term memory, the interpretation of ambiguous utterances, etc., retain their validity, even though the particular hypotheses that the experiments were designed to test (e.g. the hypothesis that utterances are processed on two levels of analysis, deep structure and surface structure) may have been abandoned. What made Chomsky's theory of language-structure so attractive to psychologists in the first place was the fact that it did yield experimentally testable hypotheses.

Needless to say, the theory itself is by no means invulnerable from a more narrow linguistic viewpoint. Also, there are philosophical reasons for calling into question, if not for rejecting, the

Chomskyan use of the term 'knowledge' in relation to linguistic competence. It has been argued that competence (i.e. the know-how that manifests itself in behaviour) is different from the kind of knowledge that is describable as true belief. More generally, it could be argued that Chomsky's theory of mind is excessively intellectualist, in that, unlike traditional views of the structure of the mind, it says nothing about the non-cognitive faculties: the emotions and the will. Chomsky himself has on several occasions defended himself against philosophical criticisms of this kind.

Although psycholinguistic research has been strongly influenced by generativism in recent years, it would be a mistake to suppose that all psychologists working on language have been concerned with the validity of this or that generative model of the language-system. Research has continued on many of the traditionally recognized topics in the psychology of language – language and thought, language and memory, etc. – within the framework of theories which do not operate with the distinction of competence and performance or are neutral with respect to its specifically Chomskyan formulation.

As far as the question of language and thought is concerned, Chomsky, as we have seen, adopts the traditional view, characteristic of the seventeenth-century rationalists, that language serves for the expression of pre-existing, full articulate thought. This view had been challenged in the eighteenth century by the French philosophers Condillac (1746) and Rousseau (1755) and somewhat later, in his famous essay on the origin of language, by the German scholar Herder (1772). Herder, in particular, took the view that language and thought had evolved together, the one being inseparable from the other, and that, in so far as the national languages of mankind differed in vocabulary and grammatical structure, they both determined and reflected national patterns of thought. There is a straight line of development, as we shall see later, from Herder, to Sapir and Whorf, who popularized essentially the same theses of linguistic determination and linguistic relativity in twentieth-century America (cf. 10.2). All that needs to be mentioned here is the fact that the so-called Whorfian hypothesis has been the subject of a certain amount of experimental research and that the results obtained are consistent with the weaker version of the hypothesis, according to which the language that one speaks influences, though it does not determine, thought.

8.6 *Cognitive science and artificial intelligence*

The principal reason for including a separate, though very short, section on **cognitive science** and **artificial intelligence** is to draw attention to what is now a recognizably distinct and expanding discipline, which draws upon philosophy, psychology and linguistics, and computer science, but cannot be classified under any one of them. The terms 'cognitive science' and 'artificial intelligence' are both somewhat misleading, in that they appear to restrict the scope of the field to the study of those mental processes which would be traditionally ascribed to the reasoning faculty; and 'cognitive science' gives no indication of what is distinctive about the approach to the study of the mind and mental processes that is followed in this new discipline. Provided that we give a broad enough interpretation to 'intelligence' we can say, following Minsky (1968: v), a prominent theorist and practitioner in the field, that what we are concerned with is "the science of making machines do things that would require intelligence if done by men". One such thing, obviously, is the production and comprehension of language.

But why should we want to try to make a machine – more particularly, a general purpose computer with an appropriate program – produce and understand language? There are, of course, many practical reasons, involving the total or partial automation of operations which at present demand many man-hours of highly skilled work: the translation of documents from one language to another; the retrieval of information from libraries; the diagnosis of illness on the basis of systematic questioning; and so on. Important though these practical applications are, they presuppose the solution of many theoretical problems that are so far unsolved. It is the theoretical problems that concern us here, and more especially the contribution that cognitive science and artificial intelligence can make to our understanding of the mental processes involved in the use of language.

But first a word of warning. Even if one were to succeed in making a computer do everything that is currently ascribed to mental processes when done by man, this would not mean that man is no more than a machine. Without its program a computer can do nothing that is of any interest to us in the present connection. It is the program, rather than the hardware, that is responsible for the computer's ability to simulate intelligent behaviour. There are those who would maintain that the program stands in much the same relation to the computer as the mind does to the brain, and that by thinking of the living human brain as a programmed special-purpose computer we can circumvent, if not solve, the traditional mind–body problem. However this may be, it must be emphasized that artificial intelligence is of itself neutral with respect to the opposition between dualism and monism, on the one hand, and between materialism and idealism, on the other. And it makes no assault on human dignity or the freedom of the will.

One of the first and most salutary lessons that comes from the attempt to write even the simplest computer program is the realization that little if anything is simple, when every step has to be prescribed in detail. We gain a new respect for the largely hidden complexity of our own everyday mental processes, including those involved in the production and comprehension of language-utterances. More important, we find our attention drawn to factors which we might otherwise take for granted because (to use the language of computer science) they are wired into our hardware or preprogrammed as genetically determined subroutines. So far, the simulation of language-processing by means of computers has not had a decisive impact upon the development of linguistic or psycho-linguistic theory. But it has influenced much of the discussion of the psychological reality problem referred to in the previous section by providing at least some measure of the complexity of different language-processing operations and of the time that it might take to perform them.

Much of the significance that we attach to cognitive science and artificial intelligence will depend upon our attitude to the explanatory role of models in the natural and social sciences. A model may successfully simulate the behaviour of a physical system, an organism or a social institution in certain respects without necessarily having the internal structure of the entity of which it is a model. On the other hand, the more complex the behaviour and the more diverse the points of contact between the model and what is known of the entity that is being modelled, the more confident we can be that they are in structural correspondence. By this criterion, any success that we have in the simulation of language-processing by computer, on the basis of what psychology can tell us about memory, perceptual strategies, reaction times, etc., and what linguists can say about linguistic structure, is bound to increase our understanding of language and mind. Whether it will ever be possible to simulate by computer all the mental processes involved in the production and comprehension of language is uncertain.

FURTHER READING

For the philosophical background: Edwards (1967) on 'Mind–body problem', 'Idealism', 'Materialism', etc.

For psycholinguistics as such: Aitchison (1976); Greene (1972); Slobin (1971) – which are all elementary and complement one another in various ways. More comprehensive is Clark & Clark (1977). Readers include Jakobovits & Miron (1967); Johnson-Laird & Wason (1977); Oldfield & Marshall (1968).

On language and the brain, aphasia, neurolinguistics, see Akmajian, Demers & Harnish (1979), chapter 13 and Fry (1977), chapter 9 for brief elementary surveys. Much of the relevant information is given, nontechnically, in Blakemore (1977).

On language-acquisition, Villiers & Villiers (1979) may be recommended as a brief, inexpensive and very readable introduction to the field. See also Donaldson (1978). Textbooks (in addition to more general textbooks of psycholinguistics) include Dale (1976); Elliot (1981); McNeill (1970). Crystal (1976) gives a non-technical account of the theoretical issues and main findings with particular reference to the needs of teachers and speech-therapists. The most comprehensive, authoritative and up-to-date survey of theory and research is Fletcher & Garman (1979).

On Chomsky's influence in philosophy and psychology: Greene (1972); Lyons (1977a), chapters 9–10; and, in addition to the works cited above for psycholinguistics and in Chapter 7 for generativism, Hacking (1975); Harman (1974); Hook (1969). On Chomsky in relation to Piaget, see Piattelli-Palmarini (1979).

On cognitive science and artificial intelligence, cf. Bobrow & Collins (1975); Boden (1977), Part 3; Charniak & Wilks (1976); Fodor (1975); Minsky (1968); Ritchie (1980); Sloman (1978); Wilks (1972); Winograd (1972).

QUESTIONS AND EXERCISES

1. "Knowledge of language results from the interplay of initially given

structures of mind, maturational processes, and interaction with the environment" (Chomsky, 1972b: 26). Discuss.

2. In what respects does Chomskyan **mentalism** differ from more traditional doctrines to which the same term is applied?

3. Explain what is meant by **lateralization** with particular reference to language-acquisition and language-processing.

4. What evidence is there for the view that there is a **critical period** for language-acquisition?

5. What is **aphasia**? Give a non-technical account of the symptoms of the most common kinds of aphasia. What do they tell us about the neuro-anatomical basis for speech and language?

6. "The language acquisition device plays two roles in Chomskyan theory: first, it accounts for the striking similarities among human languages, even those which, as far as is known, are historically and geographically unrelated . . . The second role of the language acquisition device is in accounting for the speed, ease and regularity with which children learn their first language . . ." (Smith & Wilson, 1979, 249–51). Discuss.

7. To what extent is linguistic development dependent on cognitive development? Compare the views of Chomsky and Piaget on this question.

8. Explain why the young child's apparent retrogression from saying *came*, *went*, etc., to *comed*, *goed*, etc., should be seen as evidence of normal progress in language-acquisition.

9. What role does parental reinforcement by means of rewards and punishment play in the acquisition of language by children?

10. "even in non-Western societies in which older siblings provide a great deal of the child care, the young child receives a simplified language input" (Villiers & Villiers, 1979: 99). Discuss the role of so-called **motherese** in child language-acquisition.

11. Can you supply a plausible explanation for the use of so-called **telegraphic speech** by young children?

12. Psycholinguists frequently talk about the **mental lexicon**. What do they mean? How do they go about studying it?

13. What can we learn about the storage and processing of language from the study of slips of the tongue?

14. Cite and evaluate some of the experimental evidence bearing upon the **psychological reality** of generative grammars.

15. What can the linguist and the psychologist hope to learn about language from research in **cognitive science** and **artificial intelligence**?

9
Language and society

9.1 *Sociolinguistics, ethnolinguistics and psycholinguistics*

So far there is no generally accepted theoretical framework within which language can be studied, macrolinguistically, from several different, equally interesting, points of view: social, cultural, psychological, biological, etc. (cf. 2.1). Furthermore it is doubtful, to say the least, whether any such general theoretical framework will ever be constructed. It is important to keep this in mind.

Few linguists today would subscribe to the positivistic principles of reductionism in the form in which Bloomfield and his fellow-members of the Unity of Science movement did half-a-century ago (cf. 2.2). But there are many linguists who advocate a more limited kind of reductionism, giving priority to the links between linguistics and one, rather than another, of the several disciplines concerned with language. Some, like Chomsky and the generativists, will emphasize the points of contact between linguistics and cognitive psychology; others will tell us that, since language is a socially maintained and socially functioning institution, there is ultimately no distinction to be drawn between linguistics and either sociology or social anthropology. It is natural for one group of scholars, by virtue of their bent of mind, training or special interests, to adopt one of these two points of view in preference to the other. What must be condemned is the tendency for those who do adopt a particular point of view on this question to put it forward as the only one that is scientifically justifiable. There are now several recognized branches of macrolinguistics – psycholinguistics, sociolinguistics, ethnolinguistics, etc. – which are all interdisciplinary in that, as currently practised, they involve the use of techniques and theoretical concepts coming from two or more disciplines. Despite statements to the contrary in some of the more doctrinaire introductory textbooks, linguistics is no closer to any one of the disciplines with

which it collaborates in interdisciplinary macrolinguistic research
than it is to any other.

Not only is there no generally accepted, unified theoretical
framework within which all the disciplines that deal with language
can be satisfactorily interrelated. Many of these disciplines are
engaged in demarcation disputes among themselves and have
their own internal controversies: What is the difference between
sociology and anthropology? How is cognitive psychology to
be integrated with social psychology? Questions of this kind
inevitably affect one's conception of such interdisciplinary areas as
sociolinguistics, ethnolinguistics and psycholinguistics. It is not
surprising, therefore, that there should be differences of opinion as
to the way in which one or other of these areas should be defined
and circumscribed, and that the currently available textbooks
should reflect these differences.

On the broadest definition of **sociolinguistics** (which many
specialists would reject precisely because it is so broad) we can say that
it is "the study of language in relation to society" (cf. Hudson, 1980:
1). In similar vein we can define **ethnolinguistics** as the study of
language in relation to culture – taking 'culture' in the sense in
which it is used in anthropology and more generally in the social
sciences (cf. 10.1). But culture, in this sense, presupposes society;
and society in turn depends upon culture. It follows that, on the
broadest definitions of 'sociolinguistics' and 'ethnolinguistics', the
two branches of macrolinguistics that they refer to will overlap to a
very considerable extent. Each of the branches is more narrowly
circumscribed by adding to the definitions the condition that the
aims guiding theory and research should be primarily linguistic,
rather than sociological, anthropological, psychological, etc.: that
they should relate primarily to the question "What is language?"
(cf. 1.1). But this additional condition does not significantly reduce
the degree of overlap.

From what has just been said it will be clear that the division of
material between this chapter and the next is somewhat arbitrary.
Neither chapter would in any case claim to be comprehensive in its
treatment of the field that it covers. What I have done is to take a
few of the topics that have been discussed and investigated recently
and to distribute them according to whether they relate primarily to

the structure of societies or to their beliefs and practices. In the nature of things this cannot but be, at times, a rather artificial distinction.

Even the distinction between psycholinguistics, on the one hand, and either sociolinguistics or ethnolinguistics, on the other, can cause problems – the more so if **psycholinguistics** is defined broadly as the study of language and mind. And much of what is currently handled under other branches of macrolinguistics would have been classified as psycholinguistics twenty years ago. There are fashions in these matters as in everything else. It is currently fashionable, for example, for psycholinguists to be more interested in what is biologically determined and universal than they are in socially and culturally determined variation. Sociolinguists, on the other hand, tend to be very much concerned with language-variation. But this difference of attitude and emphasis should not be taken as criterial in the definition of either 'psycholinguistics' or 'sociolinguistics'. There is no reason, in principle, why psycholinguists should not be interested in the diversity and variability of human language; or conversely why sociolinguists should not be concerned with linguistic and social universals. In the preceding chapter on language and mind, little was said about the social and cultural, as distinct from the biological, determinants of language-structure. It was noted, however, that there has been some psycholinguistic research done on the so-called Whorfian, or Sapir–Whorf, hypothesis (cf. 8.5). This will be dealt with in more detail in Chapter 10 under 'Language and culture'. It would fall just as naturally, however, under the rubric of 'Language and mind'.

9.2 *Accent, dialect and idiolect*

The dimension of language-variation that is accounted for in terms of the scale language–dialect–idiolect was introduced earlier in connection with the fiction of homogeneity (cf. 1.6). So too was the distinction between accents and dialects. In this section we are concerned with the social significance of this kind of language-variation.

The most obvious difference between the terms 'accent' and 'dialect' is that the former is restricted to varieties of pronunciation, whereas the latter also covers differences of grammar and vocabulary. In everyday usage, they are often confused. For example, someone speaking Standard English with what is popularly described as a broad regional accent might well be said to be speaking in dialect. The phrase 'in dialect' is being employed here, as it is commonly by non-linguists, to mean "in a dialect other than Standard English". The phrase 'with an accent' is similarly employed in Great Britain, and especially in England, to mean "with an accent other than RP" (cf. 3.2) or, alternatively, "with an accent other than the one I am accustomed to". Everyone speaks in one dialect or another, just as everyone speaks with one accent or another. It is quite possible for different people to speak the same dialect with strikingly different accents. Very often, terms like 'Cockney', 'Geordie' (the speech of Newcastle and Tyneside) and 'Scouse' (the speech of Liverpool) are used with reference to those whose dialect, in grammar and vocabulary, is for all practical intents and purposes classifiable as Standard English. We shall look at the social significance of the distinction between standard and non-standard dialects presently (cf. 9.3). What must be emphasized here is the importance of not confusing, say, 'RP' and 'Standard English' (in the way that they tend to be confused in the use of everyday expressions like 'The Queen's English' or 'BBC English') when one is describing the speech of inhabitants of Great Britain, and more particularly of England.

It is also worth pointing out that terms like 'British English' and 'American English' are often loosely employed, even by linguists, as if they referred to two relatively uniform dialects of the same language. There are of course many lexical differences between the speech of the average well-educated American and that of the average well-educated Englishman, Welshman, Scot or Irishman: 'elevator' vs. 'lift', 'gas' vs. 'petrol', etc. But most of the vocabulary of Standard American English and, in so far as there is such a thing, of Standard British English, is identical. So too is the grammatical structure, although there are constructions or forms of words that are characteristically American (*It is important that you not come*; *gotten*; etc.) or characteristically British (*in hospital*; *between you and I*; *move house*; etc.). But such constructions and forms are not numerous as far as the standard dialects of the two countries are concerned, and some of them are not used in all parts of either America or Great Britain.

   The term 'British English' is also misleading in a way that 'American English' (or 'Australian English', 'Indian English', 'Caribbean English', etc.) is not. What is usually meant by 'American English' is "Standard English as spoken (and written) in the United States". Most authors who use the term 'British English', however, tacitly restrict it to mean "Standard English as spoken (and written) in England". There are, of course, good sociopolitical reasons for doing so, since this was the version of Standard English that served the purposes of administration and education throughout the British Empire. The term 'British English' is nevertheless misleading in that it can conceal the fact that Scottish English and Irish English stand in much the same relation to the English of England as American English does. And both of them differ from British English, in the sense that is customarily given to the term, more than does, for example, Australian or Indian English. Indeed, it would be more reasonable to classify Australian English or Indian English under 'British English' than it is so to classify Scottish English and Irish English. Looked at from a fairly general point of view, of course, they can all be seen as being but slightly different variants of the same dialect. Compared with many languages spoken over a wide area, English is quite highly standardized, as far as grammar and vocabulary are concerned (9.3).

   As we saw earlier, two language-systems are the same (regardless of the medium in which they are manifest) if and only if they are isomorphic (cf. 2.6). It is because phonologically identical language-systems can be realized differently in the phonic medium, that it makes sense to talk of the same dialect of a language being pronounced with one accent rather than another (cf. 3.4). For 'accent' covers all kinds of phonetic variation, including that which is subphonemic in the sense that it is never made the basis of functional contrast, as this notion is usually applied by phonologists. For example, the presence or absence of the phonetic distinction between the so-called dark (i.e. velarized: cf. 3.3) and clear (non-velarized) allophones of the phoneme /l/ in English is functionally irrelevant in the narrow sense of 'functional'. It is certainly relevant to the identification of a person's accent. So too is the particular quality of the allophone that occurs in certain positions: the degree of velarization serves, with associated phonetic differences, to distinguish the accent of Bristol and South-West England from that of many other regions (cf. Hughes & Trudgill, 1979). To take another example: there is a quite noticeable degree of nasality in the pronunciation of vowels, in certain positions, in many American accents, and this is one of several clues (including other differences of vowel-quality, not to mention prosodic differences: cf. 3.5) which serve to distinguish most Americans from non-Americans by their accent. Once again, this is non-functional in the narrow sense.

But there are other differences of accent which can affect the identification of forms. For example, the phonemic difference that is exemplified, in many accents of English including RP, by the vowel-contrast of *put* : *putt*, *could* : *cud*, *butcher* : *butter*, etc., is not found in accents of the North and Midlands of England. Consequently, there are forms – notably the infinitive, the simple present tense and the present participle of 'put' and 'putt' – that are distinguished in RP, but not in a typical Northern or Midlands pronunciation. Differences of context (including those which derive from the syntactic differences between 'put' and 'putt') usually make it clear, as they do also in written English, whether *putting* is a form of 'put' or of 'putt'. Nevertheless, we here have a difference of accent, which correlates with a difference of dialect: the underlying language-systems are not isomorphic at the phonological level.

The terms 'accent' and 'dialect' are not, therefore, complementary, as might have been suggested by our earlier discussion of the possibility of speaking the same dialect – and in particular Standard English – with one accent rather than another. What is essentially a uniform dialect, as far as grammar and vocabulary is concerned, can be associated with several more or less different phonological systems. And this is the situation with Standard English. For example, the vowel systems of the various accents of Scottish English and Irish English are far from being isomorphic, in terms of the criterion of functional contrast, with RP or any other English accent.

What makes the notion of accent so important sociolinguistically, even though it overlaps with that of dialect, is that members of a language-community often react to subphonemic and phonemic differences of pronunciation in the same way as indicators of the speaker's regional or social provenance. To the extent that they do so, whether consciously or not, the so-called subphonemic differences can be said to be socially, if not descriptively, meaningful (cf. 5.1). Contrary to what many linguists have said, native speakers of a language do not necessarily fail to notice purely allophonic variation. For example, the pronunciation of a glottal stop between vowels as an allophone of /t/, which is a characteristic of many urban accents of England and Scotland (including those of London, Manchester and Glasgow), is as obvious to most speakers of English as is so-called aitch-dropping at the beginning of words. The occurrence of a glottal stop in other positions, however, may not be so obvious.

The point is that certain phonetic differences between accents may be stigmatized by society, just as certain lexical and grammatical differences between dialects are. Parents and teachers often try to eliminate what they regard as markers of lower social status or as regionalisms. Even if they do not succeed, they will have played their part in the perpetuation of the belief in the language-community at large that such and such a pronunciation is an indicator of social or educational inferiority, and this has the effect of heightening most people's sensitivity to it. Among the many differences of accent, to most of which members of a language-community respond globally, without necessarily being aware of what precisely it is in another person's speech that makes it different from their own, there may be some which are particularly significant and which they have no difficulty in identifying. In England dropped aitches and intervocalic glottal stops fall into this category, especially for those who aspire to higher social status than they feel would otherwise be ascribed to them. The absence of [r] before consonants in forms like *farm, farther*, etc., is stigmatized for similar reasons in New York, but not in New England – and not of course in England, where it is a characteristic feature of RP.

All this has long been familiar to linguists, and to any reasonably observant and intelligent layman. So too has been the fact that, in many countries, but to a particularly high degree in England, there is more regional variation in the speech of those lower on the social scale than there is in the speech of those who are higher up. It has been estimated that no more than 3 per cent of the population of

England speak with an RP accent, which gives no indication at all of the speaker's regional origins and is the product, in most cases, of a public school education. A much larger percentage of the population has an accent which approximates to RP in many criterial respects (the pronunciation of *bath*, etc.), but also contains indicators of the speaker's geographical origins. Recent sociolinguistic work has confirmed that this is so, and also that, in the vast majority of instances, the lower one is on the social scale (in terms of education, income, profession, etc.), the more one's accent will differ from RP and the more regionally marked it will be.

However, something far more interesting has also been discovered by means of survey-techniques first used by William Labov in America. This is that an individual's accent and dialect varies systematically with the formality and informality of the situation in which he finds himself. For example, New Yorkers cannot be classified simply in terms of whether they do or do not put an [r] before consonants in *farm*, *farther*, etc. Most middle-class New Yorkers have both pronunciations. Generally speaking, the higher one's social status, the greater will be the incidence of forms with a preconsonantal [r] in one's informal and relatively uncontrolled speech. When it comes to more formal situations, however, it has been found that speakers from the lower middle class have a higher incidence of preconsonantal [r] than do speakers from the upper middle class. This has been plausibly interpreted as being due to the greater sensitivity of the socially less secure and socially more ambitious. Broadly similar conclusions have been reached in the sociolinguistic investigation of accent and dialect in Great Britain (cf. Trudgill, 1978). Of particular interest is the finding that, both in America and in Britain, women are more likely than men to adopt the accent or dialect that is associated, in general, with higher social status.

There are various reasons why women might be, linguistically and otherwise, more norm-conscious and more status-conscious than men in modern Western societies. Among those that have been advanced and find some empirical support as far as the use of RP in England is concerned is the fact that, whereas the maintenance of a local accent is associated with virility and in-group loyalties for many Northern working-class men, the use of RP by Northern women leads to their being favourably rated by others on a number of evaluative dimensions, some of which are normally associated with masculinity (professional competence, persuasiveness, etc.) and others with femininity. Whether or not this is the primary causal factor in the differentiation of men's and women's speech with respect to what is, in general, socially prestigious, there is no doubt that sex is one of the principal sociolinguistically relevant variables in all languages. And there are many well-documented cases of sex-related dialect differences in the literature, which do not necessarily reflect the same attitudes towards social status or male and female roles as do the sex-related differences that exist in our own society. The relation between language-variation and its social correlates is such that broad generalizations in terms of variables like sex, age and social class soon give way, in particular instances, to more detailed and more interesting statements which make reference to the structure of different societies and to the attitudes (i.e. to the culture) of their members.

From what has been said in this section it will be clear that the notion of the **idiolect** is less useful than it might appear to be at first sight. Not only is it the case, as was mentioned earlier, that individuals may modify and extend their idiolects throughout life, though less readily, no doubt, as they get older (cf. 1.6). More important is the fact that, as we have just seen, an individual may have several dialect variants in his repertory and switch from one to the other according to the situation in which he finds himself. From a sociolinguistic viewpoint at least, it is much more useful to think of an individual as having in his linguistic competence the mastery of a set of partly isomorphic dialects, each of which he shares with fellow-members of one social group or another, than it is to think of what are normally called dialects as being sets of overlapping idiolects. Language-variation in the individual and language-variation in the community are two sides of the same coin.

The point that has just been made is relevant to what was said about expressive and social meaning in the chapter on semantics: that they merge into one another and are interdependent (cf. 5.1). In so far as we express our personality and individuality in our language-behaviour, we do so in terms of the social categories that are encoded, as it were, in language-variation in the community of which we are members. Furthermore, the social meaning that is assigned to the variables of accent and dialect is determined, for the most part, by what are called **stereotypes**. We may associate a particular accent or dialect – not to mention voice-quality, regardless of the fact that voice-quality is in part determined by purely anatomical factors – with a particular personality trait (e.g. intelligence, friendliness, virility) and, in most of our more superficial day-to-day dealings with people, judge them with reference to the stereotype. It has been demonstrated that members of a particular social group will react either positively or negatively to certain accents and dialects and, without seeing or knowing anything about the speaker, make judgements about his personality from his voice. Particularly interesting is the finding that one does not necessarily evaluate the accent or dialect characteristics of one's own social group more favourably on all dimensions of personality and character than that of a recognizably different social group. In some cases at least, members of a lower social group seem to accept the validity of the stereotype with reference to which members of socially more dominant groups evaluate them.

The implications for education and career prospects of this kind of linguistic prejudice – in so far as it is rightly called prejudice (cf. Hudson, 1980: 195) – are obvious enough. We shall return to this aspect of the question later (cf. 9.5). What should also be emphasized, however, is the more general point, that personality is, of its very nature, a social phenomenon. What we call personality is, in part at least, the product of **socialization** – the process whereby we are made members of a particular society and participants in the culture that characterizes it. And what we call self-expression is the projection of one socially interpretable image or another. It is for this reason that expressive and social meaning, both in language and in other kinds of communicative behaviour, are ultimately undistinguishable. As we have seen in this section, differences of accent and dialect can play an important role in the projection of particular social images. The point has been made with reference to English. But it holds true more generally. As we shall see later, English – partly because it is so highly standardized and partly because it is spoken as a native language in many parts of the world and also functions as the principal international language – is highly untypical, in many respects, as a specimen of human languages. Dialect-variation in India, for example, is a very different matter (cf. Burling, 1970: 103ff). However, due allowance being made for differences of social structure (e.g. for the importance of caste in Indian society), what has been said here about the social significance of differences of dialect would seem to be true of India and of all countries in which there is an appreciable degree of dialect-variation.

9.3 *Standards and vernaculars*

When the distinction between languages and dialects was first discussed in this book, I said that, although from a historical point of view the standard dialect of a language (if it has one) is no different in kind from related non-standard dialects, there are social and cultural reasons for taking a different view in the synchronic description of languages (cf. 1.6). It is now time to introduce the necessary qualifications to the statement often made by linguists, that all dialects are equal. For convenience, I will employ the term 'vernacular' in the sense that it commonly bears in everyday usage to refer, not only to non-standard dialects of the same language, but also to genetically unrelated dialects which stand in the same functional relationship to the standard in certain countries as genetically related non-standard dialects do in others. Some sociolinguists have used the term 'vernacular' in a narrower and more technical sense.

The standardization of a particular dialect in relation to one or more vernaculars is not necessarily the result of deliberate policy. For example, Standard English emerged as such over the centuries by virtue of the political and cultural importance of London; and Standard French emerged, in similar manner, as a consequence of the dominance of Paris. In each case, the standard is based upon what was in earlier times the speech of the upper classes at court or living in the capital. This is not to say that the standardization of English and French was not in part a matter of deliberate intervention. The Académie Française, founded by Richelieu in 1635, was but one of many such bodies established in Europe in the post-Renaissance period and entrusted with the task of standardizing the national literary language by compiling authoritative grammars and dictionaries; and it performs this task to this day. There is no comparable body in the English-speaking countries, so that the question whether something is or is not a feature of Standard English cannot be answered quite so readily. Nevertheless, various institutions, including the schools, universities and printing houses, influenced by the prescriptive grammarians of the eighteenth century and their successors, have played a quasi-official role in Great Britain, the United States and elsewhere very similar to that played officially by literary academies in France and many other European countries. However, for political reasons, French and English are more highly standardized, as written languages, than some of the other major languages of Europe. For example, the political unification of Italy is of relatively recent date; and there are several centres of cultural prestige, each of which still has its own somewhat different literary standard.

In all these cases, it will be noted, the written language tends to be more highly standardized than is the speech of those who use it. However, given the existence of an accepted standard for the written language, this can serve as a model of propriety and correctness for the speech of the literate in any society in which mastery of the written language brings prestige or the possibility of social advancement. The literary languages of Europe, which originated in most cases as vernaculars in relation to Latin, have for centuries exercised their own standardizing influence on the spoken dialects of the educated, and indirectly on the vernaculars in relation to which they have served as standards. This influence is at its strongest in respect of the more formal styles of speech. Consequently, what we mean when we say that someone speaks Standard English or Standard French is that the dialect that he uses in formal situations is more or less identical, in grammar and vocabulary, with the written standard. In more informal situations, however, he may well use a locally based or socially more restricted vernacular. As we shall see later, the difference between the standard and the vernacular is in many societies so sharp that their functional differentiation, whether they are dialects of the same language or not, has been classified in the recent sociolinguistic literature as a distinctive kind of bilingualism: **diglossia** (cf. 9.4).

There are obvious advantages in the standardization of one particular dialect for official purposes, especially in a modern democratic state that sets itself the ideal of universal literacy. English and French, as we have seen, were standardized over a long period of time and, in large measure, by what we may think of as a natural historical process. Very few of the languages of the world have been standardized in this way. However, several attempts have been made by governments to accelerate or by-pass the historical process by the selection and standardization of a particular vernacular for use in education, broadcasting, public meetings, official publications, etc. Apart from the practical advantages of having a single standard for such purposes, there is the force of the historic association between language and both nationhood and ethnicity. The disadvantage of attempting to implement the process of standardization by official decision, if this involves the selection of one of several distinct vernaculars already in use, is that it puts the native speakers of the chosen vernacular in a more favourable position, politically and socially, than the native speakers of other vernaculars. It is for this reason that English is still widely used in India at the national level. Although Hindi has been designated as the official national language (with several other languages similarly designated as official regional languages), it is unacceptable as the national language to most of those who speak one of the unrelated vernaculars. Many of the newly independent nations have faced similar problems. Israel, on the other hand, has avoided it by selecting classical Hebrew.

The terms 'standard language', 'national language' and 'official language' are not of course synonymous. The connection between them is that any language that is accepted by its speakers as a symbol of nationhood (i.e. of political and cultural identity) or is designated by government for official use will tend to be standardized, whether deliberately or not, as a precondition or a consequence of this very fact. The converse relation, however, does not hold. There are quite highly standardized languages which are neither national nor official languages (though they may once have been). The most obvious examples are some of the great classical languages of Europe and Asia (cf. 10.1). As for the distinction between official languages and national languages, the latter category is, in the nature of things, less sharply defined than the former. In some cases, as explained above, a country will designate a particular language as its official national language: i.e. the language which it uses for official purposes at the national level. But this is not necessarily a national language in the deeper, less easily definable, sense of the term. For example, Tanzania has adopted Swahili as its official national language. But, so far at least, this does not and cannot serve as a symbol of nationhood and cultural identity for most of the country's citizens, who belong to a very large number of distinct ethnic and linguistic groups. Finally, it should be noted that languages may be made official at lower than national level or for a relatively narrow range of official purposes, as is the case in India.

The purpose of these few remarks on the connection between standard languages, on the one hand, and official and national languages, on the other, is to draw attention to the complexity of the question and to the diversity that exists in respect of standards and vernaculars in most parts of the world. If we are monolingual native speakers of one of the very few languages of the world that are highly standardized and simultaneously serve, in one or more countries, as national and official languages (English, French, Japanese, Spanish, Russian, etc.), we may well have quite false ideas about other languages and the role that they play in the societies that use them. Indeed, we may not even understand the relation that holds between the standard and the several vernaculars in our own communities; or the feelings of those who speak a national language (e.g. Welsh, Breton, Basque) which, whether it is officially recognized for certain purposes or not, is felt to be under threat. It is not only the newly independent countries that have to face a so-called language-problem. Sociolinguistic research will not of itself solve problems. But it can provide governments with the information that is relevant to their solution (to the extent that they are soluble by political decision). More generally, and at a non-political level, it can increase everyone's, including the theoretical linguist's, understanding of the nature of language. A good deal of this information is now available in respect of certain countries.

In conclusion, mention should be made of **pidgins** and **creoles**, which originate as highly restricted vernaculars of a particular kind, but as creoles can in certain circumstances achieve the status of standards. The best-known pidgins have all developed from the contacts between people with no common language. For example, in many parts of the world there are pidgins that are English-based, in the sense that some of their grammar and vocabulary, if not their phonological structure, is derived from the English used by traders and missionaries in order to communicate with peoples whose languages they did not know. But to say that they are English-based is perhaps misleading. Usually as much, if not more, of their structure comes from other sources. Generally speaking, they are more appropriately described as mixed, or blended, languages, though it is often uncertain just what ingredients the mixtures originally contained and in what proportions. The same is true of the pidgins based on other European languages. In fact, there is a good deal of controversy attaching to the notion of **pidginization**. Whatever the details of their origin, they were presumably used, initially at least, for a very restricted range of situations and were correspondingly restricted both in vocabulary and in grammar. However, some pidgins have come to be used within particular communities for a wider range of functions and have developed, grammatically and lexically, to the point that they are reasonably described as full language-systems.

When a pidgin is acquired by children as their native language it is said to be a creole. Notable examples are the English-based creole of Jamaica and the French-based creole of Haiti. Melanesian Pidgin (Tok Pisin "pidgin talk") and Krio are now official, standard languages in New Guinea and Sierra Leone, respectively. It is not uncommon for diglossia to develop and for code-switching to occur in communities in which creoles are used as vernaculars side by side with higher-prestige languages or dialects (cf. 9.4).

It is only recently that pidgins and creoles have been investigated as language-systems in their own right, rather than as debased and reduced dialects of the European languages from which they were known or assumed to be derived. One of the consequences is that the processes of pidginization and creolization are no longer thought to have been rather marginal factors in the development of the world's languages and dialects. It is now widely believed that Black English – the vernacular dialect of lower-class urban Blacks in the northern United States – owes many of its structural features to the creoles spoken by the slave forebears of its users. If so, it is none the less as much a dialect of English nowadays as any of the other regional and social dialects. When we think of pidginization and creolization (not to mention partial decreolization as exemplified by Black English in America or the dialects spoken by some West Indian immigrants in Great Britain) in more general terms, we can see that much of the differentiation of dialects that is traditionally handled with reference to the family-tree-model of language-development in historical linguistics could be the result of essentially the same processes. For example, are the Romance languages to be regarded as having resulted from the co-existence, over a period of time, of Standard Latin and various Latin-based creoles? Once we put the question in this form, even if the question itself is in this instance less obviously pertinent than in many others, we can see there is nothing about pidginization and creolization that should lead up to associate them uniquely with the so-called expansion of Europe or the slave trade.

9.4 *Bilingualism, code-switching and diglossia*

Some countries are officially bilingual (or multilingual) in the sense that they have two (or more) official languages, national or regional (cf. 9.3). Two well-known examples of officially bilingual countries are Canada and Belgium, each of which has experienced language-problems of the kind that were referred to in the previous section. An equally well-known example of an officially multilingual country, which has not experienced any comparable language-problems, is Switzerland. Other countries, though not officially bilingual (or multilingual), have two (or more) different languages spoken within their borders. Most countries of the world fall into this latter category. Furthermore, although it does not follow from what has been said so far, in most countries, whether they are officially bilingual (or multilingual) or not, there are whole communities that are bilingual (or multilingual) in the sense that their members commonly use two (or more) languages in their daily lives. It is not the case, of course, that all the citizens of an officially bilingual (or multilingual) country use, or even know, more than one language. Bilingualism in communities – and henceforth I will use 'bilingualism' to cover multilingualism as well – is what we are concerned with here.

Obviously, a community cannot be described as bilingual unless a sufficient number of its members are bilingual. But what does it mean to say of an individual that he is bilingual? We can admit, as a theoretical ideal, the possibility of perfect bilingualism, defined as the full range of competence in both languages that a native monolingual speaker has in one. Perfect bilingualism, if it exists at all, is extremely rare, because it is rare for individuals to be in a position to use each language in a full range of situations and thus to acquire the requisite competence. However, it is not uncommon for people to approximate to perfect bilingualism by being equally competent in both languages over a fairly wide range of situations. In such cases, whether they have acquired both languages simultaneously in childhood or have acquired one as their first language and the other somewhat later, they can be classified, from a psycholinguistic point of view, as **compound** or **co-ordinate** bilinguals, according to whether the two language-systems are integrated as one at some fairly deep level of psychological organization or stored separately. So far, it is not clear whether this is a genuine dichotomy and, if so, what its neurophysiological implications are (cf. 8.3). In cases of far from perfect bilingualism, one language will be **dominant** and the other **subordinate**; and it has been suggested that the use of the subordinate language involves a process of translation from the dominant language at a fairly superficial, though not necessarily conscious, level of the psychological programming of utterances.

The classification of bilinguals just given may or may not be well founded from a psychological, and neurophysiological, point of view. But it is one that has guided a good deal of recent research. At the very least, it serves to emphasize the fact that there are many different kinds of bilingual individuals.

Similarly, there are many different kinds of bilingual communities: different in respect of whether one language is clearly dominant or not for most members; whether one language is dominant for some, but not for others; whether some members approximate to perfect bilingualism or not; whether both languages are acquired simultaneously or not; and so on. However, regardless of all these differences, there is one thing that most, if not all, bilingual communities have in common: a fairly clear functional differentiation of the two languages in respect of what many sociolinguists refer to as

domains. For example, one such domain might be the home, this being defined in terms, not simply of the actual place where the conversation occurs, but also of the participants, the topic of conversation, and other relevant variables. Thus one language might be the language of the home, in the sense that it would always be used in talking informally with other members of the family at home about domestic matters. However, another language might be used outside the home, or inside the home when strangers are present (even though they might well be bilingual too) or when the topic of conversation is other than domestic. This notion of the domain (which can be seen as subsuming a number of typical identifiable and recurrent situations) is intuitively attractive. And much of the theoretical and descriptive work in sociolinguistics inspired by Fishman (1965) attempted to identify the variables that define such intuitively recognizable domains for particular societies.

A situational change in the value of one of the variables that define a domain may result in **code-switching**. For example, two people conducting business in English in Tanzania might suddenly switch to Swahili or, if they are fellow-members of the same ethnic and linguistic subgroup, to a local vernacular, when the topic of conversation changes from business proper to more personal matters. The same kind of code-switching has been noted in many bilingual communities: in India, between English and Hindi/Urdu, Bengali, Tamil or one of the many other local languages; in Paraguay, between Spanish and Guarani; in the Puerto-Rican community in New York, between English and Spanish; and so on.

So far in this section, we have been talking as if the difference between one language and another is always as clear-cut as it is in the case of English and French, Spanish and Guarani, Hindi/Urdu and Tamil, etc. It is not. First of all, the application of the term 'language' in relation to the term 'dialect' is subject to a variety of political and cultural considerations. Second, even where the difference between two standards (whether they are called languages or dialects) is clear enough, there may be a whole range of intermediate socially or geographically determined vernaculars linking them, such that of some it is impossible to say whether they are more closely related to one standard or the other. For example, although two different literary standards, Hindi and Urdu, emerged in India under British rule in the nineteenth century (and have become more sharply differentiated since Indian independence, with the political division of India and Pakistan), the distinction of Hindi and Urdu as vernaculars, in terms of their structure, is unrealistic. And there are vernaculars that are intermediate in the same way between Hindi/Urdu and Bengali or between any two of the genetically related regional standards that share a common boundary in the Indian subcontinent. The same is true in many parts of Europe: in respect of Dutch and Low German (Plattdeutsch), Italian and (non-standard) French, English and Scots, Norwegian and Danish, and so on. In much of Western Europe, education and near-universal literacy, urbanization, increased mobility and other factors have resulted in the polarization of neighbouring vernaculars towards the national or regional standards with which communities associate themselves either politically or culturally. The fact remains that, even here, if we extend the coverage of the term 'bilingualism' to include competence in two (or more) non-standard dialects of the same language, on the one hand, or a standard and non-standard dialect of the same language, on the other, the distinction between monolingualism and bilingualism is far from clear.

We shall return presently to this point. Let us first identify a particular kind of bilingualism (in the extended sense), which linguists, following Ferguson (1959), nowadays call **diglossia**. There are many bilingual communities, the members of which regularly use one dialect for more public or formal purposes and the other in more informal, colloquial situations. Granted the validity of the distinction between the formal and the colloquial (which is perhaps definable for particular societies in terms of relevant domains), we can distinguish a high (H) and a low (L) dialect in terms of this purely functional criterion. Often the H dialect will be a literary standard, and in some cases the kind of literary standard that we call **classical**, or a dialect which approximates to it, whereas the L dialect will be a local vernacular. For example, classical Arabic is related functionally in this way, as H to L, to several different colloquial dialects in the several Arabic-speaking countries. Standard German is similarly related to Swiss German in Switzerland; Standard French to French Creole in Haiti; Katharevusa to

Demotic (Dhimotiki) in Greece; etc. And of course in much of pre-Renaissance Europe Latin was the H dialect in relation to the emergent Romance languages.

In all these cases, it must be emphasized, the distinction between the H and the L dialect is something other than a difference between two social dialects. It may well be that in many instances, only the educated classes are fully competent in both H and L. In certain cases, too, for cultural reasons, the H dialect may be thought of as being, in some sense, a more correct or purer version of the language itself: this is notably so in respect of classical Arabic, the sacred language of Islam. However, for those who have sufficient competence in H and L, the use of the one or the other is determined, not by a person's social class as such (however this is defined for the society in question), but by the situation in which he finds himself. Here, as elsewhere, the distinction between dialects and styles loses much of its force (cf. 9.6). Structurally (i.e. in terms of the degree of phonological, grammatical and lexical difference), H and L are dialects; functionally, however, they might be regarded as styles.

Most of the cases of diglossia referred to above are to be found in communities which, though they satisfy our extended definition of 'bilingualism', are normally described as monolingual: as Arabic-speaking, Greek-speaking, etc. In others, by virtue of the difficulty of saying what counts, politically or culturally, as a different language, there may be no definite consensus, even in the community itself, as to whether its members are monolingual or not. For example, there are those who would say that Swiss German is a distinct language related to, but on a par with, Standard German; there are others who would disagree. It is more important to recognize what the various cases of diglossia have in common than to separate them in terms of whether they exist in what are normally thought of as monolingual communities or not.

We now come, perhaps predictably, to the final point: in addition to those communities in which diglossia obviously exists and those in which, no less obviously, it does not, there are many that fall between the two extremes. For example, French-speaking communities in France are not generally thought to exhibit the phenomenon of diglossia. But there is a fairly clear-cut distinction between the H dialect of Standard French taught at school and used on formal occasions, especially in the written medium, and the everyday colloquial L dialect. The differences are not merely lexical, but also grammatical and, for some speakers at least, phonological. Although it is the H dialect that comes closest to the literary standard, it would be misleading to refer to the L dialect of educated Parisian circles as a non-standard vernacular.

If the concept of diglossia is applicable in respect of these two non-vernacular dialects of French, it does not seem to apply, in most parts of the English-speaking world, to English. There is a difference to be drawn, of course, between Standard English and various regional and social dialects. And within Standard English there are lexical and grammatical differences which correlate with functional differences on the formal–colloquial scale. But the difference between the formal and colloquial is less sharp for speakers of Standard English than it is for speakers of Standard French. And none of the non-standard dialects (except perhaps for some of the English-based creoles, if they are classified as English dialects) stands to Standard English in the relation of L to H. At most, what we do find are particular individuals who can switch between Standard English and a non-standard dialect as they move between one community and another. This is not uncommon. But it hardly counts as diglossia – or even, given the degree to which the non-standard vernaculars, and in particular the regional dialects, have been influenced by Standard English, as bilingualism. Once again, English-speaking communities turn out to be rather untypical of the language-communities of the world.

But then – and this is the principal lesson to be drawn so far from sociolinguistic research – there is no such thing as a typical language-community. Indeed, there is such diversity among the English-speaking language-communities that one must be hesitant about making hasty generalizations about the role that English plays in the societies in which it is used as the sole, or principal, language.

9.5 *Practical applications*

One of the points made in our discussion of the distinction between theoretical and applied linguistics was that, although this distinction is quite different in principle from the one that holds between microlinguistics and macrolinguistics, in most kinds of applied linguistics, including the application of the findings of both theoretical and descriptive linguistics to the teaching of languages, it is essential to take a macrolinguistic view (cf. 2.1). Psycholinguistics has much to contribute to our understanding of how languages are acquired, as native languages in childhood and as second languages after what is normally thought of as the critical period for language-acquisition (cf. 8.4). So too has sociolinguistics – to the extent that the distinction between psycholinguistics and sociolinguistics is anything more than a matter of methodological preferences and changing academic fashions (cf. 9.1). In particular, much of what has been mentioned in this chapter, whether it is looked at from a psychological or a sociological point of view, is very relevant to recognized areas of applied linguistics. To take first the teaching of foreign languages: although the situation in many parts of the world is now changing, foreign languages still tend to be taught without due regard to the difference between written and spoken language, on the one hand, and standards and vernaculars, on the other. The teaching of English as a foreign language has been greatly improved in recent years by the training of specialists in the relevant attitudes and skills; and they have been provided with reference grammars and teaching materials containing more accurate information about formal and colloquial Standard English than was previously available. The teaching of foreign languages in schools and universities in the English-speaking world has similarly improved, but not so far to the same extent.

The teaching of the mother tongue poses problems of a different order. There is evidence to show that teachers, like most educated members of the community whatever their own social origins, are prejudiced, in various ways, against non-standard regional and social dialects. They may even, unwittingly, judge a child to be of lower intelligence simply because his dialect (or even his accent) is broader than that of his peers. The child himself cannot but be influenced, and to the detriment of his educational prospects, by negative judgements of this kind. At the very least, therefore, a better understanding of the nature of the relationship between standards and vernaculars can reduce unintentional discrimination and injustice.

But there are deeper issues involved which sociolinguistic theory and research can illuminate, even though, in the nature of things, it cannot solve them – highly topical issues with a political dimension. It has been argued that children from working-class homes have a **language-deficit** by comparison with middle-class and upper-class children on the grounds: (a) that the non-standard dialect that they have acquired is deficient by comparison with the standard; and (b) that there is less discussion, and in general a functionally more restricted use of language, in the typical working-class home than there is in the typical middle-class or upper-class home. One version of the language-deficit theory rests upon the distinction drawn by Bernstein (1971) between so-called **restricted code** and **elaborated code**. Bernstein's work has been extremely influential among educationalists, but is highly controversial from a sociolinguistic point of view. Restricted code is said to be inexplicit and context-dependent (e.g. to make more use of elliptical expressions and pronouns, which take for granted the hearer's ability to supply contextual information) in a way that elaborated code is not. According to the theory, the working-class child is at a disadvantage at school, where elaborated code is held to be required because members of the working class, unlike those of higher social classes, use only restricted code.

As formulated by Bernstein himself, though not always by his followers, the distinction between elaborated and restricted code is not to be equated with the distinction between standard and non-standard dialects. On the other hand, it correlates with it, in that in the situations in which the competence of children is put to the test elaborated standard is compared with restricted non-standard. Given that the working-class children are likely to be on the defensive when confronted with predominantly middle-class researchers, they may not do themselves justice in the test situations in which middle-class children, with greater self-confidence, demonstrate their apparently greater control of elaborated code. Furthermore, it is argued by opponents of the theory, there has been a confusion, in practice if not in principle, of restricted code with non-standard dialects, because researchers themselves tend to be unaware of the structural complexity and the communication potential of a non-standard dialect such as Cockney or Black English. Those who maintain that non-standard dialects are not deficient but different, and that the kind of communicative competence that their users habitually draw upon is also different from that which, it is alleged, the schools require of children, have made a strong case against the language-deficit theory.

No one denies, however, that, as things are at present, children who come to school speaking a dialect that differs significantly from the standard face a problem that speakers of the standard do not have. Much of the vocabulary and grammatical structure of the materials used to teach reading may be unfamiliar to them. This particular problem can perhaps be alleviated, to some extent, by using materials carefully constructed to take advantage of the overlap between the standard and particular non-standard regional and social dialects. But this means producing different reading materials for particular subgroups; and it becomes impracticable in areas where there is a mobile and mixed population. In most societies, it would be unacceptable, on social and political grounds, to use a non-standard dialect as the medium of instruction, except perhaps orally and to a limited extent in the primary schools. On the other hand, it is possible to take advantage of the fact that, in respect of some languages at least, there is an accepted and often unnoticed range of variation within the standard. This is so, as far as English is concerned, even though English is quite highly standardized by comparison with many other languages. It would be unreasonable, for example, for a teacher to add to the learning problems of a speaker of a non-standard Edinburgh or Glasgow dialect by insisting that he use the auxiliary verbs in the way that a speaker of Standard English from the south of England normally does (cf. Hughes & Trudgill, 1979: 20ff).

The problems are particularly acute for the children of immigrants and other ethnic minorities. Torn between two cultures, they may be imperfectly bilingual in two non-standard dialects. There are, of course, advantages, as well as disadvantages, in bilingualism and biculturalism, provided that it does not stand in the way of the child's educational and social advancement. It is now more widely recognized than it used to be, in many countries, that the mother tongue of ethnic minorities should be supported, rather than discouraged as a barrier to their integration in the wider community.

What is commonly referred to as **language-maintenance** is now the official policy of many countries for some, if not all, of their minority languages, both indigenous and foreign. However, it is much easier to formulate this policy, declaring it to be politically and socially desirable than it is to implement it – or, in particular cases, even to know how to implement it.

Sociolinguistics – theoretical, descriptive and applied – has already made a great contribution to our understanding of the educational, social and political implications of this and other aspects of **language-planning**, not only in relation to the developing countries, but also – and increasingly in recent years – with particular reference to the needs of ethnic and linguistic minorities in industrialized societies. It is likely to be making an even greater contribution in the immediate future. For the so-called language-problems are part of the much larger problem of social and cultural discrimination. And this has, for political reasons, become much more urgent than it used to be in many countries.

9.6 *Stylistic variation and stylistics*

The notion of **stylistic variation** was introduced in Chapter 1, where it was contrasted, on the one hand, with differences of accent and dialect and, on the other, with differences of medium (cf. 1.7, 1.4).

One way of approaching the phenomenon of stylistic variation is by considering the fact that a language-system frequently provides its users with alternative means of saying the same thing. In so far as this is a matter of choice between lexemes, we can talk about synonymy. But synonymy, as we have seen, is rarely complete, and hardly ever absolute (cf. 5.2). Two words or phrases may be descriptively equivalent, and yet differ in terms of social and expressive meaning (cf. 'father' vs. 'daddy'). Such incompletely synonymous expressions may be referred to as **stylistic variants**: more precisely, as stylistically non-equivalent variants. Whether they are said to be semantically, as well as stylistically, non-equivalent depends, of course, on one's adoption of a broader, rather than a narrower, definition of 'meaning' and 'semantics' (cf. 5.1).

We also have to reckon with expressions that are completely, but not absolutely, synonymous: i.e. with expressions that (a) are semantically equivalent in some, but not all, of their meanings or

(b) differ with respect to the range of contexts in which they can occur. Of these other two kinds of non-absolute synonymy it is the latter – the one which depends upon context – which is most obviously relevant to the question of stylistic variation. Clearly, if one of two synonymous expressions cannot occur at all in a particular context, the question of there being a stylistically significant choice between alternatives in that context simply does not arise. However, given that two or more synonymous expressions are acceptable in a particular context, there are two further possibilities to be distinguished. Either the expressions in question will differ in respect of their degree of acceptability, appropriateness and normality or they will not. If they differ in this respect, we can once again talk of stylistic variation. If they do not, the variation is stylistically non-significant: we have a case of what might be called **completely free variation**.

Completely free variation, which subsumes complete synonymy, is relatively rare – especially in literature, where the determinants of contextual acceptability are more numerous and more diverse than they are in the everyday, unreflecting use of language. As we have seen, the term 'free variation' is customarily employed by phonologists to refer to what we may now recognize as a particular kind of incompletely free variation, in which the notion of functional contrast is restricted to the function of distinguishing one form from another (cf. 3.4). Linguists of the Prague School have always taken a broader view of the notion of functional contrast; and this is consistent with their interest in stylistic variation of all kinds (cf. 7.3).

Much, if not all, of what is covered by the term 'context' is social and falls within the scope of the sociolinguistically definable notion of the **domain** of discourse (cf. 9.4). Many authors would include within the social context of an utterance, not only the more obvious sociolinguistic variables (status, age, sex of the participants; formality or informality of the situation; etc.), but also the author's feelings and communicative intentions. I have already suggested that personality is, at least partly, the product of socialization and that so-called self-expression is the projection of one socially interpretable image or another (cf. 9.2). But this suggestion leaves open the possibility that some individuals are more capable than others of exploiting or transcending the social constraints associated with the use of particular language-systems. There is a long-standing dispute among literary critics and writers on aesthetics as to the degree to which the recognizably creative use of language by individual writers is constrained by social factors. Without prejudice to the resolution of this dispute, one can make the following purely definitional point: in so far as stylistic variation is determined, or conditioned, by the social context, it falls within the scope of the sociolinguistic concept of **register**. Other definitions of 'register' will also be encountered in the literature. But the one given here is probably the most generally acceptable.

Stylistic variation in general, and register variation in particular, is not simply a matter of vocabulary. It also affects grammar and, as far as the spoken language is concerned, pronunciation. For example, elliptical utterances (*Been shopping?*, *Just wanted to say "Thanks" for last night*, etc.) and tag-questions (*You haven't seen my pen, have you?*, etc.) are more frequent in informal English than they are in formal English. As for pronunciation, there are more cases of assimilation, of special allegro forms, etc., in casual colloquial speech than there are in a more formal style. It is important to realize that the more informal registers of English and of other languages are **rule-governed** in essentially the same way as the more formal registers are. For the most part, these rules are in both cases immanent rather than transcendent: it is the prescriptive, or normative, bias of traditional grammar which tends to obscure this fact and has promoted the view that informal usage is sloppy and unruly (cf. 2.4).

It is also important not to confuse the more informal registers of a language with non-standard dialects of that language (cf. 9.3). Speakers of Standard English will use the appropriate informal register in a whole range of recognizably informal situations: chatting with friends or colleagues, taking part in everyday family meals, and so on. Non-standard dialects may not have the same register range as the standard, simply because there are many official or semi-official situations in which non-standard dialects are not generally employed. As was pointed out earlier, in language-communities in which **diglossia** is operative the distinction between dialects and styles loses much of its force (cf. 9.4). Nevertheless, the distinction is in principle valid; and it has not always been respected in the discussion of such issues as the difference between the so-called restricted and elaborated codes of a language (cf. 9.5).

Everything that was said earlier about stylistic variation in connection with distinguishable kinds of non-absolute synonymy applies also to stylistically significant differences of grammar and pronunciation. For example, questions can be asked in English by uttering an interrogative sentence or, alternatively, by uttering a declarative sentence with a distinctive rising-intonation pattern:

(1) Is it raining?
(2) It's raining?

The question-mark attached to (2) is no more than a conventional representation in written English of its distinctive intonation-pattern; and linguists may disagree as to whether (2) is a declarative sentence uttered to ask a question (as I have classified it) or a particular kind of interrogative sentence. This difference of opinion is irrelevant to the point being made here. (1) and (2) differ in their grammatical structure; and as utterances, if not as sentences, they are partly, but not completely, equivalent. Over and above its question-asking function, (2) has the additional expressive function of indicating or revealing the speaker's surprise, distress, indignation, etc. Of course, (1) can also have an additional expressive function, conveyed by the superimposition upon it of a particular prosodic contour. But it is of itself stylistically more neutral than (2).

Another kind of contextually conditioned stylistic variation may be exemplified by

(3) We want Watney's

in contrast with

(4) What we want is Watney's

Of these, (3) is stylistically neutral and (4), like (2) in contrast with (1), is stylistically **marked** (i.e. non-neutral).[1] In this case, the stylistic difference between the marked and the unmarked, or

---

[1] Watney's is a well-known brand of beer, marketed for the most part in Britain, and (4) is one of the slogans used in several advertising campaigns.

neutral, construction would not generally be attributed to register variation. It has to do rather with what Prague School linguists have called **functional sentence perspective** and others have handled in terms of the thematic meaning of utterances or their information-structure (cf. 7.3). Although (3) and (4) are truth-conditionally equivalent and therefore have the same descriptive, or propositional, meaning, they are not equivalent with respect to the contexts in which they would normally occur. One reason why (4) is more effective as an advertising slogan than (3) would be is that (4) purports to take for granted, as given in the context, the fact that the person or persons uttering (4) are known to want something, and presumably something to drink. (Another reason, of course, is that the construction that is used in (4) produces, in this instance, alliteration and assonance.) Much of the stylistic variation that is handled by linguists in terms of functional sentence perspective, or thematic meaning, is a matter of word-order or a choice between different grammatical constructions, together with associated differences of stress and intonation, as far as the spoken language is concerned.

A speaker's ability to control the significant differences of register and to adjust the structure of his utterances to their context, in the light of his own communicative intentions, is an integral part of his linguistic competence: i.e. his knowledge of this or that language. For example, anyone whose competence in English is such that he recognizes both

(5) I have read that book

and

(6) That book I have read

as grammatically well-formed, but does not know that (6) is stylistically marked and is unable to contextualize it is, in this respect, less competent in English than someone who can use and interpret (5) and (6) as a native speaker would. Non-native speakers of a language frequently reveal themselves as such by their lapses into **stylistic incongruity**: for example, by the juxtaposition of two stylistically marked expressions, the one marked as colloquial and the other as literary. On the other hand, stylistic incongruity can be used with deliberate effect by humourists and poets. But this kind of deviation from the norm merely proves that there is a norm in the first place. Stylistic incongruity is recognized for what it is and achieves the effect that it does in relation to the norms of stylistic congruity.

Recent research has shown that the norms of stylistic congruity are, for the most part, statistical in nature. For example, although it is possible to identify certain expressions or constructions as being formal or informal, the difference between formal and informal English is not generally a matter of the one containing expressions or constructions that the other does not. It depends much more on the ratio of more formal to less formal alternatives in particular texts and discourses. Speakers do not switch between discrete registers as they move from one kind of situation, or domain, to another.

It must also be emphasized that what counts as stylistically marked in relation to what is stylistically neutral will vary according to the register that is appropriate for particular contexts. It is customary, in writing scientific papers in English, to avoid active sentences with first-person subjects ('I decided to . . .', 'We selected five specimens from each group . . .', etc.) and to make extensive use instead of impersonal passive sentences ('It was decided that . . . should/would . . .', 'Five specimens from each group were selected . . .', etc.). Although the impersonal passive in contrast with the first-person active is stylistically marked, not only in an everyday informal register, but also in most formal registers, the converse is true of what we may identify as scientific English. This point is of the greatest importance since the effect that is achieved by the deliberate use of a stylistically marked expression or construction depends upon its being stylistically marked for the register of context in which it occurs, not for the language-system as a whole.

We come now to **stylistics** as a more or less well-established branch of macrolinguistics (cf. 2.1). One definition, to which many would subscribe, might run as follows: stylistics is the study of stylistic variation in languages and of the way in which this is exploited by their users. This definition is certainly general enough: it covers everything that those who use the term 'stylistics' would want to be covered by it. But arguably it covers too much. Under

this definition, stylistics would be wholly included within sociolinguistics (broadly construed: cf. 9.1) and pragmatics (cf. 5.6).
Some scholars would be happy enough with this interpretation of
'stylistics'.

More commonly, however, the term 'stylistics' is restricted, with
or without further qualification, to **literary stylistics**: the study of
the language of literary texts. But the terms 'literary' and 'literature' can also be given a broader or a narrower interpretation.
Literature, as we normally understand the term in our culture, is by
no means universal throughout mankind. There is, however, a
more general definition of 'literature', which does not restrict it to
the written language and does not confine it within the categories
and genres of our own culture. As Bloomfield expressed it (1935:
21-2): "Literature, whether presented in spoken form or, as is now
our custom, in writing consists of beautiful or otherwise notable
utterances." One might quibble about the terms 'beautiful' and
'notable'; and one must so interpret the term 'utterance' that it
covers whole texts, not merely the products of single acts of utterance. However, Bloomfield's definition has the advantage of getting us to see that what we normally think of as literature in our own
culture is a particular manifestation of something that is found in all
cultures: the recognition that certain utterances and texts are more
worthy of preservation, repetition and commentary than others, by
virtue of their aesthetic or dramatic properties. Literature, in this
sense, is not only culturally universal; it is one of the most important
defining characteristics of cultures, distinguishing one from
another.

Regrettably, there has been something of a rift, in recent years,
between linguistic and literary studies. This is very largely the result
of misunderstanding and prejudice, on the one hand, and the
exaggerated claims of particular linguists and particular literary
critics, on the other, about the aims and achievements of their own
disciplines. Although the misunderstanding and the prejudice endure in many quarters, on both sides, it is being reduced. Linguists
are no longer as assertive as they used to be about the scientific
status of their own discipline (cf. 2.2); and they are more careful in
their formulation of the principle of the priority of spoken language
and in their criticism of the literary and prescriptive bias of tradi-

tional grammar (cf. 1.4, 2.4). And some literary critics at least are aware that the linguist's insistence that the use of language in literature is not the only, or even the basic, use of language is perfectly consistent with their view that the literary functions of language are especially worthy of study. Indeed, there are now many scholars, working in the field of literary stylistics, whose professional interests cover both language and literature, as these terms are commonly interpreted in our schools and universities.

Only cursory reference has been made to the aims of literary stylistics in this section. It will be obvious, however, that the general definition of 'stylistics' given above – the study of stylistic variation in languages and of the way this is exploited by their users – also covers literary stylistics, at least in principle. For the literary use of languages can be seen as one in which the exploitation of their resources at all levels of their structure is particularly effective and creative. Stylistic incongruity, deliberate ambiguity, the bold use of metaphor, not to mention alliteration, assonance, metre, rhythm, etc., which depend ultimately upon properties of the phonic medium – these are but some of the more obviously linguistic of the resources that a poet or an orator can draw upon in the production of "beautiful or otherwise notable utterances". Literary stylistics sets itself the task of describing these resources. Ample exemplification will be found in the works listed in the suggestions for further reading.

FURTHER READING

In addition to the treatments to be found in the more general works listed in Chapters 1 and 2, the following are recommended as introductory works in sociolinguistics and/or ethnolinguistics: Bell (1976); Fishman (1970); Hudson (1980); Pride (1971); Trudgill (1974).

Readers include Fishman (1968); Giglioli (1972); Giles (1977); Gumperz & Hymes (1972); Hymes (1964); Laver & Hutcheson (1972); Pride & Holmes (1972).

Collections of influential articles by individual scholars include Emeneau (1980); Ervin-Tripp (1973); Ferguson (1971); Fishman (1972a); Greenberg (1971); Gumperz (1971); Haugen (1972); Hymes (1977); Labov (1972).

On accents and dialects: additionally Bailey & Robinson (1973); Chambers & Trudgill (1980); Hughes & Trudgill (1979); Trudgill (1978).

On Black English (in America): additionally Burling (1973); DeStefano (1973); Dillard (1972); Shuy & Fasold (1973).

On pidgins and creoles: additionally Hymes (1971); Todd (1974); Valdman (1977).

On bilingualism, and diglossia: Ferguson (1959); Bell (1976), chapter 5. A now classic work is Weinreich (1953). See also Vildomec (1963); Haugen (1973). For some challenging suggestions about the neurophysiological aspects of bilingualism, cf. Albert & Obler (1978).

On language and social class (with particular reference to the notion of restricted and elaborated codes): additionally Bernstein (1971); Dittmar (1976); Edwards (1976); Lawton (1968); Robinson (1972); Rosen (1972).

On language planning: additionally Fishman, Ferguson & Das Gupta (1968); Rubin & Shuy (1973).

On language and nationalism: additionally Fishman (1972c).

On stylistic variation: additionally Bailey & Robinson (1973); Crystal & Davy (1969); Quirk (1968); Turner (1973).

On literary stylistics: additionally Chatman & Levin (1967); Culler (1975); Fowler (1966); Freeman (1970); Halliday & McIntosh (1966); Hough (1969); Leech (1969); Love & Payne (1969); Quirk (1968); Sebeok (1960); Ullmann (1964); Widdowson (1974).

The educational implications and practical applications of sociolinguistics and stylistics are considered in many of the works referred to above. Reference should also be made to works listed in Chapter 2 for applied linguistics and additionally to such works as Mackey (1965); Widdowson (1976, 1978); Wilkins (1972). Two readers that focus specifically on the educational implications of linguistics, including sociolinguistics and psycholinguistics, are Cashdan & Grudgeon (1972); Johnson (1976).

QUESTIONS AND EXERCISES

1. Discuss the social significance of differences of accent and dialect within a language-community. (Do they serve a generally beneficial or harmful purpose, considered from the point of view of (a) society and (b) the individual?)

2. Explain clearly the difference between RP and Standard English.

3. Linguists and others talk freely about British English, American English, Australian English, etc. Are they talking about relatively homogeneous dialects of the same language? What *is* British English or American English or Australian English?

4. "A number of British linguists have observed, informally, . . . [that] increasing numbers of speakers are using constructions such as: *He's played for us last year, They've done that three years ago*" (Trudgill, 1978: 13). Do these uses of the perfect strike you as (a) normal or (b) odd for Standard English? If they strike you, at least initially, as odd,

(a) can you say why, and (b) can you devise contexts in which they would be perfectly acceptable to you? Are there any other uses of the perfect vs. the simple past in English where synchronic variation may be indicative of what may be regarded, diachronically, as language-change? Students who know French, German, Italian or Modern Greek should also consider this question in relation to one or more of these languages.

5. "Language-variation in the individual and language-variation in the community are two sides of the same coin" (p. 274). Discuss.

6. Explain and exemplify the notion of sociolinguistically relevant **stereotypes**.

7. Do you agree that personality, in so far as it is expressed in language-behaviour, is a social phenomenon?

8. It has been suggested that all linguistics is, or should be, sociolinguistics, and again that all linguistics is, or should be psycholinguistics. What do *you* think?

9. What distinction, if any, would you draw between **bilingualism** and **diglossia**?

10. Explain what is meant by the **standardization** of languages. Should it be encouraged? If so, how?

11. How do **pidgins** differ from **creoles**?

12. Explain what is meant by **code-switching**. Does it apply to monolingual speakers or not?

13. Give a critical account of Bernstein's theory of **restricted** and **elaborated codes** with particular reference to the **language-deficit** hypothesis.

14. What is **language-planning**? Summarize the aims and findings of one or more of the case-studies referred to in suggestions for further reading.

15. "Knowing the conditions under which it would be appropriate to greet the Prime Minister with *Wotcher mate* seems to us no more a linguistic matter than knowing the conditions under which it would be appropriate to wink at him" (Smith & Wilson, 1979: 194). Discuss.

16. Consider the following three definitions of stylistics:

(a) "Stylistics . . . is the study of the social function of language and is a branch of what has come to be called sociolinguistics" (Widdowson, 1974: 202).

(b) "stylistics is that part of linguistics which concentrates on variation in the use of language, often, but not exclusively, with special attention to the most conscious and complex uses of language in literature" (Turner, 1973: 7).

(c) "stylistics is concerned with the expressive and evocative values of language" (Ullmann, 1962: 9).

Do they define the same range of phenomena? Which do you prefer and why? What distinction, if any, would you draw between literary and non-literary stylistics?

10

Language and culture

10.1 *What is culture?*

The word 'culture' (and its equivalent in other European languages) has several related senses, two of which it is important to mention and distinguish here.

There is, first of all, the sense in which 'culture' is more or less synonymous with 'civilization' and, in an older and extreme formulation of the contrast, opposed to 'barbarism'. This is the sense that is operative, in English, in the adjective 'cultured'. It rests ultimately upon the classical conception of what constitutes excellence in art, literature, manners and social institutions. Revived by the Renaissance humanists, the classical conception was emphasized by thinkers of the eighteenth-century Enlightenment and associated by them with their view of human history as progress and self-development.

This view of history was challenged, as were many of the ideas of the Enlightenment, by Herder, who said of the German equivalent of 'culture': "nothing is more indeterminate than this word, and nothing is more deceptive than its application to all nations and periods" (cf. Williams, 1976: 79). He was especially critical of the assumption that eighteenth-century European culture, dominated by French ideas and the French language, represented the high point of human progress. It is interesting to note, in this connection, that the expression 'langue de culture' (literally, "language of culture") is commonly employed by French-speaking scholars to distinguish what are held to be culturally more advanced from culturally less advanced languages. 'Kultursprache' is similarly used in German. Although there is no accepted equivalent in English, the attitude on which the use of such expressions rests is no less common in English-speaking societies. As we saw in an earlier chapter, most linguists nowadays take the view that there are no primitive languages (cf. 1.7). However, it is worth looking at this question again with particular reference to what one might call the classical conception of culture. We shall do this below (cf. 10.5).

Throughout most of this chapter, the word 'culture' is to be interpreted, not in its classical sense, but in what might be described loosely as its anthropological sense. Actually, this is the sense in which Herder proposed that the term should be used; but it was not until about eighty years later that anthropologists writing in English adopted this usage. In this second sense, 'culture' is employed without any implication of unilinear human progress from barbarism to civilization and without any prior value-judgements being made as to the aesthetic or intellectual quality of a particular society's art, literature, institutions, etc. In this sense of the term, which has spread from anthropology to the other social sciences, every society has its own culture; and different subgroups within a society may have their own distinctive subculture. Herder's promotion of the word 'culture' in this sense was bound up with his thesis of the interdependence of language and thought, on the one hand, and, on the other, with his view that a nation's language and culture were manifestations of its distinctive national spirit or mind. Many other writers in the Romantic movement had similar ideas. This is one strand in the complex historical development of the so-called Sapir–Whorf hypothesis, which dominated all discussion of language and culture, as it did of language and thought, a generation ago (cf. 10.2).

Although the term 'culture' is now widely employed in the social sciences, and especially by anthropologists, in the sense that has just been identified, it can be defined, technically, in several different ways. According to the definition with which we shall operate, culture may be described as socially acquired knowledge: i.e. as the knowledge that someone has by virtue of his being a member of a particular society (cf. Hudson, 1980: 74). Two points must be made about the use of the word 'knowledge' here. First, it is to be understood as covering both practical and propositional knowledge: both knowing how to do something and knowing that something is or is not so. Second, as far as propositional knowledge is concerned, it is the fact that something is held to be true that counts, not its actual truth or falsity. Furthermore, in relation to most, if not all, cultures we must allow for different kinds or levels of truth, such that for example the truth of a religious or mythological statement is evaluated differently from that of a straightforward factual report. Looked at from this point of view, science itself is a part of culture. And in the discussion of the relationship between language and culture no priority should be given to scientific knowledge over common-sense knowledge or even superstition.

It is customary to draw a distinction between cultural and biological (i.e. genetic) transmission. As far as language is concerned, it is quite possible that there is an innate language-acquisition faculty (cf. 8.4). Whether or not this is so, there is no doubt that one's knowledge of one's native language is culturally transmitted: it is acquired, though not necessarily learned, by virtue of one's membership of a particular society. Moreover, even if there is a genetically transmitted language-faculty, this cannot result in the acquisition and knowledge of a language unless the data upon which the language-faculty operates are supplied by the society in which the child is growing up and, arguably, in conditions which do not seriously affect the child's cognitive and emotional development. This means that the cultural and the biological in language are interdependent. Indeed, it will be obvious, on reflection, that one's linguistic competence, regardless of its biological basis, comes within the scope of our definition of culture. And it may very well be that other kinds of socially acquired knowledge – including myth, religious belief, etc. – have as much of a species-specific biological basis as language does. This point should be borne in mind when one is considering the acquisition and structure of language in terms of the opposition between the biological and the cultural. It is no longer possible to think in terms of a sharp distinction between nature and nurture.

10.2 *The Sapir–Whorf hypothesis*

The great American linguist and anthropologist Edward Sapir (1884–1939) and his pupil Benjamin Lee Whorf (1897–1941) were heirs to a tradition in European thought (mediated in all probability by Franz Boas: 1848–1942) which, as we have seen, played an important part in the development of **structuralism** (cf. 7.2). The tradition goes back at least as far as Herder and had Wilhelm von

Humboldt as one of its earliest and most influential representatives (cf. 8.1). It is marked by its emphasis of the positive value of cultural and linguistic diversity and, generally speaking, its attachment to the principles of romantic idealism.

Though hostile to the classicism, universalism and excessive intellectualism of the Enlightenment, the Herder–Humboldt tradition has not always carried its hostility as far as proclaiming that there are no universals of language and culture. Humboldt at least stressed both the universal and the particular in language. He saw the structural diversity of languages (their inner form) as the product of a universally operative and specifically human faculty of the mind. It is for this reason that Chomsky could recognize in Humboldt ("who stands directly in the crosscurrents of rationalist and romanticist thought and whose work is in many ways the culmination as well as the terminal point of these developments"; Chomsky, 1966: 2) the beginnings of generativism, and more particularly of his own notion of creativity (cf. 7.4). However that may be, the version of the Herder–Humboldt conception of the relation between language and thought to which the label 'the Sapir–Whorf hypothesis' was attached by American linguists, anthropologists and psychologists in the 1950s is usually associated with the thesis of **linguistic relativity**. Though not a necessary concomitant of structuralism as such, this thesis was one of the most conspicuous features of its American versions, including that of the post-Bloomfieldian school.

Herder, as we saw earlier, talked of the interdependence of language and thought (cf. 8.1). Humboldt comes closer to **linguistic determinism**. The Sapir–Whorf hypothesis, as it is usually presented, combines linguistic determinism ("Language determines thought") with linguistic relativity ("There is no limit to the structural diversity of languages"). In its most extreme version, the Sapir–Whorf hypothesis may be put as follows:

(a) We are, in all our thinking and forever, "at the mercy of the particular language which has become the medium of expression for [our] society", because we cannot but "see and hear and otherwise experience" in terms of the categories and distinctions encoded in language; (b) the categories and distinctions encoded in one language-system are unique to that system and incommensurable with those of other systems.

It is not clear that either Sapir or Whorf would have subscribed to the hypothesis in this form. Although I have incorporated Sapir's own expressions in the above formulation of the thesis of linguistic determinism, the famous passage from which they come (Sapir, 1947: 162) also contains a number of qualifying expressions which reduce their force.

It is worth noting that, strongly formulated though it is, the extreme version of the hypothesis that has just been presented does not of itself exclude the possibility of bilingualism. One might argue that the bilingual has two incompatible views of the world and switches from one to the other as he switches from one language to the other. However, if true, the hypothesis in its strong form is in conflict with the evident fact that bilinguals do not manifest any obvious symptoms of operating with radically incompatible world-views and often claim to be able to say the same thing in either language. Translators, too, will agree, very often if not always, that what has been said or written in one language can be said or written in another. (The qualification "very often if not always" will be taken up presently.)

Probably no one these days would defend either extreme determinism or extreme relativity. But there is much to be said in favour of a weaker – and philosophically less interesting – version of the Sapir–Whorf hypothesis in which both of its constituent theses are modified. Let us begin with determinism.

Psychologists' interest in the influence of language on thought antedates the formulation of the Sapir–Whorf hypothesis as such. It had long been known that memory and perception are affected by the availability of appropriate words and expressions. For example, experiments have shown that visual memories tend to be distorted so that they are in closer correspondence with commonly used expressions; and that people tend to notice (and remember) the things that are **codable** in their language: i.e. things that fall within the scope of readily available words and expressions. Codability, in this sense, is a matter of degree. Something which comes within the denotation of a common single word (e.g. 'uncle' in English) is more highly codable than something whose description requires a specially constructed phrase (e.g. 'parent's male sibling').

It is well known that the vocabularies of languages tend to be, to a greater or less degree, non-isomorphic (cf. 5.3). To the extent that this is so, some things will be more highly codable in one language than they are in another. For example, just as Eskimo is said to have no single word for snow, but many different words for different kinds of snow, it seems that most Australian languages have no word meaning "sand", but several words which denote various kinds of sand. The reason is obvious enough in each case. The difference between one kind of snow or sand and another is of great importance in the day-to-day life of the Eskimo, on the one hand, and of the Australian Aborigine, on the other. English has no more specific words than 'snow' and 'sand'. However, skiers, for example, who may be as interested as an Eskimo in the various kinds of snow, can use such expressions as 'powdery snow', 'spring snow', etc., which by virtue of frequent use and fixity of denotation within a particular group approximate to the status of lexemes and make certain phenomena more highly codable for them than for members of the English-speaking community at large.

The point that has just been made must be borne in mind. Codability is not necessarily constant and uniform throughout a language-community – especially when we are dealing with a community as complex, as diffuse and as varied as the native speakers of English. All too often, the correlation of language and culture is made at a very general level, and with the tacit or explicit assumption that those who speak the same language must necessarily share the same culture. This assumption is manifestly false in respect of many languages and many cultures. No less important is the fact that codability is not simply a matter of the existence of single-word lexemes. Nevertheless, provided that we do not forget that we are talking, in principle, of particular groups, rather than of whole nations, and that the productive resources of the language-system may enable the members of one group to increase for themselves the codability of what is of particular concern to them, we may continue to make use of the concept of codability as if it were a global property of language-systems.

When the Sapir–Whorf hypothesis was investigated by psychologists in the 1950s, it was demonstrated that the greater codability of certain distinctions of colour in one language than in another had the expected effect on memory and perception. For example, monolingual speakers of Zuni, an American-Indian language, which does not encode the difference between orange and yellow, had more difficulty than either monolingual speakers of English or Zuni speakers who also knew English in re-identifying, after a certain period of time, objects of a colour that was readily codable in English, though not in Zuni. However, the effect was not such that the Zuni speakers were unable to perceive the difference between a yellow and an orange object, if they were asked to compare them.

The experiments in question can be said to have partially confirmed the Sapir–Whorf hypothesis, but they did not provide evidence for the strong version of it. And the same is true of other experiments that were conducted in the 1950s and early 1960s, including a particularly interesting experiment that was designed to test the effect of differences of grammatical, rather than purely lexical, structure (cf. Slobin, 1971: 131ff). However, they did confirm a weaker version of the hypothesis: that the structure of one's language influences perception and recall. And this should not be forgotten. It may not be surprising that it should be easier to draw certain distinctions in one language than it is in another. But this is nevertheless true; and this difference seems to have a limited influence on perception and memory among languages, and on our day-to-day thinking.

Since the thesis of linguistic determinism is no longer as intensively discussed as it was a generation ago, it is difficult to know where the balance of scholarly opinion lies in relation to it. It is probably fair to say that most psychologists, linguists and philosophers would accept that language does have the kind of influence on memory, perception and thought that has just been indicated, but would be sceptical about any stronger version of the hypothesis that language determines the categories or patterns of thought. They might well add that much of the argument that Whorf and others have used in favour of a stronger and metaphysically more interesting version of the thesis is vitiated by mistranslation and circularity. For example, Whorf himself claimed that the Hopi

Indians, whose language lacks the grammatical category of tense, operate with a radically different concept of time from that with which speakers of European languages operate. But he gives no satisfactory independent evidence of differences in their behaviour or patterns of thought to justify this claim. It is also arguable that he exaggerated the difference between the grammatical category of mood in Hopi and what is traditionally classified as tense in European languages. Similarly, the absence of numerals of higher value than four in many Australian languages has often been taken as evidence of the inability of speakers of such languages to cope with the concept of number. But it turns out that Australian Aborigines who learn English as a second language have no difficulty with the numerals and can use them to count and perform calculations as readily as the average native speaker of English (cf. Dixon, 1980: 107). In short, it would seem that, despite assertions to the contrary by proponents of extreme determinism, no good reason has yet been found to jettison the more traditional view, that speakers of different languages have essentially the same world-view, or conceptual framework, as far as such deeper and philosophically more interesting concepts as time, space, number, matter, etc., are concerned.

It does not follow, however, that speakers of different languages have the same world-view in respect of other less basic concepts. For many of the concepts with which we operate are culture-bound, in the sense that they depend for their understanding upon socially transmitted knowledge, both practical and propositional, and vary considerably from culture to culture. Consider, for example, such concepts as those of "honesty", "sin", "kinship", "honour", etc. It is an accepted fact that culture-bound concepts of this kind are, to say the least, more highly codable in some languages than they are in others. Proponents of the thesis of linguistic relativity would say that many of the differences of grammatical and lexical structure found in languages are such that some things that can be said in one language cannot be said in another language. Is this true?

As we have seen, it is often possible to increase codability by drawing upon the resources of a language-system and constructing complex expressions which, by virtue of frequent use in particular contexts, may then acquire much the same specificity of meaning as lexemes. Our examples were 'powdery snow', 'spring snow', etc., for groups of English-speaking skiers. The process of increasing codability in this way depends upon the productivity of language-systems and what Chomsky has called rule-governed creativity (cf. 7.4). It is a process which goes on all the time in everyday language-behaviour. Many of the complex expressions so constructed come to be employed more widely ('arms race', 'nervous breakdown', 'drug addict', 'supply and demand', 'survival of the fittest', etc.); and there comes a time when a lexicographer will say, quite reasonably, that they have entered the vocabulary in their own right as it were. This process is one aspect of what was referred to earlier as the extensibility and modifiability of languages (cf. 1.2). It will be noted that, although in its initial stages it cannot be said to have had any effect on the language-system, it eventually results in an extension to the vocabulary. We obviously must reject any version of the thesis of linguistic relativity – and by the same token any argument that purports to refute it – which flies in the face of this kind of extensibility and modifiability.

Another way of extending the language-system itself is by the **borrowing** of lexemes from other languages (cf. 6.4). Of particular interest, in the present context, however, is so-called **loan-translation**. The most obvious kind of loan-translation involves the translation of the constituent parts of a foreign word or phrase. For example, once the English phrase 'summit conference' had been more or less lexicalized, first of all in the usage of diplomats and journalists, by means of the process outlined in the previous paragraph, it was taken over into many other languages by means of word-for-word translation: French 'conférence au sommet', German 'Gipfelkonferenz', etc.

This example illustrates the further important point that loan-translation is facilitated by the existence of formally related words, even though the words in question might not have quite the same meaning in contexts other than that created by the process of loan-translation itself. The choice of 'conférence de presse', 'Presse-konferenz' "press conference" was no doubt influenced by the existence of their formal relationship with 'conference'; and all three words are, diachronically speaking, loan-words from Latin.

As will be explained in a later section, there are subtler and less obvious kinds of loan-translation which come about by virtue of cultural contact (cf. 10.5). The point to be made here is that to extend the vocabulary of a language by means of borrowing and to modify the meaning of existing words and phrases by means of loan-translation involve changes in the lexical structure of the language-system. If this point is conceded, it is readily demonstrated, not only that some things are more highly codable in some languages than they are in others, but that there are certain things that cannot be said at all in particular languages, simply because the vocabulary with which to say them does not exist. For example, there are thousands of languages in which "They are playing cricket" cannot be said for this reason, and in all languages, except English, in which it can be said this is because the word 'cricket' or its meaning has been borrowed and, in most cases, also the word 'play' or its meaning. And to modify the vocabulary by borrowing or loan-translation is to change the language into a somewhat different one. It may seem at first sight that this is a rather trivial point. But, as we shall see later, it is of greater consequence than is generally appreciated. For a good deal of what counts as normal translation is, of necessity, loan-translation. Failure to realize that this is so has encouraged the view that a higher degree of inter-translatability holds among languages than is in fact the case (cf. 10.5).

It is not only differences of lexical structure (including, most obviously, **lexical gaps**: the absence of the appropriate words) that make exact translation between languages difficult and at times impossible. Languages can be, and often are, grammatically non-isomorphic with respect to semantically relevant categories such as tense, mood, number. The fact that this is so may not be as important, from a philosophical point of view, as Whorf and his followers thought – not to mention such predecessors as Trendelenburg, quoted earlier (cf. 8.1). But it has much the same consequences, as far as translatability is concerned, as does lexical non-isomorphism.

To take a simple example: it is strictly speaking impossible to translate into Russian (or indeed into most of the world's languages) any English noun phrase containing the definite article, since Russian does not grammaticalize the semantic distinction, or distinctions, that are grammaticalized in English by means of the presence or absence of a determiner, on the one hand, and the opposition between a definite and indefinite article, on the other. What happens in practice is that the translator usually omits entirely the information that is carried by the definite article. If this cannot be recovered from context and is judged to be of such importance that it must be conveyed in the translation, he is obliged to add something over and above what is actually said in the original. For example, he might use a demonstrative adjective meaning "this" or "that". In most contexts, the demonstrative adjectives in English and other languages are more specific in meaning than the definite article is.

Much more striking examples could be given. Boas (1911), in the immensely influential Introduction that he contributed to the *Handbook of American Indian Languages*, emphasized both lexical and grammatical differences of structure. (It was Boas, incidentally, who here used the example of the several words for snow in Eskimo, which has since been repeated in innumerable textbooks and general discussions of language and culture. Boas has several other equally persuasive examples of relevant differences of lexical structure.) As far as grammatical differences are concerned, he took the simple English sentence 'The man is sick' and showed how its translation into three different American Indian languages (Kwakiutl, Eskimo and Ponca) would oblige the translator to add information (and different information for each language) that is not contained in the original: for example, to indicate by the choice of one grammatical category rather than another whether the person being referred to is visible to the speaker or not, whether he is lying on his back, or at rest or moving, and so on; or again, to indicate whether the speaker himself can vouch for the information on the basis of direct observation or is relying on hearsay.

Following Boas, many other linguists, including Sapir and Whorf in several of their publications, have made the same general point and have convincingly demonstrated its validity. What has not been demonstrated, however, is that there is any correlation between differences of grammatical structure and differences in the mentality of speakers of grammatically different languages. Provided that we make, and insist upon, this important qualification we must, on present evidence, give our assent to a modified version of the thesis of linguistic relativity.

Since we are primarily concerned with language and culture, in this chapter, it should be added that by no means all of the lexical and grammatical differences among languages can be plausibly attributed to present, or even past, cultural differences among their speakers. Translatability can break down whether or not there are any correlated differences of culture in the two language-communities. For example, it would be hard to justify the view that the presence or absence of a definite article (cf. English and Russian) correlates with an identifiable cultural difference. But there are, of course, many differences of both grammatical and lexical structure which can be correlated with differences in the cultures with which particular languages are associated. This point will be illustrated by means of two rather different examples in the following two sections. We shall then be in a better position to evaluate the role that the cultural component plays in determining the structure of languages.

10.3 *Colour-terms*

There are several reasons for examining the vocabulary of colour in connection with the thesis of linguistic relativity. Until recently, it was the principal domain used by structuralists in order to demonstrate the fact that human languages are lexically non-isomorphic. The demonstration is the easier, and its effect the more striking, in that one can isolate the purely descriptive meaning of colour-terms from their expressive and social meaning without much difficulty. Furthermore, their descriptive meaning seems to be related to the physical world of everyday experience, in terms of denotation, in a much more straightforward way than does the descriptive meaning of lexemes in many other semantic fields (cf. 5.3). It was for this reason, too, that the vocabulary of colour was chosen by psychologists in the 1950s in their investigation of the Sapir–Whorf hypothesis (cf. 10.2).

The colour spectrum is a physical continuum. It is also a visual continuum, in the sense that any one distinguishable colour shades gradually and, at the limits of visual discrimination, imperceptibly into its neighbours. For example, blue shades gradually and imperceptibly, in this sense, into green; green shades into yellow; and so on. All languages, presumably, furnish their users with words that enable them to refer to certain areas of this visual continuum: in English, such basic colour-terms as 'black', 'white', 'red', 'green', 'blue', 'brown', etc., and such non-basic, or second-level, colour-terms as 'turquoise', 'vermilion', 'puce', etc. What counts as a basic colour-term in contrast with a non-basic, or second-level, colour-term is open to dispute, since there are several possible criteria that can be applied. For example, 'orange', by virtue of its association with the colour of the fruit, might not be regarded as a basic colour-term: like 'lemon' or 'apricot', it would count as non-basic. On the other hand, other criteria – including frequency of usage as a colour-term and familiarity of this usage to average members of the language-community – would certainly lead us to say that 'orange' is a basic colour-term in English. It is possible that by certain criteria, some languages have no basic colour-terms at all. However, most languages do and, on the whole, it is easy enough to decide what they are. Let us take for granted, then, the distinction between basic and non-basic colour-terms.

It is a well-known, and undisputed, fact that languages differ in the number of basic colour-terms that they have. It is also well known that, independently of this fact, word-for-word translation of colour-terms across languages is frequently impossible because no word in the one corresponds exactly to a word in the other. For example, there is no word in French that covers exactly what 'brown' does in English; there is no single word in Russian, Spanish or Italian that corresponds to 'blue'; no single word in Hungarian that corresponds to 'red'; and so on. Facts of this kind were frequently cited, until the end of the 1960s, as evidence, not only of the structural incommensurability, or non-isomorphism, of different lexical systems, but also of the arbitrariness of the divisions that different language-systems draw within what we have said is a physical, and also a visual (i.e. psychophysical), continuum.

Since there is now some reason to doubt whether these divisions are arbitrary, it is as well to emphasize that the structural incommensurability of the vocabularies of particular languages in respect of their basic colour-terms has not been disproved, or even called into question. For example, the English sentence 'My favourite colour is blue' cannot be translated into Russian (in any ordinary sense of the term 'translation') otherwise than by arbitrarily deciding between 'sinij' and 'goluboj', roughly "dark blue" and "lighter blue", respectively. In practice, translators are frequently obliged to make arbitrary decisions of this kind; and for the purpose in hand it is usually of no consequence. We normally think of translation as a process which holds constant at least the propositional context of what is said. But a good deal of ordinary translation does not, and in the nature of things cannot, do this.

In 1969 Berlin and Kay published an important book, *Basic Color Terms*, in which they produced evidence to show that the similarities and differences among languages in respect of the way in which they divide up the colour spectrum are not as arbitrary as they had once been thought to be. First of all, they drew attention to the importance of considering what they called the **focal meaning** of a term, rather than its peripheral meaning. As far as colour-terms are concerned, their focal meaning can be ascertained by asking speakers to point to what they would take to be a good example of the colour in question on a colour-chart. It turns out that, if this is done, there is a high degree of agreement among native speakers about the focal meaning of the basic colour-terms in their language, whereas they may have great difficulty in saying where the boundary comes between one term and another or disagree among themselves about the results of any attempt to put the boundary at a particular place in the continuum. For example, English speakers may not be able to agree where the boundary comes between blue and green on a colour-chart (or in the application of the words 'blue' and 'green' in everyday life). But they have no difficulty in saying what is typical, or focal, blue or green. So far, what Berlin and Kay discovered is consistent with the view, previously held by most structuralists, that each language imposes its own arbitrary divisions within the continuum of colour.

However, they also found that different languages tend to agree as to the focal areas of particular basic colour-terms and that this holds true independently of the number of colour-terms in the systems. For example, not only is the focal area for English 'red' and French 'rouge' the same (English and French each having the same number of basic colour-terms), but a language with far fewer

basic colour-terms may have one whose focal area coincides with
that of 'red' or 'rouge'. Even more striking is the fact – if it is a fact –
that there is a universal partial ordering, or hierarchy, among the
potential colour-terms of languages. For example, any language
with only three colour-terms will have terms whose foci correspond
with those for 'black', 'white' and 'red'; any languages with six
colour-terms will have, in addition to these three, terms whose foci
are the same as those for 'green', 'yellow' and 'blue'. The focus of
the seventh colour-term in a seven-term system is said to be brown.
(French, as noted above, has no single word for brown; but 'brun',
with contextual restrictions, and increasingly 'marron' can perhaps
be said to denote the focal area of brown.) After that come purple,
pink, orange and grey, but without any ordering within the set: i.e.
one eight-term system might have a term for purple, another a term
for pink, and so on.

The Berlin–Kay hypothesis has aroused a good deal of controversy, as far as its experimental basis is concerned. But so far,
apart from details that have not been mentioned here, it has stood
up to further empirical tests. There are two general points that can
be made with reference to the hypothesis, both of which are relevant to the thesis of relativity and the relation between language
and culture.

The first is that, although there may be a universal substructure in
the vocabulary of colour, there is quite clearly a non-universal
superstructure also. The difference between languages with a relatively rich and languages with a relatively poor system of basic
colour-terms still remains. Also, such evidence as there is for a
universal partial ordering in the set of possible basic colour-terms is
restricted, as we have seen, to the six or seven most commonly
labelled colours. Granted that these areas, more precisely the foci
associated with them, are perceptually salient for human beings, by
virtue, in part at least, of their neurophysiological make-up, there
are other non-universal and perceptually less salient areas in the
colour continuum that are given lexical recognition and fully integrated with the universally more salient areas in the colour vocabulary of particular languages. It is quite clear from discussions of
colour by anthropologists, in relation to the Berlin–Kay hypothesis
and independently of it, that cultural, as well as biologically based

perceptual, saliency plays a role in the identification of colour-terms; and, as we have seen, the biological and the cultural are, in general, interdependent in the acquisition of language (cf. 8.4). Finally, there are many everyday uses of colour-terms – and not only the most obviously symbolic (white for purity, red for danger, black for mourning, etc.) – which are culture-dependent, in the sense that one cannot acquire them without simultaneously acquiring the relevant social knowledge. The importance of this fact has been underestimated by many linguists, psychologists and philosophers who have discussed the Berlin–Kay hypothesis. What holds for the vocabulary of colour would seem to hold for any lexical domain that one cares to choose. If there is a universal substructure of semantic distinctions within it, there will also be a non-universal, and perhaps much more extensive, culture-dependent superstructure.

The second point has to do with the notion of focal areas, or foci. Although we started by talking about colour as a visual continuum, it has become clear that there is an important sense in which this is not true. Human beings are so constituted (as all animals are) as to respond neurophysiologically to particular stimuli and not to others. This may be, in part at least, the basis for the greater saliency of some colour-foci and their universality (cf. Clark & Clark, 1977: 526f). Such foci serve as the reference-points in relation to which we impose structure on the rest of the physical continuum, in so far as we do impose structure upon it. And they serve as prototypes in the acquisition of colour-terms. For example, we learn the meaning of 'red' by first associating it with its focus and then extending the denotation outwards from its focus over a somewhat indeterminate area. But the prototypical, or focal, meaning of 'red' continues to serve as the anchor-point for it thereafter; and we will tend to associate it with something that is familiar to us in our everyday environment: for example, 'red' might be defined, prototypically, in this sense, with reference to blood or fire (as many dictionaries do indeed define it). Once again, what holds for colour-terms is also true of the vocabulary in general. The world of experience does not present itself to us as an undifferentiated continuum. As we saw in an earlier chapter, it is categorized by us, to a certain extent at least, into what are traditionally called **natural kinds** (cf. 5.3).

ǀ

We also saw, first, that most lexemes in all languages do not
denote natural kinds; and, second, that the denotation of those that
do requires cultural support. The fact that particular substances are
natural kinds by virtue of their physical composition (e.g. salt) or
particular biological species by virtue of their capacity to breed and
reproduce their kind (e.g. tigers) is irrelevant, as far as the lexical
structure of language is concerned, unless these substances and
species are given cultural recognition as such. Recent work, both in
philosophical semantics and in psycholinguistics and sociolinguistics, has drawn attention to the role of culturally established prototypes for the definition of the meaning of words whether they
denote natural kinds, in the traditional sense of the term, or not.

10.4 *Pronouns of address*

The phenomenon with which we are concerned in this section has
been much discussed, by linguists and others, both for its own sake
and as an instance of a broader range·of culturally determined
distinctions in different languages. It has been chosen here because,
at first sight at least, the kind of meaning that is involved, social and
expressive, is in sharp contrast with the descriptive meaning of
colour-terms.

In most modern European languages, though not in Standard
English (as used by most groups for most purposes), there is a
distinction between what are conventionally called the polite and
the familiar pronouns of address: French 'vous' : 'tu'; German 'Sie'
: 'du'; Italian 'lei' : 'tu'; Russian 'vy' : 'ty'; Spanish 'usted' : 'tu'; etc.
The origins of this distinction are uncertain. However, it is said to
have had its source in Latin in the later period of the Roman Empire
or the early Middle Ages, and to have been taken over, at various
times, by the other languages. It is quite clearly, in its present
distribution throughout most of the languages of Europe, the result
of borrowing. In fact, there has been borrowing on several levels,
since it was not always taken directly from Latin in the first place
and over the centuries languages having the distinction have come
under the modifying influence of other languages also having the distinction. Here, as almost always, borrowing is the consequence of
cultural diffusion (cf. 10.5). For convenience and in accord with
what is now common practice, we will refer to the familiar and the

polite pronouns, regardless of the language we are dealing with, as T and V, respectively.

Social psychologists have investigated the use of T and V in terms of the concepts of power and solidarity, on the one hand, and of reciprocal and non-reciprocal usage, on the other. Generally speaking, we can say that non-reciprocal usage indicates an acknowledged difference of status. In societies in which non-reciprocal usage exists a socially superior, or otherwise more powerful, person will use T to his inferiors, but be addressed by them as V. But, non-reciprocal usage has been on the decline in most European languages since the nineteenth century, except in the case of adults and children who are not members of the same family and in one or two more special cases. This is explained historically in part by the spread of more egalitarian or democratic attitudes in Western societies and in part by the increased importance of the solidarity factor, marked not simply by reciprocal usage as such, but more particularly by the reciprocal use of T. In many countries of Europe, and notably in France, the reciprocal use of T among colleagues and acquaintances has greatly increased in recent years, at all social levels, but especially among the young and those of a politically more liberal or left-wing outlook. It is very rare nowadays, for example, for husbands and wives to use V to one another or for non-reciprocal usage to exist between parents and children. However, this was the practice in all upper-class French families in earlier times; and it has not quite disappeared.

It must be emphasized that the generalizations that have just been made about the gradual switch from power to solidarity as the dominant factor in the change that has taken place in T/V usage in European languages over the last hundred years or so are statistical in nature. It is certainly not the case that one can predict with complete accuracy whether two individuals will use T or V in a given situation on the basis solely of information about their social class, age, sex, political affiliations, etc. Also, there are differences within what appear to be comparable social groups in different countries of Europe with respect to the freedom with which T is used. However, the change described above has undoubtedly taken place at somewhat different times and at different rates.

The example has been chosen to illustrate the fact that there is,

or can be, both synchronically and diachronically, a correlation
between social structure and, not just the vocabulary, but also the
grammatical structure of languages. This correlation is much more
extensive in other languages, such as Japanese, Hindi or Javanese,
than it is in any of the European languages. But it is worth noting
that in Italian and Spanish, unlike say French, German or Russian,
there is in certain grammatical constructions an imperative/sub-
junctive distinction associated with the T/V distinction; that in
certain dialects of Southern Italian there is a further distinction,
within V as it were, of 'lei' and 'voi'; that in some, but not in all, of
the languages with a T/V distinction there is an independent singu-
lar/plural distinction associated with it; and so on. When it comes to
saying what T or V means in a particular language, a lot more detail
has to be given about social structure and social roles than is
covered by the global notions of power and solidarity. Information
must also be given about the interpretation of T and V in the
grammatical structure of each language and their use with or without titles, names and other terms of address. Nevertheless, the
general point is clear: the social and expressive meaning of T and V
is quite obviously culture-dependent; it is a matter of socially acquired knowledge. And the knowledge is practical, rather than
propositional: it falls within the scope of social know-how.

T and V may differ somewhat in meaning from language to
language. Rather striking evidence of this can be found in
nineteenth-century Russian literature, notably in the novels of
Tolstoy (cf. Friedrich, 1968). The point is that diglossia existed at
that time among the members of the Russian aristocracy, French
being the H language and Russian the L language (cf. 9.4). When
they spoke French among themselves, they would use V to one
another, regardless of bonds of family or friendship that might unite
them. In this respect they followed upper-class French usage of the
period. But when they spoke Russian, they would use either T or V,
reciprocally among themselves, non-reciprocally with their social
inferiors and subordinates. Their reciprocal usage was determined
both by long-term and also by short-term factors. The long-term
factor was what has been identified, globally, as solidarity, based on
kinship, friendship, marriage, etc. Its effect was that both men and
women either were or were not on T-terms with each of their

acquaintances. The short-term factor was the mood or emotion of the moment: Russian, unlike French for example, allowed one to pass quite freely from the long-term T of solidarity and intimacy to a highly significant short-term V of anger and estrangement; and also, though this does not concern us here, it allowed short-term solidarity to break through the social barriers, as it were, in certain highly emotional moments and triumph over the long-term non-reciprocal pattern of usage.

Tolstoy was well aware of the differences between the T/V distinction in Russian and French, as it applied to the speech of the class to which he belonged. Not only did he respect these differences in his writing, but on occasion he explicitly drew his reader's attention to them. The reason why he did this was that, especially in the later novels, much of the conversation, though it appears in Russian in the original, was intended to be understood as if it were French. It is usually possible, on the basis of internal evidence, including one's knowledge of the sociolinguistic variables, to infer whether a particular part of the text is to be construed as representing French or not. One of the clues is the pronoun of address that is employed. For example, in *Anna Karenina*, in dialogues involving any of the principal characters a T-form is (with just a couple of exceptions, explicable in context) a sure indication that Russian is being spoken (cf. Lyons, 1980). The use of a V-form, however, does not of itself imply that the conversation is to be construed as being in French. First of all, not all of the principal characters are on T-terms with one another. Second, not only do transitions occur indicating a long-term change from V to T at identifiable and highly significant points, but, as was mentioned above, switches from T to V may occur during quarrels conducted in Russian – reconciliation or tenderness then being indicated by the return to T.

Russians of the class to which Tolstoy belonged, and for whom he was writing at the period in question, would respond to these clues more or less automatically. They were bilingual in Russian and French and, as far as the T/V distinction was concerned, they used two quite different and incommensurable systems in their everyday lives, so that, knowing whether a V-form in the text had the meaning of the French V or the Russian V, they would respond unhesitatingly and for the most part unconsciously to those instances in which a transition occurs from a Russian V to T or vice versa. Many of these transitions are of great significance, and some of them, but not all, are explicitly noted as such by the author. Modern readers of the work will miss a lot unless they can acquire the sensitivity to respond appropriately in the way that Tolstoy's own Russian-speaking contemporaries did.

Now, anyone who reads an English translation cannot but miss the significant transitions: there is no way of rendering them into English – other than by using 'thou': 'you' in English to stand consistently for T: V throughout the text. But this would hardly count as translation. Nor can anything like the same effect be achieved by adding terms of endearment or other expressions of address such as first names, to the text. Standard English translations occasionally do this. But it can be readily shown that they fail of their effect (cf. Lyons, 1980).

It might be thought that a French translation could handle the problem better; and in a sense it can – by doing consistently what Tolstoy did in reverse. But whereas the Russian reader of Tolstoy's day was bilingual in both Russian and French, the average French reader of Tolstoy is not. And anyone who reads a French translation which uses 'vous' consistently for the Russian 'vy' and 'tu' for the Russian 'ty' has to interpret some of the pronouns in terms of the Russian system and some of them in terms of the quite different French system – not the French system of today but of a hundred years ago. He need not be bilingual, but he certainly must be, to a sufficient degree and in the relevant respects, bicultural.

And this is the point of the example. Most languages, if not all, exhibit distinctions in their grammatical or lexical structure that derive what meaning they have by virtue of their correlation with functional distinctions in the culture, or subculture, in which the language is used. The meaning is commonly, though not necessarily, social and expressive, rather than descriptive. But what was said in the previous section about the combination of a possibly universal substructure with a culture-dependent, non-universal, superstructure is valid in respect of this kind of meaning also. As we have seen the Russian T/V distinction differs from the French T/V distinction. But the difference can be made clear, up to a point, to

those who know neither Russian nor French in terms of very
general, if not universal, notions having to do with social status,
kinship, love, friendship, etc. In much the same way, anthropologists, sociolinguists and literary commentators can make clear
to others, more or less adequately, the meaning of unfamiliar
culture-dependent expressions of another language. This point
will be taken up and generalized in the following section. What
must be emphasized here, however, is that the ability to explain a
culture-dependent grammatical or lexical distinction, more or less
satisfactorily, by means of another language that does not have the
distinction does not imply that the distinction can be represented
in translation. Metalinguistic explanation must not be confused
with translation.[1]

10.5 *Cultural overlap, cultural diffusion and translatability*

Throughout this chapter, and indeed throughout this book, we have
been developing and exemplifying the view that language is both a
biological and a cultural phenomenon. Particular languages, it
would seem, have a universal substructure, certainly in grammar
and vocabulary and perhaps also in phonology, and a non-universal
superstructure, which is not only built upon this substructure, but is
fully integrated with it.

The universal substructure is determined in part by the genetically transmitted cognitive faculties of the human mind and, no less
important, by genetically determined human drives and appetites;
and in part by the interaction of these biologically determined
cognitive and non-cognitive factors with the physical world as it
presents itself to human beings. Whether there is also a language-
acquisition faculty as such is so far uncertain (cf. 8.4). However, the
process of language-acquisition is such that the biological transmission of whatever is universal in language is also dependent, for its
success, upon the process of cultural transmission.

As to the non-universal superstructure in languages, this is much
more obviously a matter of cultural transmission – and in two

---

[1] The term 'metalinguistic' is commonly employed nowadays to mean "pertaining to
the description or analysis of language or of a language" (cf. 'metalanguage': 5.6).
It has also been employed by post-Bloomfieldian structuralists, with reference to
the study of languages in their cultural contexts. So both senses are applicable here.

senses. Not only is this part of linguistic competence transmitted from one generation to the next by means of a particular society's institutions, but what is transmitted is itself an important component in that society's culture. If competence in a particular language implies the ability to produce and understand sentences of that language, then it is unquestionably a part of culture: i.e. social knowledge (cf. 10.1). For much of the meaning of expressions, including their descriptive as well as their social and expressive meaning, is non-universal and culture-dependent. This point has been made with reference to two very different examples in the preceding two sections. So too, however, has the no less important point that, although it may be impossible to translate all the sentences of one language into the sentences of another without distortion or makeshift compromises, it is usually possible to get someone who does not know the language and culture of the original to understand, more or less satisfactorily, even those culture-dependent expressions which resist translation into any language with which he is familiar.

This is possible because, between any two societies, there will be a greater or lesser degree of **cultural overlap**. In the limiting case, this may be no greater than is predictable from what is culturally universal by virtue of man's biological make-up and broad similarities of environment in all parts of the habitable world. But for various reasons, including what anthropologists refer to as **cultural diffusion**, the degree of overlap is far from minimal. Generally speaking, translatability is a function of the degree of cultural overlap. But, as we saw in the case of the Russian and French pronouns of address in Tolstoy, even though they cannot be satisfactorily translated into English, their use can be explained to monolingual English speakers in terms of fairly general notions that apply also, though with differences of detail, in the description of our own culture.

The same point could have been made, as far as terms of address are concerned, in relation to languages with a rich set of **honorifics** (e.g. Javanese, Korean, Thai and many languages of South-East Asia); or languages which, like Japanese, also have honorific pronouns, but make much more use of kin-terms and titles than they do of pronouns. At first sight, this seems to be very different from anything that is found in English-speaking communities. But the cultural parameters that determine non-reciprocal usage – social superiority, age, kinship, sex, etc. – are also operative in our own culture, though to a more limited degree and without the same effect upon the grammatical structure, as well as the vocabulary, of English. For example, not only is the reciprocal and non-reciprocal use of names and titles determined, in many English-speaking societies, by these same factors, but there are circumstances in which (as is more generally the case in Japanese) the superior, but not the inferior, may refer to himself by means of the same kin-term or title with which he is addressed (cf. the use of 'daddy' or 'mummy' or 'teacher': *Didn't daddy/mummy/teacher tell you to put your books away?*). Cultural overlap of this kind and to this degree enables us to understand, in a general sort of way, the descriptions of the semantic structure of other languages that appear in the sociolinguistic and anthropological literature (cf. Hymes, 1964). It would be a mistake to suppose, however, that the general understanding of the semantic structure of other languages that can be acquired in this way is anything more than superficial. Full understanding of the several kinds of meaning that are encoded in the grammar and vocabulary of a language comes only with a full understanding of the culture, or cultures, in which it operates.

What has just been said is a commonplace, not only of sociolinguistics and ethnolinguistics, but also of literary criticism. And the study of selected foreign languages in our schools and universities – all of which are judged to have the status of languages of culture ('langues de culture': cf. 10.1) in the narrower sense of 'culture' – is traditionally and rightly justified on essentially the same grounds. Particular languages are associated historically with particular cultures; the languages provide the key to the associated cultures, and especially to their literature; the languages themselves cannot be fully understood otherwise than in the context of the cultures in which they are inextricably embedded; so language and culture are studied together. The argument cannot be faulted at the level of general principle. It is of course open to debate whether the more traditional aims and methods of language-teaching are based on a sufficiently broad conception of culture. But this is another matter. Language-learning can and should be geared to particular purposes. One of these purposes is that of acquiring and participating as fully as possible in a different culture from the one in which one has been brought up.

There are certain aspects of the interdependence of language and culture that are not as widely appreciated as they ought to be. One of these, which is very relevant to the question of translatability, is the degree to which cultural diffusion reduces, and at times conceals, semantic differences between languages. The more obvious linguistic consequences of cultural diffusion have been mentioned already: borrowing and loan-translation (cf. 10.2). What we are concerned with is a less readily identifiable kind of loan-translation: a phenomenon which would not generally be regarded as such, the more so as it is difficult to distinguish it, in many cases, on the one hand from ordinary translation and on the other from creativity in the use of language which, though it may not be rule-governed, falls well within the scope of the ordinary person's linguistic competence.

Let us suppose, for example, that we are translating from Classical Greek into English and that we are confronted with the word 'sophia'. This is conventionally translated as 'wisdom'; and in many contexts this is, and more often might appear to be, a perfectly satisfactory equivalent. For example, let us suppose that a sentence containing the adjective 'sophos', related syntactically and semantically to 'sophia' as 'wise' is to 'wisdom', occurs in the Greek text of an author like Plato and is rendered into English as 'Homer was wiser than Hesiod'. Out of context, someone without either a good knowledge of Greek or a sufficient knowledge of the social and cultural background might well interpret this statement as if 'wise' were being used with the same meaning as it is in, say, 'Shakespeare was wiser than Marlowe'. But is it? Out of context the answer is uncertain, since 'sophia' undoubtedly covers, and would be the word used to refer to, what we in present-day English would identify as wisdom. But 'sophia' and 'wisdom' do not have the same range of meaning. In many contexts, the best English translation of the Greek sentence would be 'Homer is a better poet than Hesiod'. Indeed, it is arguable that this comes closest to what the Greek means when 'sophos' is being used in its **prototypical** sense. If a shoemaker or carpenter is good at his job, he is just as readily called

'sophos' as a good doctor, poet or statesman is. One might argue
that no one could be a good statesman, or possibly a good doctor,
unless he were wise, but what we normally call wisdom in English is
certainly not an essential attribute of the good shoemaker, carpenter or poet.

But translations from one language into another cannot always
respect normal usage. If someone is translating one of the many
passages in the dialogues of Plato in which the question at issue, as it
is traditionally formulated in English, is "Is virtue teachable?"
(related to the famous Socratic paradox "No one does wrong know-
ingly" and to many other equally famous theses, not only of
Greek philosophy, but of the whole Western philosophical tradition that derives from it), he will find himself obliged to use either
'wisdom' for 'sophia' (and 'virtue', or 'goodness', for the Greek
'arete') or some other word which, whatever it is, will be inappropriate, in its normal sense, in many of the collocations in
which it occurs. If he does not translate it consistently one way or
another in such passages, the structure of the argument will be
concealed and the examples that are used to support it will lose their
relevance. What this means, in practice, is that translation is relative to the purpose for which a particular translation is intended and
to the assumed background knowledge of those who will use it. It is
for this reason that so-called literal translation is at times more
appropriate than free translation.

But what is literal translation? In some cases it is the kind of
translation which fails to make adjustments for differences of sym-
bolism and metaphor in the two languages. In many instances,
however, as it would be if 'sophia' is translated consistently by
means of 'wisdom' (and 'arete' by means of 'virtue') in the passages
of the Platonic dialogues referred to above, it is simply the more or
less deliberate use of loan-translation: the difference between literal and metaphorical, or symbolic, meaning is not relevant in the
case of the present example. What is involved is a difference in the
descriptive content of words and the culture-dependent prototypes
with which they are associated. Instead of using the English word
'wisdom', we might equally well use the Greek word 'sophia' in the
English text. It amounts to the same thing; and of course this is what
one might well do in a translation that is designed primarily for the

use of English-speaking students of philosophy with a sufficient knowledge of Greek culture but an inadequate knowledge of Greek for them to read the original text. However, it requires but a moment's reflection, reinforced if possible by a little practice in translation, to see that it is not just the odd word, like 'sophia' (or 'arete') that creates problems and tends to obliterate the distinction between loan-translation and ordinary translation. The meaning of words like 'sophia' and 'arete' has been extensively discussed by virtue of the philosophical importance – and, in the narrower sense of 'culture', the cultural importance – of the texts in which they appear. One is therefore much more sensitive to the necessity of translating them with care.

Equally obvious examples can be found in any of the other classical languages of the world. For example, the Sanskrit word 'dharma' can be translated differently in different contexts: by means of 'duty', 'custom', 'law', 'justice', etc. But its prototypical meaning, in its later development and as a borrowed word in other languages, is so heavily culture-dependent, especially in Hindu and Buddhist societies, that it has been taken over with this meaning into English and other European languages. Similarly, the word 'kismet' has been borrowed, through Turkish and Persian, from Arabic with what might be referred to, briefly, as its prototypical Islamic meaning. Presumably, these words were taken over as loan-words because it was felt that to translate 'dharma' as 'duty' and 'kismet' as 'fate' or 'destiny' would be to fail to represent their highly important culture-dependent implications. Greek 'sophia', etc., might also have been borrowed into English as such if contact had been made in modern times with a society in which this Greek word was used and, let us say, a person's sophia was held to be determined, like his dharma in a Hindu society, by his caste. But of course Greek, both directly and indirectly through Latin, has exerted the same continuous influence on the languages of Europe that Sanskrit and Arabic have exerted over the centuries upon many of the languages of Asia and Africa.

Anthropologists face the same problem all the time in relation to languages which unlike Greek, Sanskrit or Arabic have not served, on a world-wide scale and for centuries, as languages of acknowledged cultural importance: i.e. as languages of culture in the sense of 'langues de culture'. They must decide whether they should borrow some word as such from the language of the society that they are describing (as 'taboo' was taken over from one of the Polynesian languages, Tongan, in the eighteenth century and subsequently generalized) or use an existing word, and adapt it more or less deliberately by loan-translation to the purpose of describing the society that they are dealing with. There is no difference, in the last resort, between what the anthropologist, or anyone else, is doing when he extends the meaning of the words of his native language by loan-translation in this way and what the translator is doing all the time when he is translating between two languages outside the area of cultural overlap.

Furthermore, there is no difference, ultimately, between loan-translation of this more or less deliberate kind and the use that a native speaker makes of his language as he extends the meaning of words beyond their prototypical sense in new situations. For example, he can bring within the denotation of 'cap', 'hat' or 'bonnet' various kinds of headgear that might be characteristic of other cultures, but not his own; he can bring within the denotation of 'boat', when he first encounters them, not only canoes, but also catamarans (whether he also borrows the local words or not); he can apply the word 'wedding' or 'funeral' to a wide range of practices which bear little resemblance to anything that would count, prototypically, as a wedding or funeral for most speakers of English.

Now, it so happens that English and the other major languages of Europe, as has been emphasized in the chapter on language and society, are, in many respects, highly unrepresentative of the languages of the world. English, in particular, has been used in the administration of an empire of great cultural diversity. It is spoken as a native language by members of many different ethnic groups and adherents of many religions, living in various parts of the world. It is widely employed by anthropologists, missionaries and writers of all kinds, not only in the description of every known society, but also in novels, plays, etc., which have their setting in countries and societies in which English is not normally spoken. This means that English, to an even greater extent than other European languages, has been enlarged and modified by loan-translation in almost every area of its vocabulary. The correlations between the semantic structure of English and the cultures of its native speakers are therefore much more complex and diverse than are the correlations between language and culture in the-vast majority of human societies. It is also much easier for a native speaker of English or one of the major languages of Europe to think that all human languages are intertranslatable than it would be for a speaker of most other languages. It is important to keep this point in mind when one is reading theoretical discussions of the nature of language with examples taken exclusively from one or other of the major European languages.

We turn now to the final point. Linguists frequently proclaim, at least as a working hypothesis, the principle that there are no primitive languages: that all languages are of roughly equal complexity and are equally well adapted to the communicative purposes they serve in the societies in which they operate (cf. 2.4). This principle does not, of itself, commit the linguist to the view that all languages are equally suitable for all communicative purposes. Indeed, as we have just seen, some languages by virtue of their role as world-languages have a flexibility and a versatility that most languages do not possess. Other languages, whether they are also world-languages or not, are associated with culture in the narrower, or classical, sense of the term (10.1). It would be paradoxical, if not absurd, to interpret the principle of the equality of languages as implying that the language that a person speaks has no effect upon the quality of his intellectual and artistic life, not to mention his career and economic prospects (cf. 9.5). There are eminently defensible reasons why some languages, rather than others, are widely taught in our schools and universities. Linguists who insist upon the equality of languages do not necessarily subscribe to the view that all cultures are equally worthy of that kind of deliberate diffusion that we call education. This is a question about which linguists, as individuals, may have their own personal opinions. There is no corporate professional view.

FURTHER READING

Generally as for Chapter 9. Of the introductory works mentioned there, Hudson (1980) and Trudgill (1974) are especially recommended for topics dealt with in this chapter; and of the readers, Hymes (1964). Also, see Burling (1970), an introduction, which covers both sociolinguistics and ethnolinguistics from an anthropological, rather than a sociological or social psychological, point of view; and Ardener (1971) for a more comprehensive work. Also, for different approaches to ethnolinguistics, Crick (1976); Greenberg (1968, 1971); Tyler (1969).

On the Sapir–Whorf hypothesis: additionally Black (1959, 1969); Carroll (1953b); Cooper (1973), chapter 5; Henle (1958); Hoijer (1954); Saporta (1961); Slobin (1971); Whorf (1956).

On the Berlin–Kay hypothesis, codability and semantic prototypes (including some relevant earlier work, other than that listed above for the Sapir–Whorf hypothesis in general): Berlin & Kay (1969); Brown (1958a, b); Clark & Clark (1977); Lloyd (1972); Lyons (1977b: 245–50); Osgood, May & Miron (1975), chapter 6; Rosch (1973, 1974, 1975, 1976).

On translation: Brower (1966); Catford (1965); Nida & Taber (1969); Olshewsky (1969), chapter 9; Savory (1957); Steiner (1975). On translating the bible: Beckman & Callow (1974); Nida (1945, 1964, 1966).

On pronouns of address and the T/V distinction: Adler (1978); Brown & Ford (1961); Brown & Gilman (1960); Brown & Levinson (1978); Friedrich (1968, 1972). A fuller account of Tolstoy's use of pronouns of address in *Anna Karenina* can be found in Lyons (1980).

On the ethnography of speaking: Bauman & Sherzer (1974); Goody (1978); Hymes (1977).

On verbal play and linguistic virtuosity: Bauman & Scherzer (1974); Burling (1970), chapters 10–11; Hymes (1964), Part 6. On rapping and playing the dozens, see the works referred to for Black English in Chapter 9 and, more especially, Abrahams (1974). On Walbiri antonymic talk, see Hale (1971).

On literacy and its cultural importance: Basso (1974); Goody (1968); Goody & Watt (1962).

QUESTIONS AND EXERCISES

1. "It is . . . something of a contradiction, an irony at least, that we have today a general linguistics that justifies itself in terms of understanding the distinctiveness of man, but has nothing to say, as linguistics, of human life. The voice is the voice of humanism, of a rational idealism; the hand, one fears, is the hand of mechanism" (Hymes, 1977: 147). Comment upon this judgement in the light of your own understanding of the aims and methodology of linguistics.

2. What distinction, if any, would you draw between a **biological** and a **cultural** approach to the study of language?

3. Give a critical account of the **Sapir–Whorf hypothesis** with particular

reference to some domain of the vocabulary other than that of colour.

4. Explain and exemplify (with examples other than those in the text) the process of **loan-translation**.

5. Discuss the validity of the notion of **codability** and its relevance to the theses of (a) **linguistic relativity** and (b) **linguistic determinism**.

6. "Languages differ from one another without limit and in unpredictable ways" (Joos, 1966: 228). Discuss this assertion with particular reference to Chomsky's theory of **language-universals** (cf. 7.4).

7. Discuss the applicability of the notion of focal, or **prototypical**, meaning to areas of the vocabularies of natural languages other than colour terminology.

8. What distinction, if any, would you draw between a **literal** and a **free translation**? Can you give a precise definition of the term 'literal' in this context?

9. "All cognitive experience and its classification is conveyable in any existing language. Whenever there is deficiency, terminology may be qualified and amplified by loanwords or loan-translations, neologisms or semantic shifts, and finally, by circumlocutions" (Jakobson, 1966: 234). Comment upon this statement, exemplifying each of the means of qualification and amplification mentioned and assessing their effect upon the existing language.

10. (a) "The unparalleled range of Bible translating, including as it does, not only all the major languages of the world but hundreds of "primitive" tongues, provides a wealth of data and background of experience in the fundamental problems of communication . . ." (Nida, 1966: 12). Why is Bible translation so special? Do the theological views of the translator make any difference to what counts, for him, as a faithful translation? If so, in what respects? (b) How many English expressions known to you can you identify as having entered the language as the result of Bible translation? How many of these do you classify, intuitively, as idiomatic, and why? Has Bible translation had any effect upon the grammatical structure of (i) colloquial and (ii) literary English?

11. What sense, if any, do you attribute to the expression 'language of culture' ('langue de culture', 'Kultursprache')?

12. Read one of the case-studies in the **ethnography of speaking** published or cited in Bauman & Sherzer (1974) and write a 1200 word summary including a brief commentary of your own.

13. If you are familiar with a language with a T/V distinction and have access to native speakers, try to determine and formulate as precisely as you can the sociolinguistic/stylistic determinants of usage. Evaluate

your results in the light of the generalizations made about **power and solidarity** in Brown & Gilman (1960), Brown & Levinson (1978) and the textbooks of sociolinguistics referred to in Chapter 9. Is there anything comparable in the grammar or vocabulary of English?

14. How is politeness expressed in English? Discuss this question with particular reference to (a) greetings and farewells and (b) the use of names and titles. Is politeness a cultural universal? If not, can it be seen as a culture-dependent manifestation of something that is truly universal in language-behaviour?

15. "Speakers of all languages in all parts of the world credit some of their fellows with superior linguistic skills, and those so recognized are often paid a special respect" (Burling, 1970: 150). Give an account of one such kind of **linguistic virtuosity** (other than what would normally count as literary composition in our culture): e.g. punning, rhyming and riddling, and other varieties of verbal play; glossolalia (speaking in tongues); rapping and playing the dozens (by speakers of Black English in America); Walbiri antonymic, or upside-down, talk. Discuss the role that this particular kind of linguistic virtuosity plays in the culture in which it operates and assess its significance for a general theory of the structure and use of language.

Bibliography

This list includes all the works referred to in the text and in the 'Further reading' and 'Questions and exercises' sections. With very few exceptions, works in languages other than English have not been mentioned unless they have also been published in an English translation. Journal articles have been cited only if they have been reprinted or excerpted in accessible readers and anthologies. Since the Bibliography itself is quite extensive, I have asterisked a smaller number of general textbooks and collections of readings. Beginning students of linguistics are advised to consult several of these in order to get a balanced view of the field.

Abercrombie, D. (1966) *Elements of General Phonetics*. Edinburgh: Edinburgh University Press & Chicago: Aldine.

Abercrombie, D. (1967) *Problems and Principles in Language Study*. London: Oxford University Press.

Abrahams, R. D. (1974) 'Black talking on the streets'. In Bauman & Sherzer (1974).

Adler, M. K. (1978) *Naming and Addressing: A Sociolinguistic Study*. Hamburg: Buske.

Aitchison, J. (1976) *The Articulate Mammal*. London: Hutchinson.

*Aitchison, J. (1978) *Linguistics*, 2nd edn. London: Teach Yourself Books. (1st edn, 1972.)

Aitchison, J. (1981) *Language Change: Progress or Decay?* London: Fontana.

Akmajian, A. & Heny, F. W. (1975) *An Introduction to the Principles of Transformational Syntax*. Cambridge, Mass.: MIT Press.

Akmajian, A., Demers, R. A. & Harnish, R. M. (1979) *Linguistics: An Introduction to Language and Communication*. Cambridge, Mass. & London: MIT Press.

Albert, M. L. & Obler, L. K. (1978) *The Bilingual Brain: Neuropsychological Aspects of Bilingualism*. New York, San Francisco & London: Academic Press.

*Allen, H. B. (ed.) (1964) *Readings in Applied English Linguistics*, 2nd edn. New York: Appleton-Century-Crofts.

*Allen, J. P. B. & Corder, S. P. (eds) (1975a) *The Edinburgh Course in

Applied Linguistics, Vol. 1: *Readings for Applied Linguistics*. London: Oxford University Press. (First published, 1973.)

Allen, J. P. B. & Corder, S. P. (eds) (1975b) *The Edinburgh Course in Applied Linguistics*, Vol. 2: *Papers in Applied Linguistics*. London: Oxford University Press.

Allen, J. P. B. & Corder, S. P. (eds) (1975c) *The Edinburgh Course in Applied Linguistics*, Vol. 3: *Techniques in Applied Linguistics*. London: Oxford University Press. (First published, 1974.)

Allerton, D. J. (1979) *Essentials of Grammar: A Consensus View of Syntax and Morphology*. London & Boston: Routledge & Kegan Paul.

Allwood, J., Andersson, L.-G. & Dahl, O. (1977) *Logic in Linguistics*. Cambridge: Cambridge University Press.

*Anderson, W. L. & Stageberg, N. C. (eds) (1966) *Introductory Readings on Language*, revised edn. New York: Holt, Rinehart & Winston.

Apresjan, J. D. (1974) *Leksičeskaja Semantika*. Moscow: 'Nauka'.

Ardener, R. (ed.) (1971) *Social Anthropology and Language*. London: Tavistock Press.

Bach, E. (1974) *Syntactic Theory*. New York: Holt, Rinehart & Winston.

Bailey, C.-J. N. & Shuy, R. W. (eds) (1973) *New Ways of Analysing Variation in English*. Washington: Georgetown University Press.

Bailey, R. W. & Robinson, J. L. (eds) (1973) *Varieties of Present Day English*. New York: Macmillan.

Baker, C. L. (1978) *Introduction to Generative-Transformational Syntax*. Englewood Cliffs, NJ: Prentice-Hall.

Barber, C. L. (1972) *The Story of Language*, revised edn. London & Sydney: Pan Books.

Basso, K. H. (1974) 'The ethnography of writing'. In Bauman & Sherzer (1974).

Baugh, A. C. (1965) *History of the English Language*, 2nd edn. London: Kegan Paul & New York: Appleton-Century-Crofts.

Bauman, R. & Sherzer, J. (eds) (1974) *Explorations in the Ethnography of Speaking*. London & New York: Cambridge University Press.

Beckman, J. & Callow, J. (1974) *Translating the Word of God*. Grant Rapids, Michigan: Zondervan.

Bell, R. T. (1976) *Sociolinguistics: Goals, Approaches and Problems*. London: Batsford.

Bergenholtz, H. & Mugdan, J. (1979) *Einführung in die Morphologie*. Stuttgart: Kohlhammer.

Berlin, B. & Kay, P. (1969). *Basic Color Terms*. Berkeley: University of California Press.

Bernstein, B. (1971) *Class, Codes and Control*, Vol. 1: *Theoretical Studies Towards a Sociology of Language*. London: Routledge & Kegan Paul.

Berry, M. (1975) *Introduction to Systemic Linguistics I: Structures and Systems*. London: Batsford.

Berry, M. (1977) *Introduction to Systemic Linguistics II: Levels and Links*. London: Batsford.

Black, M. (1959) 'Linguistic relativity: the views of Benjamin Lee Whorf'. *Philosophical Review* 68: 228–38. Reprinted in Black, M. (1962) *Models and Metaphors*. Ithaca, NY: Cornell University Press.

Black, M. (1969) 'Some problems with "Whorfianism"'. In Hook (1969).

Blakemore, C. (1977) *Mechanics of the Mind*. Cambridge: Cambridge University Press.

Bloch, B. & Trager, G. L. (1942) *Outline of Linguistic Analysis*. Baltimore: Linguistic Society of America/Waverly Press.

Bloomfield, L. (1935) *Language*. London: Allen & Unwin. (American edition, New York: Holt, Rinehart & Winston, 1933.)

Boas, Franz (1911) *Handbook of American Indian Languages*. Washington, DC: Smithsonian Institute. (Introduction excerpted in Hymes (1964).)

Bobrow, D. G. & Collins, A. (eds) (1975) *Representation and Understanding: Studies in Cognitive Science*. New York: Academic Press.

Boden, M. A. (1977) *Artificial Intelligence and the Natural Man*. Hassocks, Sussex: Harvester & New York: Basic Books.

Boden, M. A. (1980) *Piaget*. London: Fontana/Collins & New York: Viking Penguin.

Bolinger, D. L. (ed.) (1972) *Intonation*. Harmondsworth: Penguin.

*Bolinger, D. L. (1975) *Aspects of Language*, 2nd edn. New York: Harcourt Brace Jovanovich. (1st edn, 1968.)

Bright, W. (ed.) (1966) *Sociolinguistics*. The Hague: Mouton.

Bright, W. (ed.) (1968) *Sociolinguistics*. The Hague: Mouton.

Brosnahan, L. F. & Malmberg, B. (1970) *Introduction to Phonetics*. London & New York: Cambridge University Press.

Brower, R. A. (ed.) (1966) *On Translation*. London & New York: Oxford University Press. (First published, 1959.)

Brown, E. K. & Miller, J. E. (1980) *Syntax: A Linguistic Introduction to Sentence Structure*. London: Hutchinson.

Brown, G. (1977) *Listening to Spoken English*. London: Longman.

Brown, P. & Levinson, S. (1978) 'Universals in language usage'. In Goody (1978).

Brown, R. (1958a) 'How shall a thing be called?' *Psychological Review* 65: 14–21. Reprinted in Oldfield & Marshall (1968).

Brown, R. (1958b) *Words and Things*. Glencoe, Ill.: Free Press.

Brown, R. (1970) *Psycholinguistics*. New York: Free Press.

Brown, R. & Ford, M. (1961) 'Address in American English'. *Journal of Abnormal and Social Psychology* 62: 375–85. Reprinted in Hymes (1964); Laver & Hutcheson (1972).

Brown, R. & Gilman, A. (1960) 'The pronouns of power and solidarity'. In

Sebeok (1960). Reprinted in Fishman (1968); Giglioli (1972); Laver & Hutcheson (1972).

Brown, R. & Lenneberg, E. H. (1954). 'A study of language and cognition'. *Journal of Abnormal and Social Psychology* 49: 452–60. Reprinted in Brown (1970); Saporta (1961).

Burgess, A. (1975) *Language Made Plain*, 2nd edn. London: Fontana/Collins.

Burling, R. (1970) *Man's Many Voices: Language in its Cultural Context*. New York: Holt, Rinehart & Winston.

Burling, R. (1973) *English in Black and White*. New York: Holt, Rinehart & Winston.

Bynon, T. (1977) *Historical Linguistics*. Cambridge: Cambridge University Press.

Carroll, J. B. (1953a) *The Study of Language*. Cambridge, Mass.: Harvard University Press.

Carroll, J. B. (1953b) *Language and Thought*. Englewood Cliffs, NJ: Prentice-Hall.

Cashdan, A. & Grudgeon, E. (eds) (1972) *Language in Education: A Source Book*. London & Boston: Routledge & Kegan Paul, in association with The Open University Press.

Catford, J. C. (1965) *A Linguistic Theory of Translation: An Essay in Applied Linguistics*. London: Oxford University Press.

Catford, J. C. (1977) *Fundamental Problems in Phonetics*. Edinburgh: Edinburgh University Press.

Chambers, J. K. & Trudgill, P. (1980) *Dialectology*. Cambridge: Cambridge University Press.

*Chao, Y. R. (1968) *Language and Symbolic Systems*. London & New York: Cambridge University Press.

Charniak, E. & Wilks, Y. A. (eds) (1976) *Computational Semantics: An Introduction to Artificial Intelligence and Natural Language Comprehension*. Amsterdam: North Holland.

Chatman, S. & Levin, S. R. (eds) (1967) *Essays on the Language of Literature*. Boston, Mass.: Houghton Mifflin.

Cherry, C. (1957) *On Human Communication*. Cambridge, Mass.: MIT Press. (Reprinted, New York: Science Editions, 1959.)

Chomsky, N. (1957) *Syntactic Structures*. The Hague: Mouton.

Chomsky, N. (1959) Review of B. F. Skinner, *Verbal Behavior*. In *Language* 35: 26–58. Reprinted in Fodor & Katz (1964); Jakobovits & Miron (1967).

Chomsky, N. (1965) *Aspects of the Theory of Syntax*. Cambridge, Mass.: MIT Press.

Chomsky, N. (1966) *Cartesian Linguistics*. New York: Harper & Row.

Chomsky, N. (1972a) *Language and Mind*, 2nd enlarged edn. New York: Harcourt Brace. (First edn, 1968.)

Chomsky, N. (1972b) *Problems of Knowledge and Freedom*. London: Barrie & Jenkins.

Chomsky, N. (1976) *Reflections on language*. London: Temple Smith.

Chomsky, N. (1979) *Rules and Representations*. New York: Columbia University Press. (British edn, Oxford: Blackwell, 1980.)

Chomsky, N. & Halle, M. (1968) *The Sound Pattern of English*. New York: Harper & Row.

Clark, H. H. & Clark, E. V. (1977) *Psychology and Language: An Introduction to Psycholinguistics*. New York: Harcourt Brace Jovanovich.

Cook, W. A. (1969) *Introduction to Tagmemic Analysis*. Washington, DC: Georgetown University Press.

Cooper, D. E. (1973) *Philosophy and the Nature of Language*. London: Longman.

Corder, S. P. (1973) *Introducing Applied Linguistics*. Harmondsworth: Penguin.

Crick, M. (1976) *Explorations in Language and Meaning: Towards a Semantic Anthropology*. London: Malaby.

Criper, C. & Widdowson, H. G. (1975) 'Sociolinguistics and language teaching'. In Allen & Corder (1975b).

*Crystal, D. (1971) *Linguistics*. Harmondsworth: Penguin.

Crystal, D. (1976) *Child Language, Learning and Linguistics: An Overview for the Teaching and Therapeutic Professions*. London: Arnold.

Crystal, D. & Davy, D. (1969) *Investigating English Style*. London: Longman.

Culicover, P. W. (1976) *Syntax*. London & New York: Academic Press.

Culler, J. (1973) 'The linguistic basis of structuralism'. In Robey (1973).

Culler, J. (1975) *Structuralist Poetics*. London: Routledge & Kegan Paul.

Culler, J. (1976) *Saussure*. London: Fontana/Collins.

Curme, G. O. (1935) *A Grammar of the English Language*. Boston: Ginn.

Dale, P. S. (1976) *Language Development: Structure and Function*, 2nd edn. New York & London: Holt, Rinehart & Winston.

DeStefano, J. S. (1973) *Language, Society and Education: A Profile of Black English*. Worthington, Ohio: Charles Jones.

Dik, S. C. (1978) *Functional Grammar*. Amsterdam, New York & London: North Holland.

Dillard, J. L. (1972) *Black English: Its History and Usage in the United States*. New York: Random House.

Dillon, G. (1977) *An Introduction to Contemporary Linguistic Semantics*. Englewood Cliffs, NJ: Prentice-Hall.

Dinneen, F. P. (1967) *An Introduction to General Linguistics*. New York: Holt, Rinehart & Winston.

Dinnsen, D. (ed.) (1979) *Current Approaches to Phonological Theory*. Bloomington & London: Indiana University Press.

Dittmar, N. (1976) *Sociolinguistics: A Critical Survey of Theory and Application*. London: Arnold.

Dixon, R. M. W. (1980) *The Languages of Australia*. Cambridge: Cambridge University Press.

Donaldson, M. (1978) *Children's Minds*. London: Fontana/Collins.

Eco, U. (1976) *A Theory of Semiotics*. London & Bloomington, Ind.: Indiana University Press.

Edwards, A. D. (1976) *Language in Culture and Class*. London: Heinemann.

Edwards, P. (1967) *Encyclopaedia of Philosophy*. New York & London: Collier & Macmillan.

Ehrmann, J. (ed.) (1970) *Structuralism*. New York: Doubleday.

Elliot, A. (1981) *Child Language*. Cambridge: Cambridge University Press.

Elson, B. & Pickett, V. (1962) *An Introduction to Morphology and Syntax*. Santa Ana, Calif.: Summer Institute of Linguistics.

Emeneau, M. S. (1980) *Language and Linguistic Area*. Selected and introduced by A. S. Dil. Stanford, Calif.: Stanford University Press.

Ervin-Tripp, S. (1973) *Language Acquisition and Language Choice*. Selected and introduced by A. S. Dil. Stanford, Calif.: Stanford University Press.

*Falk, J. S. (1973) *Linguistics and Language*. Lexington, Mass. & Toronto: Xerox College Publishing.

Ferguson, C. A. (1959) 'Diglossia'. *Word* 15: 325–40. Reprinted in Giglioli (1972); Hymes (1964).

Ferguson, C. A. (1971) *Language Structure and Language Use*. Selected and introduced by A. S. Dil. Stanford, Calif.: Stanford University Press.

Fink, S. R. (1977) *Aspects of a Pedagogical Grammar Based on a Case Grammar and Valence Theory*. Tübingen: Niemeyer.

Firth, J. R. (1957) *Papers in Linguistics 1934–51*. London: Oxford University Press.

Fischer-Jørgensen, E. (1975) *Trends in Phonological Theory: A Historical Introduction*. Copenhagen: Akademisk Forlag.

Fishman, J. A. (1965) 'Who speaks what language to whom and when'. *La Linguistique* 2. 67–88. Revised as 'The relationship between micro- and macro-sociolinguistics in the study of who speaks what language to whom and when'. In Pride & Holmes (1972).

Fishman, J. A. (ed.) (1968) *Readings in the Sociology of Language*. The Hague: Mouton.

Fishman, J. A. (1970) *Sociolinguistics: A Brief Introduction*. Rowley, Mass.: Newbury House.

Fishman, J. A. (1972a) *The Sociology of Language*. Rowley, Mass.: Newbury House.

Fishman, J. A. (ed..) (1972b) *Advances in the Sociology of Language*, 2 vols. The Hague: Mouton.

Fishman, J. A. (1972c) *Language and Nationalism*. Rowley, Mass.: Newbury House.

Fishman, J. A., Ferguson, C. A. & Das Gupta, J. (eds) (1968) *Language Problems of Developing Nations*. New York: Wiley.

Fletcher, Paul & Garman, Michael (eds) (1979) *Language Acquisition*. Cambridge: Cambridge University Press.

Fodor, J. A. (1975) *The Language of Thought*. New York: Crowell & Hassocks, Sussex: Harvester.

Fodor, J. A. & Katz, J. J. (eds) (1964) *The Structure of Language: Readings in the Philosophy of Language*. Englewood Cliffs, NJ: Prentice-Hall.

Fodor, J. D. (1977) *Semantics: Theories of Meaning in Generative Linguistics*. New York: Crowell & Hassocks, Sussex: Harvester.

*Fowler, R. (1964) *Understanding Language: An Introduction to Linguistics*. London: Routledge & Kegan Paul.

Fowler, R. (ed.) (1966) *Essays on Style and Language*. London: Routledge & Kegan Paul.

Francis, W. N. (1967) *The English Language: An Introduction*. London: English Universities Press.

Freeman, D. C. (ed.) (1970) *Linguistics and Literary Style*. New York: Holt, Rinehart & Winston.

Friedrich, P. (1968) 'Structural implications of Russian pronominal usage'. In Bright (1968).

Friedrich, P. (1972) 'Social context and semantic feature: the Russian pronominal usage'. In Gumperz & Hymes (1972).

Fries, C. C. (1952) *The Structure of English. An Introduction to the Construction of English Sentences*. New York: Harcourt Brace.

*Fromkin, V. & Rodman, R. (1974) *An Introduction to Language*, 2nd edn. New York: Holt, Rinehart & Winston. (1st edn, 1974.)

Fry, D. B. (1977) *Homo Loquens*. Cambridge: Cambridge University Press.

Fry, D. B. (1979) *The Physics of Speech*. Cambridge: Cambridge University Press.

Fudge, E. C. (1970) 'Phonology'. In Lyons (1970).

Fudge, E. C. (ed.) (1973) *Phonology*. Harmondsworth: Penguin.

Gaeng, P. A. (1971) *Introduction to the Principles of Language*. New York: Harper & Row.

Garvin, P. L. (ed.) (1964) *A Prague School Reader on Aesthetics, Literary Structure and Style*. Washington, DC: Georgetown University Press.

Gelb, I. J. (1963) *A Study of Writing*, 2nd edn. Chicago: University of Chicago Press. (1st edn, 1952.)

Gelb, I. J. (1976) 'Writing, Forms of'. *Encyclopaedia Britannica*, 15th edn.

Giglioli, P. P. (ed.) (1972) *Language and Social Context*. Harmondsworth: Penguin.

Giles, H. (ed.) (1977) *Language, Ethnicity and Social Context*. London: Academic Press.

Gimson, A. C. (1970) *Introduction to the Pronunciation of English*, 2nd edn. London: Arnold.

*Gleason, H. A. (1961) *Introduction to Descriptive Linguistics*, 2nd edn. New York: Holt Rinehart. (1st edn, 1955.)

Gleason, H. A. (1965) *Linguistics and English Grammar*. New York: Holt, Rinehart & Winston.

Goody, E. N. (ed.) (1978) *Questions and Politeness: Strategies in Social Interaction*. Cambridge: Cambridge University Press.

Goody, J. (1968) *Literacy in Traditional Societies*. Cambridge: Cambridge University Press.

Goody, J. & Watt, I. (1962) 'The consequences of literacy'. *Comparative Studies in Society and History* 5: 304–26; 332–45. Excerpts in Giglioli (1972).

Greenberg, J. (1968) *Anthropological Linguistics*. New York: Random House.

Greenberg, J. (1971) *Language, Culture and Communication*. Selected and introduced by A. S. Dil. Stanford, Calif.: Stanford University Press.

Greene, J. (1972) *Psycholinguistics: Chomsky and Psychology*. Harmondsworth: Penguin.

Gumperz, J. J. (1971) *Language in Social Groups*. Selected and introduced by A. S. Dil. Stanford, Calif.: Stanford University Press.

Gumperz, J. J. & Hymes, D. H. (eds) (1972) *Directions in Sociolinguistics: The Ethnography of Communication*. New York: Holt, Rinehart & Winston.

Haas, W. (1976) 'Writing: the basic options'. In Haas, W. (ed.) *Writing without Letters*. Manchester: Manchester University Press.

Hacking, I. (1975) *Why Does Language Matter to Philosophy?* Cambridge: Cambridge University Press.

Hale, K. (1971) 'A note on a Walbiri tradition of antonymy'. In Steinberg & Jakobovits (1971).

Hall, R. A. (1964) *Introductory Linguistics*. Philadelphia & New York: Chilton Books.

Hall, R. A. (1968) *An Essay on Language*. Philadelphia & New York: Chilton Books.

Halliday, M. A. K. (1970) 'Language structure and language function'. In Lyons (1970).

Halliday, M. A. K. (1973) *Explorations in the Functions of Language*. London: Arnold.

Halliday, M. A. K. (1976) *System and Function in Language: Selected Papers*, ed. G. R. Cress. London: Oxford University Press.

Halliday, M. A. K. & McIntosh, A. (eds) (1966) *Patterns in Language: Papers in General, Descriptive and Applied Linguistics*. London: Longman.

Halliday, M. A. K., McIntosh, A. & Strevens, P. D. (1964) *The Linguistic Sciences and Language Teaching*. London: Longman.

*Hamp, E. P., Householder, F. W. & Austerlitz, R. (1966) *Readings in Linguistics II*. Chicago: University of Chicago Press.

Harman, G. (ed.) (1974) *On Noam Chomsky: Selected Essays*. New York: Doubleday.

Harris, Z. S. (1951) *Methods in Structural Linguistics*. Chicago: University of Chicago Press. (Reprinted as *Structural Linguistics*, 1951.)

Haugen, E. (1972) *The Ecology of Language*. Selected and introduced by A. S. Dil. Stanford, Calif.: Stanford University Press.

Haugen, E. (1973) 'Bilingualism, language contact, and immigrant languages in the United States: A research report 1956–1970'. In Sebeok, T. A. (ed.) *Current Trends in Linguistics*, Vol. 10. The Hague: Mouton.

Hawkes, T. (1977) *Structuralism and Semiotics*. London: Methuen.

Hayden, D. E., Alworth, P. E. & Tate, G. (1967) *Classics in Linguistics*. New York: Philosophical Library.

Helbig, G. (ed.) (1971) *Beiträge zur Valenztheorie*. The Hague: Mouton.

Henderson, E. J. A. (1971) 'Phonology'. In Minnis (1971).

Henle, P. (ed.) (1958) *Language, Thought and Culture*. Ann Arbor: University of Michigan Press.

Hewes, G. W. (1977) 'Language origin theories'. In Rumbaugh (1977).

*Hill, A. A. (1958) *Introduction to Linguistic Structures*. New York: Harcourt, Brace & Co.

Hinde, R. A. (ed.) (1972) *Non-Verbal Communication*. London & New York: Cambridge University Press.

*Hockett, C. F. (1958) *A Course in Modern Linguistics*. New York: Macmillan.

Hockett, C. F. (1960) 'Logical considerations in the study of animal communication'. In Lanyon, W. E. & Tavolga, W. N. (eds) *Animal Sounds and Communication*. Washington, DC: American Institute of Biological Sciences. Reprinted in Hockett, C. F. (1977) *The View from Language: Selected Essays 1948–1974*. Athens, Georgia: University of Georgia Press.

Hockett, C. F. & Altmann, S. (1968) 'A note on design features'. In Sebeok (1968).

*Hogins, J. B. & Yarber, R. E. (eds) (1969) *Language: An Introductory Reader*. New York: Harper & Row.

Hoijer, H. (ed.) (1954) *Language in Culture*. Chicago: University of Chicago.

Hook, S. (ed.) (1969) *Language and Philosophy*. New York: New York University Press.

Hough, G. (1969) *Style and Stylistics*. London: Routledge & Kegan Paul.

Householder, F. W. (1971) *Linguistic Speculations*. Cambridge: Cambridge University Press.

Householder, F. W. (ed.) (1972) *Syntactic Theory 1: Structuralist. Selected Readings*. Harmondsworth: Penguin.

Huddleston, R. (1976) *An Introduction to English Transformational Syntax*. London: Longman.

Hudson, R. A. (1971) *English Complex Sentences: An Introduction to Systemic Grammar*. Amsterdam: North Holland.

Hudson, R. A. (1976) *Arguments for a Non-transformational Grammar*. Chicago: University of Chicago Press.

Hudson, R. A. (1980) *Sociolinguistics*. Cambridge: Cambridge University Press.

Hughes, A. & Trudgill, P. (1979) *English Accents and Dialects: An Introduction to Social and Regional Variation in British English*. London: Arnold.

*Hungerford, H., Robinson, J. & Sledd, J. (1970) *English Linguistics: An Introductory Reader*. Glencoe, Ill.: Scott, Foresman.

Hyman, L. (1975) *Phonology: Theory and Analysis*. New York: Holt, Rinehart & Winston.

Hymes, D. H. (ed.) (1964) *Language in Culture and Society*. New York: Harper & Row.

Hymes, D. H. (ed.) (1971) *Pidginization and Creolization of Language*. Cambridge: Cambridge University Press.

Hymes, D. H. (1977) *Foundations in Sociolinguistics: An Ethnographic Approach*. London: Tavistock Publications. (American edn, Philadelphia: University of Philadelphia Press, 1974.)

International Phonetic Association (1949) *Principles of the International Phonetic Association*, revised edn. London: International Phonetic Association.

Ivić, M. (1965) *Trends in Linguistics*. The Hague: Mouton.

Jacobs, R. A. & Rosenbaum, P. S. (eds) (1970) *Readings in English Transformational Grammar*. Waltham, Mass.: Ginn & Co.

Jakobovits, L. A. & Miron, M. S. (1967) *Readings in the Psychology of Language*. Englewood Cliffs, NJ: Prentice-Hall.

Jakobson, R. (1966) 'On linguistic aspects of translation'. In Brower (1966).

Jakobson, R. (1973) *Six leçons sur le son et le sens* (with preface by C. Lévi-Strauss). Paris: Minuit. English translation: *Six Lectures on Sound and Meaning*. Hassocks, Sussex: Harvester, 1978.

Jespersen, O. (1909–49) *A Modern English Grammar on Historical Principles*. Heidelberg: Winter & Copenhagen: Munksgaard.

Jespersen, O. (1922) *Language: Its Nature, Development and Origin.* London: Allen & Unwin.

Johnson, Nancy A. (ed.) (1976) *Current Topics in Language.* Cambridge, Mass.: Winthrop.

Johnson-Laird, P. N. & Wason, P. C. (eds) (1977) *Thinking: Readings in Cognitive Science.* Cambridge: Cambridge University Press.

Jones, D. (1975) *An Outline of English Phonetics,* 9th edn. Cambridge: Cambridge University Press.

Jones, W. E. & Laver, J. (eds) (1973) *Phonetics in Linguistics.* London: Longman.

*Joos, M. (ed.) (1966) *Readings in Linguistics I.* Chicago: University of Chicago Press. (1st edn, 1957.)

Kempson, R. M. (1977) *Semantic Theory.* London & New York: Cambridge University Press.

Kenstowicz, M. & Kisseberth, C. (1979) *Generative Phonology.* Bloomington & London: Indiana University Press.

Keyser, S. J. & Postal, P. M. (1976) *Beginning English Grammar.* New York & London: Harper & Row.

Klima, E. & Bellugi, U. (1978) *The Signs of Language.* Cambridge, Mass.: Harvard University Press.

Koutsoudas, A. C. (1966) *Writing Transformational Grammars.* New York: McGraw-Hill.

Labov, W. (1972) *Sociolinguistic Patterns.* Philadelphia: University of Philadelphia Press & Oxford: Blackwell.

Ladefoged, P. (1962) *Elements of Acoustic Phonetics.* Chicago & London: Chicago University Press.

Ladefoged, P. (1974) 'Phonetics'. In *Encyclopaedia Britannica,* 15th edn.

Ladefoged, P. (1975) *A Course in Phonetics.* New York: Harcourt Brace Jovanovich.

Lane, M. (ed.) (1970) *Structuralism: A Reader.* London: Cape.

Langacker, R. W. (1968) *Language and its Structure,* 2nd edn. New York: Harcourt, Brace & World.

Langacker, R. W. (1972) *Fundamentals of Linguistic Analysis.* New York: Harcourt Brace Jovanovich.

Lass, R. (ed.) (1969) *Approaches to Historical English Linguistics: An Anthology.* New York: Holt, Rinehart & Winston.

Laver, J. & Hutcheson, S. (1972) *Communication in Face to Face Interaction.* Harmondsworth: Penguin.

Lawton, D. (1968) *Social Class, Language and Education.* London: Routledge & Kegan Paul.

Leech, G. N. (1969) *A Linguistic Guide to English Poetry.* London: Longman.

Leech, G. N. (1971) *Semantics.* Harmondsworth: Penguin.

Leech, G. N. (1976) *Meaning and the English Verb.* London: Longman.

Lehmann, W. P. (1973) *Historical Linguistics: An Introduction*, 2nd edn. New York: Holt, Rinehart & Winston.

Lenneberg, E. H. (1967) *Biological Foundations of Language*. New York: Wiley.

Lepschy, G. (1970) *A Survey of Structural Linguistics*. London: Faber & Faber. (Original Italian edition, *La linguistica strutturale*. Turin: Einaudi, 1966.)

Leroy, M. (1963) *Les grands courants de la linguistique moderne*. Brussels & Paris: Presses Universitaires. English translation: *The Main Trends in Modern Linguistics*. Oxford: Blackwell, 1967.

Levinson, S. (1981) *Pragmatics*. Cambridge: Cambridge University Press.

Lieberman, P. (1975) *On the Origins of Language: An Introduction to the Evolution of Human Speech*. New York: Macmillan.

Linden, E. (1976) *Apes, Man and Language*. London & New York: Penguin. (First published, New York: Dutton, 1975.)

Lloyd, B. B. (ed.) (1972) *Perception and Cognition: A Cross Cultural Perspective*. Harmondsworth: Penguin.

Lockwood, D. G. (1972) *Introduction to Stratificational Linguistics*. New York: Harcourt Brace.

Longacre, R. E. (1964) *Grammar Discovery Procedures: A Field Manual*. The Hague: Mouton.

Lounsbury, F. L. (1969) 'Language and culture'. In Hook (1969).

Love, G. A. & Payne, M. (eds) (1969) *Contemporary Essays on Style*. Glenview, Ill.: Scott, Foresman.

Lyons, J. (1962) 'Phonemic and non-phonemic phonology'. *International Journal of American Linguistics* 28: 127–33. Reprinted in Jones & Laver (1973).

*Lyons, J. (1968) *Introduction to Theoretical Linguistics*. London & New York: Cambridge University Press.

*Lyons, J. (ed.) (1970) *New Horizons in Linguistics*. Harmondsworth: Penguin.

Lyons, J. (1974) 'Linguistics'. In *Encyclopaedia Britannica*, 15th edn.

Lyons, J. (1977a) *Chomsky*, 2nd edn. London: Fontana & New York: Viking/Penguin (1st edn, 1970.)

Lyons, J. (1977b) *Semantics*, 2 vols. London & New York: Cambridge University Press.

Lyons, J. (1980) 'Pronouns of address in *Anna Karenina*: the stylistics of bilingualism and the impossibility of translation'. In Greenbaum, S., Leech, G. & Svartvik, J. (eds) *Studies in English Linguistics: For Randolph Quirk*. London: Longman.

Lyons, J. (1981) *Language, Meaning and Context*. London: Fontana/Collins.

Mackey W. F. (1965) *Language Teaching Analysis*. London: Longman.

McNeill, D. (1970) *The Acquisition of Language: The Study of Developmental Psycholinguistics*. New York: Harper & Row.

Makkai, V. B. (1972) *Phonological Theory, Evolution and Current Practice*. New York: Holt, Rinehart & Winston.

Makkai, A. & Lockwood, D. G. (eds) (1973) *Readings in Stratificational Linguistics*. Alabama: University of Georgia Press.

Malmberg, B. (1963) *Phonetics*. New York: Dover.

Malmberg, B. (1964) *New Trends in Linguistics*. Stockholm: Naturmetodens Språkinstitut.

Malmberg, B. (ed.) (1968) *A Manual of Phonetics*. Amsterdam: North Holland.

Martinet, A. (1949) *Phonology as Functional Phonetics*. London: Oxford University Press.

*Martinet, A. (1960) *Eléments de linguistique générale*. Paris: Colin. English translation: *Elements of General Linguistics*. London: Faber, 1964.

Martinet, A. (1962) *A Functional View of Language*. Oxford: Clarendon Press.

Matthews, P. H. (1974) *Morphology: An Introduction to the Theory of Word Structure*. London & New York: Cambridge University Press.

Matthews, P. H. (1979) *Generative Grammar and Linguistic Competence*. London: Allen & Unwin.

Matthews, P. H. (1981) *Syntax*. Cambridge: Cambridge University Press.

Miller, G. A. (1967) *The Psychology of Communication: Seven Essays*. New York: Basic Books.

Miller, G. A., Galanter, E. & Pribram, K. H. (1960) *Plans and the Structure of Behavior*. New York: Holt, Rinehart & Winston.

*Minnis, N. (ed.) (1971) *Linguistics at Large*. London: Gollancz.

Minsky, M. L. (ed.) (1968) *Semantic Information Processing*. Cambridge, Mass.: MIT Press.

Mohrmann, C., Sommerfelt, A. & Whatmough, J. (eds) (1961) *Trends in European and American Linguistics 1930–1960*. Utrecht & Antwerp: Spectrum.

Morton, J. (ed.) (1971) *Biological and Social Factors in Psycholinguistics*. London: Logos/Elek Books.

Nash, W. (1971) *Our Experience of Language*. London: Batsford.

Nida, E. A. (1945) 'Linguistics and ethnology in translation-problems'. *Word* 1: 194–208. Reprinted in Hymes (1964).

Nida, E. A. (1949) *Morphology: The Descriptive Analysis of Words*, 2nd edn. Ann Arbor: University of Michigan Press.

Nida, E. A. (1964) *Towards a Science of Translating. With Special Reference to Principles and Procedures Involved in Bible Translating*. Leiden: Brill.

Nida, E. A. (1966) 'Principles of translation as exemplified by Bible translating'. In Brower (1966).

Nida, E. A. & Taber, C. R. (1969) *The Theory and Practice of Translation*. Leiden: Brill.

Nilsen, D. L. F. & Nilsen, A. P. (1975) *Semantic Theory: A Linguistic Perspective*. Rowley, Mass.: Newbury House.

Norman, F. & Sommerfelt, A. (eds) (1963) *Trends in Modern Linguistics*. Utrecht & Antwerp: Spectrum.

O'Connor, J. D. (1973) *Phonetics*. Harmondsworth: Penguin.

Oldfield, R. C. & Marshall, J. C. (eds) (1968) *Language: Selected Readings*. Harmondsworth: Penguin.

Olshewsky, T. A. (ed.) (1969) *Problems in the Philosophy of Language*. New York & London: Holt, Rinehart & Winston.

Osgood, C. E., May, W. H. & Miron, M. S. (1975) *Cross-Cultural Universals of Affective Meaning*. Urban, Chicago & London: Chicago University Press.

Palmer, F. R. (ed.) (1970) *Prosodic Analysis*. London: Oxford University Press.

Palmer, F. R. (1971) *Grammar*. Harmondsworth: Penguin.

Palmer, F. R. (1974) *The English Verb*. London: Longman.

Palmer, F. R. (1976) *Semantics: A New Outline*. Cambridge: Cambridge University Press.

Paul, H. (1920) *Prinzipien der Sprachgeschichte*, 5th edn. Tübingen: Niemeyer. English translation of 2nd edn: *Principles of Language History*. London, 1890. Republished in revised edn, Maryland: McGrath, 1970.

Piaget, J. (1968) *Le structuralisme*. Paris: Presses Universitaires de France. English translation: *Structuralism*. London: Routledge & Kegan Paul, 1971.

Piattelli-Palmarini, M. (1979) *Théories du langage. Théories de l'apprentissage. Le débat entre Jean Piaget et Noam Chomsky*. Paris: Seuil. English translation: *Language and Learning: The Debate between Jean Piaget and Noam Chomsky*. Boston: Harvard University Press & London: Routledge & Kegan Paul, 1980.

Potter, S. (1950) *Our Language*. Harmondsworth: Penguin.

*Potter, S. (1967) *Modern Linguistics*, 2nd edn. London: Oxford University Press.

Poutsma, H. (1926–9) *A Grammar of Late Modern English*. Groningen: Nourdhoff.

Premack, D. (1977) *Intelligence in Ape and Man*. New York: Wiley.

Pride, J. B. (1971) *The Social Meaning of Language*. London: Oxford University Press.

Pride, J. B. & Holmes, J. (eds) (1972) *Sociolinguistics*. Harmondsworth: Penguin.

Quirk, R. (1968) *The Use of English*, 2nd edn. London: Longman. (1st edn, 1962.)

Quirk, R., Greenbaum, S., Leech, G. N. & Svartvik, J. (1972) *A Grammar of Contemporary English*. London: Longman.

Reibel, D. A. & Schane, S. E. (eds) (1969) *Modern Studies in English: Readings in Transformational Grammar*. Englewood Cliffs, NJ: Prentice-Hall.

Ritchie, G. D. (1980) *Computational Grammar*. Brighton, Sussex: Harvester & Totowa, NJ: Barnes & Noble.

Robey, D. (ed.) (1973) *Structuralism*. London: Oxford University Press.

Robins, R. H. (1971) 'The structure of language'. In Minnis (1971).

Robins, R. H. (1974) 'Language'. In *Encyclopaedia Britannica*, 15th edn.

*Robins, R. H. (1979a) *General Linguistics: An Introductory Survey*, 3rd edn. London: Longman. (1st edn, 1964.)

Robins, R. H. (1979b) *A Short History of Linguistics*, 2nd edn. London: Longman. (1st edn, 1967.)

Robinson, D. F. (ed.) (1975) *Workbook for Phonological Analysis*, 2nd edn. Huntingdon Beach, Calif.: Summer Institute of Linguistics. (1st edn, 1970.)

Robinson, W. P. (1972) *Language and Social Behaviour*. Harmondsworth: Penguin.

Rosch, E. (1973) 'On the internal structure of perceptual and semantic categories'. In Moore, T. E. (ed.) *Cognitive Development and the Acquisition of Language*. London & New York: Academic.

Rosch, E. (1974) 'Linguistics relativity'. In Silverstein, E. (ed.) *Human Communication*. Hillsdale: Erlbaum. Reprinted in Johnson-Laird & Wason (1977).

Rosch, E. (1975) 'Universals and cultural specifics in human categorization'. In Brislin, R., Lonner, W. & Bochner, S. (eds). *Cross-Cultural Perspectives in Learning*. New York: John Wiley.

Rosch, E. (1976) 'Classification of real world objects: origins and representations in cognition'. In Johnson-Laird & Wason (1977).

Rosen, H. (1972) *Language and Class: A Critical Look at the Theories of Basil Bernstein*. Bristol: Falling Wall Press.

Rubin, J. & Shuy, R. (eds) (1973) *Language Planning: Current Issues and Research*. Washington, DC: Georgetown University Press.

Rumbaugh, D. M. (ed.) (1977) *Language Learning by a Chimpanzee*. London & New York: Academic.

Russell, C. & Russell, W. M. S. (1971) 'Language and animal signals'. In Minnis (1971).

Ryle, G. (1949) *The Concept of Mind*. London: Hutchinson. (Republished, Harmondsworth: Penguin, 1963.)

Samarin, W. J. (1967) *Field Linguistics*. New York: Holt, Rinehart & Winston.

Sampson, Geoffrey (1975) *The Form of Language*. London: Weidenfeld & Nicolson.

Sampson, Geoffrey (1980) *Making Sense*. Oxford: Oxford University Press.

Sanders, Carol (1979) *Cours de linguistique générale de Saussure*. Paris: Hachette.

Sapir, E. (1921) *Language*. New York: Harcourt Brace.

Sapir, E. (1947) *Selected Writings in Language, Culture and Personality*. Edited by D. G. Mandelbaum. Berkeley & Los Angeles: University of California Press.

Saporta, S. (ed.) (1961) *Psycholinguistics. A Book of Readings*. With the assistance of J. Bastian. New York: Holt, Rinehart & Winston.

Saussure, F. de (1916) *Cours de linguistique générale*. Paris: Payot. (Critical edition by De Mauro, 1978. English translation: *Course in General Linguistics*. New York: McGraw, 1959 & London: Peter Owen, 1960.)

Savory, T. (1957) *The Art of Translation*. London: Cape.

Schane, S. (1973) *Generative Phonology*. Englewood Cliffs, NJ: Prentice-Hall.

Sebeok, T. A. (ed.) (1960) *Style in Language*. Boston, Mass.: MIT Press & London: Wiley.

Sebeok, T. A. (ed.) (1968) *Animal Communication: Techniques of Study and Results of Research*. Bloomington: Indiana University Press.

Sebeok, T. A. (ed.) (1974a) *Current Trends in Linguistics*, Vol. 12. The Hague: Mouton.

Sebeok, T. A. (1974b) 'Semiotics: A survey of the state of the art'. In Sebeok (1974a).

Sebeok, T. A. (ed.) (1977) *How Animals Communicate*. Bloomington: Indiana University Press.

Sebeok, T. A. & Ramsey, A. (1969) *Approaches to Animal Communication*.

Sebeok, T. A., Hayes, A. S. & Bateson, M. C. (eds) (1964) *Approaches to Semiotics*. The Hague: Mouton.

Shuy, R. W. & Fasold, W. (1973) *Language Attitudes: Current Trends and Prospects*. Washington, DC: Georgetown University Press.

Sinclair, J. McH. (1972) *A Course in Spoken English: Grammar*. London: Oxford University Press.

Siple, P. (ed.) (1978) *Understanding Language through Sign Language Research*. New York: Academic Press.

Skinner, B. F. (1957) *Verbal Behavior*. New York: Appleton Crofts.

Slobin, D. I. (1971) *Psycholinguistics*. Glenview, Ill.: Scott, Foresman.

Sloman, A. (1978) *The Computer Revolution in Philosophy: Philosophy, Science and Models of Mind*. Hassocks, Sussex: Harvester & New York: Humanities Press.

*Smith, N. V. & Wilson, D. (1979) *Modern Linguistics: The Results of the Chomskyan Revolution*. Harmondsworth: Penguin.

Sommerstein, A. H. (1977) *Modern Phonology*. London: Arnold.

*Southworth, F. C. & Daswani, C. J. (1974) *Foundations of Linguistics*. New York: Macmillan.

Stam, J. H. (1977) *Inquiries into the Origin of Language: The Fate of a Question*. New York & London: Harper & Row.

Steinberg, D. D. & Jakobovits, L. A. (eds) (1971) *Semantics: An Interdisciplinary Reader in Philosophy, Linguistics & Psychology*. Cambridge: Cambridge University Press.

Steiner, G. (1975) *After Babel: Aspects of Language and Translation*. London: Oxford University Press.

Stockwell, R. P. (1977) *Foundations of Syntactic Theory*. Englewood Cliffs, NJ: Prentice-Hall.

Stokoe, W. C. (1961) *The Study of Sign Language*. Silver Spring, Md.: National Association for the Deaf.

Strang, B. M. H. (1970) *A History of English*. London: Methuen.

Tesnière, L. (1959) *Éléments de syntaxe structurale*. Paris: Klincksieck.

Thorpe, W. (1974) *Animal Nature and Human Nature*. London: Methuen & New York: Doubleday.

Todd, L. (1974) *Pidgins and Creoles*. London: Routledge.

Traugott, E. C. (1972) *A History of English Syntax*. New York: Holt, Rinehart & Winston.

Trubetzkoy, N. S. (1939) *Grundzuge der Phonologie*. Prague. English translation: *Principles of Phonology*. Berkeley: University of California Press.

Trudgill, P. (1974) *Sociolinguistics: An Introduction*. Harmondsworth: Penguin.

Trudgill, P. (1975) *Accent, Dialect and the School*. London: Arnold.

Trudgill, P. (ed.) (1978) *Sociolinguistic Patterns in British English*. London: Arnold.

Turner, G. W. (1973) *Stylistics*. Harmondsworth: Penguin.

Tyler, S. A. (1969) *Cognitive Anthropology*. New York: Holt, Rinehart & Winston.

Uldall, H. J. (1944) 'Speech and writing'. *Acta Linguistica* (Copenhagen) 4: 11–16. Reprinted in Hamp *et al.* (1966).

Ullmann, S. (1962) *Semantics*. Oxford: Blackwell.

Ullmann, S. (1964) *Language and Style*. Oxford: Blackwell.

Vachek, J. (1949) 'Some remarks on writing and phonetic transcription'. *Acta Linguistica* (Copenhagen) 5: 86–93. Reprinted in Hamp *et al.* (1966).

Vachek, J. (ed.) (1964) *A Prague School Reader in Linguistics*. Bloomington: Indiana University Press.

Vachek, J. (1966) *The Linguistics School of Prague*. Bloomington: Indiana University Press.

Vachek, J. (1973) *Written Language: General Problems and Problems of English*. The Hague: Mouton.

Valdman, A. (ed.) (1977) *Pidgin and Creole Languages*. Bloomington: Indiana University Press.

Vildomec, V. (1963) *Multilingualism*. Leyden: Sythoff.

Villiers, P. A. de & Villiers, J. G. de (1979) *Early Language*. London: Fontana/Open Books.

Waldron, R. A. (1979) *Sense and Sense Development*, 2nd edn. London: Deutsch. (1st edn, 1967.)

Weinreich, U. (1953) *Languages in Contact*. New York: Linguistic Circle & The Hague: Mouton.

Wescott, R. W. (ed.) (1974) *Language Origins*. Silver Spring, Md.: Linstok Press.

Whiteley, W. H. (ed.) (1964) *Language Use and Social Change: Problems of Multilingualism with Special Reference to Eastern Africa*. London: Oxford University Press.

Whorf, B. L. (1956) *Language, Thought and Reality*. Selected writings, edited by J. B. Carroll. Cambridge, Mass.: MIT Press & New York: Wiley.

Widdowson, H. G. (1974) 'Stylistics'. In Allen & Corder (1975c).

Widdowson, H. G. (1976) *Language in Education*. London: Oxford University Press.

Widdowson, H. G. (1978) *Teaching Language as Communication*. London: Oxford University Press.

Wilkins, D. A. (1972) *Linguistics in Language Teaching*. London: Arnold.

Wilks, Y. A. (1972) *Grammar, Meaning and the Machine Analysis of Natural Language*. London: Routledge & Kegan Paul.

Williams, R. (1976) *Keywords: A Vocabulary of Culture and Society*. London: Fontana/Croom Helm.

Winograd, T. (1972) *Understanding Natural Language*. New York: Academic Press & Edinburgh: Edinburgh University Press.

Zabeeh, F., Klemke, E. D. & Jacobson, A. (eds) (1974) *Readings in Semantics*. Urbana, Ill. & London: University of Illinois Press.

Index

accent, 24–5, 268–75
adjacency, principle of, 124
affixation, 103
allophones, 85–7, 91–2, 270, 272
analogy, 200, 201–7, 208, 209
antonymy, 154–5
Aristotle, 50, 108, 201, 217, 239
artificial intelligence, 262–4
aspiration, 74–83, 90–2, 210
assimilation, 207–8, 209
Austin, J. L., 173

behaviourism, 5–6, 9, 127, 230, 231, 241, 242–3
Berlin, B., 314–16
Berlin–Kay hypothesis, 314–16
Bernstein, B., 288
Berry, M., 63n
bilingualism, 207, 213, 252–3, 277, 281–6, 289, 305
Bloch, B., 4
Bloomfield, L., 38, 39, 42, 116, 118, 153, 217, 229, 230, 231, 232, 241, 242, 243, 266, 296
Boas, F., 303, 311
borrowing, 200, 206–7, 208, 209, 309–10, 317, 325
Burling, R., 276
Burnett, J., 189

Cassirer, E., 223
Chaucer, G., 182
Chomsky, N., 7–11, 20, 22, 23, 40, 44, 59, 60, 63, 92, 104, 106, 108–9, 111, 116, 118, 121, 124–9, 164, 211, 217, 223, 224, 228–35, 239, 241, 242–7, 251, 252, 256, 257–61, 266, 304, 309
Clark, E. V., 316
Clark, H. H., 316
cognitive science, 240, 242, 262–4
communication-systems, 2–3, 16–24 *passim*, 29, 30, 245

comparative method, 180, 192–201, 210
Condillac, E., 28, 189, 261
consonants, 75–7, 80–3, 88, 95, 197–9, 255
constituency, relations of, 115–16, 119–24, 235, 246
constituent-structure, 117–24, 128
creativity, rule-governed, 23, 206, 230–1, 256, 304, 309, 325
cultural diffusion, 317, 323, 325
cultural overlap, 323–4, 328

Darwin, C., 181, 239
deixis, 168–70, 171, 174
denotation, 151–6, 161, 168, 174–5, 305–6, 316–17, 328
dependency, 116, 117, 122–3, 235
derivation, 103, 117
Descartes, R., 42, 109, 241, 244, 248
descriptivism, 217, 229
diacritics, 69–70, 74, 75
dialect, 11–12, 14, 17, 24–7, 49–50, 52, 53, 60, 180, 181–3, 207, 212–13, 268–81, 283–6, 288–9, 292–3
diglossia, 207, 213, 277, 284–6, 292
distinctive-feature theory, 88–94, 224–5, 254–5
distribution, 84–8, 93, 111–12, 117, 118, 119–23, 158
Dixon, R. M. W., 308
dualism, 241, 242, 263
Durkheim, E., 221

empiricism, 7, 40–3, 152–3, 244–8
ethnolinguistics, 36, 266–8
etymological fallacy, 55
etymology, 55–6, 147
euphemism, 151
evolutionism, 181, 189, 217–18, 239

Ferguson, C. A., 284
Fishman, J. A., 283